FOUNDATIONS WITHOUT FOU

OXFORD LOGIC GUIDES: 17

General Editors

DOV GABBAY
ANGUS MACINTYRE
JOHN SHEPHERDSON
DANA SCOTT

Foundations without Foundationalism

A Case for Second-order Logic

STEWART SHAPIRO

Department of Philosophy
The Ohio State University at Newark

CLARENDON PRESS · OXFORD

OXFORD

UNIVERSITY PRESS

Great Clarendon Street, Oxford OX2 6DP

Oxford University Press is a department of the University of Oxford.
It furthers the University's objective of excellence in research, scholarship,
and education by publishing worldwide in

Oxford New York

Athens Auckland Bangkok Bogotá Buenos Aires Calcutta
Cape Town Chennai Dar es Salaam Delhi Florence Hong Kong Istanbul
Karachi Kuala Lumpur Madrid Melbourne Mexico City Mumbai
Nairobi Paris São Paulo Singapore Taipei Tokyo Toronto Warsaw
and associated companies in Berlin Ibadan

Oxford is a registered trade mark of Oxford University Press
in the UK and in certain other countries

Published in the United States
by Oxford University Press Inc., New York

British Library Cataloguing in Publication Data

Data available

Library of Congress Cataloging in Publication Data
Shapiro, Stewart, 1951–
Foundations without foundationalism: a case for second-order
logic / Stewart Shapiro
(Oxford logic guides; 17)
Includes bibliographical references and index.
1. Logic, Symbolic and mathematical. I. Title.
II. Title: Second-order logic. III. Series.
QA9.S48 1991   511.3—dc20   91–14355 CIP
ISBN 0-19-853391-8
ISBN 0-19-825029-0 (Pbk.)

Printed in Great Britain
on acid-free paper by
Bookcraft Ltd,
Midsomer Norton, Somerset

PREFACE

An interpretation, or model, of a formal language usually contains a domain-of-discourse, or several domains-of-discourse. In effect, these domains are what the language is about. Variables that range over them are called *first-order variables*. If the language contains only first-order variables, it is called a *first-order language*. *First-order logic* includes the study of such languages. Some languages also contain variables that range over properties, functions, sets, or relations among members of the domains-of-discourse. These are *second-order variables*. A language that contains first-order and second-order variables, and no others, is a *second-order language*, the focus of *second-order logic*. The sentence 'there is a property shared by all and only prime numbers' is straightforwardly rendered in a second-order language, because of the (bound) variable ranging over properties. There are also properties of properties, relations of properties, and the like. Consider, for example, the property of properties expressed by 'P has an infinite extension' or the relation expressed by 'P has a smaller extension than Q'. A language with variables ranging over such items is called *third-order*. This construction can be continued, producing fourth-order languages, etc. A language is called *higher-order* if it is at least second-order.

The central themes of this book are the development of second- and higher-order logic, and the contention that higher-order logic has an important role to play in foundational studies. Second-order logic provides better models of important aspects of mathematics, both now and in recent history, than first-order logic does.

It is not an exaggeration to state that first-order logic dominates foundational thinking today, at least among philosophers. I believe that at least some reluctance for higher-order logic is related to remnants of what may be called *foundationalism*—the view that it is possible and desirable to reconstruct mathematics on a secure basis, one maximally immune to rational doubt. At one time, of course, it was widely held that *all* knowledge ought to be built, or rebuilt, on a secure foundation. Mathematics and logic, which are presumably near the base, should be paradigms of certainty. And, in fact, the traditional rationalists took the methodology of mathematics to be the model of all knowledge acquisition. It can be conceded that second-order logic is not as 'certain' as first-order logic in that its conceptual and ontological presuppositions are more substantial. One who employs a second-order axiomatization of a theory takes a greater risk of inconsistency and, perhaps, other errors than one who maintains a first-order axiomatization of the same theory. Moreover, it will be shown that the study of higher-order logic, especially its model-theoretic semantics, requires significant mathematical assumptions, much more than the study of first-order

logic does. Thus, second-order logic may not be appropriate for a foundationalist programme. But foundationalism, as understood here, has few proponents today, and for good reason. Some people may believe, perhaps
implicitly, that mathematics and logic are the last outpost of foundationalism,
and that canons of self-evidence are still appropriate there. As we shall see,
some theorists were even willing to cripple mathematics to make it stand on
a supporting foundation. Against this, I urge a thorough rejection of
foundationalism. One of the items before us is to examine the role of logic
and foundational studies in the anti-foundationalist climate. As indicated by
the title, we examine foundations without foundationalism.

One item on our agenda is a historical analysis of the emergence of
first-order logic as the 'standard' in current philosophical and mathematical
logic. The 'triumph' of first-order logic may be related to remnants of failed
foundationalist programmes early this century—logicism and the Hilbert
programme. It is ironic that both programmes employed higher-order
languages. The differing orientations and presuppositions of the participants
in the disputes make a fascinating study, and constitute a clear foreshadowing
of the issues in the present treatise. The conclusion is that if one is to accept
classical mathematics more or less as it stands, both historically and today,
then higher-order logic is an appropriate vehicle to develop and study its
semantics.

Today, the major opponent of higher-order logic is W. V. O. Quine (e.g.
Quine 1970). He argues that second-order logic is actually 'set theory in
disguise'. The thesis seems to be that in introducing variables over relations
or functions, one is crossing a line between logic and mathematics. Set theory
has a 'staggering ontology', while logic, presumably, should be free of
ontology. To address these arguments, we undertake a careful discussion of
the broader philosophical issues involved, including the assessment of the
ontology of a discipline, the desire to reduce ontology, and the absoluteness
of logic. In other writings, Quine has stressed a thorough holism, on strong
anti-foundationalist grounds. Drawing on a metaphor of Otto Neurath
(1932), our entire conceptual life, all of philosophy and science, is likened to
a ship which must be examined and improved while it is in the water. There
is no neutral 'dry dock' in which it can be restructured on a new foundation.
Every aspect of the enterprise is related to other aspects. In particular, Quine
holds that there is no sharp border between logic and mathematics on the
one hand and, say, physics on the other. He points out that one cannot
understand physics without mathematics, and in accepting physics one is
accepting the ontology of much mathematics. In this book, Quinean holism
is extended to logic itself. There is no sharp border between mathematics
and logic, especially the logic *of mathematics*. One cannot expect to do logic
without incorporating some mathematics and accepting at least some of its
ontology.

The book includes a technical presentation of higher-order logic. Languages, deductive systems, and several semantics are developed. The central metatheory is then presented, including the failure of the completeness, compactness, and Löwenheim–Skolem theorems for so-called 'standard semantics'. The Quinean thesis that second-order logic involves considerable mathematics is then made out in detail. It is shown that many substantial mathematical theses have counterparts in (pure) second-order logic. Thus, if there were a sharp border between logic and mathematics, second-order logic would be mathematics, and not logic. But there is no natural border to be drawn. This is to be expected of a semantics that has the expressive resources to codify mathematical theories. In effect, Quine's *reductio ad absurdum* against higher-order logic is the present defence of the (Quinean) thesis against the necessity of a sharp absolute border between logic and mathematics.

It follows from Gödel's incompleteness theorem that the semantic consequence relation of second-order logic is not effective. For example, the set of logical truths of any second-order language is not recursively enumerable. It is not even arithmetic. Thus, unlike first-order logic, there can be no complete effective deductive system for second-order logic. In many minds, this alone disqualifies second-order logic from consideration in foundational studies. Some of the discomfort with an incomplete logic may be the result of a conflation of various purposes for which logic is developed. Surely, a non-effective consequence relation cannot serve as a model of correct *deduction* for a branch of mathematics, unless some widely held views about human inference competence are incorrect. But, throughout history, logic has had a second orientation, which may be called 'semantic'. In first-order logic, the completeness theorem shows that deductive notions are coextensive with their semantic counterparts, but conceptually the notions are distinct. The 'cost' of first-order logic is an inability to account for important aspects of mathematics. In particular, semantic notions available in higher-order logic are important in accounting for how mathematical structures are described, how various mathematical structures are interrelated, and the presuppositions of various branches of mathematics. In short, there is room for a non-effective consequence relation among the tools of the logician.

The book is divided into three parts. Part I, 'Orientation', consists of two chapters. A framework for the philosophy of logic is laid, and the role of logic and foundational studies is articulated and defended.

Chapter 1, entitled 'Terms and questions', is a general discussion of the purposes of logic. Traditionally, a logic consists of a formal or informal language, together with a deductive system and/or a semantics. Each of these components is a mathematical model of various aspects of the actual language we use and reason with. A formal language is a model of a natural language, focusing attention on features relevant to description or inference.

A deductive system is a model of the practice of correctly inferring conclusions on the basis of premises, or, in other words, a model of the process of reasoning correctly in natural languages. Semantics is a model of the ways sentences come to make assertions about objects, and the ways they can be true or false. Present focus is on model-theoretic semantics. The connection between the items of a logic and the corresponding features of natural language can be good or bad, depending on the purpose at hand, but there is usually a gap between model and modelled. On the present view, there is no question of finding the 'correct' or 'true' logic underlying a part of natural language. For all we know a priori, there may be several good models that describe the phenomena being modelled, perhaps with compensating strengths and weaknesses. Moreover, different purposes may suggest different models. In this respect, first-order logic is not rejected here. Far from it. The thesis is that there is a legitimate place for higher-order logic alongside it.

Part of the controversy concerns the role of sets, or intensional counterparts like relations or propositional functions, in foundational studies. There is a tradition, dating at least from Boole, that takes collections (or properties) and the membership (or predication) relation to be within the purview of logic. By contrast, in current mathematics, class terminology is what may be called 'non-logical'. It refers to the set-theoretic hierarchy, a mathematical structure like any other. There are, in fact, two related conceptions of 'class' or 'set'. An *iterative set* is an element of the set-theoretic hierarchy. Its membership relation is the main non-logical item of current set theory. A *logical set* occurs in the context of a fixed domain of discourse, either stated explicitly or determined by context. A logical set is a subdomain of this domain of discourse. In arithmetic a logical set is a collection of numbers, in geometry a logical set is a collection of points, etc. The locution 'logical set' is similar to an indexical expression of ordinary language, in that its extension depends on the context of use. Logical sets, or something similar to them, are the range of some of the variables of higher-order languages. Confusion between these notions is most likely when the fixed context, for the logical notion, is itself the set-theoretic hierarchy. In that context, a logical set is a collection of iterative sets, what is today called a *class*. In these terms, the argument behind Russell's paradox shows that in set theory there are logical sets—classes—that are not coextensive with any iterative set. There are classes that are not members of the set-theoretic hierarchy. These are called 'proper classes'. This distinction is important in the presentation of second-order set theory, a recurring theme in this book.

Chapter 2, 'Foundationalism and foundations of mathematics', is a study of epistemological foundationalism in mathematics, and the relationship between one's views on foundationalism and one's views on the appropriate, or best, logic. Once again, the underlying agenda is to establish a role for an inherently incomplete logic. I suggest that foundationalist goals explicitly or implicitly dominated much of the work in logic and foundations of mathematics until recently. Examples include logicism and the Hilbert programme. It might be recalled that foundationalism does suggest a rather straightforward criterion for evaluating proposed logics and foundations— self-evidence. The issues here concern how much of the perspective is still plausible and how logic and foundations are to be understood in the prevailing anti-foundationalist spirit. How are candidate logics to be evaluated now?

One possible orientation is to regard logic, and perhaps mathematics in general, as an exception to the prevailing anti-foundationalism. Against this, I argue that we have learned to live with uncertainty in virtually every special subject, and we can live with uncertainty in logic and foundations of mathematics. In like manner, we can live without completeness in logic, and live well.

It is possible to distinguish two different conceptions of logic. One of them, which I call *foundational*, can be seen as an attempt to salvage logic from logicism. Accordingly, logic is the ideal of justification, or at least relative justification. An advocate of this conception of logic can concede to anti-foundationalism that we may not be able to locate a sufficient core of self-evident axioms for a given field of study, but we can at least proceed with *relative* safety. If we have true axioms, then all theorems are true. Thus, the central concern with foundational logic is deductive systems. A proposed system purports to codify all and only the arguments that conform to the postulated standard of relative ideal justification. The nature of the self-evidence necessary to support this enterprise is examined, and the extent of its use is treated. The other conception of logic is *semantic*. Although it might be traced to Aristotle, a modern exponent is Tarski. In current logic textbooks, validity is often defined in semantic terms, at least at first. An argument is said to be 'valid' if its conclusion is true under every *interpretation* of the language in which the premises are true. The semantic conception of logic is an attempt to explicate the underlying notion of 'model' or 'interpretation' that underlies this definition of validity. Although we may have pre-theoretic intuitions concerning 'models' and possible 'interpretations' of a language, and our intuitions concerning correct inference should be consistent with semantic validity, this version of a logic is not a foundationalist enterprise. The sanction of a model-theoretic semantics is a more holistic matter. In particular, the consequence relation should fit our overall intellectual system, Neurath's ship. With some hindsight, the set theory underlying current model-theoretic semantics is anything but self-evident, at least when considered prior to training.

It is possible, perhaps, to maintain both conceptions of logic. If so, then it seems desirable to have them converge on a single consequence relation.

That is, it would be nice if an argument conforms to the standard of ideal justification if and only if it is semantically valid. The soundness and completeness of a deductive system for a semantics represent counterparts of this desideratum. When these hold, the deductive system and semantics support each other. In short, the claim that the deductive system exactly conforms to ideal justification and the claim that the semantics is a reasonable codification of the relevant informal semantic notions are both sustained, at least in part, if the logic is both sound and complete. This may be the case with first-order logic. The burden of the present book, however, is to show that this *language*, with its semantics, is too weak to codify important aspects of mathematical practice. For stronger languages, without completeness, one can still maintain both conceptions of logic separately, but against this I argue that the assumptions behind the foundational conception of logic are untenable. Thus I propose to drop the foundational conception altogether. The final section concerns the role of effectiveness in logic and the relationship between reasoning and computation.

Part II contains the technical development of higher-order logic, and the bulk of the argument that higher-order notions are well suited for modelling important aspects of mathematics. The interplay between mathematical notions and those of second-order logic is described in some detail.

Chapter 3 is entitled 'Theory'. As a common core, the basic ingredients of a first-order language are presented. It is then shown how to extend this to a language with free second-order variables, to a second-order language, to a ramified second-order language, and, briefly, to third- and higher-order languages. Then deductive systems for each language are developed, with brief discussions of axioms and rules of inference. Finally, attention is turned to model-theoretic semantics. Once again, the starting point is the usual semantics for first-order languages. Three systems are developed for second-order languages. In *standard semantics*, relation variables range over the entire class of relations on the domain, and function variables range over the class of all functions on the domain. Accordingly, a standard model of a second-order language is the same as a model of the corresponding first-order language, namely a domain of discourse and appropriate referents of the non-logical terminology. That is, with standard semantics, when one specifies a domain, one thereby specifies the range of both the first-order variables and the second-order (and higher-order) variables. There is no further 'interpreting' to be done. This is not the case with the other two semantics. In both cases, one specifies a range of the first-order variables *and* a range of the higher-order variables. In *Henkin semantics*, a model consists of a domain of discourse together with subclasses of the collections of all relations and all functions on the domain, and, of course, a model specifies referents of the non-logical terminology. The designated subclasses are the range of the second-order variables. In *first-order semantics*, the second-order language is regarded as a many-sorted first-order language. A model consists of many (possibly unrelated) domains, one for the first-order variables and one for each kind of higher-order variable, and again referents for the non-logical terminology are determined. Each model also specifies appropriate relations between these domains to interpret the predication (or membership) relation between 'relations' and the items in the range of the first-order variables, and the application function between 'functions' and the items in the range of the first-order variables. In effect, in first-order semantics, predication and application are regarded as non-logical. It is shown that Henkin semantics is essentially the same as first-order semantics for higher-order languages.

Chapter 4, 'Metatheory', contains central results for second-order logic with standard and Henkin (and first-order) semantics. It sets the stage for the more philosophical discussions to follow. The first item is a review of the soundness, completeness, compactness, and downward and upward Löwenheim–Skolem theorems for first-order languages. Proofs are not given, since they are available in any competent textbook in elementary logic, and they can be reconstructed from the sketches of analogous results for Henkin semantics. Attention is then turned to second-order languages with standard semantics. The only result that carries over from the first-order case is the soundness of the deductive system for this semantics. It is shown that arithmetic and real analysis, as formulated with a second-order language, are categorical: any two models of either theory are isomorphic. The proofs are given in some detail, so that their presuppositions can be assessed later. The refutations of the completeness, compactness, and Löwenheim–Skolem theorems are corollaries of these categoricity results and the incompleteness of arithmetic. It is sometimes stated that the incompleteness, non-compactness, etc. of second-order logic are defects. In fact, these results are consequences of the crucial *strength* of second-order logic—its ability to give categorical characterizations of infinite structures. The situation with Henkin (or first-order) semantics for second-order languages is opposite to that of standard semantics. First, the semantics is *not sound* for the deductive system. Thus, one must restrict the class of acceptable Henkin models to those that satisfy the inferences and axioms of the deductive system. With this caveat, it is shown that Henkin semantics is complete and compact, and both Löwenheim–Skolem theorems hold.

The purpose of Chapter 5, 'Second-order languages and mathematics', is to discuss the prevalence of second-order notions in mathematics as practised and, conversely, the extent to which mathematical notions can be formulated in second-order logic. As noted, Quine argues that second-order logic is mathematics in disguise, 'set theory in sheep's clothing'. At least part of his argument seems to be that second-order languages can, by themselves, express a great deal of mathematics. This much is correct, and a case for it is made in this chapter. Moreover, one needs a considerable amount of set theory to study second-order logic.

There is a converse, of sorts, to the Quinean thesis about second-order logic and mathematics—namely, first-order languages, unadorned, are insufficient to codify many concepts, notions, and theories of contemporary mathematics. I shall not go so far as to assert that second-order languages and standard semantics are necessary for understanding, codifying, or explicating mathematics. Most mathematicians survive well without any logical theory and, moreover, in the anti-foundationalist spirit, there may be no single 'best' way to present and study mathematics. But second-order logic helps.

The opening section of this chapter is an account of several notions prevalent in mathematics that have adequate characterizations in second-order languages (with no special non-logical terminology). Examples include closure, well-ordering, well-foundedness, and various cardinalities. It is shown that none of these can be adequately accommodated in first-order languages. If these concepts are in fact understood and communicated in informal mathematical practice, as seems plausible (scepticism aside), then first-order languages are inadequate to the task of codifying mathematics. Section 5.2 is a discussion of first-order versions of various mathematical theories, indicating what goes wrong. The failure of categoricity is traced, and, with this as background, the assumptions that allow categoricity in the second-order cases are discussed in some detail. It is shown that any non-standard model of any of these theories—any model of the first-order theory that is not a model of the corresponding second-order theory—has features that are clearly unintended. The non-standard models are not legitimate interpretations of the original pre-formal theories. The next section is a more philosophical discussion of second-order arithmetic and analysis. Considerations, essentially due to Kreisel (1967), are brought to show that first-order languages must fail to account for epistemic, linguistic, and semantic features of mathematical practice. Second-order languages do capture these features. The final section concerns the use of second-order concepts in set theory itself. It is not claimed, of course, that second-order logic has some mystical powers that allow us to have our philosophical cake while eating it. Rather, the upshot of this chapter is that second-order logic does not presuppose any more than informal mathematics does.

Chapter 6, 'Advanced metatheory', reports a number of results about second-order logic (with standard semantics). Most of the issues involve the ability of second-order logic, with standard semantics, to make distinctions within the class of models it has in common with first-order logic. The opening section presents some caution needed concerning metatheory. It is shown in Section 6.2 that there is a sense in which nth-order logic, for $n \geq 3$, is reducible to second-order logic. The basic observation is that second-order logic has the resources to capture adequately the membership relation between collections and their elements. Consequently, the logical relations of higher-order logic can be simulated in a second-order system. This result suggests that the crucial distinction is that between first-order and second-order languages. There is a sense in which, after that, nothing new is obtained. Therefore the present focus on second-order logic is not arbitrary. Section 6.3 concerns the use of the set-theoretic hierarchy to provide the semantics of second-order logic. It turns out that reflection principles are involved, and thus we enter the realm of so-called 'small large cardinals'. In Section 6.4, analogues of the Löwenheim–Skolem theorems are presented— here we require 'large large cardinals'. Section 6.5 concerns various properties of semantical systems that, in effect, characterize first-order logic. These results are sometimes used to argue *for* first-order logic, but that depends on the indicated properties being desirable. The final section (Section 6.6) concerns definability and a few diverse matters of interest. In this chapter, most proofs are omitted, but references are provided.

Part III, 'History and philosophy', takes up the more philosophical issues relevant to the acceptance of second-order logic. Chapter 7 traces the history of the dispute, from late last century to the present, and Chapter 8 is a more direct attack on the underlying ontological and epistemic issues. It is shown that second-order logic is a remarkably clear case study for many contemporary philosophical matters of interest.

There are, in essence, three historical items, two of which overlap considerably. The first is the emergence of first-order *languages* (and semantics) as the standard in logic. The second is the development of *set theory* and the emergence of first-order *ZFC*. The third is the contemporary controversy over the status of second-order logic. Historically, the main proponents of first-order logic were Skolem, von Neumann, Weyl, and Gödel. The higher-order opposition was championed by Hilbert, Bernays, and Zermelo. In contemporary philosophy of mathematics, Quine is joined by philosophers like Tharp and Resnik against higher-order logic. The proponents include Boolos and Corcoran. It is often suggested, with hindsight, that the early historical disputes are full of confusion over the distinction between the semantics of first-order languages and the semantics of higher-order languages, confusion over the range of logic and the range of categoricity, and confusion over the applicability of the Löwenheim–Skolem theorems. The historical assertions that conform to one's views are praised as clear, while those that are incompatible are dubbed 'confused'. On the other hand, most of the remarks by the historical figures have counterparts in the current debate over second-order logic and other fundamental philosophical issues. Once presuppositions are noted, some of the pronouncements are at least relatively clear, and in some cases remarkably clear, even by modern lights. With hindsight, there are several sources of disagreement.

One concerns the distinction between syntax and semantics and, in particular, the distinction between proof theory and model theory. A closely related matter concerns the status of the second-order variables, involving what is called here the 'logical notion of set'. On one level, the question of whether this notion is a legitimate part of logic is a matter of deciding where to draw a border. Is there a notion of set in the jurisdiction of logic, or does it belong to mathematics proper? The deeper issue concerns the extent of our 'intuitive' understanding of the second-order variables and the extent to which they can be *used* in formulating the syntax and semantics of formal languages. The higher-order camp seems to hold that the terminology in question is sufficiently clear and does not stand in need of 'foundation'. Indeed, the claim is that this very terminology is at the heart of the foundational enterprise. Any successful attempt at formulating an axiomatic foundation of second-order logic would itself have terminology involving the logical notion of set (perhaps in presenting the semantics) and would thus beg the central question. The first-order advocates, on the other hand, hold that the notion of set is not clear enough for use in foundational systems, at least not as it stands. To be used at all, the relevant notions must first be formulated as part of an axiomatic theory. In short, the notion of set must be regarded as non-logical; any assertions about sets must follow from the axioms. And 'follow' here means 'follow via first-order logic'. With hindsight, the best candidate for such an axiomatic formulation is the study of the iterative hierarchy. Thus the first-order camp rejects the logical conception of set. All substantial assertions about classes are non-logical and first-order.

Chapter 8 is a philosophical recapitulation of the issues behind higher-order logic, focusing on the role of model-theoretic semantics in describing and codifying mathematics. It is shown that the debate is likely to lead to a regress or, if presuppositions are noted, a stand-off over the question of whether there is an unequivocal understanding of such locutions as 'all relations' or 'all subsets' of a fixed domain. There are, to speak roughly, three orientations towards mathematical theories and their logic. One option is to follow the Skolemite sceptic and deny that there is an intended range, unique up to isomorphism, for the variables of mathematical theories. Apparently, this outlook is not very popular among mathematicians, who use phrases like 'the natural numbers' and 'the natural number structure' with impunity. The second option is to claim that the ranges of the variables of mathematical theories are, in fact, demarcated up to isomorphism, but they are understood only informally. Model-theoretic semantics, any semantics, must of necessity fail to capture our grasp of mathematical theories. The Löwenheim–Skolem theorems are sometimes used to defend views like this, but such arguments *presuppose* that all legitimate axiomatizations are first order. In a sense, the views in question are little more than an insistence on this presupposition. The third position is the one underlying the use of second-order logic. It is to recognize the intuitive presuppositions of classical mathematics and, in effect, to include these in the logic. The claim is not that we have an esoteric grasp of the range of higher-order variables, but we do have a serviceable grasp, justified on holistic grounds. As Church (1956) puts it, the presuppositions behind second-order logic may be more perspicuous than those of contemporary mathematics, but they are not more troublesome. The rejection of foundationalism permeates the book. Logic does not need to be self-evident, nor, indeed, much more evident than the fields that it is used to codify.

With this background, the problems behind second-order logic are related to the Wittgensteinian issue of rule-following (despite Wittgenstein's later rejection of all foundational studies). One type of opponent of higher-order logic, the Skolemite sceptic, is analogous to the sceptic concerning rules. Both deny that there is an unequivocal sense in which we 'go on as before', either in following a particular rule or in the pursuit of historical mathematical theories like arithmetic and analysis. It is not that the adoption of second-order logic 'solves' the Wittgensteinian puzzles. I have no reply to scepticism. Rather, second-order logic embodies the presuppositions behind our intuitive belief that we do 'go on as before' when we follow fixed rules and when we practise mathematics. In a word, second-order logic and classical mathematics go together. What is needed here is a synthesis between the extremes of sceptical 'relativism', which holds that the constraints on the use of our language do not extend much beyond our present ability to describe and apply our rules, and traditional platonism, which holds that our minds can somehow directly grasp infinite structures, and that the concepts are thereby fixed completely, once and for all. The questions concerns the *extent* to which our present practise in, say, real analysis determines the future use of the terms or, to use another Wittgensteinian phrase, the extent to which meaning and use are and are not fixed 'throughout logical space'. I conclude with the proposal that we can shed light on the requisite concepts of meaning and reference by studying the role of second-order concepts in mathematics.

The final chapter, Chapter 9, is devoted to comparing second-order logic (with standard semantics) with some of its competitors. As noted, there is no unique 'foundation' for mathematics, nor is there a fixed 'underlying logic' for each branch of mathematics. Indeed, even the border between 'logical' and 'non-logical' terminology is not determined in advance. From this perspective, several alternative semantics, logics, and foundations are explored. Examples include Boolos' (1984) recent attempt to assimilate second-order quantifiers to the plural construction of natural language, free-variable second-order logic, infinitary logic, ω-logic, and first-order set theory.

Most of the book is accessible to readers who have had the equivalent of a graduate-level course in mathematical logic, including the completeness of first-order logic, the incompleteness of arithmetic, and the Löwenheim–Skolem theorems (e.g. Mendelson 1987, Boolos and Jeffrey 1989). The more technical parts of Chapter 5, most of Chapter 6, and parts of Chapter 9 require a more substantial background in axiomatic set theory (e.g. Jech 1971, Drake 1974). Chapter 5 contains a few references to items from abstract algebra (e.g. Mac Lane and Birkhoff 1967), but these are not essential to the development.

This project began when I was on Faculty Professional Leave from Ohio State University. During that year, I held a Fellowship from the National Endowment for the Humanities, and I was a visiting Fellow at the Center for Philosophy of Science at the University of Pittsburgh. I am grateful to all three institutions for their generous support. I would also like to thank, as groups, the Buffalo Logic Colloquium, the Hebrew University Philosophy Colloquium, the Tel Aviv Philosophy Colloquium, the University of Wisconsin Philosophy Colloquium, the Pittsburgh Logic Colloquium, the Ohio University Conference on Inference, and the Association for Symbolic Logic for devoting sessions to parts of this book. In the autumn of 1990, I gave a graduate seminar on this book at Ohio State University. In each case, the discussions were most valuable.

I also gratefully acknowledge a research grant from the Newark Campus of the Ohio State University to engage scholars and students to read the manuscript and write advisory reports on it. The participants were John Corcoran, Jill Dieterle, Harold Hodes, David Kempster, Pierluigi Miraglia, Sriram Nambiar, Woosuk Park, and Mark Steiner. They were not compensated in proportion to their efforts. Pierluigi Miraglia and Jill Dieterle also served as my research assistants during the final preparation of the manuscript.

A large number of colleagues and students provided valuable comments without compensation. The list includes Günter Asser, Nuel Belnap, George Boolos, Richard Butrick, Nino Cocchiarella, Michael Detlefsen, Matthew Foreman, Harvey Friedman, Nicolas Goodman, Yuri Gurevich, Yechiel Kimchi, Robert Kraut, Georg Kreisel, Ronald Laymon, Daniel Leivant, Azriel Levy, Giuseppe Longo, Lila Luce, Saunders Mac Lane, Penelope Maddy, Ulrich Majer, Timothy McCarthy, Charles McCarty, John McDowell, Elliot Mendelson, Gregory Moore, Calvin Normore, Charles Parsons, Robert Reilly, Michael Resnik, Michael Scanlan, Barbara Scholz, George Schumm, Allan Silverman, Robert Solovay, Robert Turnbull, and Steven Wagner. Some of these people believe that many of the theses of the book are seriously misguided and yet, in the spirit of philosophy, they generously gave their time to improve the presentation. Any errors or misrepresentations that remain can only be attributed to my stubbornness. I also thank three anonymous referees engaged by Oxford University Press who read an early draft of the manuscript. I apologize for any omissions from this list.

Finally, I thank my wife, Beverly Roseman-Shapiro, for her patience and support of the project. This book is lovingly dedicated to her.

The Ohio State University at Newark   S.S.
June, 1991

PREFACE TO PAPERBACK EDITION

During the years since the original publication of this book, there has been much discussion of second-order logic in the philosophical and logical literature. The book itself generated extensive reviews by James Robert Brown (*Dialogue*, **35** (1996), 624–6), John Burgess (*Journal of Symbolic Logic*, **58** (1993), 363–5), Nino Cocchiarella (*Notre Dame Journal of Formal Logic*, **34** (1993), 453–68), Darcy Cutler (*Philosophia Mathematica*, **5**(3) (1997), 71–91), Michael Potter (*Philosophical Quarterly*, **44** (1994), 127–9), and Gila Sher (*Philosophical Review* **103** (1994), 150–3). See also the assessment of second-order logic in Ignacio Jané, 'A critical appraisal of second-order logic', *History and Philosophy of Logic*, **14** (1993), 67–86.

The wide-ranging discussion focuses on such topics as the role and function of logic, the rationale for an effective consequence relation, the purpose of model-theoretic semantics, the notion of reference, and the nature of classes, sets, and properties—items in the range of higher-order variables. If nothing else, this shows that second-order logic provides an arena for considering some of the central issues in philosophy of language, logic, and general epistemology. I would like to mention a few areas where the views expressed in this book need to be further articulated, and in some cases, amended.

In the Preface and in Chapter 2, I defined foundationalism as the view that it is possible and desirable to put all of mathematics on an unshakeable foundation, or, failing that, to make mathematics as secure as humanly possible. I suggested that a preference for first-order logic is a holdover from failed 'foundationalist' programmes in the early twentieth century—logicism and the Hilbert programme in particular. The raw thesis was that once we give up on foundationalism, and take a more holistic approach to foundational studies, there is nothing in the way of second-order logic in foundational studies. Thus my title, *Foundations without foundationalism*. Some of the above authors (e.g. Burgess, Jané, and Cutler) took me to task for this, showing that first-order logic can be supported by epistemological considerations independent of the original foundationalist motivations. This now seems correct to me. An underlying current of the book is an eclectic approach of logic: there is no single logical system that serves every legitimate purpose of logic and foundational studies. This much stands, and most of the critics agree. The purpose of Chapter 2 was to provide some space for second-order logic in foundationalist studies.

Some of the critics (e.g. Cocchiarella and Jané) showed that my distinction between the logical and the iterative notions of set (treated in §1.3) is inadequate or, to be honest, flawed. Historically, a logical set is the extension of a property. Such items were central parts of higher-order logical systems developed by the likes of Frege and Russell, mostly because properties were thought to be under the purview of logic. A large contingent of philosophers and logicians now regard the logical notion of set to be severely flawed and not appropriate for logical studies. An iterative set is a member of the cumulative hierarchy, codified by Zermelo–Fraenkel set theory. This is the subject of a branch of mathematics. The relevant philosophical issues concern the interactions between these notions, and the items in the range of higher-order variables.

My article 'Do not claim too much: second-order logic and first-order logic' (*Philosophia Mathematica* **7**(3) (1999), 42–64) extends the treatment of these, and other issues, in response to some of the published discussion of *Foundations without foundationalism* and other work on higher-order logic. The article is a sort of sequel or follow-up to the book. I am indebted to the editor, Robert Thomas, and one of my sharpest critics, John Burgess, for supporting this genre and encouraging me to continue the discussion.

I know of no explicit criticism (or even discussion) of my anti-foundationalist stance in the philosophical or logical literature. I presume that the reviewers and critics either acquiesced in the anti-foundationalism, or else did not care much about the issue, choosing to focus on the motivation for second-order logic and other matters. However, the first part of 1999 saw an intense discussion of foundationalism on the 'foundations of mathematics' e-mail list, also known as 'fom'. A wide variety and impressive number of logicians and philosophers of mathematics participated. One useful result, I think, is an articulation of various senses of 'foundationalism', only some of which were the intended target of Chapter 2 of this book. The fom list is archived at www.math.psu.edu/simpson/fom.

Many thanks to my various critics and reviewers. The extensive discussion well illustrates the deep truth that philosophical views become enhanced through interaction with others, especially those who disagree with and thus challenge one's own views. I especially appreciate the spirit of collegiality in which the disagreements were mooted. Of course, I also appreciate the support of those who agree with me, and the wide praise for the technical aspects of the book (beginning with Chapter 3). Thanks also to Roberto Torretti, who provided a list of typos and other corrigenda.

I dedicate the paperback version of this book to the memory of George Boolos. His early defence of second-order logic provided much of the motivation for this book, and he was most helpful to me in writing it. We miss his penetrating mind and gentle humanity.

23 April, 1999   S.S.
Newark, Ohio

CONTENTS

Part I

ORIENTATION

1

Terms and questions

The purpose of this chapter is to present the broad outlines of a philosophy of logic. This sets the stage for the discussion of foundations of mathematics and second-order logic that follows. A secondary purpose is to establish terminology and make a number of distinctions, mostly between semantic and deductive concepts. Gödel's completeness theorem indicates that many of these distinctions collapse in the case of first-order logic, but they are quite significant in second-order logic.

1.1 Orientation

Define a *full logic* to be a language, together with a deductive system and a semantics. A few words on each are in order.

A *language* consists of a class of (well-formed) formulas. Typically, each formula is a finite string on a particular alphabet, but more 'abstract' sorts of languages, such as infinitary languages or languages whose formulas are numbers or sets, need not be ruled out at this point.[1]

The languages of full logics are, at least in part, mathematical models of fragments of ordinary natural languages, like English, or perhaps ordinary languages augmented with expressions used in mathematics. The latter may be called 'natural languages of mathematics'. For emphasis, or to avoid confusion, the language of a full logic is sometimes called a *formal language*. Usually, some of the terminology of formal languages either appears in natural languages, or else has analogues there. For example, the connective & corresponds to 'and', ∨ corresponds to 'or', etc. It is sometimes said that the language of a full logic is a 'cleaned up' or 'regimented' version of a natural language, but this can be misleading. As a mathematical model, there is always a gap between the language of a logic and its natural language counterpart (see, for example, Corcoran 1973). The fit between model and modelled can be good or bad, useful or misleading, for whatever purpose is at hand. For example, it is sometimes difficult to find a formula that is a suitable counterpart of a particular sentence of natural language, and moreover there is no acclaimed criterion for what counts as a good, or even acceptable, 'translation'. Many of the considerations of this book concern the match, or lack of match, between natural languages and the formal languages of various logics.

Each of the formal languages considered in this book has two important components: the class of (first-order) *terms*, and the class of *relation* symbols. Terms have a role similar to that of proper nouns and singular pronouns, which are used to designate individual objects. Relation symbols are analogues of items that designate relations among objects, or relations between relations, or even relations between objects and relations.

Define a *theory*, or a *formal theory*, to be a collection of formulas. As such, a formal theory is a rather crude model of various mathematical fields, such as arithmetic, geometry, or set theory, but the definition is useful for present purposes. In effect, each area of study is associated with a collection of assertions or, to be precise, a collection of formal language counterparts to assertions.

Define an *argument* to be a pair $\langle \Gamma, \Phi \rangle$ in which Γ is a set of formulas (of the formal language) and Φ is a single formula. The members of Γ are the *premises* of the argument, and Φ is its *conclusion*. A *deductive system* is a collection of *deductions*, each of which is associated with one or more arguments. If a deduction d is associated with argument $\langle \Gamma, \Phi \rangle$, then d is said to be a deduction of Φ from Γ. A number of different kinds of deductive systems have been developed. One of them begins with a collection of arguments, called *immediate inferences*. If $\langle \Gamma, \Phi \rangle$ is an argument, then a deduction of Φ from Γ is defined to be a finite sequence $\Phi_0, \ldots, \Phi_n$ of formulas such that Φ_n is Φ and, for each $i \leqslant n$, either Φ_i is in Γ or there is an immediate inference whose conclusion is Φ_i and whose premises all occur in the sequence before Φ_i. Alternatively, the construction of one kind of natural deduction system begins with a collection of immediate inferences and a collection of transformation rules on arguments. A deduction is defined to be a sequence of arguments, each of which is either an immediate inference or is the result of applying one of the transformation rules to previous items in the sequence. Such a sequence is a deduction of Φ from Γ if $\langle \Gamma, \Phi \rangle$ is its last member. Again, other sorts of deductive systems need not be ruled out at this point.

Let D be a deductive system. If there is a deduction of Φ from Γ in D, then we say that Φ is a *deductive consequence of Γ in D*, or that Φ *deductively follows from Γ in D*, or that the argument $\langle \Gamma, \Phi \rangle$ is *deducible in D*. This is sometimes written $\Gamma \vdash_D \Phi$. A formula Φ is a *theorem of D*, written $\vdash_D \Phi$, if Φ is a deductive consequence of the empty set. In general, if T is a theory, then Φ is a *theorem of T via D* if there is a subset Γ of T such that $\Gamma \vdash_D \Phi$. A set of formulas (or a single formula) is *deductively consistent*, or simply *consistent*, *in D* if there is at least one formula that is not a deductive consequence of it. Usually, a set Γ is consistent in D if and only if there is no formula Φ such that both Φ and its negation are deductive consequences of Γ. Mention of the deductive system D may be omitted if there is no danger of ambiguity or confusion.

If the formulas of the language are strings, then one can inquire into the string-theoretic properties of the deductive system. In particular, D is said to be *effective* if the set of well-formed formulas and the set of deductions are both recursive. This is typically established by noting that the set of immediate inferences (and/or the set of transformations) is recursive. If the deductive system is effective, then the set of deducible arguments whose premises are finite is recursively enumerable.

Deductive systems are mathematical models of actual or possible chains of reasoning in the given natural language, or languages modelled by the formal language. As above, the match between model and modelled may be good or bad, and again an evaluation of a deductive system requires a clear concept of the phenomena being modelled. In most cases, the target is not necessarily the reasoning techniques used by actual mathematicians, but rather *correct* reasoning. Accordingly, an argument $\langle \Gamma, \Phi \rangle$ should be deducible in a deductive system only if it would be correct to conclude a natural sentence corresponding to Φ on the basis of sentences corresponding to the members of Γ. The underlying issue of determining what makes a chain of reasoning in a natural language correct or incorrect is deep and interesting. It is pursued in this chapter and the next (see also Resnik 1985). Of course, when put this way, logical theory presupposes that there is such a thing as correct reasoning in the natural language (or languages) being modelled, and that people manage to reason correctly, and recognize at least some instances of correct and incorrect reasoning, without first constructing or studying a deductive system. It is not assumed, however, that the boundaries of the pre-theoretic notion of 'correct reasoning in natural language' are completely determinate and precise independent of logical theory.

Finally, a *semantics* is, in part, a collection of *models* of the formal language. Each model consists of a class (or classes), called its *domain* (or *domains*), together with an *interpretation function* which assigns appropriate items to some of the terminology of the language, the so-called 'non-logical terminology'. There are typically two other components to a semantics. The first is a *denotation function*. Given a model M and, usually, an appropriate assignment on M to the variables, the denotation function assigns a member of the domain of M to each term. The second item is a *satisfaction relation* between models, appropriate assignments to the variables, and formulas. Equivalently, the satisfaction relation may be thought of as a function from models, assignments, and formulas to the truth values {true, false}. Systems like this are sometimes called *model-theoretic semantics*. In Chapter 3 several of them are developed for higher-order languages, and in Chapter 9 a few less common specimens are presented.

Let S be a model-theoretic semantics, let M be a model in S, let Γ be a set of formulas, and let Φ be a single formula. If M satisfies Φ under every assignment, then we say that M is a *model of Φ in S*, and if M satisfies every member of Γ under every assignment, then M is a *model of Γ in S*. Thus we sometimes speak of models of theories. We say that the argument $\langle \Gamma, \Phi \rangle$ is (semantically) *valid in S*, or that Φ is a *semantic consequence of Γ in S*, written $\Gamma \vDash_S \Phi$, if each model (and assignment to the variables) that satisfies every member of Γ also satisfies Φ. A formula Φ is a *logical truth in S*, or is *valid in S*, if it is a semantic consequence of the empty set, or, in other words, if every model in S is a model of Φ. A set of formulas (or a single formula) is *satisfiable in S* if there is a model M of S (and an assignment) that satisfies every member of it. Notice that a formula Φ is a semantic consequence of a set Γ in S if and only if Γ, together with the negation of Φ, is not satisfiable in S. The semantics S need not be mentioned if it is determined by context.

The term 'model', as a component of a model-theoretic semantics, should not be confused with the locution 'mathematical model' above. The semantics, as a whole, can be thought of as a mathematical model of certain relationships between natural languages and the world. The denotation function represents the relation between, say, a name and what it is a name of, and the satisfaction relation represents the pre-theoretic notion of truth in natural languages. In a sense, satisfaction is the notion of 'truth in a model', and, as Hodes (1984) elegantly puts it, 'truth in a model' is a model of 'truth'. And, once again, a mathematical model can be good or bad depending on the purposes at hand. A good semantics will exhibit important structural features of the relationship between a natural language and whatever the natural language is used to describe. There is, of course, a vast literature on this relationship, and there is no consensus on whether, for example, natural language denotation and satisfaction (or truth) are natural, or metaphysical, or scientifically respectable relations. This book does not directly address such issues.

One important item for the present project is the distinction between logical and non-logical terminology. It is often cast in terms of *semantics*. Roughly, the *non-logical* items are those whose 'interpretation', or reference, or extension changes from model to model. In the present sketch, in each model an interpretation function assigns a referent to each non-logical item. Thus, for example, in the first-order predicate calculus, individual constants, predicate letters, and function letters are non-logical. In contrast, the extension of the *logical* terminology remains invariant from model to model. In effect, the meaning of such terms is provided by the system as a whole. In standard first-order systems, connectives and quantifiers are logical. For example, & plays the same role in the satisfaction of formulas in every model, roughly equivalent to the connective 'and' from English. Notice that two different semantics for the same language can draw the boundary differently. We shall see this in the different semantics for higher-order languages. In standard semantics, the locution for predication, or membership, is logical, while in some non-standard semantics it is non-logical.

There is a notion of logical consequence, or correct inference, that is central to the enterprise of model-theoretic semantics. An argument in ordinary language is often defined to be 'valid' if it is *not possible* for all its premises to be true and its conclusion to be false, and it is sometimes added that this 'impossibility' must be based solely on the meanings of certain linguistic expressions, the 'logical terminology'. Alternatively, one says that an argument is valid if its conclusion is true under every 'interpretation' of the language in which the premises are true. Accordingly, to show that an argument is not valid, one typically gives another argument in 'the same form' in which the premises are true and the conclusion false. The latter, called a *counter-argument* of the original argument, is presumably an interpretation of it. The requirement that both arguments have the same form is understood to entail that they have the same 'logical' terminology in corresponding places. This 'semantic' notion of logical consequence can be traced to Tarski (1935).

The central notions here are 'interpretation', or 'possible interpretation', 'form', and the related distinction between logical and non-logical terminology. A model-theoretic semantics is meant, at least in part, to characterize or 'model' these items.[2] Above, the logical–non-logical distinction is characterized for the *formal* languages of logic in terms of its model-theoretic semantics. Presumably, one can define an expression of a natural language to be logical if its counterpart in a given formal language is a logical expression. Accordingly, locutions like 'and', 'or', and 'for all' are logical expressions of English with respect to first-order logic. But this makes the distinction, and the concomitant notion of logical form, relative to a model-theoretic semantics, and a way of locating counterparts of ordinary expressions in the associated formal languages. In short, on this account, the logical–non-logical distinction would be an artefact of the logic. An item *t* in natural language would be logical *simpliciter* only if every reasonable model-theoretic semantics contains a logical item corresponding to *t*. Alternatively, one can maintain that some expressions of natural languages, or natural languages of mathematics, are logical independent of, and perhaps prior to, any model-theoretic semantics. Similarly, one can claim that each declarative sentence, or each argument, of natural language has a unique form, or forms, again independent of any semantics.[3] On such a view, a semantics is correct only if its logical terminology corresponds to the logical terminology of the natural language it models. There are a number of important philosophical issues related to this, some of which are developed in the next chapter. It is important to be as clear as possible about such matters in order to appraise the enterprise of foundations of mathematics and higher-order logic.

Many aspects of deductive systems have direct counterparts in semantics. Of those that have been introduced already, deductive consequence corresponds to validity, logical theoremhood corresponds to logical truth, and consistency corresponds to satisfiability. Many important properties of (full) logics concern the relationship between these counterparts. A logic is *weakly sound* if every theorem is a logical truth, and is *strongly sound*, or simply sound, if for every deducible argument $\langle \Gamma, \Phi \rangle$, Φ is a semantic consequence of Γ. Soundness is an indication that the deductive system is faithful to the semantics. Conversely, a logic is *weakly complete* if every logical truth is a theorem and is *strongly complete*, or simple *complete*,[4] if for each argument $\langle \Gamma, \Phi \rangle$, if Φ is a semantic consequence of Γ, then $\langle \Gamma, \Phi \rangle$ is deducible in the deductive system. If a logic is sound and complete, then a set Γ is consistent if and only if it is satisfiable.

Gödel's landmark completeness theorem (Gödel 1930; see Boolos and Jeffrey 1989, Chapter 12) applies to first-order languages with common deductive systems and semantics. It entails that, for such systems, many semantic properties are extensionally equivalent to their deductive counterparts. Logical consequence, validity, and satisfaction exactly correspond to deductive consequence, theoremhood, and consistency respectively. With the pervasiveness of first-order systems, it has become common practice to conflate the various counterparts. For example, one can establish that a given sentence can or cannot be deduced in a first-order theory by studying the models of the theory. Similarly, in treatments of independence, one readily infers that a formula is not a semantic consequence of others from the fact that it cannot be deduced from them (and, with soundness, vice versa). But, as will be shown (Chapter 4) there can be no completeness theorem for standard second-order logics (with an effective deductive system). This follows from Gödel's theorem on the *in*completeness of arithmetic. Thus it is important to the present enterprise that properties of deductive systems be kept distinct from their semantic counterparts.

Not every system studied by logicians is a full logic in the present sense. Some authors just develop a language and deductive system, and some just develop a language and semantics. To state the obvious, a given deductive system and a given semantics each presuppose a language, so we must assume at least that much. Moreover, a language in the present sense, a set of formulas, hardly deserves to be called a logic all by itself, no matter how precisely specified it is. The notion of consequence, whether semantic or deductive, must enter the picture at some point. So define a *logic* (*simpliciter*) to consist of a language, together with a deductive system, or a semantics, or both.

Call the language of a logic *uninterpreted* if there is no semantics associated with it. In an uninterpreted language, the terms have no referents. Any 'meaning' that the formulas are supposed to have is provided by the deductive system. Of course, the notions of semantic consequence and logical truth do not apply to such logics.

At the other extreme are logics whose 'semantics' consists of a single model. The language is then *fully interpreted*. An example would be an axiomatization of arithmetic whose sole intended interpretation is the natural numbers, with standard assignments to the numerals and the arithmetic function and relation symbols. Notice that in cases like this, a formula is a 'logical truth' just in case it is satisfied by the one model (under all assignments to the variables). Such formulas may simply be called 'truths'. One would not normally think of a fully interpreted language as a 'logic', unless there were a deductive system associated with it.

Notice that the distinction between logical and non-logical terminology collapses for fully interpreted languages, or at least it does under the present construal of the distinction. If there is only one model, then nothing varies, and so every item is logical. Similarly, for uninterpreted languages, there is no distinction to be made.

The usual sort of logical system developed today is neither uninterpreted nor fully interpreted. Typically, there are many models, several for each set. One can still regard some of the models as 'intended interpretations' of the language, or of a theory cast in the language. Under these circumstances, a formula is *true* if it is satisfied by the intended interpretation, or intended interpretations. Clearly, 'truth' and 'logical truth' are not the same. The latter involves all the models, intended or otherwise.

The general mathematical framework used to formulate and discuss the language, deductive system, and/or semantics of a logic is called a *metatheory*. A logic need not have all its components—language, deductive system, semantics—specified with full precision and rigour. Whatever is specified, of course, is specified with a language, often called the *metalanguage*. This metalanguage is a natural language of mathematics, and need not be one of the languages modelled by the logic in question.

Notice that the formulation of the grammar and deductive system of a logic typically presuppose the notion of finitude or natural number (in the recursion clauses). For example, we may read that 'a well-formed formula is a finite sequence of characters such that ...', and 'a formula is a theorem if there is a finite sequence of formulas such that ...'. Thus, if a metatheory is sufficient to formulate the grammar of a language and a deductive system, it must contain some arithmetic, or enough set theory to formulate the notion of finitude (see Corcoran *et al.* 1974; more on this below). Moreover, to be adequate to formulate the semantics of a logic, the metatheory must contain at least a rudimentary theory of sets, or something very similar. In particular, the resources of the metatheory should suffice to characterize the notion of 'model' (of the language of the logic) and, perhaps, to prove various theorems about the structure—some 'metatheorems'. Gödel's completeness theorem for first-order logic, for example, makes essential use of a principle of infinity. Indeed, if the semantics of a first-order language has only finite models, the usual deductive system is not complete. There are, in fact, consistent formulas that are not satisfied by any finite models.[5]

In short, the metatheory of a logic, any logic, is not free of ontological presuppositions or 'commitments'. Moreover, these presuppositions are often 'stronger' than those of the natural languages modelled by the components of the logic. One central concern of the present project is to determine the resources presumed available in certain metatheories.

1.2   What is the issue?

A decision concerning the proper status or role of higher-order logic depends on what one takes logic to *be* and, even more, on what one takes logic to be *for*. Such questions are related to the taxonomy of the previous section, since the aspects of logics that are developed and emphasized depend on what one is trying to accomplish. In addition, issues surrounding higher-order concepts are intimately related to rather basic matters in philosophy of logic and epistemology. We must address the nature and status of significant details of logic: variables, connectives, and quantifiers; the nature and status of classes and properties; the relationship between mathematics and logic. In the course of this book, we shall often return to these.

Here is the form of 'the question':

What is the [correct or best] [language or logic] in which to [   ]?

Now to the content. The important item is the goal or purpose for which a logic is chosen—what goes in the blank at the end of the form. So we begin there.

1.2.1   *The purpose*

Of course, the ends for which people study logic have evolved over time. Without attempting to be exhaustive, the possibilities include the following:

(1) to develop calculi that (more or less) accurately describe (correct) inference patterns of mathematics—each calculus is to describe correct inference for one or more areas;

(2) to carry out the logicistic programme and codify the underlying logic of *all* rational or scientific discourse—to capture the most general features of reasoning competence;

(3) to provide a framework in which all (or most) of mathematics can be (re)formulated—in short, a foundation;

(4) to formalize a particular branch of mathematics, such as arithmetic, analysis, geometry, or set theory, which can involve (4a) codifying the knowable (or deducible) propositions, or the truths, of that branch, or (4b) describing the structure (or structures) studied by that branch, or (4c) both;

(5) to enhance human reason;

(6) to carry out the positivist programme and establish a canonical language for science.

As noted, some of these goals are associated with different philosophical perspectives and programmes. By contemporary lights, some are controversial, if not dubious. Some are not, The second presupposes, or postulates, that *there is* an underlying logic of all rational or scientific discourse, presumably a single logic. The third postulates that there is (or can be) a foundation for all of mathematics. The fourth seems to involve some sort of realism towards the branch or branches in question, in that it assumes that there is a collection of knowable (or true) propositions to codify and/or a structure (or structures) to describe. On the other hand, a substantial anti-metaphysical agenda motivates the positivist programme, the sixth item in the list.

It is also clear that the above goals focus on different aspects of 'full logics'— language, deductive system, semantics. This is related to the fact that different criteria of success apply to the different goals. For example, the development of a calculus, goal (1), was a central concern of early algebraically minded logicians like Boole, Peirce, and Schröder. A calculus was also an important (but perhaps not central) feature of Frege's work in logic. In these cases, of course, an *effective deductive system* is requisite, at least if one agrees (with some hindsight perhaps) that a system must be effective in order to qualify as a calculus.[6] Notice that this has very little to do with semantics, as presently construed. The algebraists did have various interpretations of their systems in mind, but semantics was not a central concern. Also, the logicists, including Frege, did not develop model-theoretic semantics, partly because their systems were *fully interpreted*. There was no non-logical terminology whose referents would vary from model to model.[7]

Less trivially, if one is interested in *codifying correct inference* (or deducible propositions), either in a given area (goals (1) and (4a)) or in all areas at once (goal (2)), then one would want the deductive consequence relation to match human inference-competence in appropriate ways. If one further takes inference-competence to be effective in some sense, then the deductive consequence relation must also be effective. In his lecture on 'Mathematical problems' (Hilbert 1900a, Problem 2), Hilbert wrote:

> When we are investigating the foundations of a science, we must set up a system of axioms which contains an exact and complete description of the ... ideas of that science ... no statement within the realm of the science ... is held to be true unless it can be deduced from the axioms by means of a finite number of logical steps.

Wagner (1987) argues that an effective deductive consequence relation is also an essential ingredient of the Fregean programme (goal (2)). If, on the other hand, one takes human inference-competence to be more far-reaching, then an effective consequence relation is not requisite and may not be desired. As we shall see (Chapter 7), Zermelo held a view like this.[8]

The cases under consideration here (goals (1), (2) and (4a)) concern deductive systems. The goal of the enterprise is sometimes called 'completeness'. A deductive system is 'complete' in this sense if it has, as theorems or deducible arguments, all and only the items that are supposed to be characterized, be they truths, arguments, etc. Notice that this is a different, more general, use of the word 'completeness' than that of Section 1.1. In that case, the items to be codified by the deductive system are the formulas and/or arguments that are valid in the given model-theoretic semantics.

Case (4b), whose purpose is the description of a *structure* (or structures), concerns semantics, since the focus there is on the interpretations of the language. An axiomatization is successful if its models are all and only the members of the class of structures to be described. If a single structure is to be described, the goal is categoricity: an axiomatization is *categorical* if all its models are isomorphic to each other. As Veblen (1904) puts it, if an axiomatization is categorical, then it has 'essentially only one' interpretation. Moreover, he seemed explicitly aware of the fact that different goals suggest different aspects of logical systems. The purpose of his axiomatization of geometry is to *describe* Euclidean space. He noted that once a categorical characterization is accomplished, 'any further axiom would have to be considered redundant', to which a footnote is added, '... even were it not deducible from the [other] axioms by a finite number of syllogisms'. Such a 'further axiom' is redundant only to the description of Euclidean space, not to the codification of the deducible principles thereof. In his extensive study of categoricity, Corcoran (1980) constructed a set of axioms such that all its models are isomorphic to the natural numbers, but fundamental truths, like the associativity of addition, cannot be deduced from them. This establishes, in a dramatic way, that characterizing a structure and codifying a set of knowable truths are different projects. For the purpose of describing a structure, one would not insist on an effective (semantic) consequence relation.

Finally, cases like (4c), which attempt both description of structures and codification of knowable or true propositions, involve both semantics and deductive systems. These situations invite questions of soundness and completeness (in the sense of Section 1.1), questions that concern the relationship between the components of a full logic. In a sense, these questions involve the extent to which description and codification can be accomplished simultaneously with matching systems. In these terms, a major theme of this book is that in interesting cases, they cannot. First-order languages are inadequate for description and communication, while second-order logic is inherently incomplete; its semantic consequence relation is not effective.

1.2.2 *Language or logic?*

Returning to the question-form, the middle item 'language or logic' is perhaps only a matter of terminology, but clarity can forestall confusion. There are, I believe, more profound issues that lie nearby. As in the opening section, a full logic is a formal language, together with a deductive system and a model-theoretic semantics. Among these, the crucial item at present is *semantics*. Indeed, languages and deductive systems, by themselves, are neither first-order nor higher-order. The central focus of the present study is the extent of the *range* of the higher-order variables. In standard second-order systems, predicate variables range over *all* properties or relations or classes of whatever is in the range of the first-order variables. Recall that in the present orientation, a language is simply a collection of formulas and a deductive system is a collection of deductions. As will be shown (Chapter 3), neither has much to say about what the variables are supposed to range over, or what the natural languages being modelled are about. That is a question of 'meaning', at least broadly construed, and it is addressed in the model-theoretic semantics.[9]

It is possible for a deductive system to *rule out* a standard second-order interpretation in the sense that no semantics with variables ranging over *all* properties or all subsets (of the domain) is sound for it. This occurs if there are theorems corresponding to the 'non-existence' of certain classes or properties. For example, the sentence

$$\neg \exists P \forall x (\neg P x)$$

is an analogue of the denial of an empty class or property. This is false, of course, on a standard second-order reading. So define a deductive system to be *second-order sound* if it is possible to develop a sound semantics for it in which there is a sort of variable that, in each model, ranges over all classes or relations of whatever is in the range of the ordinary first-order variables of that model. Such systems are the focus of the present work.

On the other hand, languages and deductive systems, by themselves, do not determine the range or extension of the higher-order variables. It is not possible to 'guarantee' an appropriate higher-order interpretation, even if the deductive system is second-order sound. As will be shown (Chapter 3), *any* higher-order language and deductive system can be interpreted as a many-sorted first-order system (see also Gilmore 1957). That is, a first-order semantics is available for virtually all the languages and deductive systems under consideration here. The semantics will contain models in which the higher-order variables do not range over all subclasses of the domain. It will be shown (Chapter 4) that any effective deductive system which is second-order sound has an effective consistent extension (in the same language) that is not second-order sound. This is a corollary of Gödel's incompleteness theorem.

In sum, second-order logic is distinguished by the range of some of the variables (with respect to the range of the first-order variables). On the taxonomy of logic as language, deductive system, and semantics, this is a matter for semantics. Thus, for example, uninterpreted languages are neither first-order nor higher-order. If, on the other hand, a model-theoretic semantics is explicitly developed (including what are called above 'fully intrepreted languages'), the situation is straightforward, assuming that no questions are raised concerning the meaning of the terms of the metalanguage. The issue at hand depends on the *stated* range of the higher-order variables. In *standard* semantics, in each model the property variables range over the entire powerset of the domain of discourse. This makes the logic properly second-order. To specify a model, one only gives a domain and denotations or extensions of the non-logical terminology. This automatically fixes the range of the higher-order variables. There is no more 'interpreting' to be done. In *non-standard* or Henkin semantics, in each model the ranges for the first-order and higher-order variables are separately designated. In effect, this renders the logic a many-sorted *first-order* system. Details are presented below (Chapter 3).

There are, of course, situations in which a language is presented which is not intended to be uninterpreted, but no explicit model-theoretic semantics is given. The intended interpretation, or interpretations, of such a language is left intuitive or informal. The question of whether the language is higher-order is then a matter of exegesis. It depends on whether the range of the extra variables is 'intended' to include all properties or relations or classes of whatever the first-order variables range over. It may not be all that clear how to adjudicate the matter in particular cases. This issue is pursued in Chapters 7 and 8 below.

1.2.3 *Correct or best?*

In the question-form, the first item concerns the issue of whether one should strive for the 'correct' logic or the 'best' logic. The difference here is philosophical, and seems to depend on one's views concerning correct inference in the natural language that is modelled by the formal language. Once the goal for the enterprise of logic has been fixed (by filling in the blank in the question-form), one may or may not hold that there is a single correct language/logic for that goal. I suggest, however, that this question may not amount to much. The 'absolutist' who prefers the word 'correct' presumably has criteria for correctness in mind. If not, he can be accused of begging the question, or of being dogmatic, in favour of a preferred candidate logic. These criteria might very well be endorsed by the 'anti-absolutist' opposition, as criteria for 'best' logic. If philosophical rhetoric is submerged, perhaps the discourse could continue without resolving this issue of absoluteness. In the cases at hand, it might be added that, historically, disputants sometimes came from different philosophical schools, but, as will be seen (Chapter 7), the disputes themselves rarely took a purely philosophical tone —at least not over the issue of absolutism.

One difference between our advocates may be that the anti-absolutist is prepared to accept different answers to 'the question' even after the goal has been precisely formulated. Rather than a single best language/logic, there may be rivals, each with compensating strengths and weaknesses but with rough parity overall. This, I believe, is in fact the case in the present situation. But perhaps the absolutist could concede the possibility that 'the question' is ambiguous and thus does not have a unique answer.

Let us briefly consider an extreme version of absolutism, the view that there is but one correct logic, period. An advocate may claim that this logic is established through soundness and completeness theorems concerning a deductive system and semantics underlying all rational or scientific or, at least, mathematical discourse. Of course this presupposes that *there is* a (single) model-theoretic semantics that captures the central features of all relevant natural languages. This may also involve a thesis that there is a single distinction between logical and non-logical terminology for natural languages, drawn once and for all. Perhaps there would also be a single notion of logical form, and each argument in natural language would have but one form.

It is often held, and sometimes argued, that classical first-order logic is the only (real) logic there is, After all, its deductive system is sound and complete with respect to a semantics that does capture many features of natural languages of mathematics. I have argued against this extreme absolutism elsewhere (Shapiro 1989a, Section 2), and the arguments presented in this book serve as a secondary indirect attack.

It should be noted that, historically, first-order logic is only a *sub*system. The productions of Frege, Russell, Hilbert, and Peano, for example, are all higher-order. In fact, it was not until around 1915, with Löwenheim's result, that first-order logic was distinguished as even a *part* of logic for separate treatment (of which more later in Chapter 7; see also Moore (1980, 1988)). Nevertheless, it may come to pass that logicians advocate and study only classical first-order systems. We cannot rule out the possibility that the 'triumph' of first-order logic will be complete. However, if I may be permitted to be smug, both towards this possibility and towards those who currently hold that first-order logic is all there is, it might be recalled that it was once held that Aristotelian logic is the only logic there is. The considerations that toppled this view were of the same nature as those advanced in this book. The subsystems in question are not good models of important aspects of mathematics as practised.

1.3 Sets and properties

Second-order variables are commonly taken to range over concepts, properties, relations, propositional functions, or classes of whatever is in the range of the ordinary first-order variables. For the moment, let us focus on the monadic items in this list, properties (or concepts) and classes. Anything said about these will apply to the others.

Properties and classes are, of course, different. Consider the basic vocabulary associated with them. We say that object x *has* property P, P *applies to* x, and P *holds of* x. This is written Px. On the other hand, we say that x is an *element of* class C, x *is in* C, and x *belongs to* C; this is written $x \in C$. Classes are extensional: if every element of a class A is an element of a class B, and vice versa, then $A = B$. However, properties are often taken to be intensional. Equiangular and equilateral are thought to be different properties of triangles, even though any triangle is equilateral if and only if it is equiangular. In the present study, however, I propose to gloss over these differences and, in fact, sometimes the terms are used interchangeably. In fact, I have little to say about the identity relation on the items in the range of the second-order variables. For example, in the formal language developed in Chapter 3, the identity sign $=$ only occurs between first-order terms. If X and Y are second-order variables, then the expression $X = Y$ is not well-formed. For the most part, one is free to interpret the (present) second-order variables as ranging over classes or as ranging over properties, even though classes are the main ingredient of the model-theoretic semantics.

There are two plausible Quinean themes that militate against this evasion. One is that the ontology of a theory is the range of its bound variables. Since, for Quine, the term 'bound variable' is a technical term associated with *first-order* logic, the ontology of an interpreted language is to be assessed by somehow rephrasing it in a first-order language. And Quine is a steadfast opponent of higher-order logic (see, for example, Quine (1970), of which more later). Nevertheless, it is straightforward to extend the thesis concerning ontology to second-order languages, as interpreted here. Since such languages have bound variables ranging over classes or properties, they have classes or properties in their ontology. The second Quinean thesis is 'no entity without identity'. One cannot claim to speak of objects, or items in one's ontology, without an identity relation on them. If given two items, two properties for example, it must be clear and determinate whether they are the same or different.

As early as 1941, Quine attacked the system of *Principia Mathematica* on the grounds that the items in the range of the higher-order variables (attributes or propositional functions) are intensional and thus do not have a clearly defined identity relation (Quine 1941). He proposed that classes, which are extensional, be used instead. The reason that this goes so smoothly is that classes are structurally similar to properties. The predication relation between properties and objects corresponds to the membership relation between sets and elements: Px is analogous to $x \in C$. Define two properties P, Q to be *extensionally equivalent* if every object that has P also has Q, and vice versa, i.e. $\forall x(Px \equiv Qx)$. Notice that extensional equivalence is an equivalence relation on properties. Given the fact that most of standard mathematics is thoroughly extensional, extensional equivalence is also a congruence, at least in most contexts: if $\Phi(P)$ and $\forall x(Px \equiv Qx)$, then $\Phi(Q)$. If attention is restricted to such contexts, then there is no impediment to taking properties to be extensional, and systematically to conflate them with classes. In fact, $X = Y$ can be defined as $\forall x(Xx \equiv Yx)$. Nevertheless, I apologize to sensitive readers.

The relationship between congruence and identity, and thus ontology, is a version of the Leibniz principle on the identity of indiscernibles. In the contemporary setting, it is treated in Shapiro (1989b) (see also Kraut 1980). Of course, in other contexts, like modal logic and discussions of the propositional attitudes of natural languages, extensional equivalence is not a congruence among properties, and classes cannot be conflated with them.[10]

Quine (1970) holds that in invoking classes, one has somehow crossed the border between logic and mathematics; thus his opposition to second-order logic. The theory of classes, set theory, has a 'staggering ontology', while logic, properly so-called, should presuppose no ontology, or at least its ontology should be as modest as possible. This border issue is not addressed here, at least not directly. The present attitude is reflected in another of Quine's views. He has forcefully argued that there is no useful border to be drawn between mathematics and physics, or between mathematics and just about any science for that matter. Consider the amount of mathematics presupposed in even elementary science courses. The question here is why should logic, especially the logic *of mathematics*, be different? Why should it be devoid of mathematical, and ontological, presuppositions, and why should there be a useful border between logic and mathematics?

Nevertheless, the matter of ontology needs to be addressed. This concerns the notion of 'class' (or property) and its role in logic, and it concerns the status of the membership (or predication) relation. There is a tradition, dating at least from Boole, that takes classes (or properties) to be under the purview of logic. Standing in that tradition, or at least noting it, is Gödel, who in his paper on Russell (Gödel 1944) states that mathematical logic deals with 'classes [and] relations . . . instead of numbers, geometric forms, etc.'. The early algebraists, Boole, Peirce, and Schröder for example, took the subsets of a fixed domain to be under study by logic—this was one of the stated interpretations of their systems.[11] Frege also took the study of concepts, and their extensions, to be within logic (see, for example, Frege 1884). Russell also accepted classes within logic, at least before his 'no classes' interpretation. In Russell (1903, p. 11) he wrote, 'The subject of Symbolic Logic consists of three parts, the calculus of propositions, the calculus of classes, and the calculus of relations'. He also notes that 'the relation of a term to a class of which it is a member' is a primitive 'indefinable', a 'logical constant'. Two pages later, Russell comes close to the above conflation of properties and classes: '... the study of propositional functions appears to be strictly on a par with that of classes, and indeed scarcely distinguishable therefrom'.

One might think that pre-Fregean confusions are being reintroduced here, perhaps flirting with Russell's paradox. Admittedly, some care is required. There are, I believe, different orientations towards classes, or sets, and it is important to keep them distinct.

In all the cases mentioned so far, the focus is on the subsets of a *fixed* universe, or domain. That is, the context of the theory determines, or presupposes, a universe of discourse, a range of the first-order variables. A set is a subset of this universe (only). Call this the *logical sense* of 'set'. Accordingly, the word 'set' is like an indexical expression in ordinary language (e.g. 'I', 'this', 'here') in that its extension depends heavily on the context of use. Thus, in arithmetic, a logical set is a collection of numbers; in geometry, a logical set is a collection of points (or regions) etc. There are no logical sets *simpliciter*, only logical sets within a given context, although, of course, the context can be left unspecified.

In contrast, current axiomatic set theory, as it developed from the work of Cantor, Zermelo, Skolem, Fraenkel, etc., involves a binary relation on a single universe consisting of a (possibly empty) collection of urelements, sets of those, sets of sets of those, etc., with the 'set of' relation possibly iterated into the transfinite.[12] This is referred to as the *iterative sense* of 'set'. In this framework, a 'set' is sometimes called a 'well-founded set' (see Boolos 1971).

In short, an iterative set is an element of the set-theoretic hierarchy which is not an urelement. The urelements and the iterative sets form a domain of a single theory—set theory. In contemporary terms, the symbol for membership is *non-logical*. The logical notion of set, on the other hand, always refers to a domain fixed by context. A logical set is a subclass of this domain. Its membership relation is part of the logical systems of the early algebraically minded logicians, as well as the logicists Frege and Russell (at least of 1903). Part of the issue concerning higher-order logic is the extent to which the logical notion of set is a legitimate part of logic.

In every context, logical sets exemplify what may be called a *Boolean* structure. Every set x has a complement, the set of all elements of the domain that do not belong to x. There is also a 'universal set', the entire domain. The complement of the universal set is the empty set. In contrast, iterative sets are not Boolean. *No* iterative set has a complement (that is itself an iterative set). There is an empty set, but there is no universal set, since the entire set-theoretic hierarchy is not an iterative set.

Confusion between the two notions of 'set', and the danger of contradiction, should arise only in set theory and related contexts, since in such cases the 'fixed domain', the context of the logical notion, is itself the set-theoretic hierarchy. An iterative set is an element of that hierarchy (other than an urelement) and, in this context, a logical set is a *collection* of iterative sets, what is today called a 'class' or a 'set concept'. The argument behind Russell's paradox shows that in set theory there are logical sets (i.e. classes) that are not iterative sets. In other words, there are collections of iterative sets that are not elements of the set-theoretic hierarchy. They are called 'proper classes'. For example, the entire hierarchy is a proper class.

This suggests that Russell's paradox should trouble those theorists who employ both the logical notion of set *and* presuppose an all-inclusive domain of discourse, one that might be taken to contain all its subdomains as elements. To some extent, history confirms this. For the most part, only the logicists, like Frege and Russell, were affected, for they introduced variables to range over all objects whatsoever, which at least prima facie includes all collections of objects. As noted, Fregean concepts are structurally similar to the present logical sets. Although Frege clearly separated concepts from objects, he came to associate each concept with an object, its extension. The infamous Axiom V, that two concepts have the same extension if and only if they are extensionally equivalent, led to the paradox (Frege 1903). Russell himself addressed this (and other antinomies) by avoiding variables that range over the entire set-theoretic hierarchy. Instead, the all-inclusive domain is separated into individuals, classes (or properties) of individuals, classes of classes of individuals, etc. Each item must be in a fixed level, and each variable ranges over only one level.[13]

For the present purposes, the interesting cases are those authors who did *not* feel threatened by the paradox. Zermelo independently discovered Russell's paradox a full year before Russell (see Rang and Thomas 1981), but did not publish it and continued his work in set theory. Whether or not Zermelo held what I call the 'iterative notion' of set at this time, he apparently did not believe that set theory, as he construed it, was undermined.[14] In the aforementioned paper on Russell, Gödel (1944) also states that the iterative notion of set was never affected by the paradoxes. The early algebraists were also by and large untouched by Russell's paradox. In the algebraic tradition, they did not often specify a specific domain, but they only considered one domain at a time, together with its subdomains. The subdomains are not elements of the domain under consideration. Thus the logical notion of set is suitable for their work. Schröder (1980, p. 245) remarked that one cannot, without contradiction, let the fixed domain consist of all objects, which would presumably contain all collections of objects. He stated that the subsets of a domain cannot be elements of it.[15] The contrast with the logicists is striking.[16]

Cocchiarella (e.g. 1986, 1988, 1989) has distinguished a 'logical' and a 'mathematical' notion of 'class'. This has something in common with the present treatment, but there are important differences:

> ... there is a ... distinction between the logical notion of a class, i.e., the notion of a class as the extension of a concept (or property, or propositional function ...) and the mathematical notion of class, which is none other than the iterative concept of set. Thus, whereas a set, as based on the iterative concept (according to which sets are formed in stages from sets of objects of the preceding stage or stages), has its being in the objects that belong to it, a class in the logical sense, i.e., as the extension of a concept, 'simply has its being in the concept, not in the objects which belong to it'. (Cocchiarella (1989, p. 78); the passage quoted at the end is from Frege (1906))

For Cocchiarella, a mathematical class is what is called here an 'iterative set', an element of the set-theoretic hierarchy. To avoid confusion of terminology, let us use the term 'Fregean class' for what Cocchiarella calls a 'class in the logical sense'. The *extension* of a concept P is the collection of all objects that fall under P. This extension is a Fregean class. Conversely, every Fregean class is associated with a concept, the concept whose extension it is. So Fregean classes are less fundamental than concepts. And the concomitant membership relation is not primitive, since it is derived from the relation between concepts and objects that fall under them. Indeed, let P be a concept and C its extension. Then, by definition, an object x is a member of C if and only if x falls under P. With mathematical sets, on the other hand, membership is a genuine primitive. A mathematical set is composed of its elements. Also, Fregean classes have a Boolean structure because concepts do, but the structure of mathematical sets is not Boolean.

Cocchiarella agrees that Russell's paradox does not bear on the iterative notion of set, but it does have grave consequences for the Fregean notion of class. Grave, but not insurmountable. Fregean classes are objects and, as such, they are in the range of *first-order* variables. The troubling item is the extension of the concept Rx expressed by 'there is a concept P such that P is the extension of x and x does not fall under P'. One resolution is to hold that some concepts, like Rx, do not have extensions. A second option is to reject the assertion that every formula determines a concept. There simply is no concept Rx expressed by the above phrase. Cocchiarella has provided careful detailed elaborations of these and other options, and shows that the resulting theories are consistent.

The present study eschews foundational questions, such as whether the classes in the range of our second-order variables, and the concomitant membership relation, are ultimately based on concepts, or whether the classes are based on the iterative notion of set. Our languages and semantics are regarded as mathematical models of natural languages of mathematics and there is no concern with the 'primitives' of natural languages. On the other hand, the preferred model-theoretic semantics developed for second-order languages, called 'standard semantics', does make essential use of set theory. In effect, the iterative hierarchy is the background for standard semantics. Thus, for Cocchiarella, the present 'logical sets', the items in the range of the second-order variables, are iterative sets after all.

To pursue this point, let d be the range of the first-order variables under an intended interpretation of a second-order language. The question at hand is whether, for each iterative set x whose members are all in d, there is a class in the range of the second-order variables whose members are all and only the members of x. In standard semantics, the answer is 'yes'.[17] As shown in Chapters 4 and 5, this entails that the range of the second-order variables has a larger cardinality than that of d, the range of the first-order variables, and it entails that the resulting logic is incomplete. For Cocchiarella, it also entails that the items in the range of the second-order variables are iterative sets, not Fregean classes. This can be conceded if it is noted that the use of the iterative hierarchy is limited to the metatheory, which is an attempt to capture, or model, important features of natural languages, and natural languages of mathematics. The succeeding chapters of this book go to great lengths to argue that standard semantics does, in fact, capture important features of the natural languages of mathematics being modelled. I do not deny that Cocchiarella's systems also capture important features of natural languages.

Returning to the question of ontology, it should be clear that it is set theory, the theory of the iterative hierarchy, that has a 'staggering ontology'. The logical notion of set, as construed here, does not have a fixed ontology, independent of context (just as indexicals do not have denotations independent of context). Following the aforementioned Quinean thesis that the ontology of a theory is the range of its bound variables, the logical notion of set presupposes the subclasses of a domain whose members are already presupposed. But no more. In short, the logical notion does entail additional ontology, the members of one powerset of the given domain, but it is nowhere near that of set theory.[18] Second-order arithmetic, for example, presupposes the natural numbers, plus all sets of numbers. Its ontology has the size of the continuum. Second-order analysis presupposes all real numbers, plus all sets of real numbers, the powerset of the continuum. Second-order set theory does indeed have a staggering ontology, but so does first-order set theory, if taken literally.

In general, let d be a domain and let κ be the cardinality of d. Consider a second-order theory whose first-order variables are intended to range over d. The second-order variables range over the logical sets of d (in the present sense of the term). There are 2^{κ} such sets. It does not follow that the second-order language is somehow committed to a single domain consisting of the powerset of d. Having each subset of d in one's ontology is not the same as envisaging the powerset of d as a single entity. But one could make this move and develop a second-order language whose *first-order* variables range over the subsets of d, and, in keeping with the logical notion of set, the predicate variables would range over subsets of the powerset of d. Alternatively, one could develop a *third-order* language whose first-order variables range over d, whose second-order variables range over the subsets of d, and whose third-order variables range over subsets of the powerset of d. There is no reason, however, for this process to be continued indefinitely. One just develops formal languages as needed for specific purposes. If the process is continued indefinitely, one arrives at something like simple type theory (see Church 1976). This amounts to (at most) the finitary iteration of the powerset operator. The total ontology is still much less than that of an iterative set theory containing the domain d.

The situation is not quite this simple when one assesses the ontology of the *metatheory* of second-order logic, including the mathematical language used to characterize the model-theoretic semantics. Such a theory could also figure in a rigorous foundation to the work of the early algebraic logicians. It seems clear that this metatheory postulates a universe of domains, and includes a principle that, for every domain d, there is a domain consisting of all subsets of d. This, of course, is the powerset axiom. Again, thus far we are only committed to the finitary iteration of the powerset, and there is still no principle of replacement. Nevertheless, it seems that full Zermelo–Fraenkel set theory is a good metatheory for second-order logic (or first-order logic for that matter). In fact, the metatheory preferred here is *second-order* set theory (see Chapter 6, Section 6.1). It does indeed have a staggering ontology, but this does not reverse the previous claims about second-order languages. First, the standard semantics of second-order logic is much the same as that of first-order logic. Both employ the same class of models. Second, any given metatheory will have resources beyond those of some of the natural languages modelled by the formal languages subsumed under it. Tarski's theorem, and similar results, shows that a given theory cannot be used to formulate the semantic concepts for itself. The reason standard metatheory has a 'staggering ontology' is that it is rich enough to model all, or almost all, the possible domains invoked in mathematical theories.[19] This is related to the major expressive *strength* of the second-order languages, their ability to describe mathematical structures. We shall return to this theme several times in the chapters that follow.

Notes

1. Infinitary languages are briefly considered in Chapter 9.
2. See Corcoran (1983) and Etchemendy (1988) for insightful accounts of how the notion of logical consequences developed by Tarski (1935) differs from that of current model-theoretic semantics.

3. See Tarski (1986) and McCarthy (1981) for different accounts of the logical–non-logical distinction for natural languages of mathematics.

4. As formulated here, these completeness properties concern the relationship between deductive systems and semantics. However, sometimes a semantics (alone) is called (weakly) 'complete' if its set of logical truths is recursively enumerable. Wagner (1987), for example, employs the terminology this way. If a semantics is 'complete' in this sense, then there is an effective deductive system for the language such that the resulting (full) logic is weakly complete in the above sense.

5. An example is the conjunction of two standard axioms for arithmetic: $\forall x(sx \neq 0)$ & $\forall x \forall y(sx = sy \rightarrow x = y)$.

6. A calculus is a system of rules for drawing conclusions, on the analogy of calculation. As defined in the previous section, a deductive system is effective if its class of deductions is recursive. Thus the claim that a deductive system must be effective to qualify as a calculus is a variant of Church's thesis. In Shapiro (1983), I argue that problems of explicating the nature of deductive systems was a central motivation behind the development of computability in the 1930s (see also Gandy 1988).

7. This is an important difference between Frege and the algebraic logicians. See, for example, Frege (1983), and also van Heijenoort (1967b) and Goldfarb (1979). This matter is pursued in Chapter 7 below. Notice, for the present, that the systems of Frege (and of Russell and Whitehead) can be fully interpreted only because they are higher-order. They contain (quantified) predicate and relation *variables*, rather than non-logical schematic letters.

8. According to Wang (1987), Gödel also held that the human ability to reason goes beyond what can be modelled by an effective deductive system, but he still insisted on first-order logic, with its perfect match between model-theoretic semantics and an effective deductive system. It would seem, then, that Gödel did not accept the goal of describing (or extending) human inference-competence. The relationship between logic and computation is considered in the next chapter.

9. Of course, to qualify as even a *potential* component of a higher-order logic, a language must normally have more than one sort of variable. Even this requirement can be circumvented, however, if certain distinguished properties are introduced. In a single-sorted language, for example, one can have phrases corresponding to 'x is an individual object', 'x is a binary relation', etc. This approach is somewhat awkward, not to mention artificial, and it is not pursued here.

10. It might be added that it is not the case that all of mathematics is extensional. See, for example, the papers in Shapiro (1985b).

11. There is some hindsight here, however, since the algebraists did not always distinguish the membership relation from the subset relation, and sometimes conflated the singleton with its element.

12. For example, there is a set consisting of all sets obtainable by finite iteration of the 'set of' relation, and there are sets of those, sets of sets of those, etc. An *urelement* is an object in the domain that is not a set of other objects in the domain. The axioms of contemporary set theory rule out the existence of urelements.

13. The separation of the universe into such levels is, of course, only part of Russell's resolution of the antinomies. Each level (beyond the first) is further divided, or 'ramified', to avoid impredicative definitions. This is briefly developed in Chapter 3.

14. See Moore (1978). Zermelo (1908b) does mention Russell's paradox in the opening paragraph, noting that 'the very existence of [set theory] seems to be threatened'. By careful analysis of Zermelo's work in its historical context, Moore shows that the operative word here is 'seems', for Zermelo took the threat to be more apparent than real (see also Zermelo 1908a, Section 20). For example, the stated plan is to 'start with set theory as it is historically given'. This programme would be a rather poor one if set theory 'as it is historically given' is fundamentally flawed. In Zermelo's mind, the culprit is an unrestricted principle that every 'collection . . . of . . . well-distinguished objects' is a set. This seems close to the above formulation of the paradox—not every logical set is an element of the hierarchy. In Zermelo's mind, what actually *was* threatened was the general acceptance of his proof of the well-ordering theorem, and the axiomatization was addressed to that. Zermelo (1930) eventually adopted the iterative notion explicitly.

15. See Church (1976) and Rang and Thomas (1981). In the cited passage, Schröder criticizes an earlier suggestion by Boole that one interpretation of 'class 1' is the universal class, the collection of everything. This, however, is not a precursor to Russell's paradox. Schröder's text is rather obscure, and includes the conflation of the element and subset relations. Frege (1895) had little trouble dispensing with the argument.

16. This relatively neat division of historical treatment of set, class, property, concept, etc. requires some hindsight, and there are exceptions to it. Frege's correspondence with Hilbert indicates just how far the latter was from the logicists (see Resnik 1980, Chapter 3), and, as far as I know, Hilbert never considered a universal all-encompassing domain. Thus, according to the thesis at hand, he should not have been bothered by Russell's paradox. Yet after learning of the paradox, he took a cautious view of sets, while realizing their importance for logic. In 1905 he wrote:

> . . . the conceptions . . . of logic, conceived in the traditional sense, do not measure up to the rigorous demands that set theory makes . . . Yet if we observe attentively, we realize that in the traditional treatment of . . . logic, certain fundamental notions are used, such as the noton of set. (Hilbert 1905, p. 176)

This historical matter is pursued further in Chapter 7.

17. In Chapter 4, two 'non-standard' semantics are developed according to which the answer to the question is 'no'. One of these, called 'first-order semantics', is close to the semantics presented in Cocchiarella (1988, Section 6).

18. Chapter 9, Section 9.2, presents a semantics, due to Boolos (1984a, 1985), according to which the ontological presuppositions of a second-order theory are the same as those of its corresponding first-order theory. In Boolos' view, the Quinean dictum concerning ontology need not be extended to higher-order variables.

19. The first-order variables of set theory range over all iterative sets. This is enough to develop model-theoretic semantics for higher-order languages characterizing all branches of mathematics short of set theory itself (and perhaps category theory). Even set theory can be accommodated if one allows models whose domains are proper classes. As will be shown (Chapter 6), this can be accomplished in second-order set theory, if terminology for satisfaction by (proper) classes is added.

Foundationalism and foundations
of mathematics

The names of once exotic, but now commonplace, mathematical entities indicate a conservative tendency among mathematicians. Beyond the 'natural' numbers, there are 'negative', 'irrational', 'transcendental', and finally 'imaginary' numbers. Fortunately, the profession has always had its bold imaginative souls, but it seems that they do not get to provide names. Part of the purpose of foundational studies had been to respond to the desire for intellectual security.

In the preface of his landmark work on the foundations of real analysis Weyl (1917) wrote:

> With this essay, we do not intend to erect ... a ... wooden frame around the solid rock upon which rests the building of analysis, for the purpose of persuading the reader—and ultimately ourselves—that we have thus laid the true foundation. Here we claim instead that an essential part of this structure is built on sand. I believe I can replace this shifting ground with a trustworthy foundation; this will not support everything we now hold secure; I will sacrifice the rest as I see no other solution.

In this work, Weyl proposed certain 'predicative' restrictions on analysis, and later he adopted intuitionism.

As a first approximation, define *foundationalism* to be the view that it is possible and desirable to reconstruct each (legitimate) branch of mathematics on a completely secure basis, one that is maximally immune to rational doubt. It is an epistemological enterprise. For better or worse, foundationalist programmes explicitly or implicitly dominated much of the work in logic and foundations of mathematics until recently, but, for good reason, foundationalism has fallen into disrepute. The purpose of this chapter is to examine how much of the perspective of foundationalism is still plausible, and how logic and foundational studies are to be understood in the prevailing anti-foundationalist spirit. How are such studies to be evaluated now? It seems that philosophical movements spawn tendencies that remain long after the views themselves are dismissed, at least publicly. One of these tendencies, I believe, is a preference for first-order logic.

The conclusion is that just as we have learned to live with uncertainty in virtually every special subject, we can live with uncertainty in logic and foundations of mathematics, and we can live well. The first of Weyl's claims, that mathematics does not have an absolutely secure foundation, is correct.

To pursue his metaphor, it is a house build on sand. But his ultimate conclusion, that there is something wrong with this, is incorrect. The practising mathematician and the practising logician do not stand in need of a secure basis for their work; the building does not fall down when we realize its lack of grounding in bedrock. It is secure enough as it is, at least most of the time. There are important roles for foundations of mathematics, but providing maximal security is not among them. Weyl's own metaphor is suggestive. The 'foundation' is wood; the main structure, mathematics, is rock.

2.1   Variations and metaphors

Let P be a body of knowledge or a field of study. The main example, of course, is mathematics or one of its branches. A *foundation* for P is a reconstruction of its principles, either its truths or its knowable propositions. There are at least two forms that a foundation can take. One of them, the *axiomatic method*, consists of a collection of propositions, the *axioms*, together with a demonstration that all, or many, of the accepted truths of P can be derived from them. The axioms can be given in a natural language of mathematics, as in Euclid's *Elements*, or else one can specify a formal language for this purpose. As in Chapter 1, the formal language is a mathematical model of the natural language of mathematics normally used for P. One may also specify a deductive system as part of the foundation. The other sort of foundation may be called *reductive*. The basic subject matter of P is cast, or recast, in terms of another mathematical theory. The 'definitions' of integers as pairs of natural numbers, rational numbers as pairs of integers, real numbers as Cauchy sequences of rational numbers, and complex numbers as pairs of real numbers are reductive foundations of various fields. Of course, with a reductive foundation of P, there must be another field Q to which P is reduced. The definitions are cast in the terms of Q. The two sorts of foundation can be combined. One gives a reductive foundation of P in terms of Q, and also gives an axiomatic foundation of Q. For example, virtually every field of modern mathematics can be reduced to Zermelo–Fraenkel set theory which, in turn, enjoys a rigorous axiomatic foundation.

The word 'foundation' suggests an analogy with the construction of buildings. The analogue of the building is the field of study P. One striking disanalogy is that, in most cases, the field P was not developed like a building by *first* laying a foundation and then adding floors, walls, ceilings, more storeys, etc. In mathematics, foundational activity often takes place after the field P is established, sometimes long after. At most, foundational activity is contemporaneous with the development of P. To take just one example, the axiomatization of arithmetic by, say, Peano, Dedekind, or even Euclid came after the development of substantial knowledge of the natural numbers.[1]

Define *strong foundationalism* for P to be the view that there is a *single* foundation for P, one that is absolutely secure, or, failing that, as secure as is humanly possible. The metaphor is that in providing a foundation, one as attempting to 'dig' one's way to *the* ultimate basis for belief in the theses of P, an attempt to uncover what is already there for all to see.[2] From this perspective, the claim behind a reductive foundation is that the real subject matter of P has been discovered. Consequently, judgements in P are ultimately based on judgements in the reducing field. With an axiomatic foundation, the claim is that one has discovered the central core of the theses of P. This core, presumably, is self-evident, or as evident as possible, and everything else is based on it.

Define *moderate foundationalism* for P to be the view that it is possible to provide *at least one* foundation for P, again either absolutely secure or as good as possible. Here, the metaphor is that in putting forward a candidate, one is not necessarily 'digging down', but rather is 'building up' from the 'bedrock' to P. Instead of exposing what is already there, one is providing something new in the development of P. A moderate-foundationalist programme is, in effect, a *re*construction of P. A reductive foundation gives P a new subject matter, presumably one more secure than before, and an axiomatic foundation is a reorganization of the theses of P so as to make them maximally certain and hopefully not susceptible to rational doubt. Since, on such views, there may be more than one foundation, alternatives are not necessarily competitors. For all we know, the field can be rebuilt in more than one way.

The difference between these views is similar to the difference between 'best' and 'correct' in the question-form of the previous chapter. Since I do not wish to engage exegetical issues concerning the sort of foundationalism assumed by various authors, let us define *P-foundationalism (simpliciter)* to be the disjunction of strong and moderate foundationalism. The common core is a concern with rational certainty. The 'bedrock' is the material from which foundations are made, the reducing field and/or the axioms, and perhaps the deductive system. If the bedrock is self-evident, then well and good. If not, the foundationalist can be consoled with the belief that he has reached a (or the) place beyond which no further building, rebuilding, digging, or general 'securing' is humanly possible. To continue the metaphors, even if it is possible to dig below the bedrock, there is no point.

The last hundred years (or so) has seen a number of major foundationalist efforts. Two of them, logicism and the Hilbert programme, are considered here.[3] Both have been evaluated and analysed in enormous detail, but I will indulge in a few words since the issues surrounding the present project developed in this context.

In both cases, the plan of reconstruction includes the familiar axiomatic method, with attention to foundationalist detail. A core basis of the tenets of the field are identified and labelled 'axioms' or 'definitions'.[4] Then one shows how the entire body of knowledge can be developed step by step from the axioms by methods of reasoning. Unlike prior axiomatic treatments (such as Euclid's *Elements*), both foundationalist programmes require that the *logic* itself be made explicit through a deductive system. One must precisely delimit the notion of *correct inference*. In short, both the basis and the methods of proof are to be fully stated without gaps.

Probably the most important difference between the two programmes concerns how the security is to be guaranteed. For Hilbert, only a certain 'finitary' core of mathematics is meaningful, even though most branches go well beyond this (see, for example, Hilbert 1925). In the programme, one reformulates each branch in a deductive system, thought of as a *calculus*, a collection of mechanical rules operating on the formulas of a formal language. Once this is accomplished, we need some assurance that none of the theorems of the deductive system correspond to incorrect finitary statements. This reliability is secured with a *proof* that the deductive system is consistent. Following a theme introduced in the previous chapter, this requires a metatheory in which to carry out the consistency proof. The subject matter of this metatheory is formulas of the formal language, regarded as strings on a finite alphabet. For purposes of the consistency proof, the formal language is uninterpreted—no semantics is envisaged. Indeed, the programme has been called 'logic as calculus'. Noting that the structure of strings is equivalent to that of natural numbers, the metatheory is to be finitary arithmetic, presumably regarded by all as unquestioned. This may not produce *absolute* reliability, in that the metatheory does not have an independent foundation, but presumably it is the best we can do. There is no *more* preferred standpoint from which to evalute, criticize, or secure the envisaged metatheory used to secure the deductive system that models the branch in question (see Tait 1981).

With logicism, the older programme, the situation is not like this. As emphasized by van Heijenoort (1967b) and Goldfarb (1979), the language and deductive system envisaged are to be characterized with sufficient precision to allow alleged derivations to be checked mechanically, but this is not the crucial aspect of the programme. The formal language is to be *completely interpreted*, the diametric opposite of the idea that it is a meaningless uninterpreted formal system. Moreover, the language should be universal—completely general—in that it applies to all subject matters. Every item in the language is what is today a logical term, such as a variable, connective, or quantitier.[5] As Frege, following Leibniz, elegantly put it, the system is to be at once a *calculus ratiocinator* and a *lingua characterica*. There can be no other standpoint from which to verify the correctness of the deductive system of logicism. There is no independent metatheory. The language in question is already universal, indeed *the* universal language. Thus the axioms and inferences of the system must *themselves* be self-evidently reliable. There is nothing extra we can do to 'establish' the reliability of this logic. The perspective has been called 'logic as language'.[6]

As Goldfarb (1988) notes, this programme invites a charge of circularity. If one does not accept the proposed language and deductive system as *characterizing* the reliability of mathematical inference, then one can doubt the reliability of the deductive system. To follow the construction metaphor, the system is to provide a blueprint for the building after (or while) it is built. When we study the blueprint, we are to be assured that the building will not collapse. But if we doubt that the given system is the blueprint, we shall not be assured of anything. But, as Goldfarb adds, the circle is hard to resist, especially in retrospect. The logicists claim that the deductive system makes explicit the standards of rigour already implicit in at least careful mathematical practice.[7]

Both these programmes failed to achieve the foundationalist goal and, for various reasons, few people seriously hold out hope for repairs.[8] To be brief, concerning logicism, it was concluded that the reduction of mathematics to logic requires the incorporation of a considerable set theory, or something similar, into the universal language. The development of this was rather arduous—the proposed blueprint proved hard to read. As noted in the previous chapter, this was in large part due to Russell's paradox. There is no question concerning the power and fruitfulness of axiomatic set theory, the offspring of this work, but history shows that its theses are anything but self-evident, at least prior to training. As for the Hilbert programme, with hindsight it is surely reasonable to insist that any deductive system within its framework must be effective[9] and, of course, consistent. Some of the languages should be sufficient to model elementary arithmetic. Gödel's second incompleteness theorem shows that one cannot prove the consistency of such a deductive system D in D, much less in a theory weaker than D, one *more* evident.

This is not to belittle the accomplishments of these programmes. They spawned entire branches of mathematics, and, after all, set theory is a good foundation of mathematics. But it does not satisfy the epistemic goals of foundational*ism*, as defined here.

Writing after the dust had settled, Skolem (1950) sketched three possible desiderata of foundational research in mathematics. The 'logicist' desire is

> ... to obtain a way of reasoning which is logically correct so that it is clear and certain in advance that contradictions will never occur, and what we prove are truths in some sense.

This, of course, is a foundationalist goal; and it is not limited to logicism. Another, more modest, aim is 'to have a foundation which makes it possible to develop present day mathematics, and which is consistent so far as is known yet'. Skolem calls this the 'opportunistic' outlook. We might say that it is foundations without foundationalism. Skolem states that it has the 'unpleasant' feature that we are never certain when the foundational work is complete. He makes liberal use of the construction metaphor:

> We are not only adding new floors at the top of our building, but from time to time it may be necessary to make changes at the basis.

I presume that this is not a sound way to erect buildings, but metaphors only go so far. Skolem's third 'desire' is the 'Hilbert programme', which is a result of 'giving up the logicist standpoint and not being content with the opportunistic one'.

Skolem was, of course, aware of the difficulties with the foundationalist programme, but apparently he was reluctant to give up on foundationalism altogether. Today, some decades later, it is generally held that *nothing* can satisfy the requirements of foundationalism. That level of security cannot be attained. We are left with Skolem's 'opportunistic' option and anti-foundationalism.

This raises two kinds of questions. First, *to what extent* is foundationalism impossible to sustain? Perhaps *part* of the goal can be achieved. Second, what are the purposes and goals of an 'opportunistic' foundation? Why do we want one, and how do we evaluate candidates? These questions are, of course, interrelated.

To be sure, there are a number of purposes of foundational studies that are independent of foundationalism, and many of these are shared by foundationalist authors, in particular Hilbert, Frege, and Russell. An axiomatic foundation represents the codification of the reasoning in a branch of mathematics, and a reductive foundation forges a connection between two fields of study. Neither of these has to be construed as yielding absolute security, a foundation in bedrock. Nor should a foundation be criticized for failing to provide this.

If there happens to be a doubt about a branch of mathematics, a reductive foundation might provide some security. Perhaps reservations concerning negative or irrational numbers were alleviated when it was shown that they can be modelled in, or reduced to, natural numbers. At best, however, this security is relative. One who is content with the arithmetic of natural numbers has no reason (or less reason) to reject rational numbers.[10]

Even at this level, quieting scepticism is only part of the enterprise. There is surely a gain in insight when whole branches of mathematics are codified, and relations between them are articulated. Such studies have opened fruitful lines of research in mathematics itself. For example, when complex numbers are identified with pairs of real numbers, or vectors, they acquire properties they did not have before, such as length and direction. There is no question concerning the power of these notions. They lead to the notion of 'radius of convergence', which has proved useful even in the study of real numbers. Similarly, the Weierstrass foundation of calculus revealed interesting and important ambiguities in the notions of continuity and convergence.[11] Foundational studies have also opened whole new fields of mathematics, like set theory and recursive function theory.

Foundations of mathematics also has philosophical value. The connection between fields often allows a reduction of ontology. We have learned, for example, that one can maintain that sets are the only mathematical items in one's ontology. More substantially, if one adopts a philosophical view that places limits on the conceptual resources available to humans as knowers (e.g. nominalism), one would like to ascertain how much mathematics and science is possible. A coherent grasp of a semantics of ordinary mathematics, and its conceptual presuppositions, is surely a helpful, if not necessary, ingredient in this assessment.

2.2   Foundations and psychologism

The metaphorical talk of building, digging, and securing suggests that foundational studies may be a psychological enterprise—even a therapeutic one. Returning to our generic field of study P, the appearance is that one sees some value in P and either feels threatened (e.g. by antinomies) or worries about future attacks on P. The foundation seems designed to alleviate these worries and make the P-theorist feel secure once again.

There is some historical support for this orientation. Recall, for example, Hilbert's (1925) quip about never having to leave Cantor's paradise. In many minds, however, this outlook is dangerously misleading. Define *psychologism* to be the view that the aim of logic is to characterize a certain kind of subjective certainty and the aim of foundational studies is to study subjective certainty. On such a view, an argument from natural language is correct if and only if a given person, or most people, assent to it. Accordingly, logic is a branch of psychology and, as such, it is an empirical discipline. Most foundationalist authors reject psychologism, claiming that logic deals with objective norms of actual correct inference, not with what is felt to be correct by this or that person, or even by this or that community. The aim of a foundation of P is to clarify or develop a basis for *justification* of the theses of P, or in the case of the Hilbert programme, the finitary theses of P. From this anti-psychologistic perspective, the question is not 'What can make us feel better about believing, pursuing, or practising P?', but rather 'Why or how are we justified in practising P?' If we *only* want to relieve anxiety about P, then we could engage a therapist (or a hyponotist, or a pharmacist). There is surely more to the goal of logic and foundational studies than a licence to go on working in P with abandon.

There are two contrasts that are in play here. One is the distinction between what is objective and what is subjective or, better, between what is objective and what is 'intersubjective', the judgements shared by a large body of subjects. The other distinction is between fact and value, between what is and what ought to be. The anti-psychologist holds that logic and foundations are both objective and normative. A foundation should correspond to objective norms of justification and knowledge. These distinctions, of course, have been well discussed in the history of philosophy, and there is no consensus concerning what they amount to. In the present case, the central matter is the question of what counts as a justification, and there is the rub.

The charge against the role of psychology in foundational work is, I believe, unfair. The *P*-theorist certainly does not want *merely* to go on doing *P*, and certainly not with abandon. The antinomies and threats do, after all, tell us something, and we have to figure out what the pitfalls are and how to avoid them. Both advocates and opponents of psychologism agree that *P* plays a role in our overall intellectual life, and we need some assurance that this role can continue. So, on all accounts, the desire is to put *P* on solid ground with reason. In some cases at least, the attacks on *P* leave an unclarity concerning just what *P* is. It is not all that clear *how to go on* with the practice.[12] At least part of the goal of foundations is to provide guidance on this. This goal, at least, is independent of the issues of psychologism. Indeed, it is independent of foundational*ism*.

An extreme version of psychologism, the idea that there is nothing more to logic and foundations than psychology, does not merit a revival today. But the other extreme, that psychology is in no way relevant to logic and foundations, is also misguided. Even if we did have a candidate for a foundationalist system, the relevant epistemic issues would be difficult, perhaps impossible, to resolve on neutral ground. Poincaré launched a broad attack on the emerging field of logic, partly on psychologistic grounds. He argued that some theses of the new logic (ramified type theory; see Chapter 3) are certainly not self-evident, and that the counterparts of simple arithmetic statements in its language are far *less* evident than the originals. The supposed foundation is less solid than the enterprise it is supposed to support (see, for example, Poincaré 1908). The logicist response is that this charge confuses psychological certainty with epistemic warrant. Poincaré held his ground:[13]

> M. Russell will doubtless tell me that these are not matters of psychology, but of logic and epistemology. I shall be driven to respond that there is no logic and epistemology independent of psychology. This profession of faith will probably close the discussion ... (Poincaré 1909, p. 482)

The main question here is whether epistemic matters *can* ultimately be divorced from psychological ones. We need an account of *what it is* for an argument to be an epistemic warrant, independent of whether most thoughtful people (in the right frame of mind) will, as a matter of fact, be convinced by it.

If logicism could get off the ground, it would provide the beginning of a response to this query. An argument in ordinary language is an epistemic warrant if and only if it is accurately modelled by a deducible argument in the formal language. As noted above, this would be a circle. One who rejects the logicistic deductive system as a codification of objective norms of correct inference could also reject the distinction between intersubjective certainty and epistemic warrant, as Poincaré did. But perhaps the circle is not all that vicious.

But logicism failed and we still have no received account of what an epistemic warrant is. Whether we can obtain one may depend on the extent to which *part* of the logicist programme can be salvaged. Suppose that one had a candidate (partial) logicist deductive system that is purported to model accurately the notion of epistemic warrant. We would thus be confronted with the 'circle' and would have to decide whether to 'enter' it. It is surely out of the queston to demand that the proponent *prove* to us that the system does capture the notion of epistemic warrant—or even that the system is consistent. Again, the very matter at issue is what *counts* as a justification. As noted, the logicists did not embrace such metatheoretic studies.

Continuing the subjunctive mood, there would be two questions to be settled about the candidate deductive system. First, does every deducible argument correspond to a correct inference in the natural language of mathematics under study? Second, is the system *exhaustive* in the sense that every correct inference of the natural language corresponds to a deducible argument in the formal language? There are two philosophical stances that would be available to our logicist (plus the possibility of a combination). One is to make a concession to psychologism and assert that the inferences that correspond to the deducible arguments all *seem* certain, or are obvious, and, as far as we can tell, every inference that we are in fact certain of (on reflection) is modelled by a deducible argument. Of course, this *is* a concession, but it does not suffer from the worst psychologistic excesses. The concession is limited to the initial defence of the language and deductive system. The other stance is to postulate a faculty of normative epistemic judgement, a faculty outside the purview of psychology.[14] The claim is that we somehow recognize the correctness of at least some inferences in natural language, and that we do in fact recognize the correctness of inferences modelled by deducible arguments. Notice, however, that neither of these moves could assure us that the system is exhaustive, that *every* correct inference of the natural language is modelled in the deductive system. It is surely far-fetched to hold that a faculty of epistemic judgement could tell us this. At best, it would judge individual inferences of natural language, and perhaps the extent to which an argument in the formal language corresponds to one in the natural language. Perhaps the logicist can live with the possibility that the deductive system may have to be expanded one day. New deductions may be added to it. This is an 'incompleteness' of sorts.

Notice that, on both of these stances, the programme is a familiar one in philosophical theory-building. We start with pre-theoretic or 'intuitive' beliefs, instincts, dispositions to judge, etc. Formalization begins with these as 'data'. The difference between the two stances is over the nature of the *original* 'intuition'—whether it is subjective or objective, natural or normative, etc. (see Resnik 1985).

A more important issue concerns the status of our instincts and dispositions to judge *after* theory has been established. I confess to some sympathy for the views of both Poincaré and Russell. Poincaré is correct on the original motivation or origin of logical theory and foundational study. At the outset of theory, when considering the 'data' with which one is to begin, 'there is no logic and epistemology independent of psychology'. It is, in effect, a working hypothesis that the inferences and propositions that seem correct are correct. What else is there to go on? The stronger our intersubjective certainty about a given inference, the less likely it is that it will be challenged or revised in the light of theory. In some cases, we simply cannot imagine revision, at least not now. This applies to logic, with our instincts concerning correct inference, and to basic fields like arithmetic, with our intuitive feelings towards, say, simple sums. The products of the translations provided by the logicists are certainly less evident than the simple identities they translate. However, once theory has begun and shows signs of success (whatever that may be), then our intuitions can be modified by its light. That is, theory can guide our dispositions to judge, just as dispositions guide theory. Indeed, at any given time, these 'intuitions' are the product of one's background and training, and that is, at least in part, the product of previous intellectual endeavours. This also applies to our beliefs concerning what is more basic, or fundamental, in a discipline.[15]

On the other hand, once a successful logic is in place, one can make a coherent distinction between intersubjective certainty and epistemic warrant, against Poincaré. The deductive system can acquire a normative status within the community. For example, one can criticize an argument in natural language by showing how it is modelled by an argument in the formal language that is not deducible or not valid in the model-theoretic semantics.

As for the details of the debate, the surviving variants of the logicistic systems are more or less correct as far as they go, i.e. correct to the extent that they are consistent, not overly cumbersome, and able to express mathematics. But, unlike Poincaré, we now have the benefit of historical hindsight. The systems have proved fruitful and they do conform to our *current* dispositions concerning correct inference. Theory has guided intuition just as intuition has guided theory.

Without question, the most widely acclaimed surviving fragment of the aforementioned foundationalist programme is classical first-order logic. It is a central component of contemporary views on correct inference, *as opposed to* subjective certainty. But, given the failure of the foundationalist programmes, one should not be overly confident that first-order logic is the only system worthy of our attention. Indeed, is any given logic, no matter how well established, the *whole story*? Does it model *every* correct inference of the natural language of mathematics? The burden of this book is to show that first-order logic is not adequate. We should further weaken foundationalist aims and accept, at least provisionally, a 'stronger' logic, one less secure and less 'certain' than first-order logic.

2.3   Two conceptions of logic

There are at least two different orientations towards modern logic. Distinguishing these can help expose philosophical prejudices and can forestall discussion at cross-purposes. I call the orientations the *foundational* and the *semantic* conceptions of logic. They suggest different kinds of systems and have different criteria for the acceptance of the components of a logic. As will be shown, there is a sense in which the conceptions coincide when attention is restricted to first-order languages. This is related to the fact that first-order logic is complete, unlike higher-order logic. The foundational and semantic conceptions are not necessarily competitors, but (to undermine the dialectical drama), our conclusion is that the semantic one is more plausible.

2.3.1   *The foundational conception*

In modern foundations of mathematics, the axiomatic method has two stages (unlike, say, Euclid's *Elements*). One gives axioms *and* one gives rules for deducing theorems—a deductive system. In principle, of course, there is not much difference between axioms and rules. Any axiom can be thought of as a rule of inference, and many rules can be recast as single statements in the form of conditionals. In practice, however, axioms often concern the special subject under study, while rules of inference concern the logic. The latter are rules for deducing arguments that are supposed to be correct in any field.[16] Perhaps the concession to anti-foundationalism can be limited to the search for a central core of evident propositions among the truths of a given branch of mathematics, typically the axiom-providing stage. According to this proposal, it may not be possible to locate a sufficient core of self-evidence among the theses of a given field, but it *is* possible to provide rules of inference that are self-evidently reliable, or maximally immune to rational doubt. We cannot be absolutely sure that our starting axioms are true, but *if* they are, *then* we can be certain that the deductive system will not lead us astray.

This programme is an attempt to salvage 'logic' from logicism. Following Wagner's (1987) lucid account, a logic is seen as the ideal of what may be called *relative justification*, the process of coming to know some propositions *on the basis of* others. Define an argument in natural language to be *ideally justified* if its premises lead to its conclusion by a self-evidently reliable chain of reasoning. That is, an argument is ideally justified if it meets the postulated standard of relative justification. In such circumstances, we also say that the conclusion of the argument is *ideally justified on the basis of* its premises. Wagner calls the attempt to characterize this notion the 'rationalist conception of logic', but this can be misleading.[17] Call it the *foundational conception* of logic.

Since the central concern with foundational logic is deduction, the main item is a deductive system. It should codify all and only the ideally justified arguments, those that meet the standard of relative justification. There are two questions to be asked of each deductive system. First, do all its deducible arguments correspond to ideally justified arguments? Is it the case that an argument $\langle \Gamma, \Phi \rangle$ in the formal language is deducible only if a sentence in the natural language that corresponds to Φ can be justified on the basis of sentences corresponding to those in Γ? Call this the issue of *conformity*. Second, does every ideally justified argument in the natural language correspond to a deducible argument in the formal language? Call this the issue of *sufficiency*. Conformity and sufficiency are informal counterparts of soundness and completeness. They concern the match (in extension) between a precisely defined formal notion and an intuitive pre-formal counterpart.[18] Together, they indicate that the deductive system is an accurate model of relative justification.

Since the enterprise at hand is a limited version of logicism, we may expect a similar disavowal of a foundational role for model-theoretic semantics and metatheory in general. As will be seen, this would be premature, but it is certainly correct that metatheory cannot help with the *conformity* issue. The deductive system is to model ideal justification itself. There is no more secure perspective from which to justify the conformity of the system. No proof in the metatheory can have premises that are more evident than deductions it is meant to secure. In particular, a proof of consistency would not help. The advocate of the foundational conception of logic sides with Frege against Hilbert (see Resnik 1980, Chapter 3).

It seems plausible that a foundational deductive system ought to be at least a crude model of the *process* of justification. It might be constructed by specifying a collection of *immediate inferences* and defining a deduction of Φ from Γ to be a finite sequence $\Phi_1 \ldots \Phi_n$ of formulas in the formal language such that Φ_n is Φ and, for each $i \leqslant n$, Φ_i is either in Γ or follows from previous formulas by an immediate inference. In this framework, the conformity of a deductive system would come down to whether every natural language argument that corresponds to an immediate inference is ideally justified.[19] It seems reasonable to require that this be true of any deductive system that purports to conform to the foundational conception of logic, and that it be knowable beyond dispute. In particular, it must be assumed that our intuitive pre-theoretic ability to detect correct justification suffices to sanction counterparts of each immediate inference. Moreover, there should be only finitely many immediate inferences to check, or, at most, each immediate inference should be an instance of one of finitely many inference schemes, where it is evident that every instance of each scheme corresponds to an ideally justified argument.

Notice that we have, as yet, no way to determine that a given argument in natural language is *not* ideally justified. The question of *sufficiency* is related to this. We may, for example, find an argument in the formal language that is a good model of the natural language argument at hand, and we may show somehow that the formal language argument is not deducible, but without sufficiency this would not imply that the original argument is not ideally justified.

It is too much to expect that our powers of recognition determine whether a given deductive system is sufficient, whether every ideally justified argument of natural language has a deducible counterpart. It is even too much to expect our intuitive pre-theoretic abilities to determine whether, for every natural language argument that *does* correspond to one in the formal language, the former is ideally justified only if the latter is deducible. That would require an intuitive ability that not only checks individual inferences for correctness, but also provides some sort of pre-theoretic 'map of logical space', determining its boundaries. This, I believe, is more than a foundationalist can reasonably postulate, much less defend.

Thus, for the question of sufficiency, the standards must be relaxed—self-evidence is out of the question. Sufficiency is a theoretical question, not an intuitive one, and requires some theory, or metatheory, for an answer.

2.3.2 *The semantic conception*

Wagner (1987) argues that a foundational conception of logic underlies the work of the logicists, most notably Frege. It is a natural successor (or correction) to earlier ideas of logic as the 'laws of thought'. As Wagner observes, there is a second conception of logic, a semantic or model-theoretic one, in which validity is characterized in terms of models or interpretations of the language in question. I shall not venture any detailed statements about its pedigree, but I believe that it can be traced to Aristotle. The modern version can be seen in Hilbert and Ackermann (1928). The semantic conception of logic is often associated with Tarski (e.g. Tarski 1935).[20]

As noted in the previous chapter, in textbooks and courses in elementary logic, validity is often characterized informally in either semantic or modal terms, at least at first. One asserts that an argument is 'valid' if it is not *possible* for the premises to be true and the conclusion false, and this impossibility is based solely on the meaning of certain expressions, the logical terminology. Alternatively, we may read that an argument is valid if any *interpretation* of it that makes the premises true also makes the conclusion true. The semantic conception of logic is part of an explication of these definitions. To characterize the notions, one provides a collection of models and defines 'correct inference' in terms of (semantic) validity. That is, an argument $\langle \Gamma, \Phi \rangle$ in the formal language is valid if and only if Φ is satisfied by every model that also satisfies every member of Γ.

This notion of logic depends on a distinction between the 'logical terminology' and the 'non-logical terminology' of the language in question. To reiterate, the non-logical items are those whose referents vary from model to model, while the logical items are those whose meaning is the same in all the models. In a sense, the references or usage of the logical terminology are determined by the model-theoretic semantics as a whole.

The extension of 'valid' depends on where the line between logical and non-logical terminology is drawn. Focus, for the moment, on a common (first-order) language of arithmetic, augmented with a predicate letter D. Let Nx be a predicate corresponding to 'x is a natural number'. Consider the following two arguments.

The ω-rule: $\langle \{D0, Ds0, Dss0, \ldots\}, \forall x(Nx \rightarrow Dx) \rangle$.

The principle of induction: $\langle \{D0, \forall x(Dx \rightarrow Dsx)\}, \forall x(Nx \rightarrow Dx) \rangle$.

In standard first-order semantics, neither of these is valid. Consider a model whose domain is the set of all countable ordinals, with 0 and the successor symbol s given their usual readings. Let the extension of N be the entire domain and let the extension of D be the set of finite ordinals. In this model, the premises of both arguments are satisfied, but the conclusions are not.[21]

The informal 'reason' one might give for the invalidity of these arguments is that the premises *only* say that D holds of 0, $s0$, $ss0$, etc.; they do not say that 0, $s0$, $ss0$, etc. are *all* the natural numbers there are. The above counter-interpretation exploits this fact by *re*interpreting the numerals as ordinals. Such is common practice. But suppose someone were to challenge the reasoning, and assert that both inferences are valid *as they stand*. The claim is that the proposed model is not a legitimate interpretation of the language. Accordingly, the predicate N, the numerals, and the successor symbol would be logical terms, not subject to reinterpretation in the models of a semantics. Even if we could, we do not have to state explicitly in the premises of an argument that 0, $s0$, $ss0$, etc. are all the natural numbers there are.[22]

Notice the analogy between this disputant's remarks and ours if we were confronted with a claim that $P \& Q$ does not imply P, owing to the interpretation (over the natural numbers) of P as $s0 = 0$, Q as $0 = 0$, and the ampersand as 'or'. We would (justly) protest that this is not a legitimate interpretation. The ampersand is a logical term, not subject to reinterpretation.

In effect, if there is to be *no* logical terminology in the language (the opposite of logicism), then no arguments are semantically valid except those whose conclusion is one of the premises. This is surely an extreme not worth pursuing. Following Tarski (1935), it may well be that the distinction between logical and non-logical terminology is not to be determined in advance of logical theory. As noted in the previous chapter, the logical–non-logical distinction may hold for a natural language only relative to a model-theoretic semantics for a formal language that corresponds to it. As will be seen, it is fruitful to think of the difference between first- and second-order logic as a difference concerning the border between logical and non-logical terms. The philosophical issues are discussed in Chapters 7 and 8.

On the semantic conception of logic, the plausibility of a proposed semantics depends on the extent to which the class of models corresponds to the intuitive notion of 'interpretation' or 'possible world', the one active in pre-formal judgements of validity. Analogous to the foundational programme, there are two questions for each system. First, does the model-theoretic semantics *conform*? That is, does each model thereof correspond to a legitimate interpretation of a natural language modelled by the formal language? Second, is the proposed semantics *sufficient* in the sense that it has 'enough' models? In other words, is it the case that for each set Γ of formulas of the formal language, if there is an 'intuitive' interpretation of the natural language that makes the sentences corresponding to the members of Γ true, then there is a model in the semantics that satisfies every member of Γ?[23]

Our judgements concerning correct inference are relevant in answering these questions in a given case, but other kinds of judgements are relevant also. The natural languages in question are used to *describe* structures as well as to justify propositions, and we have at least tentative pre-formal beliefs or, for lack of a better term, 'intuitions' about possibility and interpretation. After all, the above *informal* semantic-model characterization of validity is phrased in those terms, and when newcomers to logic hear it, they have *some* idea of what is meant. To be sure, such pre-formal ideas, and original intuitions, must be refined by theory, radically in some cases, but everyone starts from somewhere.

It seems that on the semantic conception of logic, pre-formal judgements, whether they concern inference, description, or interpretation, are tentative data, subject to correction in some cases. Suppose, for example, that there were an argument in a natural language that seems 'correct' but its counterpart in the formal language is not valid, according to a proposed model-theoretic semantics. That is, suppose that the conclusion of the argument is obtained from the premises by a chain of short steps, each of which is 'self-evidently correct', and suppose also that in the semantics there is a model that satisfies the counterparts of the premises but not the counterpart of the conclusion. There would be tension; *something* must be changed. One option would be to modify the semantics and excise the offending model, perhaps by moving the boundary between the logical and the non-logical terminology. Or we could modify our 'intuitive' judgements about the chain of reasoning in question. Or we could decide that the argument in the formal language is not a good counterpart of the natural language argument after all. Of course, in a case like this, *some* explanation of where our pre-formal intuition went wrong is called for. For example, we could locate an offending step in the informal argument chain and make explicit an 'assumption' (or, to use Lakatos' phrase, a 'hidden lemma') of the derivation. It seems that evaluating semantics is a complex holistic matter. It is not a fundationalist enterprise, although it might augment one. Let us turn to the relationships between the two conceptions of logic.

2.4   Marriage: Can there be harmony?

If we focus on a *fixed* formal language *L* and the fragments of natural language that it models, it is possible that the two conceptions of logic converge on a single consequence relation. It might be the case that for every natural language argument *A* that has a counterpart in *L*, *A* is ideally justified if and only if the counterpart is semantically valid. This may in fact occur in the case of first-order languages, but let us be more general for the moment.

Suppose that one develops a deductive system as a candidate for the codification of ideal justification, and a model-theoretic semantics as a candidate for characterizing the pre-formal semantic conception of logic. Then there would be two mathematical structures. Let us assume that they employ the same formal language *L*. Relations between the structures could then be investigated. In particular, one could try to prove soundness and completeness theorems. Recall that soundness is the statement that every deducible argument is valid in the semantics. Completeness is the converse, that every argument valid in the semantics is deducible in the deductive system. The question at hand is whether such results would strengthen *either* the claim that the deductive system is correct for ideal justification or the claim that the semantics is true to the pre-formal notion of semantic validity. This, it seems, depends on the relationship between the pre-formal notions themselves.

In the imagined scenario, there would be several 'philosophical' theses to investigate. Some of these have been encountered already. Let us recapitulate, and add to the list.[24]

(1a) The proposed deductive system is a correct or acceptable codification of ideal justification for the language at hand. That is:

(1a1) If Φ is deducible from Γ, then any natural language sentence corresponding to Φ is ideally justified on the basis of sentences corresponding to the members of Γ (conformity).

(1a2) If a natural language argument A corresponds to an argument $\langle \Gamma, \Phi \rangle$ in L, and A is ideally justified, then Φ is deducible from Γ (sufficiency).

(1b) The proposed semantics is faithful to the pre-formal notions of 'possible interpretation' and 'validity'. That is:

(1b1) Each model in the semantics corresponds to a legitimate interpretation of the natural language. If a natural language argument A corresponds to an argument $\langle \Gamma, \Phi \rangle$ in L, and A is 'valid' in the sense that its conclusion is true under every interpretation of the natural language in which its premises are true, then Φ is satisfied by every model of the semantics that also satisfies every member of Γ (conformity).

(1b2) There are 'enough' models in the semantics. If a natural language argument A corresponds to an argument $\langle \Gamma, \Phi \rangle$ in L, and $\langle \Gamma, \Phi \rangle$ is valid in the model-theoretic semantics, then the conclusion of A is true under every interpretation of the natural language that makes the premises of A true. This amounts to a statement that if there is an interpretation of the natural language that makes every member of a set S of sentences true, and if every member of Γ corresponds to a member of S, then Γ is satisfiable in the semantics (sufficiency).

(2a) If an argument A of the natural language is ideally justified, and A has a counterpart in L, then the conclusion of A is true under every interpretation of the language in which the premises of A are true (pre-formal soundness).

(2b) If the conclusion of a natural language argument A is true under every interpretation of the language in which the premises of A are true, and A has a counterpart in L, then A is ideally justified (pre-formal completeness).

Notice that all these theses only concern sentences and arguments from natural language that have counterparts in the formal language L. This will play a large role in what follows.

In a sense, the conformity of the deductive system (1a1) is 'internal' to the foundational conception of logic. As noted, it can probably be verified by checking each axiom and rule of inference against our intuitions concerning relative justification. On the other hand, (1a2) is more 'theoretical', and we shall presently look to semantics for help. Similarly, (1b1) is more or less 'internal' to the semantic conception, and we can probably rely on pre-formal intuition there, at least at first. However, (1b2) is more theoretical, and requires some analysis of the purpose of the language and logic.

Item (2a) is a deeply held thesis among those who employ *both* a foundational and a semantic conception of logic. The two *must* be related this way. If confronted with an alleged counter-example, we would have to explain it away, or else our intuitions would have to be repaired in its light. Of course, the very intelligibility of (2a) would be challenged by both someone who uses the foundational conception alone, such as a logicist, and someone who rejects the foundational conception. But for those who accept both conceptions, (2a) is a substantive, if uncontroversial, thesis.

Item (2b) asserts that idealized human ability suffices to justify *every* (intuitively) semantically correct argument that has a counterpart in the formal language L. If L has any complexity, this is prima facie unlikely. Indeed, the variable in the definition of 'semantically correct' ranges over *all* interpretations. On most accounts, there is a proper class of models, some of which are (uncountably) infinite. Our abilities, even idealized, surely have some limit.

The argument, of course, is defeasible, and will not convince those familiar with the Löwenheim–Skolem theorems for first-order logic. These theorems indicate that the existence of very large interpretations does not add much complexity to the semantic consequence relation. Thus, item (2b) is very plausible for the fragments of natural languages that can be modelled in first-order formal languages. But the Löwenheim–Skolem theorems do not hold for higher-order languages (see Chapter 4).

Notice that (1a) and (1b) *and* the soundness and completeness of the semantics and the deductive system for each other imply (2a) and (2b). In particular, it is straightforward that (2a) follows from (1a2), soundness, and (1b2), and that (2b) follows from (1b1), completeness, and (1a1).

But (2a) and (2b) are not the primary matters at hand. The success of the programmes associated with our two conceptions of logic, when considered separately, is summed up in (1a) and (1b), and we want to examine the extent to which soundness and completeness bear on *these* issues.

For what it is worth, (1a1) follows from soundness, (1b2), and (2b). More substantially, (1a2) follows from (2a), (1b1), and completeness. Combined, (1a) follows from (1b), (2a), (2b), soundness, and completeness. Similarly, (1b1) follows from (2b), (1a2), and soundness, and (1b2) follows from completeness, (1a1), and (2a). Combined, (1b) follows from (1a), (2a), (2b), soundness, and completeness.

It can be concluded on the basis of all this that if soundness and completeness have been established, then (1a), (1b), (2a), and (2b) give mutual support to each other. Any one of these follows from the other three.[25] So, for the given language, we can regard the adequacy of *both* the semantics and the deductive system to be strengthened by soundness and completeness theorems. In that case, the systems support each other. This would not be conclusive, of course, but it helps. In philosophy, we rarely have more.

I suggest that, in some minds at least, this mutual support is in fact enjoyed by current first-order logic. For those who accept both the semantic and the foundational conceptions of logic, the soundness and completeness of first-order logic provide some assurance that we have it right on both counts—a good marriage.[26]

2.5   Divorce: Life without completeness

The above discussion concerns a single formal language *L*, held fixed throughout and not questioned. The harmony we found concerning first-order logic should not blind us to the possibility that this *language*, and its semantics may not be adequate to codify the descriptive and deductive components of actual mathematical practice. After all, both Aristotelian logic and propositional logic are complete,[27] but surely neither is an acceptable model of substantial mathematical practice.

The main theme of this book is to argue that first-order languages and semantics are also inadequate models of mathematics. As will be seen (Chapter 4), the favoured alternative, higher-order logic, is inherently incomplete in that there is *no* effective, sound, and complete deductive system for the semantics. Moreover, the considerations show that *any* language and model-theoretic semantics that overcomes the deficiencies of first-order logic is also inherently incomplete.

There are, however, good effective deductive systems for second-order logic, but they are all incomplete. One of them, presented in the next chapter, is a straightforward extension of a deductive system for first-order logic. The question at hand concerns the status of our two conceptions of logic under these circumstances. There are three possibilities: one can maintain both conceptions separately, one can jettison the foundational one, or one can jettison the semantic one. The last would be a return of sorts to logicism, and is not pursued here. A few remarks on the other two options are in order.

2.5.1   *Joint custody*

Suppose, then, that one has a model-theoretic semantics regarded as adequate for natural language arguments that have counterparts in a formal language *L*, and suppose that one has a deductive system that is purported to codify ideal justification for those arguments. The deductive system is sound for the semantics, but not complete. Under these circumstances, item

(2b) above, stating that informal semantic validity entails ideal justifiability, would have to be regarded as very unlikely, if not false. As noted, this is to be expected. If L is complex, it would take a fair amount of pre-established harmony for the human ability to justify arguments to match up to the semantic notion of validity. Never mind that there is such harmony in the case of first-order logic. The converse (2a) can, and probably should, be maintained. If an argument can be justified, it is semantically valid.

Clearly, without the completeness of the deductive system and without (2b), we do not have the mutual support between the adequacy of the semantics and the adequacy of the deductive system. We can coherently maintain the *conformity* of the deductive system to the foundational standard of ideal justification (1a1). Once again, the axioms and rules of inference could be directly verified against our ability to detect justifications. But there seems to be no reason to accept the *sufficiency* of the deductive system (1a2). By hypothesis, one of the three premises used to establish it is false and another is unlikely at best. Under these circumstances, it is hard to imagine a form of argument that would establish sufficiency.

Of course, there could be inductive evidence for the sufficiency of a deductive system. It may be that for every natural language argument A that we consider, if A conforms to our intuitions of ideal justification and has a counterpart in the formal language L, then the latter is deducible. Even in such a case, the best outlook would be to regard the sufficiency of the prevailing deductive system to be open. Unlike the scenario above, where completeness was assumed, one should admit the possibility that we may one day discover arguments that conform to foundational standards of ideal justification, but have counterparts in L that are not deducible in the deductive system. We might then augment the deductive system, but of course the new candidate might also be incomplete for the semantics. In short, the extension of the notion of 'ideal justification' may be open-ended. This is consonant with the essential incompleteness of the logic.

To extend the point, suppose that it is known that an argument $\langle \Gamma, \Phi \rangle$ in L is valid in the model-theoretic semantics, and that Φ cannot be deduced from Γ in the deductive system. Both of these, of course, would be established in the metatheory (see Chapter 4 for examples in the case of second-order logic). One might be tempted to claim that a natural language sentence corresponding to Φ is, after all, ideally justified on the basis of sentences corresponding to those in Γ (alone). Have we not *proved* that $\langle \Gamma, \Phi \rangle$ is valid? But this would conflate semantic validity and ideal justification. The problem is that the *metatheory* may have axioms or presuppositions which are not self-evident, or which otherwise do not conform to foundationalist standards. Typically, model-theoretic semantics is formulated in set theory, and the proof that $\langle \Gamma, \Phi \rangle$ is valid may have substantial assumptions about the 'universe' of sets. So we cannot conclude from a proof that $\langle \Gamma, \Phi \rangle$ is semantically valid that sentences corresponding to Φ can be justified from those corresponding to the members of Γ, at least not without further ado. On the other hand, we can, and should, hold open the possibility that we may one day discover a compelling justification of a natural language argument corresponding to $\langle \Gamma, \Phi \rangle$, one that does meet the postulated standard of ideal justification.

2.5.2   *Foundationalism denied*

Most of the present study of higher-order logic is consistent with the outlook of the previous subsection. Indeed, I have little to say on how one settles on a deductive system (in light of incompleteness). Nevertheless, I do not favour such an amiable divorce, and I reject the foundational conception of logic altogether.

Let us consider the central notions of ideal justification and self-evidence. To pursue the above scenario, suppose that it is known that an argument $\langle \Gamma, \Phi \rangle$ in L is semantically valid, but that Φ cannot be deduced from Γ in the currently favoured deductive system. What would we do if we were given an *informal* derivation of a sentence corresponding to Φ from those correspond- ing to Γ, a derivation that purports to conform to ideal justification? Presumably, we would attempt to check if it does so conform, whether it shows that the sentence corresponding to Φ really is ideally justified on the basis of those corresponding to Γ. What tools and measures are to be used in this check? Presumably, our intuitive judgements of correct inference and self-evidence. And there lies the problem.

It is possible that 'intuitions' simply run out at this point. Intuitive judgement seems to be based on paradigm examples, and it may not pronounce on every case. If our intuitions are silent about the purported derivation, then we simply cannot judge on an *intuitive pre-theoretical* level whether the sentence corresponding to Φ really is ideally justified on the basis of those corresponding to Γ. Of course, advocates of the foundational conception of logic may contend that there is nevertheless a fact of the matter as to whether or not the argument meets the standard of ideal justification. One might claim that the *lack* of judgement about the informal derivation in question indicates that the sentence corresponding to Φ is not (yet) justified on the basis of the sentences corresponding to Γ. On the other hand, the situation as described could equally be taken as indicating that the notions of ideal justification, self-evidence, etc. are *vague*. They may have genuine borderline cases, which might turn out to borderline cases of 'correct inference' itself. I leave it to foundationalists to determine whether the vagueness of these central notions is consistent with the aims of the programme.

There is a deeper problem, or at any rate a deeper difference between the foundational outlook and that of the present study. According to the former, judgements of correct justification at the basic level are *prior* to theory, and thus *independent* of theory. Deductive systems are to codify the pre-existent and independent conception of ideal justification. Lacking a completeness theorem, model-theoretic semantics is irrelevant to this enterprise. I propose that, against this, justification is a holistic matter. Our post-theoretic judgements regarding correct inference are guided by our work in logical theory—both deductive and semantic. To borrow an overworked phrase, some of the 'data', judgements of correct inference or 'intuitions', are heavily laden with theory, at least at this point in history.[28]

A foundationalist might concede this, perhaps using a phrase like 'corrupted by theory' instead of 'laden with theory', but she would insist that the basic pre-theoretic notion survives. Otherwise, even the limited retrenched logicist claims would be compromised. Even relative ideal justification would be anchored in sand, not bedrock.

Consider, once more, the situation in which it has been established (in the metatheory) that an argument $\langle \Gamma, \Phi \rangle$ is semantically valid and that Φ cannot be deduced from Γ in the deductive system. Suppose also that we have an informal derivation of a sentence corresponding to Φ from those corresponding to Γ. The question at hand is whether the informal derivation shows that the sentence corresponding to Φ is ideally justified on the basis of those corresponding to Γ (alone). Call this situation T (for theory). Contrast it with another, call it NT (for no theory), which is identical, except that there is no proof in the metatheory that $\langle \Gamma, \Phi \rangle$ is semantically valid. That is, in NT a (different) community knows that Φ cannot be deduced from Γ in the deductive system, but has an informal derivation of a corresponding natural language argument, the same derivation as envisaged in situation T, and in this community the question of whether $\langle \Gamma, \Phi \rangle$ is semantically valid is still open, or perhaps it does not have a model-theoretic semantics at all.

We assume that both communities are honest and straightforward in their efforts, and that both have the same *pre-theoretic* capacities for judging correct inference. The foundational assumption is that the community in situation T can, in effect, go back to their uncorrupted pre-theoretical judgement where ideal justification is a matter of self-evidence. It would undermine the foundational enterprise if the semantical results of a substantial set-theoretic metatheory were allowed to affect judgements of ideal justification, self-evidence, and the like. So, under these assumptions, the informal derivation (in T and NT) is to be evaluated the same way in both situations, and both communities should come to the same conclusion *with the same confidence*. It is similar to two people measuring the length of one object using the same ruler under relevantly ideal conditions (assuming similar capacities to read rulers). Indeed, the only difference in the two situations here is the presence of the metatheoretic proof (in T) that the argument in

L is valid, and that is not relevant to the foundational conception of logic.

This scenario does not constitute a *reductio ad absurdum* against the foundational conception of logic, but the conclusion it points to is counter-intuitive. It seems evident that the community in situation *T* would be more confident in the judgement that the sentence corresponding to *Φ* is ideally justified on the basis of counterparts of those in *Γ* simply because the informal derivation is supported by a model-theoretic proof of semantic validity. That is, community *T* would be more willing to accept the informal derivation, other things being equal. In actual cases, we do rely on metatheoretic results in judging correctness, or at least take them to be relevant (especially within set theory itself). In short, (semantic and deductive) theory guides our judgements of correct inference. To be sure, we have an 'intuitive' feel for correct argument, and we rely on this as well. Indeed, it is on intuitive judgement that logical theory begins. However, I take it as uncontroversial that intuitive judgements (of correct inference) are dynamic. They vary over time and are affected by successful theory and education.[29] The question at hand is whether there is a core of this intuitive judgement that survives all the metatheory, and remains prior to it. Even if there is such a core, can we now confidently 'identify' it and separate it from the rest—the 'corrupted' part of our intuitive judgement? Even more, is there any reason to attempt such a separation and build a philosophy of logic on it? I leave this part of the discussion with these questions, and my preference for negative answers.

2.5.3 *Deductive systems without foundationalism*

A natural question at this point concerns the role of deductive systems, and criteria for evaluating them, on the present semantic conception of logic. Historically, the codification of correct deduction is a central task of logic, and it remains so in current studies. Proof theory has not been replaced by model theory; the two work together. In making the semantic conception of logic primary, it is necessary at least to establish a connection with the traditional concern with deduction.

For present purposes, the goal of developing deductive systems is cast in the same terms as that given by the foundational conception. It is to model the practice of giving proper (relative) justifications in mathematics. The difference, of course, is that I do not employ the same notion of 'justification'. What does that mean now?

Recall the last two thesis given in Section 2.4.

(2a) If an argument *A* of the natural language is ideally justified, and *A* has a counterpart in *L*, then the conclusion of *A* is true under every interpretation of the language in which the premises of *A* are true.

(2b) If the conclusion of a natural language argument *A* is true under every interpretation of the language in which the premises of A are true, and A has a counterpart in L, then A is ideally justified.

In Section 2.4 these were regarded as substantive statements on the relationship between the semantic and the foundational notions of logic, both regarded as autonomous. It was suggested that under these assumptions, (2b) is unlikely, especially in cases where there is no completeness theorem linking the deductive system and the semantics. Here, though, the foundational conception of logic and the autonomy of the notion of justification, however idealized, are both rejected.

A first attempt might be to use theses (2a) and (2b) as a *definition* of ideal justification. That would make justification *completely* subordinate to semantics. In effect, this attempt is the extreme opposite of foundationalism. It simply eliminates the notion of justification, replacing it with semantic validity. This is also counter-intuitive, at least with regard to second-order logic. As pointed out by critics of second-order logic, there are cases in which the metatheoretic *proof* that a given argument $\langle \Gamma, \Phi \rangle$ is semantically valid requires a substantial amount of set theory (see Chapters 4–6), enough that one can hardly say that a sentence corresponding to Φ is ideally justified on the basis of those corresponding to Γ alone. An advocate of this subordinate notion of justification could retort that, in such cases, the informal argument is indeed justified, but one needs a substantial theory of sets in order to see this. After all, set theory is the vehicle for the semantics, the basis of justification so construed.

This is an uncomfortable philosophy. According to it, there would be no standpoint from which one could *criticize* a deductive system, except by relating it to semantics. Here, I adopt a middle course in which we keep an 'intuitive' notion of justification and use it to guide our theorizing, both semantic and deductive, and to evaluate deductive systems. There are several important differences between this notion of justification and its foundational counterpart. There is no problem here with justification's being laden with theory, even being laden with set theory. Neurath's (1932) metaphor of the ship is apt. Logic is an integral part of the intellectual enterprise, and its boundaries cannot be sharply delimited. In particular, there is no sharp distinction between logic and mathematics. Second, the present notion of justification is admittedly vague. In at least some cases there is no need for there to be determinate facts as to whether a given sentence of natural language really is ideally justified on the basis of others. Borderline cases are to be expected when dealing with 'intuitions' which are, after all, matters of training, experience, and temperament. The reason that these differences are not problematic, and that the present view does not entail extreme psychologism, is that no central foundational role is accorded to intuition. Once again, logical theory is a holistic enterprise. It aims at precision, but does not have to start with something precise. Theory corrects as well as codifies our intuition (see Tarski 1935).

The theory-laden notion of justification sketched here allows an intersubjective theory-laden variation of the foundationalist programmes. In the development of a field *P*, a theorist may find certain beliefs especially compelling. To adopt a remark by Gödel (1964), some statements may force themselves on us. Further, it may be discovered that all, or most, of the beliefs concerning *P* can be justified on the basis of these axioms, according to the prevailing standards of justification. If other theorists at the time (when else?) find the axioms and justifications compelling, the programme has succeeded, at least tentatively. The system may come to constitute the norms of justification in *P*, as a dictionary can come to constitute the norms of correct spelling and language use. If there is no consensus, the group can work towards a core that is compelling to them and adequate for justification. As part of this, intuitions are made explicit and, if necessary, defended. In the process, intuitions concerning what is compelling and what is a justification are refined and, perhaps, modified. To return to a theme from the opening paragraphs of this chapter, there is surely value in regimenting a field in this way. Once again, we have foundations without foundationalism.

2.6 Logic and computation

It is widely believed that there is a close relationship between logic and computation. The historical roots of this run deep. For example, the Greek word for 'syllogism' is cognate with 'logistic', the theory of computation. In the early modern period, we have Hobbes' famous 'By ratiocination, I mean computation' (*On the body*, Part I, Chapter VI), and from a different philosophical perspective, Leibniz' Universal Characteristic is a forerunner of mathematical logic:

> What must be achieved is in fact this: That every paralogism be recognized as an *error* of *calculation*, and that every *sophism* when expressed in this new kind of notation ... be corrected easily by the laws of this philosophic grammar ... Once this is done, then when a controversy arises, disputation will no more be needed between two philosophers than between two computers. It will suffice that, pen in hand, they sit down ... and say to each other: 'let us calculate' (Leibniz 1686, XIV)

On the contemporary scene, it is no accident that recursive function theory, the study of computability as such, is a branch of mathematical logic. In Shapiro (1983), I argue that a major motivation for the rigorous development of computability in the mid 1930s was to clarify the notion of an acceptable deductive system with respect to the Hilbert programme (see also Gandy 1988).

Along these lines, it is commonplace to insist that deductive systems be effective in the sense that the collection of deductions ought to be recursive.

This is particularly reasonable if the deductive system is to model the *process* of ideal justification, be the latter foundational or otherwise. As suggested by Leibniz' metaphor, the deductive system is to be *used* as a calculus to model *and check* actual informal reasoning. If so, then a human should (ideally) be able to determine reliably whether a given sequence of formulas is a deduction in the deductive system. It thus seems plausible to insist that there be an *algorithm* for determining whether a given sequence is a deduction. Church's thesis, the assertion that every algorithm computes a recursive function, is pretty much beyond dispute nowadays. It follows that the collection of deductions should be recursive.

Conversely, for any recursive set of sequences of strings, there is a deductive system in a formal language whose 'deductions' are all and only those sequences. Thus a relationship between reasoning and computation amounts to a relationship between reasoning and deductive systems in formal languages. And this goes to the heart of the issues under discussion here. What is the relationship between reasoning and deductive systems?

The sort of connection between computation and reasoning envisaged here has had its detractors. One of them was Brouwer, with his attacks on formalism and, for that matter, the field of logic. Brouwer was sceptical of the idea that any deductive system in a formal language could adequately model mathematical reasoning. He believed that mathematics is inherently non-linguistic. As will be seen (Chapter 7), Zermelo and Gödel also rejected the connection between computation and reasoning. They held that the human ability to reason in mathematics goes beyond what can be captured in any effective deductive system. This is not to mention opposition from general philosophy, notably the later Wittgenstein, who held that in reasoning one is not, or not merely, following a rule.

Detlefsen (1990) suggests a programme for distinguishing two schools of thought concerning reasoning. The 'logic-intensive' model focuses on deduction and, in particular, on the *rules* one follows in reasoning correctly. The philosophical view behind this is that reasoning correctly is *constituted by* following the correct rules. The 'intuition-intensive' model rejects this idea. Reasoning is accomplished by some (other) faculty we possess; it is not simply obedience to a rule. Detlefsen argues that Brouwer held a view like this, and therein lies his main objection to classical logical theory.

We are now in a position to shed some light on the relationship between computation and reasoning, and to delimit areas of genuine controversy. To mention the obvious, no one would go so far as to *identify* correct reasoning with computation (despite the above sentence from Hobbes). Most algorithms do not correspond to reasoning in any sense, even if we restrict attention to those that act on linguistic items, such as sentences. The thesis at hand is that correct reasoning is a type of computation. If attention is restricted to a fixed fragment of natural language, there is an algorithm that adequately *represents* correct reasoning in that fragment. By the above equation, the thesis is that there is a particular deductive system in a formal language that adequately represents correct reasoning in that fragment.

A central item is to articulate the notion of 'representation' that is in place here. In what sense is it claimed that an algorithm or formal system 'represents' reasoning? There are at least two interpretations, a strong one and a weak one. The strong thesis asserts that, in order to reason correctly, one must *grasp* and *execute* an appropriate algorithm, or, equivalently, one must grasp and follow an appropriate deductive system. The weak thesis is that for a fixed fragment of a natural language, the collection of correct chains of reasoning in that fragment is recursive.

The strong theses is a form of the 'logic-intensive' view of reasoning. According to it, correct reasoning is literally constituted by following particular rules. The view is consistent with the foundational conception of logic, and may underlie it. Once again, the advocate of the foundational conception holds that there is a fixed (a priori) notion of ideal justification. With this presupposition, the above argument that deductive systems must be effective suggests a thesis that correct reasoning is itself effective, and thus that there is an effective deductive system that codifies ideal justification (see Wagner 1987).

There are, however, deep problems with this strong equation between reasoning and computation, independent of the above attack on foundationalism. To sustain the thesis, we need an account of the notion of 'grasping' that is in use when it is claimed that to reason correctly, one must grasp a particular algorithm or deductive system. It cannot be a *conscious* grasping, in the sense that the grasper can *articulate* the relevant algorithm (as, for example, many people can articulate an algorithm for addition). Most people who manage to reason correctly are not directly aware of any algorithm that they may be following in the process. At the very best, only (some) logicians are consciously aware of the appropriate algorithm. There is a second problem concerning how the fragment of natural language is rendered into the syntax of the algorithm's inputs and outputs, or into the formal language of the deductive system. The thesis that reasoning is constituted by following an algorithm requires a much stronger connection between formal language and natural language than that between a mathematical model and what it is modelling. The formal language must somehow *be* the medium that the subject reasons in, in some literal sense. Finally, there is a problem of characterizing how a reasoner (correctly) applies the requisite algorithm. That is, are there to be rules for applying the 'reasoning-algorithm'?[30]

The second, weaker articulation of the thesis connecting reasoning and computation is that the collection of correct chains of reasoning in a given fragment of natural language is recursive. Equivalently, there is an effective deductive system that describes the *extension* of correct reasoning in that fragment. On this view, a reasoner does not have to be aware of and consciously execute such an algorithm, and, even more, one who does execute such an algorithm may not be reasoning. Moreover, it may not be known, or even knowable, of any particular algorithm (or formal system) that it describes all and only the correct inferences in the fragment of natural language. This version of the thesis is consistent with the 'intuition-intensive' view of reasoning which, as it stands, does not say anything about the extension of 'correct reasoning'.

The problem of how the fragment of natural language is rendered in the formal language remains. If we are to speak of a deductive system as describing *the extension* of correct reasoning, even for a fragment of natural language, then in a sense the formal language must be the fragment of the natural language in question.

The weak thesis draws some support from Church's thesis and the philosophy of mechanism. The relevant premises are that a human being can be described at some level as a complex machine, a mechanical system, and that the total linguistic output of any given mechanical system is recursively enumerable. But this is not enough to imply the thesis. The supposed algorithm is not to describe the method by which *one* particular person *actually* reasons (even if we idealize on memory, attention span, etc.), but rather the extension of *correct* reasoning as such. Even if we allow that there is an effective way to determine the portion of a person's 'output' that is reasoning, it would not follow that we can effectively delimit her *correct* reasoning. Thus the argument from mechanism to our weak thesis needs another premise to the effect that it is possible for a human to reason correctly all the time. Even this is not sufficient. It is not enough that our idealized mechanical reasoner never make mistakes—dead people accomplish this much. The person must produce *all and only* correct inferences. But this further premise concerning a possible human super-reasoner does no more than beg the question. The idealized super-reasoner must still fall within the scope of mechanism. We have no reason to believe that there can be such a person unless we already believe that the extension of correct inference in the fragment in question is effective. Without a completeness theorem coupled to a good model-theoretic semantics, it is empty optimism to think that there is an effective deductive system that not only 'gets it right' but 'gets all of it'.

More importantly, the present (weak) thesis connecting reasoning and computation assumes that, for the fragment of natural language under consideration, the extension of 'correct inference' is fixed. That is, the statement that there is a deductive system that describes the extension of correct inference presupposes that *there is* such an extension. To proceed any further it is necessary to be more specific about the notion of 'correct inference' that is in play here.

One possibility would be to revive the foundational conception of logic and define 'correct inference' in terms of the notion of ideal justification. Presumably, the extension of this is not only fixed, but fixed once and for all, a priori. Such a move would support the strong thesis, and the weak one as a corollary, but foundationalism is not worth reviving.

A second possibility is to define 'correct reasoning' in terms of semantic model-theoretic validity. An argument is 'correct' if and only if it is semantically valid. If this route is taken, and if there is a fixed model-theoretic semantics for the fragment in question, then there is indeed a fixed extension for 'correct inference' in that fragment (if we manage to put aside the problem of how the natural language is rendered into the formal language). But under these circumstances, we have no reason to think that the collection of valid arguments (whose premises are finite) is recursively enumerable, at least not without a look at the details. As Wagner (1987) points out, by opting for a *thoroughly* semantic conception of correct inference, we have divorced it from the reasoning abilities of humans, however idealized. It would be fortuitous if validity ended up being recursively enumerable (as it does with first-order logic), but we cannot *start* with this assumption.

The best course, I believe, is the intermediate one sketched in the previous subsection. The semantic conception of logic is adopted, but the notion of correct inference is not identified with semantic validity. On this view, ideal justification is *not* regarded as fixed, at least not fixed once and for all. There are two senses to this, each of which yields a modification of the connection between reasoning and computation. First, the notion of ideal justification is *dynamic*. The extension of 'correct inference' is moulded by successful theory, both semantic and deductive. To accommodate this, one can fix attention on a fixed time t and consider the notion of ideal-justification-at-t, those inferences that are justified by resources available at time t. The weak thesis is now the assertion that there is an algorithm or formal system that describes correct-inference-in-the-fragment-at-t. Second, the notion of ideal justification (at time t) is, or may be, vague—there might be borderline cases of correct reasoning. If so, our weak thesis loses much of its force, if not its sense. Surely, an algorithm or formal system cannot *exactly* describe the extension of a vague concept. Nevertheless, one can still hold that the inferences sanctioned by a given formal system more or less coincide with correct-reasoning-in-the-fragment-at-t. This is another modification of our weak thesis, but now it is plausible. Indeed, our retrenched weak thesis is a presupposition, or regulative ideal, of proof theory. We would not even try to develop formal deductive systems if we did not believe that a reasonable model could be achieved. But the present version of the thesis is a far cry from the original equation between reasoning and computation.

The theme of this chapter is the rejection of the remnants of epistemological foundationalism in logic and foundational studies. To conclude, there is room in the current philosophical and technical climate for a non-effective consequence relation, based on a model-theoretic semantics. It is time to turn to details.

Notes

1. The connection between a field and its foundations is not always remote. Some branches of abstract algebra began with the formulation of axioms, and proceeded from there. Set theory was also given an axiomatic treatment relatively early in its history (see Chapter 7), and the axiomatization still plays a large role in the pursuit of the subject.
2. It is interesting to compare this orientation to foundations of mathematics with the discussion of what may be called 'foundations of ethics' in Chapter 1 of John Stuart's Mill's *Utilitarianism*. Mill makes an analogy between the foundations of a field and the roots of a plant.
3. A list of twentieth century foundationalist programmes must include intuitionism. Whatever the fate of other efforts, it is clear that intuitionism will be alive in the 21st century. It will be pursued, not just discussed. Here, however, intuitionism would take us too far afield, partly because it goes in a direction radically different from the others and partly because it is revisionist. Present focus is on the foundations of classical mathematics, programmes that leave the field (more or less) as it is found.
4. The logicist programme includes both reductive and axiomatic foundations. Statements of arithmetic are recast in terms of logic, and the logic is axiomatized. The Hilbert programme is axiomatic.
5. This is possible because the languages of logicism are higher-order. They contain predicate and relation *variables* instead of non-logical schematic letters. The predicate and relation variables can be bound with quantifiers. See Chapter 7 below.
6. In addition to van Heijenoort (1967b) and Goldfarb (1979), the distinction between a universal language and a formal language, between 'logic as language' and 'logic as calculus' is discussed in more detail in Hintikka (1988) and Cocchiarella (1988). Resnik (1980) traces the discussion at cross purposes in the (early) correspondence between Frege and Hilbert to their different orientations.
7. The epistemological goals of foundationalism may not have been Frege's primary aim. He had an ontological orientation as well. The question is not necessarily (or not only) how we can be certain of arithmetic truths, but what arithmetic is about. The latter can be addressed without increasing epistemic security, and perhaps in the case of arithmetic, no increase is needed. It is curious that hardly anyone harbours serious doubts concerning arithmetic propositions, but there is no consensus on what the subject matter of arithmetic is. Many of the criticisms of logicism do not apply to this ontological agenda.
8. There are exceptions; see Detlefsen (1986).
9. The role of effectiveness in deductive systems is taken up in Section 2.6.
10. It might be added that, once forged, connections between fields go both ways. If misgivings about real or complex numbers persist, one can doubt the coherence of the talk of sets or sequences of rational numbers.
11. In correspondence, Mark Steiner has emphasized the importance of these examples.
12. Kitcher (1983) argues, for example, that the Cauchy–Weierstrass foundation of analysis, the familiar ε–δ formulations of limit, continuity, etc., were accepted only because the previous techniques involving infinitesimals, divergent sequences, and the like were breaking down in practice. Mathematicians were no longer

sure whether a given process, or inference, would reliably lead to correct results. At least this time, the rigour of the Cauchy–Weierstrass definitions was needed on internal grounds.

13. See Goldfarb (1988) for a lucid presentation of this dispute in the context of Poincaré's contribution to the development of logic and foundations of mathematics; see also Steiner (1975).

14. At least part of the Fregean goal was to rid arithmetic of Kantian intuition. The proposed move would not necessarily reintroduce it, since the postulated faculty need not be directly related to the structure of sensory perception. The nature of intuition is a recurring theme in Parsons (1983).

15. An interesting case study is Bolzano's (1817) proof of the intermediate value theorem (see note 12). It was based on careful rigorous definitions of continuity, limit, and the like (and it included a demonstration of the Bolzano–Weierstrass theorem that every bounded infinite set of points has a cluster point). Bolzano's proof was certainly a major achievement— a hallmark of modern analysis. A century or so earlier, however, mathematicians would probably balk at the idea that the intermediate value theorem *needed* a proof. What could be more evident than the statement that a continuous curve which passes from below the x-axis to above it must cross the axis somewhere. At some point, however, it became clear that intuitive conceptions of, say, continuity, were not sufficient. To use a Kuhnian phrase, the paradigm was breaking down, and explicit definitions were needed (see Coffa (1982) and the last chapter of Kitcher (1983)). In short, it became evident that what was previously thought to be obvious is problematic. This is closely related to a 'gap' in Euclid's elements: the principle that if a line goes through a circle, it must intersect it somewhere.

16. There are exceptions. Many treatments of first-order logic (including the one sketched in the next chapter) contain 'logical axioms', and the ω-rule only applies to arithmetic. The principle of mathematical induction can also be formulated as a rule.

17. In the history of philosophy, rationalism is associated with a number of philosophical claims, notably anti-empiricism. The present concern is the connection with foundationalism, the alleged self-evidence of relative justification. It should be noted that the traditional empiricists did not deny the self-evidence of simple correct deductions. Moreover, the present study does not concern the issue of whether the self-evidence of correct justification entails that it is not empirical. The holism that is defended here is limited to mathematics, at least on the surface, and no stance is taken on the extent to which mathematics is or is not empirical. Wagner (1991) and recent correspondence indicate that he is more concerned with the non-empirical nature of relative justification than with its indubitablity. Thus, he and I may be at cross purposes, notwithstanding the fact that Shapiro (1985a) is one of the main targets of Wagner (1987).

18. In this respect, sufficiency and conformity are the same kind of thing as Church's thesis: the statement that the mathematically precise notion of recursive function is extensionally equivalent to the pre-formal notion of computable function.

19. This assumes that the pre-formal notion of ideal justification is 'transitive' in the sense that if Φ is ideally justified on the basis of Γ_1 and every member of Γ_1 is ideally justified on the basis of Γ_2, then Φ is ideally justified on the basis of Γ_2. No finite bound is placed on the 'length' of a justification.

20. As noted in the previous chapter, Etchemendy (1988) shows that, although Tarski eventually adopted the current model-theoretic conception of logical consequence, there are important differences between it and the notion developed by Tarski (1935) (see also Corcoran 1983). Hintikka (1988) argues that Hilbert held a 'model-theoretic' conception of logic. The best case for this applies to Hilbert's relatively early period, when he corresponded with Frege. The later Hilbert programme was more concerned with proof and deductive systems than with interpretation and semantics. The programme prescribed languages that might as well be *uninterpreted*. That is the whole point. But this perspective is compatible with the idea of *different interpretations* of the formal languages, and thus with the semantic conception of logic. After all, the metatheoretic completeness problem, linking deductive systems and model-theoretic semantics, did emerge from the Hilbert school. Thus, with Hintikka, the Hilbert programme need not be seen as a repudiation of the semantic conception of logic. Proof theory can augment model theory: it need not supplant it.

21. For a second example, consider any model whose domain contains at least two elements, *s* denotes the identity function, *N* holds of everything, and *D* holds only of the item denoted by 0.

22. Tarski (1935) also raises the ω-rule, and suggests that it may be valid. The perspective that arithmetic terminology is not to be interpreted differently in different models, that it be 'logical terminology', is sometimes called ω-logic, and is briefly presented in Chapter 9, Section 9.1. As will be shown (Chapters 4 and 5), it follows from the compactness theorem that the 'assumption' that 0, $s0$, $ss0$, etc. are all the natural numbers cannot be stated in a first-order axiomatization, but it can in a second-order axiomatization. In a sense, ω-logic lies between first-order logic and second-order logic.

23. Questions like this are central in Kreisel's (1967) analysis of informal rigour. The question of sufficiency is similar to one concerning the distinction between what Kreisel calls 'informal validity' and what may be called 'set-theoretic validity': a sentence Φ is *informally valid* if it is true under *all* interpretations of the language, and Φ is *set theoretically valid* if Φ is true under all interpretations of the language *whose domain is a set*. The principle that informal validity is coextensive with set-theoretic validity is treated in Chapter 6, Section 6.3, in the context of higher-order languages.

24. See Etchemendy (1988) for a discussion of questions like this in a historical context.

25. To become frivolous about this exercise, it might be noted that soundness follows from (1a1), (2a), and (1b1), and completeness follows from (1b2), (2b), and (1a2). But soundness and completeness are mathematical matters, internal to the developed structures.

26. There is an analogy with Church's thesis, which is supported by the fact that several different (independent) attempts to codify computability all have the same extension. Here we have different orientations to 'correct inference' leading to a common consequence relation, at least in the formal language. See Shapiro (1981).

27. For Aristotelian logic, see Corcoran (1972); for propositional logic, see any competent textbook in symbolic logic (e.g. Mendelson 1987, Boolos and Jeffrey 1989).

28. See Etchemendy (1988) for an insightful discussion of the contrast between pre-theoretic logical notions and their (current) 'theory-laden' manifestations.
29. The law of the excluded middle, the axiom of choice, and impredicative definition make interesting historical case studies. See Moore (1982).
30. This, of course, is a Wittensteinian problem. See Wright (1980) and Blackburn (1984).

Part II

LOGIC and MATHEMATICS

3

Theory

3.1 Language

A series of formal languages, each of which is, in part, a set of strings, are presented in this section. The strings in a language are called *well-formed formulas*, or simply *formulas*. For each language, a set K consisting of the *non-logical* terminology is designated. In arithmetic, for example, K would be $\{0, s, +, \cdot\}$, the symbols for zero, succesor, addition, and multiplication. Schemes for constructing formulas from K are presented. Deductive systems and model-theoretic semantics are developed in succeeding sections.

3.1.1 *First-order*

The reader is assumed to be familiar with first-order logic (see, for example, Mendelson 1987, Boolos and Jeffrey 1989). We only need to establish notation. The first group of languages is called $L1K$, first-order *without* identity[1]. *Variables* are lower case letters near the end of the alphabet, with or without numerical subscripts. The variables of $L1K$ are called *first-order variables*. The *connectives* are material implication $\rightarrow$ and negation $\neg$. Other connectives are introduced as abbreviations:

$$\Phi \vee \Psi: \neg\Phi \rightarrow \Psi \qquad \text{disjunction}$$

$$\Phi \,\&\, \Psi: \neg(\Phi \rightarrow \neg\Psi) \qquad \text{conjunction}$$

$$\Phi \equiv \Psi: (\Phi \rightarrow \Psi) \,\&\, (\Psi \rightarrow \Phi) \qquad \text{material equivalence.}$$

The language also has a *universal quantifier* $\forall$. The existential quantifier is defined as follows:

$$\exists x\Phi: \neg\forall x\neg\Phi.$$

A *sentence* is a formula without free variables, and, as in Chapter 1, a *theory* is a set of formulas.

If the set K of non-logical terminology is empty, then there are no atomic formulas in the language and thus no formulas at all. This is not the case with the other languages to be examined. So, in this one case, we require that K be non-empty. If K is countable,[2] then there is a denumerable infinity of formulas and sentences. If K is uncountable, then the cardinality of the set of formulas $L1K$ is the same as the cardinality of K.

A *first-order language with identity* $L1K =$ is obtained from $L1K$ by adding a binary relation symbol $=$. Thus, if t and u are terms of $L1K$, then $t = u$ is an atomic formula of $L1K =$. The identity symbol is regarded as logical and is not in K. Two more abbreviations are

$$t \neq u: \neg(t = u)$$

$$\exists!x\,\Phi(x): \exists x \forall y(\Phi(y) \equiv x = y).$$

The former, of course, is used to express distinctness. The latter $\exists!x\,\Phi(x)$ can be read 'there is a unique x such that $\Phi(x)$'.

Notice that, even if K is empty, $L1K =$ has a non-empty set of formulas. In general, formulas of a language that have no occurrences of members of K are called *purely logical*. Examples include

$$\exists x \exists y(x \neq y)$$

$$\exists x \exists y \exists z \exists u[(x \neq y \,\&\, y \neq z \,\&\, x \neq z) \,\&\, \forall w(w = x \lor w = y \lor w = z \lor w = u)].$$

We have not developed a semantics yet, or otherwise discussed the 'meaning' of the formulas of $L1K =$, but the first sentence 'says' that there are at least two things. The second says that there are either three things or four things. As will be seen, in higher-order languages there are more substantial purely logical sentences.

3.1.2 *Second-order*

3.1.2.1 *Free-variable*

Our first extension of first-order language is one in which relation and function variables can occur free, but not bound. In other words, higher-order *quantifiers* are not introduced. On the standard semantics, this is the same as allowing only prenex universal quantification for relation and function variables.

The language $L2K -$ is obtained from $L1K =$ by adding a stock of relation variables and function variables. These are called *second-order variables*. Relation variables are upper-case italic letters, and function variables are lower-case italic letters near the beginning of the alphabet, typically f, g, and h. A superscript is used to indicate the *degree*, or number of places, of each second-order variable. Thus, for example, X^1 is a monadic predicate variable, X^2 is a binary relation variable, f^1 is a unary function variable, and f^2 is a binary function variable. If the context determines the degree of a variable, or if it does not matter, the superscript may be omitted. We let $\langle t \rangle_n$ represent a finite sequence of terms $t_1 \ldots t_n$, and let $\langle x \rangle_n$ represent a finite sequence of *distinct* first-order variables $x_1 \ldots x_n$. The form $\forall \langle x \rangle_n$ is an abbreviation of $\forall x_1 \ldots \forall x_n$. There are two new formation rules.

If f is an n-place *function variable* and $\langle t \rangle_n$ is a sequence of n terms, then $f \langle t \rangle_n$ is a term.

If R is an n-place *relation variable* and $\langle t \rangle_n$ is a sequence of n terms, then $R \langle t \rangle_n$ is an atomic formula.

An alternative would be to introduce relation variables only. As will be seen, no generality is lost, since $(n + 1)$-place relation variables can serve as surrogates for n-place function variables. If F^{n+1} is such a variable, then the clause $\forall\langle x\rangle_n \exists! y F\langle x\rangle_n y$ indicates that F can play the role of an n-place function. This option is somewhat awkward, however.

Another alternative would be to include only monadic predicate variables.[3] In such languages, surrogate n-place relation (and function) variables can be introduced if there is a notation for a fixed *pairing function*, a one-to-one binary function from the domain to itself. If u and v are terms, let $\langle u, v \rangle$ denote the corresponding 'pair', the value of the pairing function at arguments u and v. The formula $X^2 xy$ could be replaced by $X^1\langle x, y\rangle$. This option would simplify the exposition in places, but it brings the cost of an arbitrary posit, the pairing function. It might be added that a pairing function amounts to a principle of infinity, since there is no such function on finite domains. Another option would be to introduce a pairing function on a case-by-case basis, using available non-logical terminology.

3.1.2.2   *Full second-order*

Notice that since $L2K-$ is an extension of $L1K=$, the identity symbol is maintained as a logical item. In contrast, the language $L2K$ is obtained from $L1K$, not $L1K=$. Relation and function variables are added, together with universal quantifiers binding them. The existential quantifier is defined as above:

$$\exists X \Phi\!: \neg\forall X \neg \Phi$$

$$\exists f \Phi\!: \neg\forall f \neg \Phi.$$

Thus, for example, $\exists X \forall x \neg X x$ asserts the existence of an 'empty' property, one which applies to nothing.

The symbol for identity between (first-order) objects is introduced as an abbreviation. The relevant principle is the *identity of indiscernibles*

$$t = u\!: \forall X(Xt \equiv Xu)$$

in which t and u are terms. I do not intend to assert a deep philosophical thesis about identity with this definition. As will be seen, on the standard semantics, for each object m in the range of the first-order variables, there is a property which applies to m, and m alone. It can be taken as the singleton set $\{m\}$.

As noted in Chapter 1, the present study has very little to say about identity between relations or about identity between functions. For the most part, one can think of relations and functions as extensional, or intensional, or one can leave it open. Little turns on this here, and in fact words like 'property', 'class', and even 'set' are used interchangeably since the differences among these items are not of present concern. The issues pursued here concern the intended *range* or *totality* of the higher-order items, and not the nature of individual specimens.

As indicated, if pressed, I would adopt an extensional interpretation. In fact, symbols for identity between relations and identity between functions could easily by accommodated. The familiar character = would do, since context would indicate its meaning. One option would be to take it as an abbreviation, using the *principle of extensionality*

$$P = Q\colon \forall \langle x \rangle_n (P\langle x \rangle_n \equiv Q\langle x \rangle_n)$$

$$f = g\colon \forall \langle x \rangle_n (f\langle x \rangle_n = g\langle x \rangle_n)$$

for each sequence $\langle x \rangle_n$ of first-order variables, each pair P, Q of n-place relation variables, and each pair f, g of n-place function variables. An alternative would be to take the symbol as a (logical) primitive, as in the first-order case.

Let $L2$ be the second-order language in which the set of non-logical terminology is empty. This language and, in general, the purely logical part of $L2K$ are rather substantial. Consider, for example, the sentences

$$\exists f[\forall x \forall y(fx = fy \rightarrow x = y) \,\&\, \exists x \forall y fy \neq x]$$

$$\exists f \exists x \forall P[(Px \,\&\, \forall w(Pw \rightarrow Pfw)) \rightarrow \forall x Px].$$

The first 'asserts' that the domain is (Dedekind) infinite, while the second asserts that the domain it as most countable.

3.1.2.3 *Ramified second-order*
I do not have much to say about ramified, or predicative, languages, except by way of comparison. The idea behind these systems is that relations are to be defined or constructed in *levels*. Relations defined at a given level become available for use in definitions at later levels. So it is stipulated that each higher-order variable has a numerical subscript to indicate its level. Call the resulting language $L2Kp$, where the p stands for 'predicative'. To take up one example, the sentence $\forall P_3 \exists Q_1 \forall x(Q_1 x \equiv P_3 x)$ asserts that for each level 3 predicate there is a level 1 predicate with the same extension. For simplicity, we do not include function variables in $L2Kp$.

3.1.3 *Onward and upward*
There are two directions for further expansion of our languages. One concerns the set K of non-logical terminology. Second-order variables, as well as non-logical predicate, relation, and function names, may be called 'higher-order terms', items that 'denote' relations and functions. By way of analogy, this opens the possibility of relations of relations, functions on relations, etc. These may be called *higher-order non-logical terms*. An example

would be a property TWO of properties such that TWO(P) 'asserts' that P applies to exactly two things. A relevant 'definition' would be

$$\text{TWO}(P) \equiv \exists x \exists y [x \neq y \ \& \ \forall z (Pz \equiv (z = x \vee z = y))].$$

A more complicated example would be a predicate UNC(P) asserting that P applies to uncountably many things.[4]

A second expansion is to introduce *variables* for relations of relations, functions of predicates, functions of functions, etc. These would be *third-order* variables. Then one could add non-logical constants (to K) for relations on functions of predicates, and the like, and one could add *fourth-order* variables ranging over such things, thus producing a fourth-order language, and so on. If the language contains nth-order variables, for each natural number n it is of order ω. We can go on from here, but will not. It will be shown (in Chapter 6, Section 6.2) that there is a sense in which second-order is enough.

These higher-order languages can also be *ramified*. Each variable would be annotated somehow to indicate both its *type* (the kinds of objects, relations, etc. it applies to) and its *level* (the place in the hierarchy at which it is defined). A type 3 level 0 predicate would be a predicate of type 2 predicates defined by reference only to type 2 relations. A type 3 level 1 predicate would be a predicate of type 2 predicates defined by reference to type 3 level 0 relations, etc.

3.2 Deductive systems

A standard deductive system for the first-order languages is sketched here, beginning with $L1K$. Since familiarity with first-order logic is assumed, most detail is omitted.

The following are *axiom schemes*. Any formula obtained by substituting formulas for the Greek letters is an *axiom*:

$$\Phi \to (\Psi \to \Phi)$$
$$(\Phi \to (\Psi \to \chi)) \to ((\Phi \to \Psi) \to (\Phi \to \chi))$$
$$(\neg \Phi \to \neg \Psi) \to (\Psi \to \Phi)$$
$$\forall x \Phi(x) \to \Phi(t)$$

where t is a term free for x in Φ.[5]

Let Γ be a set of formulas and Φ a single formula. We define a *deduction of Φ from Γ* to be a finite sequence $\Phi_1 \ldots \Phi_n$ such that Φ_n is Φ and, for each $i \leq n$, Φ_i is in Γ, Φ_i is an axiom, or Φ_i follows from previous formulas in the sequence by one of the following rules of inference.

Modus ponens: from Φ and $\Phi \to \Psi$, infer Ψ.

Generalization: from $\Phi \to \Psi(x)$ infer $\Phi \to \forall x \Psi(x)$, provided that x does not occur free in Φ or in any member of Γ (i.e. any premise of the deduction).

Call this deductive system $D1$. If there is a deduction of Φ from Γ in $D1$, then we write $\Gamma \vdash_{D1} \Phi$, or $\Gamma \vdash \Phi$ if the context indicates the deductive system.

The above axioms and rules make a proof of the following metatheorem a rather straightforward exercise. Details are omitted.

THEOREM 3.1 (Deduction theorem).   If $\Gamma \cup \{\Phi\} \vdash_{D1} \Psi$, then $\Gamma \vdash_{D1} \Phi \to \Psi$.

Unless stated otherwise, all the deductive systems presented here satisfy this theorem. It is tedious but routine to derive the usual 'axioms' and 'rules' associated with the other connectives, here regarded as abbreviations. An example is the rule of existential introduction.

From $\Phi(x) \to \Psi$ infer $\exists x \Phi(x) \to \Psi$, provided that x does not occur free in Ψ or in any premise.

Once again, a competent text in elementary logic will suffice for details.

A deductive system for $L1K=$, a first-order language with identity, is obtained by adding axioms for identity:

$\forall x(x = x)$

$\forall x \forall y(x = y \to (\Phi(x) \to \Phi(y)))$, provided that y is free for x in $\Phi(x)$.

The latter scheme is the 'indiscernibility of identicals', the opposite of the identity of indiscernibles.[6] Call the resulting deductive system $D1=$.

As will be seen, these deductive systems are complete for the common semantics (on the respective languages). Since this is not the case for *any* effective deductive system for a second-order language, there is no theoretically unique candidate to present. There are, however, natural extensions of $D1$ to second-order languages.

The next item is a deductive system for $L2K$, the full (non-ramified) second-order language. The extension of the quantifier axioms and rules to the second-order variables is straightforward.

$\forall X^n \Phi(X^n) \to \Phi(T)$, where T is either an n-place relation variable free for X^n in Φ or a non-logical n-place relation letter.[7]

$\forall f^n \Phi(f^n) \to \Phi(p)$, where p is either an n-place function variable free for X^n in Φ or a non-logical n-place function letter.

From $\Phi \to \Psi(X)$ infer $\Phi \to \forall X \Psi(X)$, provided that X does not occur free in Φ or in any premise of the deduction.

From $\Phi \to \Psi(f)$ infer $\Phi \to \forall X \Psi(f)$, provided that f does not occur free in Φ or in any premise of the deduction.

We also add the *axiom scheme of comprehension*:

$\exists X^n \forall \langle x \rangle_n (X^n \langle x \rangle_n \equiv \Phi \langle x \rangle_n)$ provided that X^n does not occur free in Φ.

This scheme asserts, in effect, that every formula (of $L2K$) determines a relation, or, more precisely, that for every formula there is a relation with the same extension. If the formula Φ itself contains bound higher-order variables, then the corresponding instance of the comprehension scheme is called *impredicative*. An alternative scheme, involving the predicative language $L2K$p, is briefly presented below.

The final item is a form of the axiom of choice:

$$\forall X^{n+1}(\forall\langle x\rangle_n\exists y X^{n+1}\langle x\rangle_n y \;\rightarrow\; \exists f^n\forall\langle x\rangle_n X^{n+1}\langle x\rangle_n f\langle x\rangle_n).$$

The antecedent of this conditional asserts that for each sequence $\langle x\rangle_n$ there is at least one y such that the sequence $\langle x\rangle_n y$ satisfies X^{n+1}. The consequent asserts the existence of a function[8] that 'picks out' one such y for each $\langle x\rangle_n$.

The axiom of choice has a long and troubled history (see Moore 1982), but it is now essential to most branches of mathematics. In fact, a corresponding metatheoretic principle is necessary for many of the theorems reported here. Mathematical logic also thrives on the axiom of choice. If, however, the axiom of choice is dropped from the present deductive system, it should be replaced by the weaker principle of *comprehension for functions*:

$$\forall X^{n+1}(\forall\langle x\rangle_n\exists! y X^{n+1}\langle x\rangle_n y \;\rightarrow\; \exists f^n\forall\langle x\rangle_n X^{n+1}\langle x\rangle_n f\langle x\rangle_n).$$

The comprehension scheme and the principle of comprehension for functions underscore the above assertion that function variables can be eliminated in favour of relation variables. Informally, if f is an n-place function, define the *graph* of f to be the $(n + 1)$-place relation that holds a sequence $\langle x\rangle_n y$ if and only if $f\langle x\rangle_n = y$. The statement that every function has a graph

$$\forall f^n\exists X^{n+1}\forall\langle x\rangle_n\forall y(X^{n+1}\langle x\rangle_n y \equiv (f\langle x\rangle_n = y))$$

can be derived from an instance of the comprehension scheme. There is a converse of sorts to this. Define an $(n + 1)$-place relation R to be *single valued* if for each sequence $\langle x\rangle_n$ there is exactly one object y such that R holds of $\langle x\rangle_n y$. The principle of comprehension for functions asserts that every single-valued $(n + 1)$-place relation is the graph of an n-place function.

Call this deductive system $D2$. Recall that $L2K$ does not contain a primitive symbol for (first-order) identity. Rather, $x = y$ is taken to be an abbreviation of

$$\forall X(Xx \equiv Xy).$$

To justify this, derivations of the counterparts of the identity axioms of $L1K=$ are sketched. First, $\forall x(x = x)$ is $\forall x\forall X(Xx \equiv Xx)$. In the light of the deduction theorem, it is trivial[9] that this is derivable from no premises in

*D*2. Next, $\forall x \forall y(x = y \to (\Phi(x) \to \Phi(y)))$ is

$$\forall x \forall y[\forall X(Xx \equiv Xy) \to (\Phi(x) \to \Phi(y))],$$

recalling the proviso that y be free for x in $\Phi(x)$. Take $\forall X(Xx \equiv Xy)$ and $\Phi(x)$ as premises (to deduce $\Phi(y)$). Let us take $\forall z(Yz \equiv \Phi(z))$ as a further premise (where neither Y nor z occur in $\Phi(x)$, relettering if necessary). Then $Yx \equiv \Phi(x)$ and thus Yx can be derived. We also have $Yx \equiv Yy$ (an instance of $\forall X(Xx \equiv Xy)$) and thus Yy. By our added premise, we obtain $\Phi(y)$. From the deduction theorem, $\forall x(Yz \equiv \Phi(z)) \to \Phi(y)$ can be derived from the first two premises alone. From the second-order version of existential introduction, we obtain $\exists Y \forall z(Yz \equiv \Phi(z)) \to \Phi(y)$. The antecedent of this is an instance of the comprehension scheme, and so the consequent $\Phi(y)$ follows from the same two premises. Two applications of the deduction theorem show that

$$\forall X(Xx \equiv Xy) \to (\Phi(x) \to \Phi(y))$$

follows from no premises. It is then a short path to

$$\forall x \forall y[\forall X(Xx \equiv Xy) \to (\Phi(x) \to \Phi(y))],$$

the required 'axiom'.

It is tedious, but straightforward, to establish a corresponding indiscernibility principle for relation variables:

$$\vdash_{D2} \forall\langle x\rangle_n(P\langle x\rangle_n \equiv Q\langle x\rangle_n) \to (\Phi(P) \to \Phi(Q))$$

for each formula Φ such that Q is free for P in $\Phi(P)$. The (metatheoretic) proof of this principle proceeds by induction on the complexity of the formula Φ. This partly justifies the present extensional orientation towards the higher-order terminology.

We now consider the free-variable second-order languages $L2K-$. Notice that one cannot formulate the instances of the comprehension scheme in such a language because of the existential quantifier binding a second-order variable. As a result, the deductive system for $L2K-$ is a little more complicated.

Let Φ and $\Psi(\langle x\rangle_n)$ be formulas of $L2K-$, the latter possibly containing $\langle x\rangle_n$ free, and let R^n be an n-place relation variable. Define $\Phi[R/\Psi(\langle x\rangle_n)]$ be the formula obtained from Φ by replacing each occurrence of $R\langle t\rangle_n$ (where $\langle t\rangle_n$ is a sequence of terms) with $\Psi(\langle t\rangle_n)$, making sure that there are no free variables in $\langle t\rangle_n$ that are bound in $\Psi(\langle t\rangle_n)$ (relettering bound variables if necessary). For example, if Φ is $Rf(w) \vee \forall y(Ry \to Qy)$ and $\Psi(x)$ is $\forall z X xz$, then $\Phi[R/\Psi(x)]$ is $\forall z X f(w)z \vee \forall y(\forall z X yz \to Qy)$.

The deductive system for $L2K-$ consists of the schemes and the rules of $D1=$, together with the following *substitution rule*:[10]

$$\text{from } \Phi \text{ infer } \Phi[R/\Psi(\langle x\rangle_n)]$$

where Ψ does not contain any free variables that are bound in $\Phi[R/\Psi(\langle x \rangle_n)]$, i.e. where Ψ is free for R in Φ. The substitution rule has the effect of treating any formula with relation variables as a scheme whose 'place holders' are the relation variables and whose substitution instances are the appropriate formulas of $L2K-$.

We also add a rule allowing one to derive from any formula Φ an equivalent formula Φ^* that contains no function variables. The procedure for constructing Φ^* from Φ is tedious but straightforward.[11]

Call this deductive system $D2-$. It does *not* have an unrestricted deduction theorem. Indeed, if it did, then since $\neg Xx \vdash_{D2-} \neg(x = x)$, we would have $\vdash_{D2-} \neg Xx \rightarrow \neg(x = x)$ and so $\vdash_{D2-} Xx$. But any formula can be deduced from Xx. Thus, if the deduction theorem held for $D2-$, it would be inconsistent, and so would $D2$.[12]

However, the following is straightforward.

THEOREM 3.2 (Restricted deduction theorem).   If there is a deduction in $D2-$ of Ψ from $\Gamma \cup \{\Phi\}$ in which the substitution rule is not applied to a relation variable that occurs in Φ or Φ^*, then $\Gamma \vdash_{D2-} \Phi \rightarrow \Psi$.

This difference between $D2$ and $D2-$ is due to an ambiguity in the interpretation of free variables in contemporary logic. Sometimes they are taken as surrogate names for (unspecified) individuals. On this reading, a formula $\Phi(x)$ asserts that the object named by x has the property represented by Φ. The phase *free constant* might be better than 'free variable' in such cases. In other contexts, free variables are taken as if they are bound by prenex universal quantifiers. Accordingly, $\Phi(x)$ says that *everything* has the property represented by Φ, in which case the variable may be called *implicitly bound*. Some authors employ different notation for free constants and (implicitly or explicitly) bound variables, but the more common practice of conflating the two is followed here. The substitution rule presupposes that all second-order variables of $L2K-$ are *implicitly bound*. Thus a formula $\Phi(X)$ of $L2K-$ can be 'translated' into $L2K$ as $\forall X \Phi(X)$. Assume that Φ and Ψ are in $L2K-$, Φ has only X free, and Ψ has no free variables. Suppose also that $\Phi \vdash_{D2-} \Psi$. This amounts to $\forall X \Phi \vdash_{D2} \Psi$. So, from the deduction theorem, $(\forall X \Phi) \rightarrow \Psi$ can be deduced from no premises in $D2$. But in $D2-$, the conclusion of a deduction theorem would be $\vdash \Phi(X) \rightarrow \Psi$, which amounts to $\vdash \forall X[\Phi(X) \rightarrow \Psi]$. This does not match the result in $D2$ under the 'translation'.

Along these lines, in $L2K-$, $\neg \Phi(X)$ amounts to $\forall X(\neg \Phi(X))$, which is *not* the 'contradictory opposite' of $\Phi(X)$. In general, $L2K-$ is not closed under 'contradictory opposition' in that there are formulas $\Phi(X)$ with X free, such that there is no formula of $L2K-$ equivalent to $\neg \forall X \Phi(X)$.

Let us briefly take up the ramified language $L2Kp$. Recall that each relation variable of $L2Kp$ is to contain a subscript to indicate its level in the hierarchy of definition. Each relation must be definable in terms of variables ranging over lower-level relations. The axioms and rules of the first-order $D1$ are to be systematically extended to the ramified variables and quantifiers. First, if $j \leq i$ and X_j has the same degree as X_i and is free for X_i in Φ, then $\forall X_i \Phi(X_i) \rightarrow \Phi(X_j)$ is an axiom. That is, if Φ holds for all relations of a given level and degree, then Φ holds of any given relation of the same degree and the same or lower level. Next we have the rule of generalization: from $\Phi \rightarrow \Psi$ infer $\Phi \rightarrow \forall X_i \Psi$ provided that X_i does not occur free in Φ or in any premise of the deduction. The distinctive feature of this deductive system is the axiom scheme of *ramified comprehension*:

$\exists X_i \forall \langle x \rangle_n (X_i \langle x \rangle_n \equiv \Phi(\langle x \rangle_n))$ provided that X_i has degree n and the level of each relation variable (free or bound) that occurs in Φ is *less than i*.

Thus, level 0 relations are those 'definable' in terms of formulas containing no relation variables, i.e. first-order formulas. Level 1 relations are those definable in terms of formulas containing (at most) level 0 relation variables etc.

Call this deductive system $D2p$. The axiom of choice is *not* included. Indeed, the philosophical tendency underlying ramified systems is to restrict the variables to *definable* relations. There seems to be good reason to think that a general 'choice relation' is not definable.[13] The above derivations in $D2$ of the (unabbreviated versions) of the first-order identity axioms cannot be carried out in $D2p$, since they involve the full comprehension principle. In fact, it is not clear that a satisfactory characterization of identity can be given in $L2Kp$. Of course, one can introduce it as a primitive.

Some ramified systems, like that of *Principia Mathematica*, have an *axiom of reducibility*

$$\forall X_i \exists Y_0 \forall x (Y_0 x \equiv X_i x)$$

which asserts that for every level i relation, there is a level 0 relation with the same extension. This appears to simplify the theory, but it has the effect of collapsing the levels (see, for example, Ramsey 1925).

Deductive systems for the further extensions of $L2$ and $L2p$ are straightforward extensions of those considered here, but I shall not present details. The bulk of the present study is devoted to unramified (i.e. impredicative) second-order systems. Hazen (1983) gives an insightful analysis of ramified type theory, and Hilbert and Ackermann (1928) remains a good rudimentary source for impredicative ω-order deductive systems.

3.3 Semantics

Three model-theoretic semantics for second-order languages are presented in this section. A discussion of a more recent semantics proposed by Boolos

(1984, 1985a) is postponed to Chapter 9, Section 9.1. The systems developed here all use the resources of ordinary set theory. For the present, the metatheory is left informal. Later, we shall have occasion to be more explicit and careful.

Familiarity with standard model-theoretic semantics for first-order languages is assumed. Again, a rough sketch is offered, mostly to establish notation.

Each *model* of $L1K$ or $L1K=$ is a structure $M = \langle d, I \rangle$, in which d is a non-empty set, the *domain* of the model, and I is an *interpretation function* that assigns appropriate items constructed from d to the non-logical terminology, the members of K. For example, if b is an individual constant in K, then $I(b)$ is a member of d, and if B is a binary relation symbol, then $I(B)$ is a subset of d $\times$ d. A *variable-assignment* s is a function from the variables of $L1K$ (and $L1K=$) to d. Sometimes 'assignment' is elliptical for 'variable-assignment'.

For each model and assignment, there is a *denotation function* that assigns a member of d to each term of the language. The relation of *satisfaction* between models, assignments, and formulas (of $L1K$ and $L1K=$) is then defined in the usual manner. Again, consult any competent text in first-order logic for details. We write $M, s \vDash \Phi$ for 'M and s satisfy Φ'. As in Chapter 1, if $M, s \vDash \Phi$ for every assignment s, then we say that M is a *model of* Φ. If s and s' are any two assignments that agree on the free variables of Φ. then $M, s \vDash \Phi$ if and only if $M, s' \vDash \Phi$. Thus, if Φ is a sentence (i.e. a formula with no free variables), the assignment makes no difference and one can unambiguously write $M \vDash \Phi$.

A formula Φ is (semantically) *valid*, or is a *logical truth*, if $M, s \vDash \Phi$ for all models M and all assignments s on M. In other words, Φ is a logical truth if every model is a model of Φ. A formula Φ is *satisfiable* if $M, s \vDash \Phi$ for some model M and assignment s on M. A set Γ of formulas is *satisfiable* if there is a model M and assignment s on M such that $M, s \vDash \Phi$ for every Φ in Γ. Finally, a formula Φ is a *semantic consequence* of Γ, or $\langle \Gamma, \Phi \rangle$ is *valid*, if the union of Γ with $\{\neg \Phi\}$ is not satisfiable. In other words, Φ is a semantic consequence of Γ if for every model M and assignment s on M, if $M, s \vDash \Psi$ for every Ψ in Γ, then $M, s \vDash \Phi$. This is sometimes written $\Gamma \vDash \Phi$.

Notice that a formula Φ is a logical truth if and only if the result of prefixing it with universal quantifiers over its free variables is a logical truth. Similarly, Φ is satisfiable if and only if the result of prefixing it with existential quantifiers over its free variables is satisfiable. Because of this, when discussing single formulas, one can often restrict attention to sentences.

To follow up a previous discussion, the definition of satisfaction seems to take free variables as 'free constants'. The assignment function, in effect, specifies an individual in the domain as the denotation of each (free) variable. The definition of validity, on the other hand, has a universal quantifier ranging over all assignments of each model. Thus, in that context, free variables are 'implicitly bound'.

We now turn to the second-order languages $L2K$ and $L2K-$, and present three semantics. In each case, every model contains a substructure $\langle d, I \rangle$ where, as above, d is a non-empty set, the *domain* of the model, and I is the interpretation function of the model. What is added is a range of the relation and function variables.

First, there is *standard semantics*, which makes the logic properly second-order. A *standard model* of $L2K$ and $L2K-$ is the same as a model of the first-order $L1K$ and $L1K=$, namely a structure $\langle d, I \rangle$. A *variable-assignment* is a function that assigns a member of d to each first-order variable, a subset of d^n to each n-place relation variable, and a function from d^n to d to each n-place function variable. Thus, for example, a variable-assignment is, in part, a function from the collection of n-place relation variables to the collection of *all* n-place relations on d, the *powerset* of d^n. The denotation function for the terms of $L2K$ is a straightforward extension of the denotation function from $L1K$. The new clause is as follows.

> Let $M = \langle d, I \rangle$ be a model and s an assignment on M. The denotation of $f^n \langle t \rangle_n$ in M, s is the value of the function $s(f^n)$ at the sequence of members of d denoted by the members of $\langle t \rangle_n$.

The relation of *satisfaction* between models, assignments, and formulas is also extended to $L2K$ (and thus to $L2K-$) in a straightforward manner. There are three new clauses.

> If X^n is a relation variable and $\langle t \rangle_n$ is a sequence of n terms, then $M, s \vDash X^n \langle t \rangle_n$ if the sequence of members of d denoted by the members of $\langle t \rangle_n$ is an element of $s(X^n)$.

> $M, s \vDash \forall X \Phi$ if $M, s' \vDash \Phi$ for every assignment s' that agrees with s at every variable except possibly X.

> $M, s \vDash \forall f \Phi$ if $M, s' \vDash \Phi$ for every assignment s' that agrees with s at every variable except possibly f.

The notions of validity and satisfaction are defined as above: Φ is *standardly valid*, or is a *standard logical truth*, if $M, s \vDash \Phi$ for every M, s; Φ is *standardly satisfiable* if $M, s \vDash \Phi$ for some M, s; Γ is *standardly satisfiable* if there is an M, s such that $M, s \vDash \Phi$ for every Φ in Γ; Φ is a *standard consequence* of Γ if the union of Γ with $\{\neg \Phi\}$ is not standardly satisfiable. As abbreviations, 'valid' is used for 'standardly valid', 'satisfiable' for 'standardly satisfiable', etc.

Some of these semantic notions are not as useful with respect to free-variable second-order languages $L2K-$ in the light of the treatment of free second-order variables as *implicitly bound* (i.e. as if they were bound by

a universal quantifier ranging over the entire formula). If Φ is a formula of
$L2K-$, we say M, s *quasi-satisfies* Φ if $M, s' \vDash \Phi$ for every assignment s' on
M that agrees with s on the first-order variables. So, if X is the only free
second-order variable in Φ, then M, s quasi-satisfies Φ if and only if
$M, s \vDash \forall X \Phi$ in $L2K$. Notice that if a formula Ψ has no free first-order
variables, then for any assignments s, s', M, s quasi-satisfies Ψ if and only if
M, s' quasi-satisfies Ψ. So, for such formulas Ψ, we can unambiguously say
that M quasi-satisfies Ψ. We say that Φ is *quasi-satisfiable* if there is a model
M and assignment s such that M, s quasi-satisfies Φ; Γ is *quasi-satisfiable* if
there is an M, s such that M, s quasi-satisfies every member of Γ; and Φ is
a *quasi-consequence* of Γ if, for each M, s if M, s quasi-satisfies every member
of Γ, then $M, s \vDash \Phi$. The notion of validity is acceptable for $L2K-$ as it stands.

It is worth emphasizing the fact that a standard model for $L2K$ (and
$L2K-$) is the same as a model of its first-order counterpart $L1K$, namely
a domain and an interpretation of the non-logical terminology. That is, in
standard semantics, by fixing a domain one thereby fixes the range of both
the first-order variables and the second-order variables. There is no further
'interpreting' to be done. This is not the case with the next two semantics.
In both cases, one must separately determine a range for the first-order variables
and a range for the second-order variables. That is the crucial difference.

Next is Henkin semantics. The central facet is that in a given model, the
relation variables range over a *fixed collection* of relations on the domain,
which may not include all the relations, and the function variables range
over a fixed collection of functions on the domain. A *Henkin model of L2K*
(and $L2K-$) is a structure $M^H = \langle d, D, F, I \rangle$ in which d is a domain and
I is an interpretation function (for the terminology in K) as above. The items
D, F are a sequence of collections of relations and a sequence of collections
of functions respectively. In particular, for each n, $D(n)$ is a non-empty subset
of the powerset of d^n and $F(n)$ is a non-empty collection of functions from
d^n to d. The idea is that $D(n)$ is the range of the n-place relation variables
and $F(n)$ is the range of the n-place function variables. A *variable-assignment*
is a function that assigns a member of d to each first-order variable, a member
of $D(n)$ to each n-place relation variable, and a member of $F(n)$ to each
n-place function variable. The rest of the presentation of this semantics is
essentially the same as that of standard semantics. There are four new clauses.

Let $M^H = \langle d, D, F, I \rangle$ be a Henkin model and s an assignment on M^H.
The denotation of $f^n \langle t \rangle_n$ in M, s is the value of the function $s(f^n)$ at a
the sequence of members of d denoted by the members of $\langle t \rangle_n$.

If X^n is a relation variable and $\langle t \rangle_n$ a sequence of terms, then $M^H \vDash X^n \langle t \rangle_n$
if the sequence of members of d denoted by the members of $\langle t \rangle_n$ is an
element of $s(X^n)$.

$M^H, s \vDash \forall X \Phi$ if $M^H, s' \vDash \Phi$ for every assignment s' (on M^H) that agrees with s at every variable except possibly X.

$M^H, s \vDash \forall f \Phi$ if $M^H, s' \vDash \Phi$ for every assignment s' (on M^H) that agrees with s at every variable except possibly f.

Of course, the nature of the phrase 'every assignment' (in the third and fourth clause) is what distinguishes Henkin semantics from standard semantics. Here the assignments are restricted to those that assign members of the various $D(n)$ and $F(n)$ to the higher-order variables. The notions of *Henkin-validity*, *Henkin-satisfaction*, and *Henkin-consequence* are defined in a straightforward manner: Φ is Henkin-valid if $M^H, s \vDash \Phi$ for every Henkin model M^H and assignment s; Φ is Henkin-satisfiable if $M^H, s \vDash \Phi$ for some Henkin model M^H and assignment s; Γ is Henkin-satisfiable if there is a Henkin model M^H and an assignment s such that $M^H, s \vDash \Phi$ for each Φ in Γ; Φ is a Henkin-consequence of Γ if for every Henkin model M^H and assignment s if $M^H, s \vDash \Psi$ for every Ψ in Γ, then $M^H, s \vDash \Phi$. It is straightforward to extend these notions to $L2K-$ (e.g. quasi-Henkin-satisfaction etc.).

It is immediate that a standard model of $L2K$ is equivalent to the Henkin model in which, for each n, $D(n)$ is $\mathscr{P}(d^n)$ and $F(n)$ is the collection of all functions from d^n to d. Such Henkin models are sometimes caled *full models*.

THEOREM 3.3.   Let M be a standard model and M^F the corresponding full model. Then for each assignment s and each formula Φ, $M^H, s \vDash \Phi$ if and only if $M^F, s \vDash \Phi$.

COROLLARY 3.4.   If Φ is Henkin-valid, then Φ is (standardly) valid. If Φ is a Henkin-consequence of Γ, then Φ is a consequence of Γ. If Φ is standardly satisfiable, then Φ is Henkin-satisfiable.

It will soon become clear that the converses of Corollary 3.4 fail.

In the third model-theoretic semantics, each model consists of separate, possibly unrelated, domains for each kind of variable. In effect, the languages $L2K$ and $L2K-$ are regarded as *multi-sorted* first-order languages. Each model also determines a 'predication' relation between the items in the range of the relation variables and appropriate sequences of items in the range of the first-order variables, and each model determines an 'application' function from items in the range of the function variables and appropriate sequences to the range of the first-order variables. In short, in the present semantics, 'predication' and 'application' are non-logical,[14] on a par with the items in K.

By way of analogy, our third system is designated *first-order semantics*. Each *first-order model* of $L2K$ (and $L2K-$) is a structure

$$M^1 = \langle d, d_1, d_2, \langle I, p, a \rangle \rangle,$$

in which d is a non-empty set and I is an interpretation function assigning items constructed from d to the items in K, as above. For each natural number n, $d_1(n)$ and $d_2(n)$ are non-empty sets, the ranges of the n-place relation variables and the n-place function variables respectively. For each n, $p(n)$ is a subset of $d^n \times d_1(n)$ and $a(n)$ is a function from $d^n \times d_2(n)$ to d. Here, the idea is that $p(n)$ is the interpretation of the n-place 'predication' relation, the relation between a sequence of length n and an n-place 'relation' that 'holds' of it. Similarly, $a(n)$ is the interpretation of the n-place 'application' function, from the collection of sequences and functions to the first domain. A *variable-assignment* is a function that assigns a member of d to each first-order variable, a member of $d_1(n)$ to each n-place relation variable, and a member of $d_2(n)$ to each n-place function variable. The denotation function is adapted from that of $L1K$. The new clause is as follows.

Let M^1 be a first-order model and s an assignment on M^1. If $f^n\langle t\rangle_n$ is a term and $\langle u\rangle_n$ is the sequence of elements of d denoted by the members of $\langle t\rangle_n$, then the denotation in M, s of $f^n\langle t\rangle_n$ is $a(n)(\langle u\rangle_n, s(f^n))$.

In other words, the denotation of $f^n\langle t\rangle_n$ is determined by the 'application' function $a(n)$, evaluated at the denotations of the items in $\langle t\rangle_n$ and the item in $d_2(n)$ denoted by f^n. Once again, the relation of satisfaction is straightforward. The new clauses are as follows.

Let X^n be an n-place relation variable and $\langle t\rangle_n$ a sequence of terms. Let $s(X^n) = v$ (an element of $d_1(n)$) and let $\langle u\rangle_n$ be the sequence of elements of d denoted by $\langle t\rangle_n$. Then $M^1, s \vDash X^n\langle t\rangle_n$ if the pair $\langle u\rangle_n, v$ is in $p(n)$.

$M^1, s \vDash \forall X \Phi$ if $M^1, s' \vDash \Phi$ for every assignment s' (on M^1) that agrees with s at every variable except possibly X.

$M^1, s \vDash \forall f \Phi$ if $M^1, s' \vDash \Phi$ for every assignment s' (on M^1) that agrees with s at every variable except possibly f.

As above, the semantical notions are straightforward: Φ is *first-order-valid* if $M^1, s \vDash \Phi$ for every first-order model M^1 and assignment s; Φ is *first-order-satisfiable* if $M^1, s \vDash \Phi$ for some first-order model M^1 and assignment s; Γ is *first-order-satisfiable* if there is a first-order model M^1 and an assignment s such that $M^1, s \vDash \Phi$ for each Φ in Γ; Φ is a *first-order-consequence* of Γ if for every first-order model M^1 and assignment s, if $M^1, s \vDash \Psi$ for every Ψ in Γ, then $M^1, s \vDash \Phi$.

It is easy to see that a given Henkin model $\langle d, D, F, I\rangle$ simply *is* the first-order model $\langle d, d_1, d_2, \langle I, p, q\rangle\rangle$ such that d_1 is D, d_2 is F, p is the 'real' predication (or membership) relation between d and D, and F is the 'real' application function from the various $F(n)$ and d^n to d. That is, $\langle u, v\rangle$ is in $p(n)$ if and only if $u \in v$, and $a(n)(u, w) = w(u)$. Thus, for every Henkin model M^H there is a first-order model M^1, and for every assignment s on M^H there is an assignment s^1 on M^1, such that for every formula Φ of $L2K$, $M^H, s \vDash d$ *if and only if* $M^1, s^1 \vDash \Phi$. There is a converse.

THEOREM 3.5. Let $M^1 = \langle d, d_1, d_2, \langle I, p, a\rangle\rangle$ be a first-order model of $L2K$. Then there is a Henkin model $M^H = \langle d, D, F, I\rangle$ and, for every variable-assignment s on M^1, there is an assignment s^H on M^H such that for every formula Φ of L2K, $M^1, s \vDash \Phi$ if and only if $M^H, S^H \vDash \Phi$.

Proof. For each natural number n and each $v \in d_1(n)$, let $S(n, v) = \{u \in d^n \mid \langle u, v \rangle \in p(n)\}$. That is, $S(n, v)$ is the set of members of d^n that bear the M^1-interpretation of 'predication' to v. Let $D(n) = \{R \subseteq d^n \mid R = S(n, v)$ for some v in $d_1(n)\}$, and let D be the sequence of the $D(m)$. Similarly, for each natural number n and each $w \in d_2(n)$, let $T(n, w)$ be the function from d^n to d whose value at each $\langle u \rangle_n$ is $a(n)(\langle u \rangle_n, w)$. That is, $T(n, w)$ is the function obtained from w by the M^1-interpretation of the 'application' function. Let $F(n) = \{T(n, w) \mid w \in d_2(n)\}$, let F be the sequence of the $F(m)$, and let M^H be the structure $\langle d, D, F, I \rangle$. Let s be a variable assignment on M^1. If x is a first-order variable, then let $s^H(x)$ be $s(x)$, if X is an n-place relation variable, then let $s^H(X)$ be $S(n, s(X))$, and if f is an n-place function variable, then let $s^H(f)$ be $T(n, s(f))$. Notice that for every assignment s' on M^H, there is an assignment s on M^1 such that $s^H = s'$. The only thing left to show is that for each Φ of L2K, $M^1, s \vDash \Phi$ if and only if $M^H, s^H \vDash \Phi$. But this is a straightforward induction on the complexity of Φ.   □

To take a frivolous example, suppose that in M^1, d is a set of apples and $d_1(1)$ is a set of oranges. Then in M^H, each orange is 'replaced' by the set of apples that bear the M^1-interpretation of the predication relation to it.[15]

COROLLARY 3.6.   For each Φ of L2K (and L2K−), Φ is Henkin-valid if and only if Φ is first-order-valid, and Φ is Henkin-satisfiable if and only if Φ is first-order-satisfiable. For each set Γ of formulas, Γ is Henkin-satisfiable if and only if Γ is first-order-satisfiable, and Φ is a Henkin-consequence of Γ if and only if Φ is a first-order-consequence of Γ.

In short, Henkin semantics and first-order semantics are pretty much the same.

Notes

1. Names of languages here begin with the letter L. The numeral 1 indicates that this language is first-order, and, as noted, K is the set of non-logical terminology.
2. Throughout this book, 'countable' is taken as 'either finite or denumerably infinite'. Sometimes the phrase 'finite or countable' is used for emphasis.
3. This option, which is sometimes called 'monadic second-order logic', is briefly discussed in Chapter 9, Section 9.1.
4. Along these lines, quantifiers binding first-order variables can also be thought of as higher-order predicates. Accordingly, $\forall x P$ is a property of properties, asserting that P holds of everything.
5. A term t is free for x in $\Phi(x)$ if no variable has an occurrence that is both free in t and bound in $\Phi(t)$.
6. Again, this not meant as a philosophical thesis about identity. If anything, it follows from the assumption that the present languages are extensional.

7. In $L2K$, the only 'relation terms' and 'function terms' are variables and, possibly, members of K. In third- and higher-order languages, more complex 'higher-order terms' would be included here.
8. Chapter 5 contains a discussion of the axiom of choice in the context of second-order logic. See also the last chapter of Hilbert and Ackermann (1928). A stronger version of the axiom of choice involves relations. It is a scheme:

$$\forall x \exists X \, \Phi(x, X) \rightarrow \exists Y \, ^2 \forall x \forall Z (\forall z (Zz \equiv Y\, ^2 xz) \rightarrow \Phi(x, Z)).$$

The antecedent asserts that for each x there is a property X such that x, X satisfies the formula Φ. Using the axiom of choice informally, we can 'pick' one such property for each x. Call it P_x. The consequent holds if there is a relation whose extension is all pairs x, z such that P_x holds of z. It is straightforward to formulate versions of this scheme with n-place relations X^n instead of properties X.
9. An actual derivation of $\forall x \forall X (Xx \equiv Xx)$ in $D2$ requires 15 lines.
10. In $D2$ one can derive $\Phi[R/\Psi(\langle x \rangle_n)]$ from $\forall R \Phi$, using an instance of the comprehension scheme, provided that Ψ does not contain any free variables that become bound in $\Phi[R/\Psi(\langle x \rangle_n)]$. A variant of the substitution rule holds in $D2$. If $\Gamma \vdash_{D2} \Phi$, then $\Gamma \vdash_{D2} \Phi[R/\Psi(\langle x \rangle_n)]$, provided that R does not occur free in any formula in Γ and no free variable of Ψ is bound in $\Phi[R/\Psi(\langle x \rangle_n)]$. Henkin (1953) given an insightful account of the relationship between substitution rules and principles of comprehension.
11. Suppose that Φ has $f_1 \ldots f_n$ as its only function variables. Let $F_1 \ldots F_n$ be a sequence of relation variables that do not occur in Φ, such that, for each $i \leq n$, the degree of f_i is one less than the degree of F_i. Each of these relation variables is to replace the corresponding function variable. Suppose that R has exactly m occurrences of function variables. Define a sequence of formulas $\Phi_0 \ldots \Phi_m$ as follows: Φ_0 is Φ. Suppose that Φ_i has been defined for $i < m$. Let $f_j \langle t \rangle_r$ be the leftmost term that occurs in Φ_i such that f_j is a function variable and no function variables occur in the members of $\langle t \rangle_n$. Let z be a first-order variable that does not occur in Φ_i. Then Φ_{i+1} is $\forall z [F_j \langle t \rangle_r z \rightarrow \Phi_i']$ where Φ_i' is the result of replacing the first occurrence of $f_j \langle t \rangle_r$ with z. Notice that the last item in the sequence, Φ_m, has no function variables. Let Ψ be the conjunction of the formulas $\forall \langle x \rangle_r \exists! y F_i \langle x \rangle_r y$, for $1 \leq i \leq n$ and r the degree of f_i. Informally, this asserts that each F_i is the graph of a function. Finally Φ^* is $\Psi \rightarrow \Phi_m$.
12. The consistency of $D2$ and $D2-$ follows from their soundness. See Chapter 4.
13. For example, it is consistent with contemporary set theory (ZFC) that there is no set-theoretic definable choice function on the powerset of the set of real numbers.
14. In the previous chapters, the logical–non-logical distinction applies to the *terminology* in various formal languages. Notice, however, that $L2K$ and $L2K-$ do not have special symbols for predication and application. Simple concatenation is used for this; for example, Px expresses the predication of x by P. It may be appropriate to say that these instances of concatenation are non-logical in first-order semantics for $L2K$.
15. See Gilmore (1957). Our decision not to introduce a (primitive) symbol for identity between relations simplifies the present treatment. Suppose, for example, that in M^1, there are two *different* elements of $d_1(1)$, v and w, such that for each $u \in d$, $\langle u, v \rangle \in p(1)$ if and only if $\langle u, w \rangle \in p(1)$. Since v and w are 'extensionally equivalent' in this model, both are assigned to the same subset of d by S:

$S(1, v) = S(1, w)$. Now, let s assign v to X and w to Y. Then, if identity were a logical primitive, we would have $M^1, s \vDash X \neq Y$, but $M^H, s^H \vDash X = Y$. If a primitive symbol for identity among relations (or functions) were in the language, one option would be to restrict the class of first-order models to those that satisfy the principles of extensionality:

$$\forall P \forall Q [\forall \langle x \rangle_n (P \langle x \rangle_n \equiv Q \langle x \rangle_n) \rightarrow P = Q]$$

$$\forall f \forall g [\forall \langle x \rangle_n (f \langle x \rangle_n = g \langle x \rangle_n) \rightarrow f = g].$$

An alternative would be a variation of the technique used in first-order logic—we could introduce certain equivalence classes among the sets $\{R \subseteq d^n \mid R = S(n, v)\}$, $\{f \mid f = T(n, w)\}$. Notice, incidentally, that the functions S and T in the above proof need not be one-to-one. In full generality, the axiom of choice is needed to carry out the 'straightforward induction' mentioned at the end of the proof.

4

Metatheory

4.1 First-order theories

There are a number of well-known results that apply to first-order logic. The major theorems are stated in order to make the contrast with second-order languages with standard semantics. Proof sketches of corresponding results are found in Section 4.3 on Henkin and first-order semantics. The reader may also consult any competent text devoted to first-order mathematical logic (e.g. Mendelson 1987, Boolos and Jeffrey 1989).

THEOREM 4.1 (Soundness). Let Γ be a set of formulas and Φ a single formula of $L1K=$. If Φ is deducible from Γ in $D1=$, then Φ is a semantic consequence of Γ. *A fortiori*, if Φ is a logical theorem, then Φ is a logical truth.

The proof of this is straightforward. One checks each axiom and rule of inference. Virtually no substantial assumptions about the set-theoretic semantics are employed. The converse holds, but it is far from simple.

THEOREM 4.2 (Completeness) (Gödel 1930). Let Γ be a set of formulas and Φ a single formula of $L1K=$. If Φ is a semantic consequence of Γ, then $\Gamma \vdash_{D1=} \Phi$. Equivalently, if Γ is consistent then Γ is satisfiable.

As noted in Chapter 1, the completeness of first-order logic depends on a principle of infinity (in the metalanguage). If the model-theoretic semantics had no models with infinite domains, the completeness theorem would be false.[1]

THEOREM 4.3 (Compactness). Let Γ be a set of formulas. If every finite subset of Γ is satisfiable, then Γ itself is satisfiable.

Proof. This is a corollary of the completeness and soundness theorems. If Γ is not satisfiable, then, by completeness, Γ is not consistent: $\Gamma \vdash_{D1=} (\Phi \,\&\, \neg \Phi)$. But each deduction (in $D1=$) can contain only finitely many premises. So there is a finite subset Γ' of Γ such that $\Gamma' \vdash_{D1=} (\Phi \,\&\, \neg \Phi)$. By soundness, Γ' is not satisfiable. □

Let $M = \langle d, I \rangle$ and $M' = \langle d', I' \rangle$ be two models of $L1K=$. Define M' to be a *submodel* of M if $d' \subseteq d$, I and I' give the same denotation to each individual constant, and the interpretation of each relation and function symbol under I' is the restriction to d' of the corresponding interpretation under I. If there are any function letters in K, then d' must be closed under the functions they denote. For example, if f is a unary function letter, then for every $m \in d'$, $I(f)(m)$ must also be in d'. $I'(f)$ is the restriction of $I(f)$ to d'.

THEOREM 4.4 (Downward Löwenheim–Skolem theorem). Let M be a model of $L1K=$. Then M has a submodel M' whose domain is at most denumerably infinite (or the cardinality of K, whichever is larger), such that for each assignment s on M' and each formula Φ, $M, s \vDash \Phi$ iff $M', s \vDash \Phi$.

The proof of this theorem makes essential use of the axiom of choice (in the metatheory).

THEOREM 4.5 (Upward Löwenheim–Skolem theorem). Let Γ be a set of formulas of $L1K=$. If, for each natural number n, there is a model of Γ whose domain has at least n elements, then for any *infinite* cardinal κ, there is a model of Γ whose domain has cardinality at least κ.

In the rest of this chapter, the set K of non-logical terminology is assumed to be at most countable, unless explicitly noted otherwise. Theorems 4.4 and 4.5 entail that no first-order theory with an infinite model is categorical. Indeed, if Γ has an infinite model, then Γ has a model of *every* infinite cardinality. It is a corollary that first-order languages are not adequate to characterize infinite structures. Indeed, let M be any structure with an infinite domain, and let Γ be the set of first-order sentences satisfied by M (i.e. $\Gamma = \{\Phi \mid M \vDash \Phi\}$). According to Theorems 4.4 and 4.5, for any infinite cardinality κ, there is a structure of cardinality κ that is a model of Γ. This property, I would say 'defect', of first-order logic is not shared by second-order languages with standard semantics. There are many important structures with categorical second-order characterizations. In fact, the counterparts of 4.2–4.5 all fail for second-order languages with standard semantics. However, the counterparts do hold for second-order languages with Henkin or first-order semantics. In this respect, such logics are much like first-order logic.

4.2   Second order—standard semantics

One result does carry over from first-order logic to second-order logic with standard semantics.

THEOREM 4.6 (Soundness). Let Γ be a set of formulas and Φ a single formula of $L2K$. If Φ can be deduced from Γ in $D2$, then Φ is a semantic consequence of Γ. *A fortiori*, if Φ is a logical theorem, then Φ is a logical truth.

Like the first-order case, this is straightforward. One checks each axiom and rule of inference. Most of the axioms and rules require no substantial assumptions about the set-theoretic universe underlying the model theory. The clause involving the comprehension scheme uses the comprehension principle that every formula *in the metatheory* determines a relation, and it uses a (metatheoretic) principle of separation: if d is a set and P is a property, then there is a set containing all and only the members of d that have P. Similarly, the clause involving the axiom of choice uses a principle of choice in the metatheory.

In these cases, then, we have an apparent circularity. A certain axiom (or scheme) is shown to be sound by using that very principle. It is not a real circularity, however, because the principle to be sanctioned is in the formal language $L2K$, while the principle used is in the metatheory. Moreover, exactly the same situation occurs with respect to the soundness of first-order logic. For example, one cannot prove in the metatheory that a formula in the form $\forall x \Phi(x) \rightarrow \Phi(t)$ is a logical truth, or that *modus ponens* preserves satisfaction, without using the metatheoretic principles modelled by those schemes. The purpose of the soundness theorem is not to establish that, say, *modus ponens* or the axiom of choice is justified, but only to verify that the principle is sanctioned by the semantics. People who have doubts about separation, comprehension, or choice, as applied to the present model-theoretic semantics, may drop the corresponding axioms from the deductive system $D2$. However, one should be forewarned that the metatheoretic principles in question have a significant role to play in the sequel.

Recall that the deductive system $D2-$ for the free-variable second-order language $L2K-$ can be regarded as a subsystem of $D2$, if the free relation and function variables are bound by universal quantifiers ranging over the entire formula. Because of the difference in the treatment of variables, the soundness theorem does not hold as stated for free-variable second-order logic. For example, the sentence $\exists x(x \neq x)$ follows from $\exists xXx$ by the substitution rule, but the former is not a semantic consequence of the latter. Indeed, let M be any model and let s assign the entire domain of M to the variable X. Then $M, s \vDash \exists xXx$, but of course M, s does not satisfy $\exists x(x \neq x)$. In Chapter 3, Section 3.3, a formula Φ of $L2K-$ is defined to be a quasi-consequence of a set Γ if, for each M, s, if M, s' satisfies every member of Γ for every assignment s' that agrees with s on the first-order variables, then $M, s \vDash \Phi$. This is the appropriate consequence relation for $L2K-$. It is vacuous that $\exists x(x \neq x)$ is a quasi-consequence of $\exists xXx$, since the latter is not quasi-satisfiable. In general, we have the following corollary.

COROLLARY 4.7.   Let Γ be a set of formulas and Φ a single formula of $L2K-$. If Φ can be deduced from Γ in $D2-$, then Φ is a quasi-consequence of Γ.

The primary business in this section is the *refutation* of the analogues of 4.2–4.5: completeness, compactness, and the Löwenheim–Skolem theorems.

The categoricity of second-order Peano arithmetic will be established in some detail (for the purposes of later examination). This is followed by a sketch of a proof of the categoricity of real analysis and a similar, but weaker, result for set theory. The indicated refutations are corollaries of these results.

The *language of arithmetic* has $A = \{0, s, +, \cdot\}$ as its set of non-logical terminology.[2] The first-order language is $L1A =$, and the second-order languages are $L2A$ and $L2A -$. The following axioms are first-order:

$\forall x(sx \neq 0)$ & $\forall x \forall y(sx = sy \rightarrow x = y)$ (successor axiom)

$\forall x(x + 0 = x)$ & $\forall x \forall y(x + sy = s(x + y))$ (addition axiom)

$\forall x(x \cdot 0 = 0)$ & $\forall x \forall y(x \cdot sy = x \cdot y + x)$ (multiplication axiom).

Then there is the induction axiom

$$\forall X[(X0 \ \& \ \forall x(Xx \rightarrow Xsx)) \rightarrow \forall x Xx]$$

which is a proper second-order statement. Let AR be the conjunction of these four axioms, and let $AR-$ be the conjunction of the first three and the result of removing the opening $\forall X$ from the induction axiom. The latter is a formula of $L2A -$.

Let N be the model of $L2A$ whose domain is the set of natural numbers and which assigns zero to 0, and assigns the successor function, the addition function, and the multiplication function to s, $+$, and $\cdot$, respectively. Then $N \vDash AR$ and N quasi-satisfies $AR-$. Indeed, N is the *intended* model of these formulas. The next theorem is that, in an important sense, N is the *only* model.

THEOREM 4.8 (Categoricity of arithmetic) (Dedekind).   Let $M1 = \langle d_1, I_1 \rangle$ and $M2 = \langle d_2, I_2 \rangle$ be two models of $L2A$. For $i = 1, 2$, let 0_i be the interpretation of 0 in d_i, and let s_i, $+_{i, \cdot i}$ be the respective interpretations of successor, addition, and multiplication. If $M1 \vDash AR$ and $M2 \vDash AR$, then $M1$ and $M2$ are *isomorphic*: there is a one-to-one function f from d_1 onto d_2 such that $f(0_1) = 0_2$, and for each a, b in d_1, $f(s_1 a) = s_2(f(a))$, $f(a +_1 b) = f(a) +_2 f(b)$, and $f(a \cdot_1 b) = f(a) \cdot_2 f(b)$. That is, f preserves the structure of the models.

Proof.   Define a subset S of $d_1 \times d_2$ to be *successor closed* if (i) $\langle 0_1, 0_2 \rangle \in S$ and (ii) if $\langle a, b \rangle \in S$ then $\langle s_1 a, s_2 b \rangle \in S$. Let f be the intersection of all successor closed subsets of $d_1 \times d_2$. Clearly, f is not empty, since $d_1 \times d_2$ itself is successor closed and $\langle 0_1, 0_2 \rangle$ is in every successor closed set. Also, f is successor closed. A series of lemmas establishes the theorem.

1. For each $a \in d_1$ there is a $b \in d_2$ such that $\langle a, b \rangle \in f$. Let P be the set $\{a \in d_1 \mid$ there is a $b \in d_2$ such that $\langle a, b \rangle \in f\}$. That is, P is the domain of f. Clearly, $0_1 \in P$, since $\langle 0_1, 0_2 \rangle$ is in f. Suppose that $a \in P$. Then there

is a $b \in d_2$ such that $\langle a, b \rangle$ is in f. Thus, $\langle s_1 a, s_2 b \rangle$ is in f (since f is successor closed) and so $s_1 a \in P$. In sum, P contains 0_1 and is closed under s_1. Since $M1$ satisfies the induction axiom, P contains every member of d_1.

2. If $\langle a, b \rangle \in f$ and $\langle a, c \rangle \in f$, then $b = c$ (i.e. f is a function). Let $P = \{a \in d_1 \mid \exists! b \in d_2 (\langle a, b \rangle \in f)\}$. Assume that 0_1 is not in P. Then there is a $c \neq 0_2$ in d_2 such that $\langle 0_1, c \rangle$ is in f. Let $S = d_1 \times d_2 - \{\langle 0_1, c \rangle\}$. Clearly, $\langle 0_1, 0_2 \rangle \in S$, and if $\langle a, b \rangle \in S$, then $\langle s_1 a, s_2 b \rangle \in S$, since $s_1 a \neq 0_1$. Thus S is successor closed, but $\langle 0_1, c \rangle$ is not in S, contradicting our assumption that $\langle 0_1, c \rangle$ is in f, the intersection of every successor closed set. So $0_1 \in P$. Now let $a \in P$, and let b be the unique member of d_2 such that $\langle a, b \rangle \in f$. Then since f is successor closed, $\langle s_1 a, s_2 b \rangle \in f$. Now assume that $s_1 a$ is not in P. Then there is a $c \in d_2$ such that $c \neq s_2 b$ but $\langle s_1 a, c \rangle$ is in f. Let $T = f - \{\langle s_1 a, c \rangle\}$. Since $s_1 a \neq 0_1$, $\langle 0_1, 0_2 \rangle \in T$. Suppose $\langle u, v \rangle \in T$. Then $\langle u, v \rangle \in f$ and so $\langle s_1 u, s_2 v \rangle \in f$. If $u \neq a$, then since $M1$ satisfies the successor axiom, $s_1 u \neq s_1 a$ and thus $\langle s_1 u, s_2 v \rangle \in T$. If on the other hand $u = a$, then since $a \in P$, $v = b$ and $s_2 v = s_2 b \neq c$. Thus $\langle s_1 u, s_2 v \rangle \in T$. Hence, T is successor closed, and so $f \subseteq T$, a contradiction. To sum up, $0_1 \in P$ and P is closed under successor. Thus, by induction in $M1$, P contains every member of d_1.

We can now employ functional notation, writing $f(a) = b$ for $\langle a, b \rangle \in f$.

3. f is one-to-one and onto d_2. This is exactly similar to 1 and 2, using the fact that $M2$ satisfies the successor and induction axioms.

4. f preserves the structure of the models. Clearly $f(0_1) = 0_2$. The clause for successor, $f(s_1 a) = s_2(f(a))$, is a consequence of the fact that f is successor closed. The clauses for addition and multiplication follow in a similar manner, using the addition and multiplication axioms in $M1$ and $M2$.   □

It follows that if M is a model of AR, then the domain of M is denumerably infinite. Notice that $M \vDash AR$ if and only if for every assignment s on M, $M, s \vDash AR-$. Thus M is isomorphic to the natural numbers if and only if M, s quasi-satisfies $AR-$ for every assignment s on M.

COROLLARY 4.9.   Let Φ be a sentence of $L2A$. Then Φ is true of the natural numbers (i.e. $N \vDash \Phi$) if and only if $AR \rightarrow \Phi$ is a logical truth. Let Ψ be a sentence of the first-order $L1A=$. Then Ψ is true of the natural numbers if and only if Ψ is a quasi-consequence of $AR-$.

In *real analysis*, the non-logical terminology is $B = \{0, 1, +, \cdot, \leq\}$. The first axioms are those of an ordered field, all of which are first order.[3] The sole second-order statement is the *axiom of completeness*, asserting that every bounded property (or set) has a least upper bound:

$$\forall X\{\exists x \forall y(Xy \rightarrow y \leq x) \rightarrow \exists x[\forall y(Xy \rightarrow y \leq x)$$

$$\& \ \forall z(\forall y(Xy \rightarrow y \leq z) \rightarrow x \leq z)]\}.$$

Let AN be the conjunction of the axioms of real analysis, and let $AN-$ be the conjunction of these axioms with the opening $\forall X$ removed from the completeness axiom. In both cases, the real number structure constitutes the intended model, and AN is categorical.

THEOREM 4.10 (Categoricity of analysis). Let $M1 = \langle d_1, I_1 \rangle$ and $M2 = \langle d_2, I_2 \rangle$ be two models for the language $L2B$. If $M1 \vDash AN$ and $M2 \vDash AN$, then $M1$ and $M2$ are isomorphic.

Proof sketch. We construct a subset f of $d_1 \times d_2$ in stages. Since, at each stage, f is one-to-one, we sometimes employ functional notation, writing $f(a) = b$ for $\langle a, b \rangle \in f$. Define the *natural numbers of* each model to be the smallest set containing the denotations of 0 and 1 and closed under the denotation of addition.[4] It is easy to show that in any model that satisfies AN, these 'natural numbers' are unbounded. Moreover, in any such model, the submodel whose domain is these 'natural numbers' satisfies a variant of the axiom (AR) of arithmetic, and thus, by Theorem 4.8, the natural numbers of $M1$ are isomorphic to the natural numbers of $M2$. So we begin by including all pairs $\langle a, b \rangle$ in f in which a and b are corresponding natural numbers of d_1 and d_2 respectively. The field axioms entail that each number has a unique additive inverse, and each number except 0 has a unique multiplicative inverse. So we define the *rational numbers of* each model to be the smallest set that contains the natural numbers of the model and is closed under additive inverse, multiplication, and multiplicative inverse. The above isomorphism between the respective 'natural numbers' of the models is easily extended to the 'rational numbers'. So we have $\langle a, b \rangle \in f$ if a is a 'rational number' of $M1$ and b is the corresponding 'rational number' of $M2$. It can be shown that the 'rationals' are *dense* in each model in the sense that for each x and y, if $x \leq y$ and $x \neq y$, then there is a rational number q such that $x \leq q \leq y$. Now, let c be any non-rational member of d_1. Consider the set

$$C = \{a \in d_1 \mid a \text{ is a rational number of } M1 \text{ and } a \leq c \text{ in } M1\}.$$

This set is bounded in $M1$ and, in fact, c is its least upper bound (since the rationals are dense). Define $f(C)$ to be $\{f(a) \mid a \in C\}$, a subset of d_2. Since C is bounded and the natural numbers of $M1$ are not, let n be a natural number of $M1$ that is greater than or equal to every member of C. Then $f(n)$ is an upper bound in $M2$ for $f(C)$. So $f(C)$ is bounded and thus it has a least upper bound, say d. Then include the pair $\langle c, d \rangle$ in f. It is straightforward to show that f has been extended to an isomorphism between $M1$ and $M2$.   □

It follows that all models of AN have the cardinality of the continuum. Thus, by Cantor's theorem, none are countable. The proofs of Theorems 4.8 and 4.10 are analysed in Chapter 5, Section 5.2, and it is shown why they fail in the respective first-order theories.

The language of *set theory* has only one non-logical term, the binary membership symbol $\in$. We write $x \notin y$ for $\neg(x \in y)$. This part of this section assumes some familiarity with first-order set theory ZFC (see, for example, Fraenkel *et al.* 1973).

As with arithmetic and analysis, all but one of the axioms are first-order:

$$\forall x \forall y [\forall z (z \in x \equiv z \in y) \to x = y] \qquad \text{(extensionality)}$$

$$\forall x [\exists y (y \in x) \to \exists y (y \in x \ \& \ \forall z (\neg (z \in y \ \& \ z \in x)))] \qquad \text{(foundation)}$$

$$\forall x \forall y \exists z \forall w (w \in z \equiv (w = x \ \lor \ w = y)) \qquad \text{(pairs)}$$

$$\forall x \exists y \forall z (z \in y \equiv \exists w (z \in w \ \& \ w \in x)) \qquad \text{(unions)}$$

$$\forall x \exists y \forall z (z \in y \equiv \forall w (w \in z \to w \in x)) \qquad \text{(powerset)}$$

$$\exists x [\exists y (y \in x) \ \& \ \forall z (z \in x \to \exists w (w \in x$$

$$\& \ \forall v (v \in w \equiv v \in z \ \lor \ v = z)))] \qquad \text{(infinity)}.$$

Finally, the second-order *axiom of replacement* asserts that if f is a function and x a set, then the range of f restricted to the members of x is also a set:

$$\forall f \forall x \exists y \forall z (z \in y \equiv \exists w (w \in x \ \& \ z = fw)).$$

Let $Z2$ be the conjunction of these seven sentences.[5]

The deductive system obtained from $D2$ by adding $Z2$ as an axiom is equivalent to that of Morse–Kelley (MK) set theory (see Fraenkel *et al.* 1973, Chapter II). It is not a conservative extension of first-order ZFC in that there are first-order sentences that are deducible in MK but not in first-order ZFC. Von Neumann–Gödel–Bernays (NGB) set theory is obtained from MK by restricting the comprehension scheme (of $D2$) to formulas that lack bound relation and function variables. That is, impredicative instances of comprehension are not axioms of NGB. The latter is a conservative extension of first-order ZFC.

Let $M = \langle d, I \rangle$ be a model of the language of set theory. Define M to be a *set model* if d is an element of the iterative hierarchy (formed without urelements) and I assigns the membership relation to $\in$. That is, M is a set model if d is a set of sets and $\in$ is interpreted as membership. In this case, M can be identified with d. If, for every $b \in d$, $a \in b$ entails that $a \in d$, then d is said to be *transitive*. In other words, d is transitive if it contains every member of each of its members. It is a theorem of set theory that for any structure $M' = \langle d', I' \rangle$, if the interpretation of $\in$ in M' is extensional and well-founded, then M' is isomorphic to a transitive set model.[6] It follows that any model that satisfies the axioms of extensionality, foundation, and replacement is isomorphic to a transitive set-model. Moreover, the following theorem holds.

THEOREM 4.11. Let $M \vDash Z2$. Then M is isomorphic to an inaccessible rank.

Let $M1 = \langle d_1, I_1 \rangle$ and $M2 = \langle d_2, I_2 \rangle$ both satisfy $Z2$. Then $M1$ is isomorphic to a transitive set model a_1 and $M2$ is isomorphic to a transitive set model a_2. If $a_1 = a_2$, then of course $M1$ is isomorphic to $M2$. If on the other hand $a_1 \neq a_2$, then either $a_1 \in a_2$ or $a_2 \in a_1$. In effect, if $M1$ is not isomorphic to $M2$, then one of them is isomorphic to what may be called an 'initial segment' of the other. Because of this, Weston (1976) calls second-order set theory 'almost categorical' (although he denies that this is significant).

We now proceed, rapid-fire, to refute the analogues of Theorems 4.2–4.5 for $L2K$ with standard semantics. The Löwenheim–Skolem theorems are easiest. Second-order arithmetic AR is categorical (Theorem 4.8). It has denumerably infinite models and no uncountable models. Second-order analysis AN is also categorical (Theorem 4.10). It has uncountable models and no countable models. Thus we have the following.

THEOREM 4.12.   Both Löwenheim–Skolem theorems fail for second-order languages with standard semantics.

The same applies to the free-variable second-order languages $L2K-$, provided that the theorems are formulated in terms of quasi-satisfaction in place of satisfaction. In particular, the formula $AN-$ is quasi-satisfiable, and for every model M and assignment s, M, s quasi-satisfies $AN-$ only if the domain of M is uncountable. And $AR-$ is quasi-satisfiable, and for every model M and assignment s, M, s quasi-satisfies $AR-$ only if the domain of M is denumerably infinite.

As in the previous chapter, there is a sentence

$$\forall f \neg (\forall x \forall y (fx = fy \rightarrow x = y) \ \& \ \exists x \forall y (fy \neq x))$$

which is satisfied by all and only those models whose domains are finite. Let Γ be the set consisting of this sentence and

$$\{\exists x_1 \exists x_2 (x_1 \neq x_2), \ \exists x_1 \exists x_2 \exists x_3 (x_1 \neq x_2 \ \& \ x_1 \neq x_3 \ \& \ x_2 \neq x_3), \ldots\}.$$

In other words, the set Γ contains a formula asserting that the domain is finite and, for each natural number n, Γ contains a formula asserting that the domain has at least n elements. Notice that the members of Γ have no non-logical terminology, so they are in every language $L2K$. Let Γ' be a finite subset of Γ, and let n be the maximum number of occurrences of the existential quantifier in any one member of Γ'. Then any structure whose domain has at least *n* elements satisfies every member of Γ'. Thus Γ' is satisfiable, but Γ is not. Indeed, suppose that $M \vDash \Phi$ for every Φ in Γ. Then the domain of M is finite. Let *m* be its cardinality. But Γ contains a sentence asserting that the domain has at least $m + 1$ elements, which is a contradiction. Thus we have the following theorem.

THEOREM 4.13. Standard semantics for $L2K$ is not compact.

A similar argument establishes that there is a set Γ of formulas of $L2K-$ such that Γ is not quasi-satisfiable, but every finite subset of Γ is quasi-satisfiable. Thus, $L2K-$ is also not compact, if this is formulated in terms of quasi-satisfaction.

The last item is the refutation of completeness. There is no effective sound deductive system that is complete for standard semantics.[7] *A fortiori*, D2 is incomplete. Let us focus, for the moment, on the language $L2A$ of arithmetic.

THEOREM 4.14. Let *D* be any effective deductive system that is sound for $L2A$. Then *D* is not weakly complete: there is a logical truth that is not a theorem of *D*. In short, standard semantics is *inherently incomplete*.

Proof. Let $T = \{\Phi \mid \Phi$ is a sentence with no relation or function variables and $\vdash_D AR \rightarrow \Phi\}$. Since *D* is effective, the set *T* is recursively enumerable. Since *D* is sound, every element in *T* is true of the natural numbers (see Corollary 4.9). It follows from the proof of Gödel's *in*completeness theorem (e.g. Gödel 1934) that the collection of true first-order sentences of arithmetic is not recursively enumerable. So let Ψ be a true sentence of first-order arithmetic that is not in *T*. Then, $AR \rightarrow \Psi$ is not provable in *D*, but $AR \rightarrow \Psi$ is a logical truth (Corollary 4.9). Thus, *D* is not weakly complete.   □

It follows that the set of standardly valid formulas of $L2A$ is not recursively enumerable. A refinement of this is presented in Chapter 6, Section 6.6.

Things are not quite this smooth for free-variable second-order languages $L2K-$. If Φ is a formula of $L2K-$, let Φ' be the result of uniformly replacing each relation variable of Φ with a different non-logical relation term (of the same degree), not in Φ already, and replacing each function variable of Φ with a different non-logical function letter also not in Φ already. Then Φ' is first-order. Notice that Φ is valid iff Φ' is valid. So Φ is valid iff Φ' is deducible from no premises in $D1=$. But any deduction of Φ' in $D1=$ is readily transformed into a deduction of Φ in $D2-$. Thus $D2-$ (even without the substitution scheme and the rules for eliminating function variables) is weakly complete. Similar reasoning establishes that if Γ is a set of formulas of $L2K-$ and $\Gamma \vDash \Phi$, then $\Gamma \vdash_{D2-} \Phi$. Thus $D2-$ is strongly complete. But, as we have seen, this is not the natural notion of consequence for $L2K-$, in the light of the treatment of second-order variables as implicitly bound. Let Ψ be a first-order sentence in the language of arithmetic. By Corollary

4.9, Ψ is true of the natural numbers if and only if $AR-$ *quasi-satisfies* Ψ. So the collection of quasi-consequences of $AR-$ is not recursively enumerable.

There is nothing special about the non-logical terminology used in the statement and proof of Theorems 4.12–4.14 concerning full second-order logic. Similar results hold for $L2$, the second-order language with no non-logical terminology. There is a technique, attributed to F. P. Ramsey (in another context), for translating each formula of $L2K$ into one in $L2$. The idea is to replace each non-logical symbol with an appropriate variable. For example, the following are analogues of the successor and induction axioms:

$$\forall x(fx \neq w) \ \& \ \forall x \forall y(fx = fy \rightarrow x = y)$$

$$\forall X((Xw \ \& \ \forall x(Xx \rightarrow Xfx)) \rightarrow \forall xXx).$$

Here, w is the analogue of 0 and f is the analogue of the successor symbol s. Let $AR(w, f)$ be the conjunction of these two formulas. Notice that since there is no non-logical terminology to 'interpret', a model of $L2$ is just a domain d. The *sentence* $\exists w \exists f(AR(w, f))$ is satisfied by d if and only if d is denumerably infinite. That is, $\exists w \exists f(AR(w, f))$ has denumerably infinite models and no uncountable models. In a similar fashion, the refutation of the second-order analogues of Theorems 4.2–4.4 can be carried out for $L2$.

As pointed out in Chapter 2, deductive systems must be effective if they are to serve some of their purposes. The upshot of Theorem 4.14 is that no effective deductive system is sound and complete for standard semantics. It will be shown in the next section that completeness *can* be obtained for $D2$ by an *extension of the semantics*. It remains to be seen whether this extension is reasonable and, for that matter, whether completeness is a reasonable goal. That is taken up in the next chapter.

4.3   Non-standard semantics—Henkin and first-order

Theorem 3.5 of Chapter 3 indicates that for the second-order languages $L2K$ and $L2K-$, Henkin semantics and first-order semantics are essentially the same—for any model of one sort, there is an equivalent model of the other sort. Thus each of the present results is given in terms of only one of these semantics. Application to the other is automatic.

The first thing to notice is that, as formulated above, *neither of these semantics is sound* for $D2$. It is routine to verify that every Henkin model satisfies the axioms and rules of $D1$. But some Henkin models do not satisfy the comprehension scheme, and some do not satisfy the axiom of choice (or the principle of comprehension for functions). Consider, for example, a structure $M = \langle d, D, F, I \rangle$ in which d is any set with at least two members

$a \neq b$, $D(2)$ has a single member, the relation $\{\langle x, a \rangle \mid x \in d\}$, and $F(1)$ has a single member, the function whose value at any $x \in d$ is x. Then M does not satisfy the following instance of the comprehension scheme:

$$\exists X \forall x \forall y (Xxy \equiv x \neq x).$$

In effect, this formula asserts the existence of an empty binary relation, but M does not have one. Similarly, M does not satisfy the axiom of choice. If s assigns the one relation in $D(2)$ to the variable X, then M, s satisfies $\forall x \exists y Xxy$, but there is no appropriate choice *function* in $F(1)$. So M, s does not satisfy $\exists f \forall x Xxfx$, the consequent of the axiom of choice. The one binary relation in M is the graph of a function, but this function is not in $F(1)$.

Similar considerations apply to the free-variable second-order language $L2K-$ and its deductive system $D2-$. The above model satisfies and quasi-satisfies $\exists x Xxx$, since M only contains the one binary relation. But $\exists x (x \neq x)$ follows from $\exists x Xxx$ by the substitution rule.

Define a Henkin model (or a first-order model) to be *faithful to D2*, or simply *faithful*, if it satisfies the axiom of choice and every instance of the comprehension scheme. And define a Henkin model to be *faithful to D2−* if it quasi-satisfies every instance of the substitution rule and the rules for eliminating function variables. All subsequent discussion is restricted to faithful models.

Recall that a Henkin model $M = \langle d, D, F, I \rangle$ is *full* if, for each n, $D(n)$ is the entire powerset of d^n and $F(n)$ is the collection of all functions from d^n to d. Since every full model $\langle d, D, F, I \rangle$ is equivalent to the standard model $\langle d, I \rangle$, full models are faithful to $D2$ and $D2-$ (by the soundness of standard semantics). As will be shown, there are faithful models that are not full models.

The remainder of this section concerns second-order languages $L2K$. In most cases, corresponding results for $L2K-$ are either corollaries or are similar.

Soundness is now immediate.

THEOREM 4.15 (Soundness).   If $\Gamma \vdash_{D2} \Phi$, then Φ is satisfied by every faithful Henkin model that satisfies every member of Γ. A fortiori, if Φ is a theorem of $D2$, then Φ is Henkin-valid in the sense that Φ is satisfied by every faithful Henkin model.

There are also analogues to Theorems 4.2–4.5: Henkin semantics (restricted to faithful models) is complete, compact, and satisfies both Löwenheim–Skolem theorems. I provide brief sketches of the proofs, assuming that the reader is familiar with the first-order versions.

THEOREM 4.16 (Completeness) (Henkin 1950).   Let Γ be a set of formulas and Φ a single formula of $L2K$. If Γ is consistent in $D2$, then Γ is

Henkin-satisfiable in a faithful model. Equivalently, for every formula Φ and set Γ, $\Gamma \vdash_{D2} \Phi$ if $M, s \vDash \Phi$ for every faithful Henkin model M and assignment s that satisfies every member of Γ.

Proof sketch. For convenience, we restrict attention here to sets of sentences; no generality is lost. The first item is the *Lindenbaum lemma*.

1. Let S be a consistent set of sentences of any second-order language $L2K$. Then there is a set S' of the same language such that $S \subseteq S'$ and S' is *maximally consistent* in the sense that S' is consistent, and for each sentence Φ of $L2K$ either Φ is in S' or $\neg \Phi$ is in S'.

   The proof of this lemma is exactly the same as the first-order version. Let $\Phi_1, \Phi_2, \ldots$ be an enumeration of the sentences of $L2K$. Define a sequence $S_1, S_2, \ldots$ of sets of sentences as follows: $S_1 = S$; if $S_n \vdash_{D2} \neg \Phi_n$, then $S_{n+1} = S_n$; otherwise, $S_{n+1} = S_n \cup \{\Phi_n\}$. That is, if Φ_n is consistent with S_n, then we add it to S_{n+1}. Let S' be the union of the sets S_n. Of course $S \subseteq S'$ and it is straightforward to verify that S' is maximally consistent.[8]

Notice that if S is maximally consistent, then for every sentence Φ of the same language, if $S \vdash_{D2} \Phi$ then $\Phi \in S$. Let Γ be a consistent set of sentences of $L2K$. We construct a model of Γ in first-order semantics. Consider the language obtained from $L2K$ by adding a denumerably infinite stock of new individual constants $c_0, c_1, \ldots$, a denumerably infinite stock of n-place relation letters $C_0^n, C_1^n, \ldots$ for each natural number n, and a denumerably infinite stock of n-place function letters $g_0^n, g_1^n, \ldots$ for each natural number n. Let $\Psi_1, \Psi_2, \ldots$ be an enumeration of the formulas of the expanded language that have only x free, let $\chi_1, \chi_2, \ldots$ be an enumeration of the formulas of the expanded language whose only free variable is one of $X^1, X^2, \ldots$, and let $\Phi_1, \Phi_2, \ldots$ be an enumeration of the formulas of the expanded language whose only free variable is one of $f^1, f^2, \ldots$. Define a sequence $T_0, T_1, \ldots$ of sets of sentences as follows:

$$T_0 = \Gamma$$

$$T_{m+1} = T_m \cup \{\exists x \Psi_m(x) \rightarrow \Psi_m(c_i), \exists X^n \chi_m(X^n) \rightarrow \chi_m(C_j^n),$$

$$\exists f^p \Phi_m(f^p) \rightarrow \Phi_m(g_k^p)\}$$

where c_i is the first constant in the above list that does not occur in Ψ_m, χ_m, Φ_m, or any member of T_m, n is the degree of the free relation variable in χ_m, C_j^n is the first relation letter in its list that does not occur in Ψ_m, χ_m, Φ_m, or any member of T_m, p is the degree of the free function variable in Φ_m, and g_k^p is the first function letter in its list that does not occur in Ψ_m, χ_m, Φ_m, or any member of T_m. Let T be the union of the sets T_m. It can then be shown that T is consistent.[9] Applying the Lindenbaum lemma, let T' be a maximally consistent set of sentences (of the expanded language) that contains T. So, of course, T' contains Γ. Define a first-order model $M = \langle d, d_1, d_2, \langle I, p, a \rangle \rangle$ as follows: the first domain d is the set of new individual constants $c_0, c_1, \ldots$, for each n the set $d_1(n)$ consists of the set of new n-place relation symbols $C_0^n, C_1^n, \ldots$, and for each n the set $d_2(n)$ consists of the set of new n-place function symbols $g_0^n, g_1^n, \ldots$. It remains to provide the 'predication' relation p on the items in the various $d_1(n)$, the 'application' function on the items in the various $d_2(n)$, and the interpretation function I for the non-logical terminology in K. We give only a few examples here. The interpretation function I assigns each of the new individual constants to itself. If c is an individual constant in K, then $I(c)$ is the first c_i such that the sentence[10] $c = c_i$ is in T'. If R is a binary relation letter, either in K or one of the C_i^2, then $I(R) = \{\langle c_i, c_j \rangle \mid Rc_ic_j \in T'\}$. If f is a unary function letter, then $I(f)$ is the function whose value at any c_i is the first c_j in the list such that the sentence $fc_i = c_j$ is in T'. The 'predication' relation and the 'application' function are defined similarly. Let $\langle c \rangle_n$ be a sequence of n of the members of d. Then the pair $\langle c \rangle_n$, C_i^n is in $p(n)$ if and only if $C_i^n \langle c \rangle_n$ is in T'. In effect, $p(n)$ assigns the relation $I(C_i^n)$ to C_i^n. Similarly, the value of $a(n)$ at $\langle c \rangle_n$ and g_j^n is the first c_k in the list such that $g_j^n \langle c \rangle_n = c_k$ is in T'. To sum up, in our model M, each constant, predicate, and relation is interpreted as it is in T'. It is straightforward to verify that M is faithful. The final item is the following lemma.

2. For each sentence Φ of the expanded language, $M \vDash \Phi$ if and only if $\Phi \in T'$.

The proof of this proceeds by induction on the complexity of Φ. The details, which are exactly the same as those of the first-order version, are omitted.[11] It follows that M is a model of T' and, *a fortiori*, M is a model of the original set Γ.   □

There are several things worthy of note concerning this proof. First, if K is countable, then the constructed model M might be called *doubly countable* in that the domain d *and* each $d_1(n)$ and $d_2(n)$ are denumerably infinite. In the corresponding Henkin model, the first domain D and each $D(n)$, $F(n)$ is either finite or denumerably infinite. Since each infinite domain has uncountably many n-place relations for each n, some (indeed, most) are not in the second domain of the indicated Henkin model. Thus, if the Henkin model has an infinite domain, it is not a full model.

Second, recall that the identity symbol is not a primitive in $L2K$. Rather, $t = u$ is defined as $\forall X(Xt \equiv Xu)$. As indicated above, this is adequate in standard semantics because a formula in this form is satisfied by a standard model (and assignment) if and only if the denotations of t and u are the same. The reason is that for each item a in the domain of a standard model, there is a subset whose sole member is a. But such singleton sets need not be in every faithful Henkin model. In fact, there is no formula $\Psi(x, y)$ of

$L2K$ such that for any Henkin model M and assignment s, $M, s \vDash \Psi(x, y)$ iff s assigns the same thing to x and y. In short, unlike standard semantics, identity cannot be defined in Henkin (or first-order) models[12] of $L2K$.

Nevertheless, since the formula $\forall X(Xx \equiv Xy)$ does define a congruence relation, identity can be accommodated in Henkin semantics, somewhat along the same lines as its incorporation in first-order languages without identity. Call a Henkin model M *identity-standard* if, for every assignment s, $M, s \vDash \forall X(Xx \equiv Xy)$ only if s assigns the same element of the domain to x and y. Notice that full models are all identity standard. In general, every Henkin model is equivalent to one that is identity standard, along the same lines as the corresponding theorem for first-order logic. The construction behind the proof of Theorem 4.16 can be modified to establish that for every satisfiable set Γ of sentences of $L2K$, there is a faithful identity-standard Henkin model that satisfies Γ.

THEOREM 4.17 (Compactness).   Let Γ be a set of formulas of $L2K$. If every finite subset of Γ is satisfiable in a faithful (identity-standard) Henkin model, then Γ itself is satisfiable in a faithful (identity-standard) Henkin model.

Proof.   This is exactly the same as in the first-order case (Theorem 4.3). If Γ is not satisfiable in a faithful Henkin model, then by completeness Γ is not consistent. That is, $\Gamma \vdash_{D2} (\Phi \ \& \ \neg \Phi)$. But deductions must be finite, so there is a finite subset Γ' of Γ such that $\Gamma' \vdash_{D2} (\Phi \ \& \ \neg \Phi)$. By soundness, Γ' is not satisfiable in a faithful Henkin model.   □

The statement of the downward Löwenheim–Skolem theorem requires that the notion of 'submodel' be extended to Henkin (and first-order) semantics. Let $M = \langle d, D, F, I \rangle$ be a Henkin model. Define $M' = \langle d', D', F', I' \rangle$ to be a *Henkin submodel* of M if (1) $d' \subseteq d$, (2) for each n and each set $P' \in D'(n)$ there is at least one $P \in D(n)$ such that $P' = P \cap (d')^n$, (3) for each n and each function f' in $F'(n)$ there is at least one f in $F(n)$ such that f' is the restriction of f to $(d')^n$, (4)I' and I assign the same elements (of d') to each individual constant, and (5) the interpretation of each predicate, relation, and function symbol under I' is the restriction to d' of its interpretation under I'. It is, of course, required that d' be closed under the functions in the various $F'(n)$ and the functions assigned to the function letters by I. For example, if g is in $F(1)$, then for every c in d', $g(c)$ is in d'.

Let $M' = \langle d', D', F', I' \rangle$ be a Henkin submodel of $M = \langle d, D, F, I \rangle$. Define k to be a *correspondence function between* M' *and* M if, for each $P \in D'(n), k(P) \in D(n)$ and $P = k(P) \cap (d')^n$, and for each $g \in F'(n), k(g) \in F(n)$ and g is the restriction of $k(g)$ to $(d')^n$. If k is a correspondence function and s is a variable assignment on M', then define s^k to be the assignment on M that agrees with s on the first-order variables; for each relation variable X^n, if s assigns P to X^n, then s^k assigns $k(P)$ to X^n, and for each function variable f^n, if s assigns g to f^n, then s^k assigns $k(g)$ to f^n.

THEOREM 4.18 (Downward Löwenheim–Skolem theorem). Let $M = \langle d, D, F, I \rangle$ be a Henkin model of $L2K$. Then there is a Henkin submodel $M' = \langle d', D', F', I' \rangle$ of M and a correspondence function k between M' and M such that (1) d' and each $D'(n)$, $F'(n)$ are all at most denumerably infinite (or the cardinality of the set K of non-logical terminology, whichever is greater), and (2) if Φ is any formula and s any assignment on M', then $M', s \vDash \Phi$ iff $M, s^k \vDash \Phi$.

Proof.   Let Ch be a choice function on d, D, and F. In particular, if $a \subseteq d$ and a is not empty, then $Ch(a) \in a$, and if $A \subseteq D(n)$ or $A \subseteq F(n)$ for some n, and A is not empty, then $Ch(A) \in A$.

Let s be an assignment on M, and let Ψ be a formula of $L2K$ and x a first-order variable free in Ψ. Define the *x-witness of Ψ over s*, written $w_x(\Psi, s)$, as follows. If M, s does not satisfy $\exists x \Psi$, then $w_x(\Psi, s)$ is $Ch(d)$, the choice function applied to the domain d. If $M, s \vDash \exists x \Psi$, then let q be the set of all $c \in d$ such that there is an assignment s' on M such that $M, s' \vDash \Psi$, s' agrees with s except possibly at x, and s' assigns c to x. In short, q is the set of elements of the domain d that can go for x in Ψ. By hypothesis, q is not empty. Let $w_x(\Psi, s) = Ch(q)$. We need a similar construction for the relation and function variables. Let Φ be a formula of $L2K$ and X an n-place relation variable free in Φ. Define the *X-witness of Φ over s*, written $w_X(\Phi, s)$ as follows. If M, s does not satisfy $\exists X \Phi$, then $w_X(\Phi, s)$ is $Ch(D(n))$. If $M, s \vDash \exists X \Phi$, then let Q be the set of all members P of $D(n)$ such that there is an assignment s' such that $M, s' \vDash \Phi$, s' agrees with s except possibly at X, and s' assigns P to X. By hypothesis, there are such assignments s' and thus Q is not empty. Let $w_X(\Phi, s) = Ch(Q)$. Let χ be a formula of $L2K$ and f an n-place function variable free in χ. Define the *f-witness of χ over s*, written $w_f(\chi, s)$ in a similar fashion.

Let $b \subseteq d$ be non-empty, let B be a sequence of sets $B(1), B(2), \ldots$ such that each $B(n)$ is a non-empty subset of $D(n)$, and let E be a sequence of sets $E(0), E(1), \ldots$ such that each $E(n)$ is a non-empty subset of $F(n)$. Define a $\langle b, B, E \rangle$-*assignment* to be a variable assignment on M that assigns a member of b to each first-order variable, a member of $B(n)$ to each n-place relation variable, and a member of $E(n)$ to each n-place function variable. Now define the *Skolem hull* of $\langle b, B, E \rangle$ to be the triple $\langle b', B', E' \rangle$ such that

$$b' = b \cup \{w_x(\Psi, s) \mid \Psi \text{ is in } L2K, x \text{ is free in } \Psi, \text{ and } s \text{ is a } \langle b, B, E \rangle \text{ assignment}\}$$

and, for each n,

$$B'(n) = B(n) \cup \{w_X(\Phi, s) \mid \Phi \text{ is in } L2K, X \text{ is an } n\text{-place relation variable free in } \Phi, \text{ and } s \text{ is a } \langle b, B, E \rangle \text{ assignment}\}$$

$$E'(n) = E(n) \cup \{w_f(\chi, s) \mid \chi \text{ is in } L2K, f \text{ is an } n\text{-place function variable free in } \chi, \text{ and } s \text{ is a } \langle b, B, E \rangle \text{ assignment}\}.$$

Finally, define a sequence of triples $\langle a_m, A_m, C_m \rangle$ as follows: a_0 is $Ch(d')$, together with the denotations under I of any individual constants in K; for each n, $A_0(n)$ is $Ch(D(n))$ and $C_0(n)$ is $Ch(F(n))$ (this is only to assure that all the relevant sets are non-empty); for each m, let $\langle a_{m+1}, A_{m+1}, C_{m+1} \rangle$ be the Skolem hull of $\langle a_m, A_m, C_m \rangle$. We are now in position to characterize the model M': d' is the union of the sets a_m; for each n, $D'(n)$ is $\{P \cap (d')^n \mid P \in A_m(n)$ for some $m\}$; for each n, $F(n)$ is $\{f' \mid$ for some m and f in $C_m(n)$, f' is the restriction of f to $(d')^n\}$. And define I' in such a way that $M' = \langle d', D', F', I' \rangle$ is a Henkin submodel of M. The relevant closure properties are straightforward. For example, let g be a unary function assigned to a function letter f by I. If $c \in d'$, then $c \in a_m$ for some m. Then $g(c)$ will be the x-witness of $fy = x$ under any s that assigns c to y. So $g(c) \in a_{m+1}$. Next we define the correspondence function k. If $B \in D'(n)$, then let $k(B)$ be a member of some[13] $A_m(n)$ such that $B = k(B) \cap (d')^n$, and if $g \in F'(n)$, then let $k(g)$ be a member of some C_m such that g is the restriction of $k(g)$ to $(d')^n$. Two lemmas and we are done.

1. The sets d', $D'(n)$, and $F'(n)$ are all at most denumerably infinite, or the cardinality of the set K, whichever is greater.

   Proof. Let λ be the maximum of $\aleph_0$ and the cardinality of K. In the light of the axiom of choice, we need only show that each a_m, $A_m(n)$, and $C_m(n)$ has cardinality at most λ. But this is a straightforward calculation, based on the fact that there are at most λ-many formulas, and thus at most λ-many witnesses at each stage.

2. Let s be an assignment on M'. Then, for each formula Φ, $M', s \vDash \Phi$ iff $M, s^k \vDash \Phi$.

   The proof, which proceeds by induction on the complexity of Φ, is virtually the same as the corresponding first-order case. So we omit it. $\square$

Notice that, as with the completeness theorem, if K is at most countable, the model M' is doubly countable in that both the primary domain and the collections of relations and functions are all at most denumerably infinite.

THEOREM 4.19 (Upward Löwenheim–Skolem theorem). Let Γ be a set of sentences of $L2K$. If, for each natural number m, there is a (faithful identity-standard) Henkin model $M_m = \langle d_m, D_m, F_m, I_m \rangle$ such that d_m has at least m elements and M_m is a model of Γ, then for every infinite cardinal κ there is a (faithful identity-standard) Henkin model $M_\kappa = \langle d_\kappa, D_\kappa, F_\kappa, I_\kappa \rangle$ such that d_κ has cardinality at least κ and M_κ is a model of Γ.

Proof. This is a corollary of the compactness theorem (Theorem 4.17). Let K' consist of K together with κ-many new individual constants $\{c_\alpha \mid \alpha \in \kappa\}$. Consider the set $\Gamma' = \Gamma \cup \{\exists X(Xc_\alpha \,\&\, \neg Xc_\beta) \mid \alpha < \beta < \kappa\}$. The hypothesis entails that every finite subset of Γ' is Henkin-satisfiable (in a faithful identity-standard model). Clearly, any Henkin model of Γ' is a model of Γ in which the denotations of the c_α are all different. $\square$

It might be added that if the hypotheses of Theorem 4.19 are satisfied and κ is infinite and greater than or equal to the cardinality of K, then the proofs of the last two theorems together indicate that there is a faithful identity-standard Henkin model M of Γ such that the first domain of M has cardinality exactly κ.

As in the first-order case, Theorems 4.18 and 4.19 indicate that no theory with an infinite Henkin model is what may be called 'Henkin-categorical'. Thus second-order languages with Henkin (or first-order) semantics are not adequate to characterize infinite structures up to isomorphism.

Notes

1. The reason is that there are satisfiable sentences that have no finite models. An example is the successor axiom of arithmetic. See Section 4.2.
2. The symbols for addition and multiplication are not necessary in the second-order case, since there are formulas $A(x, y, z)$ and $M(x, y, z)$ that define those functions:

$$A(x, y, z)\colon \forall f^2(\forall u \forall v(f^2u0 = u \ \& \ f^2usv = sf^2uv) \rightarrow f^2xy = z)$$
$$M(x, y, z)\colon \forall g^2(\forall u \forall v(g^2u0 = 0 \ \& \ A(g^2uv, u, g^2usv)) \rightarrow g^2xy = z).$$

That is, $A(x, y, z)$ says that z has the value at x, y of every binary function that satisfies the two clauses of the addition axiom. This entails that $A(x, y, z)$ holds if and only if $x + y = z$. In $D2$, one can deduce $\forall x \forall y \exists ! z A(x, y, z)$ and $\exists f^2 \forall x \forall y A(x, y, f^2xy)$ from the successor and induction axioms below. Similar remarks apply to multiplication and the formula $M(x, y, z)$. As to be discussed later (Chapter 5), an analogous move is not available in the first-order (or the free-variable second-order) version of arithmetic. This illustrates the fact that a second-order theory can be more expressive than its first-order counterpart. In this case, more functions can be defined in the second-order version.
3. The axioms for an ordered field state that addition and multiplication are associative and commutative, multiplication is distributive over addition, 0 is the additive identity, 1 is the multiplicative identity, every element has an additive inverse, every element but 0 has a multiplicative inverse, $\le$ is a linear order, and the elements greater than or equal to 0 are closed under addition and multiplication. They are as follows:

$\forall x \forall y \forall z((x + y) + z = x + (y + z))$ $\forall x \forall y(x + y = y + x)$
$\forall x(x + 0 = 0)$ $\forall x \exists y(x + y = 0)$

$\forall x \forall y \forall z((x \cdot y) \cdot z = x \cdot (y \cdot z))$ $\forall x \forall y(x \cdot y = y \cdot x)$
$\forall x(x \cdot 1 = x)$ $\forall x(x \ne 0 \rightarrow \exists y(x \cdot y = 1))$

$\forall x \forall y \forall z(x \cdot (y + z) = (x \cdot y) + (x \cdot z))$

$\forall x \forall y \forall z((x \le y \ \& \ y \le z) \rightarrow x \le z)$ $\forall x \forall y(x \le y \ \lor \ y \le x)$
$\forall x \forall y((x \le y \ \& \ y \le x) \rightarrow x = y)$

$\forall x \forall y((0 < x \ \& \ 0 < y) \rightarrow (0 < x + y \ \& \ 0 < x \cdot y)).$

For more details, seee any treatment of abstract algebra (e.g. Mac Lane and Birkhoff 1967, Chapters IV and V).

4. In $L2B$, there is an explicit definition of these 'natural numbers'. The formula

$$\forall Q([Q0 \ \& \ Q1 \ \& \ \forall y \forall z(Qy \ \& \ Qz \ \rightarrow \ Q(y+z))] \rightarrow Qx)$$

holds of a given x if and only if x is a 'natural number'. The 'rational numbers' of a model of analysis are also explicitly definable, in similar fashion.

5. The axiom of choice is not included since it can be deduced from $Z2$ using the version of the axiom of choice in the deductive system $D2$. In fact, in the context of set theory, the axiom of choice in $D2$ amounts to a principle of 'global choice', since it asserts the existence of a choice function on the entire universe. This theme is taken up in Chapter 5.

6. A binary relation R is *extensional* if, for every a, b in the domain, if Rxa iff Rxb for every x, then $a = b$. Notice that the interpretation of $\in$ in a model M is extensional if and only if M satisfies the axiom of extensionality. A relation R is *well-founded* if there is no infinite sequence $a_0, a_1, \ldots$ such that $Ra_1a_0, Ra_2a_1, \ldots$ all hold. It will be shown in the next chapter that the property of well-foundedness cannot be adequately characterized in any first-order language.

7. Actually, it follows from the Rosser (1936) extension of the incompleteness theorem that no *consistent* extension of $D2$ (whether sound or not) is complete for standard semantics.

8. The proof of Theorem 4.16, like that of its counterpart 4.2, does not use the axiom of choice (in the metatheory). In both cases, however, the Lindenbaum lemma makes essential use of the law of excluded middle. In Shapiro (1988), I show that this proof cannot, in general, be made constructive. This is significant because D. C. McCarty (McCarty and Tennant 1987) has established that the compactness of first-order intuitionistic predicate calculus cannot be proved in intuitionistic set theory. Indeed, first-order intuitionistic arithmetic is *categorical* in a reasonable intuitionistic metatheory. A detailed account of this would take us too far afield. Let it suffice to state that McCarty's results are part of a good case for the viability of intuitionistic logic and, thus, complement the present case against logical absolutism, the view that there is but one logic (see Shapiro 1989a).

9. This is straightforward for those familiar with the completeness theorem for first-order logic. The details are the same.

10. There is such a c_i, since T' is maximally consistent, and it contains both the theorem $\exists x(c = x)$ and a sentence of the form $\exists x(c = x) \rightarrow c = c_i$.

11. The foregoing proof is a straightforward adaption of the Henkin proof of the completeness of first-order logic. In a presentation to the conference honouring Alonzo Church (Buffalo, May 1990), Henkin remarked that the discovery of the completeness of higher-order logic (with Henkin semantics) was made first; his proof for the first-order case was an adaption of that.

12. As noted above, first-order semantics regards $L2K$ as a two-sorted first-order language. Recall that identity cannot be defined in a first-order theory in which it is not a logical primitive.

13. In fact, there is only one choice for each $k(B)$: if $C_1 \in A_m(n)$, $C_2 \in A_q(n)$, and $C_1 \neq C_2$, then $C_1 \cap (d')^n \neq C_2 \cap (d')^n$. There is also only one choice for each $k(f)$.

Second-order logic and mathematics

Among contemporary writers, the most influential opponent of second-order logic is W. V. O. Quine. In Quine (1970), he argues that second-order logic is mathematics in disguise, calling it 'set theory in sheep's clothing'. The main premise seems to be that pure second-order languages can express a great deal of mathematics, and they have substantial mathematical and ontological presuppositions. This much is correct and, indeed, I shall presently make out a case for it in some detail. It will be shown (here and in the next chapter) that a considerable amount of mathematics can be expressed in (pure) second-order languages and, moreover, second-order logic is thoroughly intertwined with set theory. Quine concludes that these presuppositions are too great for second-order logic to bear the honorific label of 'logic'.[1] But this is incorrect. If there were a sharp border between logic and mathematics, second-order logic would go on the 'mathematics' side. A main theme of this book, however, is that there is no natural boundary to be drawn. The Quinean perspective of the 'web of belief' holds here. Quine himself has argued that mathematics is necessary for understanding just about anything. Why should logic, especially the logic *of* mathematics, be different?

There is a converse, of sorts, to the thesis connecting second-order logic and mathematics. First-order languages, unadorned, are insufficient to codify many concepts, notions, and theories of contemporary mathematics. I do not claim, of course, that second-order languages and standard semantics are in some sense necessary for understanding mathematics. Most mathematicians manage well without any formal languages and metatheory whatsoever, and, in the anti-foundationalist spirit, there is no single 'best' way to present and study mathematics. But second-order logic does help. Parts of this chapter (and the next) require a basic grasp of axiomatic set theory (see, for example, Jech 1971, Fraenkel *et al.* 1973).

5.1 Mathematical notions

5.1.1 *Minimal closure*

It is common in mathematics to define sets in terms of what may be called a 'closure' condition. Let *B* be a set, called the *basis*, and let *H* be a collection of one or more functions, or operations, or relations. Define M to be the *minimal closure* of B under H if M is the smallest set that includes B and is closed under the members of H. It is sometimes described as *the* set obtained from B by closure under the operations in H, or one says that y is in M just in case y is the result of iterating the operations in H on members of B finitely many times. There are a number of ways of formulating the notion of minimal closure more precisely. Consider, for simplicity, a case in which H consists of a single binary relation R. The first method, essentially due to Frege, is based on the *ancestral relation*[2] induced by R. The idea is that y is in the minimal closure of B under R if y is in *every* set (or has every property) that includes B and is closed under R. Notice the universal quantifier ranging over sets (or properties). The following second-order formula says, of x, that it is in the minimal closure of the extension of Y under R:

$$MC(x, Y, R): \forall X [(\forall y(Yy \rightarrow Xy) \ \& \ \forall y \forall z((Xy \ \& \ Ryz) \rightarrow Xz)) \rightarrow Xx].$$

The existence of this minimal closure is an instance of the comprehension scheme of $D2$:

$$\exists Z \forall x (Zx \equiv MC(x, Y, R)).$$

Notice that this formula is impredicative, because $MC(x, Y, R)$ has a bound variable with the same range as Z.

Another method of characterizing minimal closures makes essential use of natural numbers.[3] Define the relation T as follows:

$T0y$ holds iff y is in B
$T(n + 1)y$ holds iff there is a z such that Tnz and Rzy.

Then x is in the minimal closure of B under R if and only if $\exists n Tnx$.

There are instances of the minimal closure construction throughout mathematics. To mention a few, if R and S are two rings, $R \subseteq S$ and $a \in S$, then the ring $R[a]$ is the minimal closure (within S) of $R \cup \{a\}$ under the functions of S-addition and S-multiplication. It is the smallest subring of S that includes R and contains a. In a given field, the *rational subfield* is the minimal closure of the multiplicative identity under the field functions and their inverses. In mathematical logic, collections of terms, well-formed formulas, and theorems are defined as minimal closures of sets of strings.

The Dedekind (1888) definition of the natural numbers is also a minimal closure. Let C be a set, $c \in C$, and let f be a one-to-one function from C to C. The triple $\langle C, c, f \rangle$ is said to be a *simply infinite system* if c is not in the range of f and C itself is the minimal closure of $\{c\}$ under f. A simply infinite system is none other than a standard model of arithmetic (with f as the successor function and c as zero).[4]

The categoricity arguments in the previous chapter involve several minimal closures. For example, the 'natural numbers' of a given model of real analysis are defined to be the minimal closure of (the denotations of) 0 and 1 under (the denotation of) the addition function, and the 'rational numbers' are the minimal closure of the 'natural numbers' under additive inverse, multiplication, and multiplicative inverse (i.e. the rational subfield). Thus the categoricity arguments presuppose that our metatheory contains enough higher-order terminology (or set theory) to carry out the Fregean construction of minimal closures, or else it contains enough arithmetic to execute the construction in terms of natural numbers. These presuppositions are reasonable—one can hardly do serious mathematics, or metamathematics, without them.

From the practice of mathematics, I submit that the use of minimal closures is now well understood, at least as much as anything in mathematics, and there is no ambiguity concerning the constructed set. It would seem, then, that it is a requirement on languages and semantics of foundational research that they be capable of characterizing minimal closures, at least if they are to capture our ability to describe and communicate what we are doing, the intended meaning of our natural languages. There is a straightforward argument, relying on the compactness theorem, that no collection of first-order formulas can successfully characterize any non-trivial minimal closure. This is evidence that first-order languages are inadequate.

Fix a first-order theory T and a model M with domain d. Let Γ be a set of formulas, containing a predicate letter P (not occurring in T), that purports to characterize the minimal closure of the extension of a formula $\Phi(x)$ under a unary function p. Assume that the given structure M is a model of $T + \Gamma$ in which the extension of P includes the minimal closure of the extension of Φ under (the denotation of) p. This is surely necessary for Γ to be a characterization of the minimal closure in question. Assume also that in M, for each natural number n, the extension of P contains at least one element that cannot be obtained from anything in the extension of Φ by n (or fewer) applications of p. That is, the n-fold application of p to the extension of Φ does not exhaust the extension of P. This is a requirement of non-triviality.[5] Under these conditions, there are models of $T + \Gamma$ in which the extension of P is not the relevant minimal closure. Indeed, let b be a constant that does not occur in $T + \Gamma$, and consider the set of formulas:

$$T': T \cup \Gamma \cup \{Pb, \neg \Phi(b), \forall x(\Phi(x) \rightarrow px \neq b), \forall x(\Phi(x) \rightarrow ppx \neq b), \ldots\}.$$

On the above assumptions, every finite subset of T' is satisfiable in M. Indeed, let S be a finite subset of T', and let n be the largest number of occurrences of p in any one member of S. Then since the n-fold application of p to the extension of Φ does not exhaust the extension of P, we can find an appropriate denotation for b in M such that every element of S is satisfied. Thus, by compactness, T' itself is satisfiable. Let M' be any model of T'. Then in M', the denotation of b cannot be in the extension of Φ, nor can it be the result of applying p to anything in the extension of Φ, nor the result of applying p twice to anything in the extension of Φ, etc. In short, the denotation of b in M' cannot be in the minimal closure of the extension of Φ under p. But the denotation of b is in the extension of P, since Pb is in T'. Thus the extension of P is not the relevant minimal closure in any model of T'.

Call a set of formulas Γ a *partial characterization* of the minimal closure of Φ under p if every model of T can be extended to a model of $T + \Gamma$ in which the extension of P is the minimal closure of Φ under p. The above argument shows that if Γ is a partial characterization of a non-trivial minimal closure, then there are models of T that can be extended to models of $T + \Gamma$ in more than one way. Thus, following the main result reported by Corcoran (1971), Γ fails to be a legitimate definition at all, let alone a definition of minimal closure.[6]

Someone may object that the foregoing considerations beg the question. The significance of the fact that second-order languages characterize minimal closures presupposes that there is an unambiguous minimal closure to describe. The compactness argument above may indicate that the construction is equivocal. There may be no such thing as *the* minimal closure of, say, B under R. One may suggest, for example, that the model-theoretic analysis shows that there are several different notions of minimal closure, just as the pre-formal notion of continuity emerged into two different properties, pointwise continuity and uniform continuity. But the present situation is not like this. In the above model M', it is evident that the extension of P is *not* the relevant minimal closure. Nevertheless, I have no definitive refutation of scepticism concerning minimal closures. The outlook of this study is that the minimal closure construction is sufficiently determinate, and it is a datum to be accommodated in a model-theoretic semantics. Similar remarks apply to the rest of the items considered in this section. The notions of finitude and well-ordering, for example, are other data. The sceptical arguments are considered in Chapter 8.

5.1.2 *Cardinality*

The second-order formula

$$\text{INF}(X): \exists f[\forall x \forall y(fx = fy \rightarrow x = y) \ \& \ \forall x(Xx \rightarrow Xfx)$$

$$\& \ \exists y(Xy \ \& \ \forall x(Xx \rightarrow fx \neq y))]$$

asserts that there is a one-to-one function from X to X whose range is a proper subset of X. This is the usual definition of (Dedekind) infinite. The formula $\text{INF}(X)$ is satisfied by a model and assignment if and only if the class assigned to X is infinite.[7] It immediately gives rise to a characterization of finitude:

$$\text{FIN}(X): \neg \text{INF}(X).$$

Since both these formulas have no non-logical terminology, they are in the pure second-order language $L2$.

As noted in several places above, there are first-order formulas (with identity) that are satisfiable only in infinite domains. Here is one:

$$I[s, 0]: \forall x \forall y (sx \neq 0 \ \& \ (sx = sy \rightarrow x = y))$$

where 0 is an individual constant and s is a non-logical function letter. In a similar manner, for any formula Φ there is a formula $I[s, 0](\Phi)$ such that in any model that satisfies $I[s, 0](\Phi)$, the extension of Φ is infinite:

$$I[s, 0](\Phi): I[s, 0] \ \& \ \Phi(0) \ \& \ \forall x (\Phi(x) \rightarrow \Phi(sx)).$$

But these are not full characterizations of infinitude. In particular, the negation of $I[s, 0]$ does not guarantee that the domain is finite, and the negation of $I[s, 0](\Phi)$ does not guarantee that the extension of Φ is finite. In any model M (of any cardinality), if the function denoted by s is not one-to-one, or if the denotation of 0 is in its range, then $M \vDash \neg I[s, 0]$. It is true that for any natural number n and any formula Φ, there is a first-order formula that is satisfied by a given model if and only if Φ has at most n elements in its extension.[8] For $n = 3$, an example is:

$$\exists x \exists y \exists z \forall w (\Phi(w) \rightarrow (w = x \ \lor \ w = y \ \lor \ w = z)).$$

But this is not enough. In mathematics, there are many situations in which one wants to assert that a given extension, or a given domain, is finite without specifying a (finite) upper bound on its size. For example, there is a theory that applies to all finite groups, no matter how large. Similarly, in the theory of computability, a Turing machine is characterized as a finite table of states and instructions, and it is essential that there be no fixed finite upper bound on the sizes of machine tables. It is this general notion of *finitude* that cannot be captured in a first-order language, any first-order language.

THEOREM 5.1.   Let S be a set of first-order sentences and let $\Phi(x)$ be any first-order formula containing x free. If, for each natural number n, there is a model of S in which the extension of Φ has at least n members, then there is a model of S in which the extension of Φ is infinite.

Proof.   This is another corollary of the compactness theorem. Let $c_0, c_1, \ldots$ be a sequence of constants that do not occur in Φ or in any sentence in S. Consider the set

$$S' = S \cup \{c_i \neq c_j \mid i < j\} \cup \{\Phi(c_i) \mid i \in \omega\}.$$

By hypothesis, every finite subset of S' is satisfiable. Indeed, if a subset T of

S' has n members, then T is satisfiable in any model of S in which the extension of Φ has at least $2n$ elements. One simply assigns different members of the extension of Φ to the new constants that occur in T. Thus, by compactness, S' is satisfiable. But any model of S' is a model of S in which the extension of Φ is infinite. $\square$

Finitude is a widely used notion, occurring throughout mathematics. It is clear and determinate, at least at this point in history. If, for example, a mathematician asserts that a given extension is finite, then her listeners understand, without ambiguity, what she means. Therefore the language and model-theoretic semantics used to formalize mathematical practice should be capable of expressing this notion. But, as we have seen, no first-order theory can do this.[9]

In a similar vein, Boolos (1981) shows that theories formulated in first-order languages cannot express simple cardinality comparisons like 'the extension of Φ is at least as large as the extension of Ψ', except on a limited *ad hoc* basis. By contrast, second-order languages, even the pure $L2$, can express straightforward comparisons of cardinalities. First, the cardinality of X is *less than or equal to* the cardinality of Y if and only if there is a one-to-one function from X into Y:

$$|X| \leq |Y|: \exists f(\forall x \forall y((Xx \,\&\, Xy \,\&\, fx = fy) \to x = y) \,\&\, \forall x(Xx \to Yfx)).$$

The cardinality of X is *equal to* the cardinality[10] of Y if and only if there is a one-to-one function from X *onto* Y:

$$|X| = |Y|: \exists f(\forall x \forall y((Xx \,\&\, Xy \,\&\, fx = fy) \to x = y) \,\&\, \forall x(Xx \to Yfx)$$

$$\&\, \forall y(Yy \to \exists x(Xx \,\&\, fx = y))).$$

The Schröder–Bernstein theorem can then be stated in $L2$, our pure second-order language, and, as an exercise in deduction, it can be *proved* in $D2$:

THEOREM 5.2 (Schröder–Bernstein). $\vdash_{D2} (|X| \leq |Y| \,\&\, |Y| \leq |X|) \to |X| = |Y|$.

Proof. The derivation is presented informally. Take the antecedent as a premise. Let f be a function that is one-to-one from X into Y and let g be a function that is a one-to-one from Y into X. Let X_0 be the complement in X of the range of g on Y, i.e.

$$\forall x(X_0 x \equiv (Xx \,\&\, \neg \exists y(Yy \,\&\, gy = x))),$$

and let X_1 be the minimal closure of X_0 under the composition of f with g, i.e.

$$\forall x(X_1 x \equiv \forall Z[(\forall y(X_0 y \to Zy) \,\&\, \forall y(Zy \to Zgfy)) \to Zx]).$$

Now define H, a relation between X and Y, as follows:

$$\forall x \forall y (Hxy \equiv (X_1 x \,\&\, fx = y) \vee (Xx \,\&\, \neg X_1 x \,\&\, Yy \,\&\, gy = x)).$$

The 'rule for applying' H is as follows: given x in X, if x is in the minimal closure of X_0 under the composition of f with g, then apply f; otherwise apply the inverse of g. The existences of X_0, X_1, and H are all instances of the comprehension scheme. A few lemmas and we are done.

1. H is a function on X, $\forall x(Xx \rightarrow \exists! y Hxy)$. If $X_1 x$ then there is a unique y such that $fx = y$ and thus Hxy. If Xx and $\neg X_1 x$, then, in particular, $\neg X_0 x$. Thus x is in the range in X of g on Y. Since g is one-to-one on Y, there is a unique y in Y such that $gy = x$ and thus Hxy.

2. H is one-to-one on X. Suppose that $Xx_1 \,\&\, Xx_2 \,\&\, Hx_1 y \,\&\, Hx_2 y$. If x_1 and x_2 are both in X_1, then $x_1 = x_2$, since f is one-to-one on X. If neither x_1 nor x_2 are in X_1, then $x_1 = x_2$, since g is a function. Suppose that $X_1 x_1$ and $\neg X_1 x_2$. So $fx_1 = y$ and $gy = x_2$. So $gfx_1 = x_2$. But this entails that x_2 is in the minimal closure of X_0 under the composition of f with g. That is, x_2 is in X_1, which is a contradiction. The assumption that $\neg X_1 x_1$ and $X_1 x_2$ is similarly dismissed.

3. The range of H is Y. Suppose Yy. Then Xgy. If gy is not in X_1, then $Hgyy$ and thus y is in the range of H. Suppose, then, that $X_1 gy$. Since gy is in the range of g, gy is not in X_0, the basis of the minimal closure X_1. But gy is in X_1. So there is an x such that $X_1 x$ and $gfx = gy$. But since g is one-to-one on Y, $y = fx$. Thus Hxy, and so y is in the range of H.

It is then straightforward to deduce $\exists h \forall x(Xx \rightarrow Hxhx)$ from this, and so $|X| = |Y|$.   □

Our next example is *Cantor's theorem* that the powerset of any set is larger than the set. When put this way, of course, the statement refers to sets of sets and thus involves either a powerset operator or a third-order variable. But (pure) second-order languages can be used to simulate *some* statements about sets of sets. Let R be a binary relation and define R_x to be the set $\{y \mid Rxy\}$. In $L2K$, we could write $\forall y(R_x y \equiv Rxy)$. We say that R_x is the set[11] *coded by x in R*, and the relation R *represents* the set of sets $\{R_x \mid x$ is in the domain of discourse$\}$. The correspondence between x and R_x is, in effect, a function from the domain onto the collection of sets represented by R. In these terms, Cantor's theorem amounts to a statement that no binary relation can represent the collection of all subsets of its domain, or, in other words, for every relation there is a set that is not represented by it. This can be expressed in $L2$.

THEOREM 5.3 (Cantor). $\vdash_{D2} \forall R \exists X \forall x \exists y[(Rxy \& \neg Xy) \lor (\neg Rxy \& Xy)]$.

Proof.   The usual diagonal proof of Cantor's theorem can be carried out in $D2$. Working informally, let R be binary. From an instance of the axiom scheme of comprehension, there is a set X such that

$$\forall x(Xx \equiv \neg Rxx).$$

Notice that for every x, either $Rxx \& \neg Xx$ or $\neg Rxx \& Xx$. The result follows immediately.   □

The notion of 'being countable' can be characterized in $L2$:

$$\text{COUNT}(X): \forall Y(\forall x(Yx \to Xx) \to (\text{FIN}(Y) \lor |Y| = |X|)).$$

Denumerably infinite is characterized as

$$\text{ALEPH-0}(X): \text{COUNT}(X) \& \text{INF}(X),$$

and further

$$\text{ALEPH-1}(X): \neg \text{FIN}(X) \& \neg \text{ALEPH-0}(X) \& \forall Y(\forall x(Yx \to Xx) \to$$
$$(\text{FIN}(Y) \lor \text{ALEPH-0}(Y) \lor |Y| = |X|)),$$

$$\text{ALEPH-2}(X): \neg \text{FIN}(X) \& \neg \text{ALEPH-0}(X) \& \neg \text{ALEPH-1}(X)$$
$$\& \forall Y(\forall x(Yx \to Xx) \to (\text{FIN}(Y) \lor \text{ALEPH-0}(Y)$$
$$\lor \text{ALEPH-1}(Y) \lor |Y| = |X|)),$$

and so forth for any finite aleph. This process does not stop here. The cardinality of a set S has *cofinality omega* if S is the union of a denumerably infinite sequence of infinite sets such that for every item in the sequence, there is another that is larger. Again, as it stands, this definition refers to sequences of sets, and thus it cannot be formulated directly in $L2$. However, the definition can be simulated using the techniques presented in the statement of Cantor's theorem above. Consider a formula asserting that there is a relation R such that (1) the domain of R is a denumerably infinite set, (2) the range of R is X, and (3) for each x, R_x is infinite, and there is a z such that R_x is (strictly) smaller than R_z. This is equivalent to an assertion that the cardinality of X has cofinality omega. Here goes:

$$\text{COF-OMEGA}(X): \exists R[\forall Y(\forall x(Yx \equiv \exists y Rxy) \to \text{ALEPH-0}(Y))$$
$$\& \forall y(Xy \equiv \exists x Rxy) \& \forall x(\text{INF}(R_x))$$
$$\& \forall x \exists z(|R_x| \leq |R_z| \& \neg(|R_x| = |R_z|))].$$

We can now define another cardinality:

$$\text{ALEPH-OMEGA}(X): \neg \text{COUNT}(X) \& \text{COF-OMEGA}(X)$$
$$\& \forall Y((\forall x(Yx \to Xx) \& \neg \text{COUNT}(Y)$$
$$\& \text{COF-OMEGA}(Y)) \to |Y| = |X|).$$

Enough. It is straightforward to go on even further, to develop formulas characterizing ALEPH-OMEGA-PLUS-ONE(X), ALEPH-TWO-OMEGA(X), etc. The above techniques indicate that for any cardinal κ, if κ can be characterized in some $L2K$, then so can the next cardinal κ^+. Moreover, for any well-ordering w definable in $L2K$, we can formulate the notion of cofinality w and thus the corresponding aleph.[12]

There are different ways of defining various cardinalities in $L2$ and so, as in set theory, statements of comparison can be formulated. I present the most famous instance of this, the continuum hypothesis. Recall that the *continuum* is the cardinality of the powerset of a denumerably infinite set. Once again, a direct formulation of this would require sets of sets, third-order items, but a paraphrase in $L2$ is possible. Notice that a set X has the cardinality of the continuum[13] if there is a denumerably infinite set C and a relation R, whose domain is X and whose range is C, such that (1) for each $Y \subseteq C$ there is an x in X such that R_x is Y, and (2) for every x and y in X, if $R_x = R_y$ then $x = y$. Under these circumstances, the association of x with R_x is a one-to-one function from X onto the powerset of C:

CONTINUUM(X): $\exists C \exists R [\text{ALEPH-0}(C)$ & $\forall x \forall y(Rxy \rightarrow (Xx$ & $Cy))$
$$\&\ \forall Y(\forall y(Yy \rightarrow Cy) \rightarrow \exists x \forall y(Rxy \equiv Yy))$$
$$\&\ \forall x \forall y(Xx\ \&\ Xy\ \&\ \forall z(Rxz \equiv Ryz)) \rightarrow x = y)].$$

It follows that the continuum hypothesis can be formulated in the language $L2$ of pure second-order logic:

$$CH: \forall X(\text{ALEPH-1}(X) \equiv \text{CONTINUUM}(X)).$$

This sentence is a (semantic) logical truth if and only if the continuum hypothesis is true (in the set-theoretic hierarchy). Notice, however, that its negation $\neg CH$ is not a logical truth, even if the continuum hypothesis is false. Indeed, CH is satisfied in every countable model, no matter what. However, there is an analogue of the negation of the continuum hypothesis. The following sentence of $L2$ is a logical truth if and only if the continuum hypothesis is false:

$$NCH: \forall X(\text{ALEPH-1}(X) \rightarrow \neg \text{CONTINUUM}(X)).$$

Thus, either CH is a logical truth, or else NCH is a logical truth. Chuaqui (1972) has shown that standard forcing techniques can be applied to second-order set theory using Henkin models (see also Weston 1977). It follows that neither CH nor NCH (nor their negations) can be deduced in $D2$ from $Z2$, our axiomatization of second-order set theory (provided only that the latter is consistent; see Chapter 4, Section 4.2). *A fortiori*, neither can be deduced in $D2$ alone. This is an instance of the incompleteness of second-order logic. One of CH, NCH is an unprovable logical truth.

The same technique can be used to formulate a version of the generalized continuum hypothesis in $L2$. There is a formula $POWER(X, Y)$ asserting that Y has the cardinality of the powerset of X, and there is a formula $NEXT(X, Y)$ asserting that Y has the smallest cardinality that is larger than that of X. The generalized continuum hypothesis is

$$GCH: \forall X \forall Y(INF(X) \to (POWER(X, Y) \equiv NEXT(X, Y))).$$

For a final example, recall that all models of $Z2$ are inaccessible ranks (Chapter 4, Section 4.2). It is possible to modify $Z2$ to produce a formula $INNAC(X)$ of $L2$ asserting that there is a binary relation E on X such that X is a model of $Z2$ with E as membership. Then $INNAC(X)$ is satisfied by a given model if and only if the cardinality of X is (strongly) inaccessible. The sentence $\forall X \neg INNAC(X)$ is a logical truth if and only if there are no inaccessible cardinals. This is also independent of $Z2$ (if consistent with it) and thus is not decided by $D2$ alone.

5.1.3 Well-ordering and choice

A *well-ordering* of a set X is an irreflexive, transitive, and binary relation on X in which every non-empty subset of X has a least element. This definition can be rendered in $L2$ in a straightforward manner. Let R be a binary relation variable and X a predicate variable. Then the following formula of $L2$ is the statement that R is a well-ordering of X:

$$WO(R, X): \forall x \neg Rxx \ \& \ \forall x \forall y \forall z((Rxy \ \& \ Ryz) \to Rxz)$$
$$\& \ \forall Y((\exists x Yx \ \& \ \forall x(Yx \to Xx))$$
$$\to \exists y(Yy \ \& \ \forall z(Yz \to (z = y \ \vee \ Ryz)))).$$

There is no adequate formulation of this notion in a first-order language except in the trivial cases in which the extension of X has a fixed finite bound on its cardinality. To be specific, let T be a first-order theory containing a non-logical binary relation symbol W. If, for each natural number n, there is a model of T in which the extension of W is a linear order on at least n elements of the domain, then there is a model of T in which the extension of W is not a well-ordering. This is another corollary of the compactness of first-order logic. It has the same form as the others.

The *well-ordering principle* states that every set has a well-ordering:

$$WOP: \forall X \exists R(WO(R, X)).$$

It is well known that in the context of (first-order) Zermelo–Fraenkel (ZF) set theory, the well-ordering principle, restricted to iterative sets, is equivalent to the (local) axiom of choice, the statement that for every set x of non-empty sets there is a function whose value at every $y \in x$ is a member of y (Zermelo 1904).

Recall that our deductive system $D2$ contains a version of the axiom of choice. One instance is

$$AC: \forall X(\forall x \exists y Xxy \rightarrow \exists f \forall x Xxfx).$$

In second-order set theory $Z2$, AC is a rather strong principle. It entails what is called *global choice*, the existence of a single choice function for the entire universe. Indeed, it follows from an instance of the comprehension scheme that there is a binary relation E such that Exy holds iff either x is empty or $y \in x$. Then, clearly, $\forall x \exists y Exy$. An application of AC yields a single function whose value at any non-empty x is a member of x. The graph of this global choice function is not an iterative set; it is a proper class.

In the light of Zermelo's theorem, one may query whether the well-ordering principle WOP, as formulated in $L2$, can be derived in $D2$ (which includes AC). The answer is that it cannot. If x and y are sets, then define y to have *x-choice* if, for every function f whose value at each $z \in x$ is a non-empty subset of y, there is a function g_f such that if $z \in x$ then $g_f(z)$ is a member of $f(z)$. In other words, y has x-choice if there is a choice function for every set of non-empty subsets of y that is 'indexed' by x. For example, y has ω-choice if there is a choice function for every countable set of non-empty subsets of y. Say that y has *continuum-choice* if y has 2^ω-choice. The so-called *principle of determinacy* has been well studied by set theorists (see, for example, Jech 1973, Section 12.3). Since it entails that there is no well-ordering of the continuum, determinacy is inconsistent with the axiom of choice. There is a somewhat stronger principle, called 'real-determinacy' that entails that the continuum has continuum-choice.[14] The stage is now set.

THEOREM 5.4.   *WOP is not a theorem of $D2$.*

Proof.   Actually, we only show that this theorem follows from the consistency of the principle of real-determinacy with (first-order) ZF set theory.[15] Let m be a model of this theory. Define a Henkin model M^H of $L2$ as follows. The first domain of M^H is the set d of all subsets of ω that are in m. The second domain D of M^H is the amalgamation of all relations on d that are in m, and the third domain F is the amalgamation of all functions on d whose graphs are in m. Note the following.

1. M^H satisfies the comprehension scheme. This follows from the fact that m satisfies the replacement scheme.

2. M^H satisfies AC. For example, suppose that there is a relation R in $D(2)$ such that $M^H \vDash \forall x \exists y Rxy$. Consider the collection $R' = \{R_x \mid x \in d\}$. By replacement, R' is in m and thus, by continuum-choice, there is a function g whose graph is in m, such that for every $x \in d$, $gx \in R_x$. But then g is in $F(1)$, and so $M^H \vDash \exists f \forall x Rxfx$. The situation with n-place functions is similar.

Taking 1 and 2 together, M is faithful to the deductive system $D2$.

3. M does not satisfy *WOP*. If it did, there would be a well-ordering of d in $D(2)$ and thus a well-ordering of d in m, contradicting the fact that m satisfies the determinacy principle.

Thus, by the soundness of faithful Henkin models (Chapter 4, Theorem 4.15), *WOP* is not provable in $D2$.   □

On the other hand, the converse holds. Let $D2^*$ be the deductive system obtained from $D2$ by dropping AC. It is straightforward that $WOP \rightarrow AC$ is a theorem of $D2^*$.

These results shed some light on the relationship between choice and well-ordering. In set theory, the usual proof that a given set x has a well-ordering uses a choice function on the *powerset* $\mathcal{P}(x)$ of x. That is, if $\mathcal{P}(x)$ had $\mathcal{P}(x)$-choice, then there is a well-ordering of x. The present discussion indicates that, in general, x-choice does not entail the existence of a well-ordering[16] of x.

5.1.4   *Well-foundedness*

Recall that a binary relation E is *well-founded* if there is no infinite sequence $a_0, a_1, \ldots$ such that $Ea_1a_0, Ea_2a_1, \ldots, Ea_{i+1}a_i, \ldots$ all hold. To indulge in jargon, a relation E is well-founded if there are no 'infinite descending E-chains'.

Once again, the notion of well-foundedness cannot be characterized in a first-order framework. Indeed, let T be a first-order theory containing a binary relation symbol E. Suppose that for each natural number n, there is a model of T in which there are $n + 1$ elements $a_0; \ldots, a_n$, such that $\langle a_1, a_0 \rangle, \ldots, \langle a_n, a_{n-1} \rangle$ are all in the extension of E. Then there are models of T in which the extension of E is not well-founded. This is yet another corollary of the compactness of first-order logic.

Notice that every well-ordering R is well-founded, since if there were an 'infinite descending R-chain', it would not have a 'least' element. Conversely, it follows from (a version of) the axiom of choice in the metatheory that if a linear order R is not a well-ordering, then it is not well-founded.

A second-order formulation of well-foundedness is straightforward:

$$\forall X [\exists x Xx \rightarrow \exists x (Xx \ \& \ \forall y (Xy \rightarrow \neg Eyx))].$$

That is, E is well-founded if and only if every non-empty set X has an element x that is E-minimal in the sense that nothing in X bears E to x.

Again, I submit that the notion of well-foundedness is both clear and unambiguous. In arithmetic, for example, proofs by induction and definitions by recursion presuppose that the predecessor relation and the 'less than' relation are well-founded. In set theory, it is central to the iterative conception that the membership relation is well-founded (see Boolos 1971, Parsons 1977).

Putnam (1980) argues against a type of 'realism' in set theory. In one section (Putnam 1980, pp. 468–9), he claims that the Löwenheim–Skolem theorems indicate that there is no 'fact of the matter' whether all sets are constructible, or even whether some particular countable set of real numbers is constructible. To support this, he refers to a theorem that for every countable set s of real numbers, there is an ω-model of set theory which contains s and satisfies a sentence asserting that every set is constructible.[17] Of course, a realist will maintain that the given set s may nevertheless be non-constructible 'in reality'. Putnam replies:

> But what on earth can this mean? It must mean, at the very least, that … the model $[M]$ we have described would not be *the intended model*. But why not?

He then goes on to argue that there are no grounds to claim that M is 'unintended' since M satisfies all the 'theoretical constraints' that have been placed on the notion of 'intended model' of set theory. But the only 'theoretical constraints' on models that Putnam seems to consider are that they satisfy the axioms of *first-order* set theory and that their 'finite ordinals' have the right structure. But one can surely insist that the well-foundedness of the membership relation is a 'theoretical constraint' on intended models of set theory. Few set theorists would regard a structure with a non-well-founded 'membership' relation to be an 'intended model'. Yet it follows (from a result that Putnam indicates) that if a given set t is non-constructible, then any model (containing t) that satisfies 't is constructible' is not well-founded. Thus, against Putnam, in the above scenario, if the set s is non-constructible, then there is indeed a clear sense in which M is an unintended model of set theory. Its membership relation is not well-founded.

Once again, someone might claim that I am begging the question here. If one does not believe that there is an unequivocal notion of well-foundedness, then it is not a 'theoretical constraint' that the membership relation is well-founded, and one cannot fault first-order logic for failing to capture this notion. And again, I have no independent argument in favour of well-foundedness and the other items considered here. From the practice of mathematics, they are data to be accommodated by semantics. This is not to say that there are no philosophical problems with second-order set theory (determining the range of its variables etc.) nor that the Löwenheim–Skolem theorems are irrelevant. These matters are considered in the historical and philosophical context in Chapters 7 and 8.

5.2 First-order theories—what goes wrong

The usual first-order versions of arithmetic, analysis, and set theory are obtained by replacing the second-order axioms with *schemes*. The theories are not finitely axiomatized.

First-order arithmetic consists of the successor, addition, and multiplication axioms (see Chapter 4, Section 4.2), together with the *axiom scheme of induction*:

$$\text{In}(\Phi): [\Phi(0) \ \& \ \forall x(\Phi(x) \rightarrow \Phi(sx))] \rightarrow \forall x \Phi(x),$$

one instance for each formula Φ of the first-order language of arithmetic.

First-order real analysis is obtained from the second-order version AN by replacing the completeness axiom with the *completeness scheme*:

$$C(\Phi): \exists x \forall y(\Phi(y) \rightarrow y \leq x) \rightarrow \exists x[\forall y(\Phi(y) \rightarrow y \leq x)$$
$$\& \ \forall z(\forall y(\Phi(y) \rightarrow y \leq z) \rightarrow x \leq z)],$$

one instance for each formula Φ of the first-order language of analysis, provided that Φ contains neither x nor z free.

First-order Zermelo–Fraenkel set theory (*ZFC*) is obtained from the second-order $Z2$ by exchanging the replacement axiom with the *replacement scheme*:

$$R(\Phi): \forall w \forall z_1 \forall z_2(\Phi(w, z_1) \ \& \ \Phi(w, z_2) \rightarrow z_1 = z_2)$$
$$\rightarrow \forall x \exists y \forall z(z \in y \equiv \exists w(w \in x \ \& \ \Phi(w, z))),$$

one instance for each formula Φ of the respective first-order language (not containing y free). First-order ZFC also includes an *axiom of choice*:

$$\forall x[\forall y \forall z(y \in x \ \& \ z \in x \rightarrow \neg \exists w(w \in y \ \& \ w \in z))$$
$$\rightarrow \exists v(\forall y(y \in x \ \& \ \exists w(w \in y) \rightarrow \exists! w(w \in y \ \& \ w \in v)))]$$

since there is no corresponding principle in the first-order metatheory.

The instances of these schemes can be derived from the corresponding second-order axiom, using the comprehension scheme of $D2$ (or, in the free-variable case, the substitution rule). The second-order theories of arithmetic and set theory are *not* conservative extensions of their first-order counterparts.[18] That is, in each case there is a formula Φ of the *first-order* language, such that Φ can be deduced from the second-order axiom (AR or $Z2$), but Φ is not a deductive consequence of the first-order axioms (nor, by completeness, is it a semantic consequence). For example, in second-order arithmetic and second-order set theory, one can formulate a 'truth' definition for the corresponding first-order theory and thus one can deduce the consistency of the first-order theory.[19]

There are a few items of interest concerning the deductive strength of $Z2$

over that of first-order *ZFC*. To take one example, it is a deductive consequence of *Z*2 that there is a countable model *M* such that for every sentence Φ of first-order set theory, $M \vDash \Phi$ iff Φ holds in the set-theoretic hierarchy. This is a rather natural extension of the downward Löwenheim–Skolem theorem. Yet the result in question cannot be stated, much less proved, in first-order *ZFC*.

In general, however, the deductive differences between our counterpart theories are not that significant. The consistency of second-order set theory *Z*2 can be proved in first-order *ZFC* augmented with an axiom asserting the existence of an inaccessible cardinal. The latter entails the existence of an inaccessible rank which, by Theorem 4.11 of Chapter 4, is a model of *Z*2.

The important differences between the first-order and second-order theories lie in semantics. Since the first-order versions are subject to the compactness and Löwenheim–Skolem theorems, there are uncountable models of first-order arithmetic and countable models of analysis and set theory. Following Montague (1965), call a model of each of our second-order theories *standard*, and call a model of any of our first-order theories that is not a model of the respective second-order theory, *non-standard*.

There are, in fact, non-standard models of the following sets of first-order formulas:

AR-1: $\{\Phi$ is in the language of first-order arithmetic and $\vDash AR \rightarrow \Phi\}$

AN-1: $\{\Phi$ is in the language of first-order analysis and $\vDash AN \rightarrow \Phi\}$

*Z*2-1: $\{\Phi$ is in the language of first-order *ZFC* and $\vDash Z2 \rightarrow \Phi\}$.

By Corollary 4.9 of Chapter 4, *AR*-1 is the set of first-order arithmetic *truths*. There are uncountable models of it. Similarly, *AN*-1 is the set of first-order truths of analysis, and it has countable models. An example will be presented shortly. Finally, there are countable models of *Z*2-1, the set of first-order formulas satisfiable in all inaccessible ranks. This is despite the fact that one can *prove* (in first-order *ZFC*) that there are uncountable *sets* (Cantor's theorem). This is the *Skolem paradox*, a recurring theme in this book. Let us see where the proofs of the categoricity theorems fail in the first-order cases.

The second-order axioms of induction, completeness, and replacement apply to any subset of the domain, whether definable in the language or not. For example, the induction axiom asserts that *every* set that contains (the denotation of) 0 and is closed under (the denotation of) the successor function is the whole domain. Since principles like this cannot be stated in the first-order language, the instances of the various schemes serve as surrogates. But these schemes apply *only* to sets that are *definable by formulas*—formulas of the respective first-order languages. The proofs of the categoricity theorems in the previous chapter begin with 'arbitrary' models of the theories. Certain subsets of (or relations on) their domains are determined, and the appropriate second-order axiom is applied to them. To reiterate, the constructions are carried out in the metatheory, which contains at least a rudimentary theory of sets, enough to determine the existence of the relevant subsets or relations.

By contrast, let $M = \langle d, I \rangle$ be a model of one of the first-order theories. To apply a first-order *scheme* to a given subset p of d, one must first establish that there is a *formula* in the first-order language in question that 'defines' p in the model M. To be specific, we require a formula $\Phi(x)$ and an assignment s on M such that for all assignments s' that agree with s, except possibly at x, $M, s' \vDash \Phi(x)$ if and only if s' assigns a member of p to x. Then, and only then, there would be an instance of the scheme that applies to p. Call a set p that meets this condition *first-order M-definable* (with parameters), and define a relation or function to be first-order M-definable similarly. Each of the first-order theories, formulated with a scheme, entails that for each model M, the relevant principle (induction, completeness, or replacement) applies to every first-order definable subset of, or function on, the domains of M. But that is all. They do not, and cannot, state that the principle applies to every subset of the domain.

In short, then, the categoricity theorems fail in the first-order cases because certain subsets of the domains, constructed in the metatheory, may not be first-order definable. This is a manifestation of the phenomenon (familiar since Tarski and Gödel) that the resources of an adequate metatheory are often stronger than the theories modelled by the formal language in question. In the present case, the focus is on the resources of set definition. Let us take up some examples.

Consider the proof of the categoricity of arithmetic (Theorem 4.8 of Chapter 4). In effect, the isomorphism f between our two models, $M1 = \langle d_1, I_1 \rangle$ and $M2 = \langle d_2, I_2 \rangle$ is the minimal closure (within $d_1 \times d_2$) of the single element $\langle 0_1, 0_2 \rangle$ under the function whose value at $\langle a, b \rangle$ is $\langle s_1 a, s_2 b \rangle$. In establishing that this set of pairs is a one-to-one function from d_1 onto d_2, we defined certain subsets of d_1 and d_2 (e.g. the domain of f and the range of f) and then applied the induction principle (satisfied by both $M1$ and $M2$) to conclude that these subsets are the whole domain. This does not work in the first-order case because one cannot show that the indicated subsets of d_1 are *first-order M1-definable*, nor can one show that the relevant subsets of d_2 are first-order $M2$-definable. Notice that we had to refer to *both* structures (in the metatheory) to define the function f, and then we used f to define the indicated subsets of the domains. These resources are not available in the first-order theories themselves.

Let $M = \langle d, I \rangle$ be a *non-standard* model of arithmetic.[20] Let $d' \subseteq d$ be the minimal closure of the denotation of 0 under the denotation of the successor function. Since M is non-standard, there are elements of the domain d that are not in d'. Thus d' is not first-order M-definable. If it were, the induction scheme would entail that d' is the whole domain. It is the burden of compactness that such models cannot be ruled out.

In analysis, a model $M = \langle d, I \rangle$ is said to be *Archimedean* if, for any p, q in d such that $p > 0$ and $q > 0$, there is a natural number m such that the result of adding p to itself m times is greater than q. In other words, an ordered field is Archimedean if it contains no 'infinitesimals'. It is essential to the (post-Weierstrass) understanding of the real numbers that the structure is Archimedean. And it follows from the foregoing considerations that all models of the second-order axiomatization AN are Archimedean. Indeed, in such a model let $p > 0$ and P be the minimal closure of $\{p\}$ under addition. It is easy to see that P cannot have a least upper bound, and so, by the completeness axiom, P is unbounded. But there are non-Archimedean models of first-order analysis. The reason is that even such simple minimal closures as P (or, for that matter, the 'natural numbers' and 'rational numbers' of a given model) may not be first-order definable.

Recall that the last part of the proof sketch of the categoricity of analysis (Theorem 4.10 of Chapter 4) involved defining sets in one model $M2$ in terms of another model $M1$. We began with an arbitrary element c of the domain of $M1$ and defined the set C of rationals of $M1$ that are less than c. Then we let $f(C)$ be the image in the domain of $M2$ of this set under the isomorphism between the rational numbers of the models. Finally, we applied the completeness axiom to $f(C)$ in $M2$. This argument fails in the first-order case, because the set $f(C)$ need not be first-order $M2$-definable (even if the rational numbers of $M2$ are first-order $M2$-definable). The metatheoretic definition of the set $f(C)$ makes mention of *another structure*, the model $M1$. To repeat, the completeness scheme can only be applied in $M2$ to sets that are first-order $M2$-definable; the defining formula cannot refer to elements of any other structure.

In set theory, the situation is similar. There are essential aspects of our (post-Zermelo) understanding of set theory that are missing from some models of first-order ZFC.

We have just encountered one of these, the notion of well-foundedness. The purpose of the axiom of foundation is to state that the membership relation is well-founded. Recall that it is a *first-order* sentence

$$\forall x[\exists y(y \in x) \rightarrow \exists y(y \in x \ \& \ \forall z(\neg(z \in y \ \& \ z \in x)))]$$

asserting that every non-empty set x has an element y such that x and y are disjoint. In every model of the *second-order* theory $Z2$, the membership relation is in fact well-founded. Indeed, suppose that $M = \langle d, I \rangle$ satisfies $Z2$ and let $a_0, a_1, a_2, \ldots$ be a sequence of members of d such that, for each i, the pair $\langle a_{i+1}, a_i \rangle$ is in the extension of the membership relation of M. Let $A = \{a_0, a_1, a_2, \ldots\}$. Now $A \subseteq d$ and A is countable. The axioms of infinity and replacement entail that there is a member b of d whose 'elements in M' are precisely $\{a_0, a_1, a_2, \ldots\}$. This set is a counter-example to the axiom of foundation. Any 'element' of b, say a_i, has an 'element', namely a_{i+1}, in common with b.

In first-order ZFC, however, the axiom of foundation only prevents infinite descending membership chains that are *first-order definable* (in the given model). This entails, for example, that there are no elements x such that $x \in x$ (which would produce the descending chain $x, x, x, \ldots$), and there are no finite closed chains: $x_1 \in x_0, x_2 \in x_1, \ldots, x_{n+1} \in x_n$, and $x_0 \in x_{n+1}$. But, as noted, one cannot prevent non-well-founded models of any substantial axiomatization of first-order set theory. Any consistent extension of first-order ZFC has such models. In sum, the axiom of foundation, a first-order sentence, only 'works' in the second-order theory.

Here is a fact, mentioned earlier, about well-founded structures:

Let $M = \langle d, I \rangle$ be a model of the language of set theory such that (1) the relation assigned to the symbol $\in$ is well-founded, and (2) M satisfies the axiom of extensionality. Then M is isomorphic to a model whose domain is a transitive set s and whose interpretation of $\in$ is the membership relation on s.

That is, every extensional well-founded structure is isomorphic to a transitive set (under membership). Thus the discussion of well-founded models of set theory can be limited to transitive *set models*, structures in which the domain is a set and the membership relation is assigned to $\in$. We identify each such model with its domain.

Thus, if first-order ZFC has a well-founded model at all, then it has a transitive set model d. It is a consequence of the downward Löwenheim–Skolem theorem that there is a *countable* subset $d' \subseteq d$ that is also a set model. The set d' may have uncountable elements, but there is no puzzle over countable sets with uncountable elements. However, it follows from the fact cited above that there is a *transitive* set m that is isomorphic to d'. This m is also a set model, and every element of m is countable.[21]

Let C be the statement of *Cantor's theorem*. It entails that the powerset of the collection of finite ordinals is not countable. Since C is a theorem of first-order ZFC, $m \vDash C$, but, as just stated, m is itself countable and so are its elements. This, again, is the so-called Skolem paradox.

A few observations suffice to clear up any confusion. As usual, let ω be the set of finite ordinals. One can show that $\omega \in m$. Let $S(y)$ be a formula asserting that $y \subseteq \omega$ (i.e. that every member of y is a finite ordinal) and let $O(z, x)$ be a formula asserting that z is a function from ω *onto* x. The powerset axiom entails $\exists x \forall y (y \in x \equiv S(y))$ and Cantor's theorem is

$$\forall x [\forall y (y \in x \equiv S(y)) \rightarrow \neg \exists z O(z, x)].$$

Both of these sentences are satisfied by m.

Clearly, since every element of m is countable, the powerset of ω cannot be a member of m. But there *is* an assignment s such that $m, s \vDash \forall y(y \in x \equiv S(y))$. Let p be the set assigned by s to the variable x. Then p 'plays the role' of the powerset of ω in m. Again, it does not contain every subset of ω. In fact, p contains all and only those subsets of ω that are in m. This set is countable. So let f be any function from ω onto p. Now, by Cantor's theorem, for this same assignment s, we have $m, s \vDash \neg \exists O(z, x)$. That is, '$p$ is not countable' is satisfied by m. But this (only) means that functions like f are *not in* m. In sum, the set p is in fact countable, but no function from ω onto p is a member of m, nor is such a function first-order m-definable.

Although there is no contradiction here, it should be clear that m is an unintended model of set theory. The powerset axiom is a first-order sentence:

$$\forall x \exists y \forall z(z \in y \equiv \forall w(w \in z \rightarrow w \in x)).$$

It is supposed to assert the existence of the set of all subsets of each set. But the variables (like all first-order variables) range over the elements of the model. So the powerset axiom only guarantees the existence of a set of all subsets of (say) ω *that are in the model*. The subsets of ω that are 'guaranteed by the axioms' to exist in a given model m are those that are first-order m-definable, and only those. In some cases there are only countably many of them.

Skolem himself drew some radical conclusions about the nature of cardinality from considerations like these. We shall return to this later (Chapters 7 and 8). For the present, let us continue the analysis of the phenomena of non-standard models.

Define a set m to be *closed by subsets* if, for every $c \in m$ and $b \subseteq c$, $b \in m$. That is, m is closed by subsets if m contains every subset of each of its members. Countable models of ZFC are not closed by subsets and are, for this reason, unintended. The Löwenhaim–Skolem theorems indicate that no first-order set theory has all its set models closed by subsets (unless, of course, it has no set models at all).

In contrast, the set models of $Z2$ are all closed by subsets. Indeed, suppose that c is an element of such a model m and $b \subseteq c$. If b is empty, then $b \in m$. If b is not empty, then let $q \in b$, and let f be the function whose value at x is x if $x \in b$ and whose value at x is q if $x \notin b$. Then $b \in m$ follows from the replacement axiom applied to the function f and the element c. Of course, this function need not be first-order m-definable.

It can be shown that if m is a transitive set model of first-order ZFC and m is closed by subsets, then m is a rank V_α, and α is a limit ordinal. Such sets are called *rank models*. Conversely, every rank model is closed by subsets. These models of ZFC are all uncountable, but nevertheless some are non-standard. There is, in fact, an ordinal β with cofinality ω such that V_β is a model of first-order ZFC. That is, there is a countable sequence of ordinals that is unbounded in β, or in other words, there is a one-to-one function f from ω to β such that $\beta = \bigcup \{ f(n) \mid n \in \omega \}$. Of course, the function f is not in V_β, nor is it first-order definable in V_β. If it were, then since V_β is a model of first-order set theory, $\beta \in V_\beta$ would follow from the replacement scheme, which is a contradiction.

This point can be generalized. If α is not a regular cardinal, then the replacement property fails on V_α. Indeed, if α is not regular, then there is an ordinal $\beta < \alpha$ and a function $f: \beta \rightarrow \alpha$ such that $\bigcup \{ f(\gamma) \mid \gamma \in \beta \}$ is α. If the second-order replacement property held in V_α, then, since $\beta \in V_\alpha$, $\{ f(\gamma) \mid \gamma \in \beta \}$ would be in V_α, and so $\alpha \in V_\alpha$, which is a contradiction. I suggest that such a model is unintended, because the replacement property fails.

We have reached the end of this story. If V_κ is a model of first-order ZFC and κ is a regular cardinal, then κ is inaccessible and thus V_κ is a model of the second-order $Z2$. It is standard.

To summarize, let $M = \langle d, I \rangle$ be any model of first-order ZFC that does not satisfy $Z2$. Then M may not be well-founded. If it is well-founded, then it is isomorphic to a transitive set which is either not closed by subsets or is a rank model V_α in which α is not a regular cardinal. In all three cases, M is 'unintended', but these cases cannot be ruled out with a first-order theory.

5.3 Second-order languages and the practice of mathematics

I submit that having to check whether a given set is first-order definable is little more than an artefact of logical theory. Mathematicians, other than those explicitly studying first-order logic, do not do it. In practice, induction, completeness, and replacement are applied to classes and functions no matter how they are defined. It follows that mathematical theories are better cast in second-order languages. Kreisel makes a similar point:

> ... Bourbaki [for example] is extremely careful to isolate the assumptions of a mathematical theorem, but never the axioms of set theory implicit in a particular deduction, e.g., what instances of the comprehension axiom are used. This practice is quite consistent with the assumption that what one has in mind when following Bourbaki's proofs is the second-order axioms ... (Kreisel, 1967, p. 151)

The purpose of this section is to extend the argument that the restriction to first-order logic is often awkward and artificial. The discussion focuses on three considerations suggested by Kreisel (1967) concerning arithmetic and analysis, and concludes with a few remarks on lengths of deductions. Second-order set theory is treated in the next section.

5.3.1 *Epistemics*

It is widely held among mathematicians that arithmetic, real and complex analysis, and, perhaps, set theory are not hypothetical systems. Arithmetic is about the natural numbers, real analysis is about the real numbers, and set theory is about the iterative hierarchy. For now, let us call this attitude 'working realism', since no stance is taken so far about the nature and ontological status of the presumed intended interpretations of these theories. Working realism is little more than an insistence that most serious mathematical discourse be taken literally (see Chapter 8).

From this perspective, one can inquire as to why any given statement, even an axiom, is believed or accepted either by a particular mathematician or by the community as a whole. The request that an axiom be justified is not necessarily a demand that it be made evident, all by itself, and it is certainly not a demand for self-evidence. That would be a return to the foundationalism that is rejected here. Theories can be justified by the role they play in the overall intellectual enterprise, and axioms can be justified in terms of their role in a theory. But some explanation can be requested. Of course, one cannot expect illuminating replies to *every* such question, all at once, without introducing an infinite regress, and certainly not while maintaining an ontological neutrality. All explanations and justifications must eventually end. But, from the present perspective, there is no a priori reason why the axioms of a given formulation of a theory should be immune from epistemic query.

Kreisel wrote:

> A moment's reflection shows that the evidence of the first-order schema derives from the second-order [axiom]; the difference is that when one puts down the first-order schema, one is supposed to have convinced oneself that the particular formulae used ... are well-defined in any structure one considers. (Kreisel 1967, p. 148)

Kreisel's point seems to be that a given mathematician believes or accepts the individual instances of the first-order *scheme* only because she (already) believes or accepts the second-order *axiom*. Suppose, for example, that one is given an instance of the completeness scheme $C(\Phi)$, perhaps one in which the indicated formula Φ is rather complicated, and suppose that the person is asked whether it is true of the real number structure and, if it is, why she believes it. On the basis of the first-order formulation, one answer might be something like 'I accept this formula because it is an axiom—it has the form of the completeness scheme', or perhaps 'this formula is one of the *basic* or *defining characteristics* of the real number structure'. It is as if one had asked why he believes that every group has an identity element. This would be the place where justification ends. I would suggest, however, that in the case at hand, such an answer is artificial, especially if the instance is complex. A more holistic justification of such an instance is also implausible. It is unlikely that such a complicated formula has any role at all in the development of real analysis, let alone a significant role. A more natural response to the original query would be: 'The subformula $\Phi(x)$ determines a set of real numbers.[22] The formula in the form $C(\Phi)$ asserts that if *this* set is bounded, then it has a least upper bound. I accept the formula because it follows, via universal instantiation, from the completeness axiom—a statement that characterizes the real number structure.'

Of course, some philosophers are dubious of second-order languages, often on ontological grounds. A like-minded mathematician might argue that by employing first-order analysis, one is sacrificing epistemic clarity and simplicity for a theory that is more acceptable on philosophical grounds. The onus on such a mathematician is to show why he accepts each instance of the scheme. A separate justification for each axiom is out of the question—there are infinitely many. Moreover, the mathematician cannot claim that the instances of the scheme are acceptable *because* they are the 'safe' or 'reasonable' consequences of the second-order completeness axiom, the consequences that do not involve the undesirable or dubious second-order language. If one rejects the second-order axiom on philosophical grounds, then one cannot use it as a premise to justify other sentences.

A better plan, perhaps, would be for our advocate of first-order analysis to attempt a justification of the completeness scheme as such, either by reference to the role of the scheme or with some sort of informal 'justification scheme' covering each instance. But any role played by the scheme is also played by the second-order completeness axiom. One possibility is simply to claim that the scheme itself *characterizes* the real numbers, and so no justification of its instances is required. But, as indicated by the Löwenheim–Skolem theorems (Chapter 4, Section 4.1), the scheme does not characterize the real numbers. Non-standard models abound. A second possibility would be to formulate an informal principle like 'every appropriately definable, bounded set of real numbers has a least upper bound' and then point out that the instances of the completeness scheme are instantiations of this statement. Notice, however, that the statement in question has a variable ranging over (definable) sets of real numbers, which is prima facie second-order. Moreover, it presupposes a concept of *definability*, which is usually characterized as a minimal closure. Again, this construction cannot be modelled with a first-order language.

It may be that a plausible justification of the first-order scheme that does not involve a second-order or set-theoretic language is possible, but such a justification has yet to be given.

5.3.2 *Languages*

Since the second-order axiomatizations of arithmetic, real analysis, and set theory are finite and do not contain schemes, they are somewhat independent of the non-logical terminology available in the language. For example, the characterization of the natural numbers in a second-order language containing only the constant 0 and a name for the successor function is essentially the same as the characterization in a language containing names for other functions, such as addition and multiplication. Since the only difference between the two is that the latter contains axioms that define the new functions of addition and multiplication, the presence of the new terminology does not affect the fundamental description of the structure. This is not the case with the first-order versions. In arithmetic, the extension of the induction scheme $(In(\Phi))$ is determined by the available *formulas* Φ, and this depends on the non-logical terminology of the formalizing language.

Kreisel wrote:

> The choice of the first-order schema is not uniquely determined by the second-order axiom! Thus, Peano's own axioms mentions explicitly only the constant 0 and the successor function, ... not addition nor multiplication. The first-order schema built up from 0 and [the successor function] is a weak, ... decidable, subsystem of classical first-order arithmetic ... and quite inadequate for formulating current informal arithmetic. (Kreisel 1967, p. 148)

Suppose, for example, that in the course of a treatise on the natural numbers, a mathematician decides to introduce a new function f. She proceeds by adding a new function letter to the terminology, giving a description of the function, such as a recursive derivation of it, and proving that a unique function is thereby described. Clearly, it is assumed that the mathematician has introduced a new function on the *same* domain as the one she was working in before the introduction. A theorem (which does not mention the function f) in the extended theory is taken to be *true of* the natural numbers, even if it could not be deduced from the previous axioms alone.

The orientation is accurately modelled by the second-order axiomatization of arithmetic. The introduction of the function f does not alter the basic description of the natural numbers, as given by the second-order axiomatization. Moreover, the indicated proof that a unique function has been introduced amounts to a proof of what may be called 'unique extendibility'— each model of the original theory can be extended to a model of the new theory in exactly one way. As indicated in note 6, it follows from the result reported by Corcoran (1971) that that characterization of f is semantically eliminable and non-creative. In short, the standard requirements of an acceptable definition have been met and thus, in the second-order theory, all is as it should be.

It might be added that if the new function f is introduced by primitive recursion, the extended theory is a conservative extension of the original (Dedekind 1988). That is, any formula lacking the new symbol that is provable in the extended theory is also provable in the original theory. To take one example, it was pointed out in the previous chapter that the extension (or graph) of addition and multiplication can be *explicitly* defined in second-order arithmetic with successor alone:

$$A(x, y, z): \quad \forall f^2(\forall u \forall v(f^2 u 0 = u \ \& \ f^2 usv = sf^2 uv) \rightarrow f^2 xy = z)$$

$$M(x, y, z): \quad \forall g^2(\forall u \forall v(g^2 u 0 = 0 \ \& \ A(g^2 uv, u, g^2 usv)) \rightarrow g^2 xy = z).$$

That is, $a + b = c$ corresponds to $A(a, b, c)$, and $a \cdot b = c$ corresponds to $M(a, b, c)$. It is straightforward to show (in second-order arithmetic with successor alone) that both formulas define functions and that the addition and multiplication axioms hold of the respective defined functions. It is then immediate that AR (second-order arithmetic with successor, addition, and multiplication) is a conservative extension of second-order arithmetic with successor alone. Conceptually, the addition and multiplication symbols are excess baggage (but, of course, they are very convenient).[23]

Let us pursue Kreisel's remark that things are not so smooth in the first-order cases. Continuing our example of arithmetic, let A_0 be $\{0, s\}$, the numeral 0 and the successor symbol. Let A_1 be $\{0, s, +\}$, and let A_2 be $\{0, s, +, \cdot\}$, the set we called A in the presentation of arithmetic in Chapter 4. For each $i = 0, 1, 2$, let $AR1_i$ be the corresponding first-order arithmetic, consisting of the successor axiom, recursive derivations of the included binary functions (if any), and the induction *scheme* (see Chapter 4, Section 4.2). The crucial observation is that the induction scheme of $AR1_i$ is only to include formulas from the first-order language $L1A_i =$. Thus, the scheme of $AR1_0$ does not contain formulas with occurrences of the addition and multiplication symbols, and the scheme of $AR1_1$ does not contain formulas with occurrences of the multiplication symbol. First-order arithmetic with addition only, $AR1_1$, is sometimes called *Presburger arithmetic*. For each i, let $AR2_i$ be the corresponding *second-order* theory, consisting of the successor axiom, recursive derivations of the included binary functions, and the induction *axiom*.

It might be objected that in the expanded second-order $AR2_2$ and $AR2_1$, the new terminology is included in the instances of the comprehension scheme (in the deductive system $D2$), and that this is how the terminology finds its way into the deductive consequences of the induction axiom. To see that this is misleading, it need only be repeated that addition and multiplication are explicitly definable in the 'impoverished' $AR2_0$. In short, $AR2_0$, $AR2_1$, and $AR2_2$ are mere notational variants of each other.

In fact, *any* function defined by primitive recursion is explicitly definable in $AR2_0$ (as a minimal closure). But, since the defining formulas are second-order, the same does not automatically hold in the first-order theories. The full $AR1_2$ is a rich and interesting theory sufficient to formulate a substantial amount of number theory. For example, every primitive recursive function is definable in $AR1_2$ (see Gödel 1931).[24] For this reason, $AR1_2$ is incomplete. By contrast, $AR1_0$ and $AR1_1$ are both deductively *complete* (and decidable). Thus, for example, if Φ is a sentence of $L1A_1=$, then either $AR1_1 \vdash \Phi$ or $AR1_1 \vdash \neg \Phi$ (see Presburger 1930, Hilbert and Bernays 1934). It is too weak to formulate much number theory and elementary syntax. Clearly, $AR1_2$ is not a mere notational variant of $AR1_1$ and $AR1_0$.

The situation regarding the semantics of these theories is similar. There is a model of $AR1_1$ that cannot be extended to a model of $AR1_2$, and there is a model of $AR1_1$ that can be extended to a model of $AR1_2$ in more than one way. Thus, following the result reported in Corcoran (1971), the requirements of a successful definition have not been met. That is, in the first-order theories, recursive derivations are *not* implicit definitions.[25]

Real analysis offers an interesting variation on this theme. Recall that we began with the axioms of an ordered field, which are finite in number and first-order. In addition, the second-order AN contains the axiom of completeness stating that every set with an upper bound has a least upper bound, and the first-order version contains each instance of the completeness scheme $C(\Phi)$ above. A landmark result of Tarski (1948, 1967) is that the first-order theory is complete and thus decidable. Moreover, exactly the same theory is obtained from the axioms of an ordered field together with an intermediate value scheme for polynomials:

$$[\exists x(t(x) \le 0) \ \& \ \exists x(t(x) \ge 0)] \rightarrow \exists x(t(x) = 0)$$

for each term t of the language of real analysis (i.e. each term constructed from variables and the symbols 0, 1, +, ·).

It follows, for example, that the ordered field of real algebraic numbers is first-order equivalent to the ordered field of all real numbers. That is, any first-order sentence Φ is satisfied by the real numbers if and only if Φ is satisfied by the real algebraic numbers. In particular, the real algebraic number structure is a (countable) model of first-order analysis.

These observations represent good reasons why the first-order theory is far too impoverished to be an adequate formalization of classical analysis. First, analysis is traditionally taken to be an *extension* of arithmetic.[26] Indeed, as noted above in several places, every ordered field includes a copy of the natural numbers, the minimal closure of $\{0, 1\}$ under addition, and this substructure satisfies a variant of the axiom of second-order arithmetic. But the collection of 'natural numbers' of a given ordered field F need not be first-order definable in F. If it were in general, the incompleteness theorem would apply and first-order analysis would not be complete. Second, the fact that the real algebraic numbers form a model of first-order analysis indicates that transcendental numbers (like e and π) are not definable, nor are any transcendental functions. In short, only a small fragment of traditional analysis remains in the first-order theory. Of course, we could add terminology for such numbers and functions as they are needed, together with appropriate axioms (or schemes), and we could extend the completeness scheme to include the formulas of the expanded language as we go.[27] This is the sort of thing done in first-order arithmetic when addition and multiplication are added.

The second-order *AN* does not share this defect. As noted in the categoricity theorems of the previous chapter, the 'natural numbers' of any model of *AN* are a readily definable minimal closure, and it can be shown that this set satisfies the axioms of second-order arithmetic. Thus second-order real analysis is a clear *extension* of arithmetic, as it should be. It follows, incidentally, that the incompleteness theorem does apply to *AN*, but the undecidable sentences are not in the first-order language. One can also use minimal closures (together with the completeness axiom) to state and prove the existence of transcendental numbers and to define common numbers and functions. Thus, I submit that *AN* comes a lot closer to modelling traditional analysis than does its first-order counterpart.

In sum, the second-order theoreis of arithmetic and analysis are quite powerful when formulated with only the terminology necessary to state the central axioms (induction or completeness). Other elements, functions, and sets can be explicitly defined as needed. One adds new terms with definitions, without modifying the central theses of the theory (and, in most cases, the new terms are eliminable). In the first-order cases, the central schemes are modified as we go, and it is a non-trivial affair to determine just when we have added 'enough' new terminology.

Although this is ahistorical, one can think of the second-order variables and quantifiers as a 'primitive' to be added to a first-order theory. One has a choice between this and the collection of individual functions and predicates needed to extend the minimal first-order theories to an acceptable level. Conceptual simplicity indicates the second-order route.

5.3.3 *Interrelations and models*

Another consequence of the close tie between schemes and languages is that the various first-order theories are presented as if they were isolated not only from each other but from the rest of mathematics as well. This is not in accord with the extremely fruitful practice of viewing mathematical structures as interrelated. One manifestation of this is the common technique of 'embedding' or 'modelling' one structure in another. We have already made use of this in defining the 'natural numbers' and 'rational numbers' of models of real analysis. But the technique is not limited to logic. In Kreisel's words:

> ... very often the mathematical properties of a domain D become only graspable when one embeds D in a larger domain D'. Examples: (1) D integers, D' complex plane; use of analytic number theory. (2) D integers, D' p-adic numbers; use of p-adic analysis. (3) D surface of a sphere, D' three-dimensional space; use of three-dimentional geometry. Non-standard analysis [also applies] here ... (Kreisel 1967, p. 166)

To take a simple example, when one realizes that the complex plane (or, for that matter, the set-theoretic hierarchy) contains an 'isomorphic copy' of the natural numbers, then one can use complex analysis (or set theory) to shed light on the natural numbers. That is, since isomorphic structures satisfy the same sentences, a theorem of complex analysis that only refers to the natural numbers of the complex plane is true *of* the natural numbers. As Kreisel notes, another example is non-standard arithmetic and analysis. This is particularly relevant here since it involves a careful and often insightful combination of first-order logic and second-order notions. One begins with a non-standard model M of the set of all first-order sentences true of the real numbers. Then one points out that M includes (an isomorphic copy of) the real numbers as a (proper) substructure. Call this substructure M'. It is the 'standard part' of M. That is, we embed the standard real numbers in a non-standard model. The metatheory of first-order logic indicates that results can be 'translated' between M and M'. Indeed, sentences satisfied by M hold in M' and thus are true of the real numbers. There is a vast literature that testifies to the productivity of this technique. The relevant fact here is that the domain of the standard part M' is not first-order definable in M. If it were, the completeness scheme would entail the existence of a least upper bound of the standard reals in M, which is impossible. Thus non-standard analysis works because in the metatheory we are able to look beyond the first-order theory to define sets that are not first-order definable. We use a categorical characterization of the real numbers to study the first-order models of analysis, all this to learn something about the real numbers.

It is well known that general embedding techniques can produce results that are not obtainable in the original theories. This occurs because there are *subsets* of the original (embedded) structures that are definable in the larger context, but not in the original theories alone. Thus, for example, there are sets of natural numbers definable in set theory, but not in arithmetic. One who accepts first-order arithmetic as adequate cannot make the straightforward claim that certain theorems of complex analysis and set theory reflect truths of the natural numbers.[28] In other cases, the results of embedding are obtainable in the original theories alone, but the derivations in the more expansive contexts are shorter or more insightful. This often occurs with deductions in non-standard arithmetic and analysis.

Embedding represents another instance in which categoricity is important. In order to embed a structure D into a structure E, one must have a means of recognizing a substructure of E as isomorphic to D. Otherwise, one cannot be certain that D really is a substructure of E. The analogue of this requirement of (re)identification is a categorical characterization. Suppose, for example, that someone comes to believe that a certain structure M 'includes' the natural numbers and thus that the study of M may produce new theorems of arithmetic, or more perspicuous derivations of old theorems. In attempting to verify this, suppose that he defines a certain substructure M' of M and shows that M' satisfies the axioms of *first-order* arithmetic. Then, of course, we can conclude that every theorem of first-order arithmetic holds of M', but here we are interested in a converse of sorts, whether certain facts about M correspond to facts about the natural numbers. Since no first-order theory with an infinite model is categorical, the mathematician cannot conclude that M' is isomorphic to the natural numbers, nor can he conclude that all theorems of M whose variables are restricted to the domain of M' are true of the natural numbers. For all he knows so far, the structure M' may be a non-standard model of first-order arithmetic. The situation is somewhat analogous to an observation that a certain structure is a group. Since the group axioms are not categorical, it does not follow that properties of this structure are 'truths' of group theory. But, unlike arithmetic, group theory is not about any one particular structure. In the example at hand, the situation would be different if the mathematician showed that the structure M' satisfies the axioms of *second-order* arithmetic. Then he can conclude that M' is isomorphic to the natural numbers and thus that any theorem about M whose variables are restricted to the domain of M' is true of the natural numbers.

5.3.4   *A note on speed-up*

There is an interesting phenomenon concerning sentences that are deducible in both a given nth-order theory and its $(n + m)$th-order counterpart. Sometimes the deductions in the higher-order theories are shorter, a lot shorter.

Gödel (1936) states, but does not prove, that for any recursive function f and any natural number n, there are infinitely many sentences Φ of the language of first-order arithmetic, such that Φ is derivable in both nth-order and $(n + 1)$th-order arithmetic, but if m is the number of formulas in the shortest $(n + 1)$th-order deduction of Φ, then there is no nth-order deduction of Φ with fewer than $f(m)$ formulas. That is, there is no recursive bound on how much longer the shortest nth-order deduction is over the shortest $(n + 1)$th-order deduction of the same formula. Mostowski (1952) contains a proof of a similar result (using the Gödel number of a deduction as the measure of its length, rather than the number of formulas it contains). Statman (1978) gives a general study of the length of deductions in the context of predicate calculus, our deductive systems $D1 =$ and $D2$. One result of note is that there is no function f that is provably recursive in second-order arithmetic that represents a bound on how much longer the shortest first-order derivation of a (first-order) logical truth is over the length of a second-order derivation of the same logical truth.[29] That is, there is no (second-order) provably recursive f such that for each first-order logical truth Φ, if Φ has a deduction of length m in a certain deductive system for second-order logic, then Φ has a deduction of length $f(m)$ in a corresponding first-order system.

Boolos (1987) concerns the following argument I, whose premises and conclusion are all first-order sentences:

$$\forall y(fy0 = s0)$$
$$\forall x(f0sx = ssf0x)$$
$$\forall y\forall x(fsysx = fyfsyx)$$
$$D0$$
$$\forall x(Dx \rightarrow Dsx)$$

Therefore,

$$Dfssss0ssss0.$$

The language contains an individual constant 0, a unary function symbol s, a binary function symbol f, and a predicate symbol D. Consider a model whose domain consists of a set that includes the natural numbers, s denotes the successor function (when restricted to the natural numbers), f denotes an Ackermann-type function defined by double recursion, and the extension of D is any set that contains 0 and is closed under s. It is easy to see that the premises and conclusion of I are all satisfied by such a model. Indeed, the extension of D must contain every natural number, and the Ackermann function is closed under the natural numbers (i.e. if m and n are natural numbers, then so is fmn). The conclusion simply states that D holds of the result of applying f to a particular pair of natural numbers.

It is almost as easy to see that I is (semantically) valid. Indeed, let $M = \langle d, I \rangle$ be any model satisfying the premises. Let Z be the minimal closure (within d) of the denotation of 0 under the function denoted by s. It is clear that Z is a subset of the extension of D, since the latter contains 0 and is closed under s. A double induction then shows that Z is closed under $I(f)$. So $M \vDash Dfssss0ssss0$.

This reasoning can readily be transformed into a deduction of I in the deductive system $D2$ of *second-order* logic. The main element in the above reasoning is the minimal closure construction which, as we have seen, can be rendered in a second-order language. See Boolos (1987, Appendix) for a more detailed sketch of the deduction. With full details, and no abbreviations, it would not take up more than a page or two.

Since I is valid and first-order, it follows from the completeness theorem that there is also a deduction of I in the first-order deductive system $D1=$. Moreover, one can see how such a deduction could proceed. Repeated use of the first three premises yields a formula in the form $fssss0ssss0 = p$, where p is a term consisting of many occurrences of s followed by an occurrence of 0. Then one use of the fourth premise, many instantiations of the fifth premise, and many *modus ponens* allow the derivation of Dp for the aforementioned term p. The conclusion is but a single step away, an application of an identity axiom. The problem is that the term p is *very* long, containing many more occurrences of s than there are particles in the known universe. Boolos sketches a proof that the shortest deduction of I in a typical first-order system (like the present $D1=$) is also extremely long. It is not possible for such a deduction to be written in this universe, nor is it possible for a human to come to know that I is valid by such a derivation. Boolos concludes:

> ... the fact that we so readily recognize the validity of I would seem to provide as strong a proof as could be asked for that no standard first-order logical system can be taken to be a satisfactory idealization of the psychological mechanisms or processes ... whereby we recognize (first-order!) logical consequences. 'Cognitive scientists' ought to be suspicious of the view that logic as it appears in logic texts adequately represents the whole of the science of valid inference.

It would seem that these 'psychological mechanisms' are either modelled by second-order logic, or they otherwise involve some set theory.

It is sometimes argued that first-order logic has some sort of epistemic significance, since its consequence relation is recursively enumerable, unlike that of second-order logic (e.g. Wagner 1987). If an argument modelled in a first-order language is valid, then there is a mechanically checkable deduction of its conclusion from its premises. Presumably, this feature of logic is necessary if it is to be an accurate model of the ways in which humans ought to reason or, to be precise, the ways in which humans come to know that conclusions follow from premises. The above example undermines this consideration. The fact that a consequence relation is recursively enumerable does not entail that it is feasible, and it does not entail that the deductive system models all the processes that we use, or could use, or ought to use in reasoning. We have before us an argument that we know to be valid, but could not know to be valid by deducing it in the acclaimed first-order deductive systems. On the other hand, we could know this argument to be valid by deducing it in a second-order deductive system.

5.4   Set theory

The epistemic matters of Section 5.3.1 apply to set theory with the force that they have in arithmetic and analysis. One accepts the instances of the first-order replacement scheme $R(\Phi)$ only because one accepts the second-order axiom of replacement. The instances of the scheme are not taken to be separate entities, but rather each is a consequence of a general principle, one best formulated in terms of functions on sets or, equivalently, in terms of (possibly proper) classes.[30]

It is conceded, however, that the other considerations of the last section apply to set theory only to a limited extent. The possibility of introducing new terminology to the language, which would extend the replacement scheme, is moot. One could make up examples of this sort of thing, but I do not know of any that are relevant to the practice of set theory. It seems that the language whose only non-logical term is the membership symbol is sufficient for current practice in set theory. The construction of Boolean-valued models (to obtain independence results) is prima facie an embedding of the set-theoretic hierarchy in a richer structure (see Jech 1971, Section 17), but such constructions can be reinterpreted within the set-theoretic hierarchy.

One reason for the limited range of these considerations is the wide applicability of (even first-order) set theory. It is *a* reasonable foundation for contemporary mathematics. With few exceptions, mathematical terms and notions have analogues in the set-theoretic hierarchy that can be defined in first-order *ZFC*. Virtually every structure is isomorphic to either a member of the set-theoretic hierarchy or a structure constructed from it. The natural numbers correspond to the finite ordinals, the real numbers to the powerset of the set of finite ordinals, etc., and all the usual functions and relations are definable in set theory. In short, one can hold that 'embeddings' stop at the set-theoretic hierarchy and that everything can be described in first-order set theory.[31]

On the other hand, it seems that terminology for proper classes is at least prima facie implicit in informal treatments of set theory. First, the terms V for the entire set-theoretic hierarchy, ON for the class of ordinals, and L for the class of constructible sets are common items in the set theorist's vocabulary. At least on the surface, these are names of proper classes (or set-theoretic properties). But, again, such terminology is readily paraphrased away, if anyone wants to bother. Parsons writes:

> ... talk of classes and some sort of distinction between sets and classes is a quite standard part of the conceptual apparatus of set theory. It is used by workers in the field even when the *formal* theory they work with (for example, the familiar ... system *ZF*) [affirms] the nonexistence of the 'paradoxical' [collections]. (Parsons 1983, p. 209)

The latter are the proper classes (like V, ON, and L) that are not *members* of the set-theoretic hierarchy, and thus are not in the range of the first-order variables. Parsons supports this conclusion with an elaborate discussion of Takeuti and Zaring (1971). Another example is the excellent textbook by Jech (1971), in which variables ranging over 'classes' are introduced informally as proxies for 'arbitrary' formulas (with free variables). In short, formulas with class terms are thought of as schemes. For example, the separation principle is first given its official formulation as a scheme and then is succinctly reformulated with a class variable:

$$\forall x \exists y (y = C \cap x).$$

Similarly, after the replacement principle is given as a scheme, several versions with class variables are presented. One is

$$\text{If } F \text{ is a function, then } \forall x \exists f (F \upharpoonright x = f)$$

and this is glossed 'if a class is a function, then its restriction to any set can be replaced by a function which is a set'. For the most part, class terminology is used throughout the volume, usually without supplying the equivalent scheme. For example, the theorem supporting transfinite induction on ordinals is stated thus:

> Let C be a class of ordinals and assume that
> (1) $0 \in C$
> (2) $\alpha \in C \rightarrow (\alpha + 1) \in C$
> (3) $s \subseteq C \rightarrow \lim s \in C$.
> Then $C = ON$.

Again, Jech (1971) explicitly asserts that statements like this are to be understood as schemes. The phrase '$\alpha \in C$', for example, is rendered '$\Phi(\alpha)$, for some arbitrary appropriate formula Φ'. We have dwelt on schemes above. It seems that such locutions are meant as general statements about *all* their instances. In the Quinean tradition, one can ask 'all of what', and thus make an inquiry into the best way to formulate the generality of these locutions.

Parsons suggests that there are two ways to regiment the generality expressed by statements containing class variables. First, they can be taken literally as statements *about* classes. This makes the theory at least prima facie second-order, but does not determine a range for the class variables. The other reading is to take formulas with class terms

> ... as assertions that every statement in the language of ZF of which it is an instance is *true* (or true of all the values of its free variables). (Parsons 1983, p. 211)

This seems to be the reading intended by Jech (1971). In such cases, the natural way to formulate the talk of classes would be to introduce terminology for *truth* or, better, *satisfaction*.[32]

There is a sense in which these two proposals are equivalent. Parsons establishes that extensions of first-order set theory containing class terminology are mutually translatable with extensions of the same theory involving terminology for satisfaction. For example, a sentence $\exists X \forall x(Xx)$ corresponds to 'there is a formula that is satisfied by everything'. In either case, if formulas containing the new terminology are *not* included in the replacement scheme, the theory is a conservative extension of first-order ZFC. The class theory is essentially the same as the von Neumann–Gödel–Bernays (NGB) set theory. But Parsons suggests that it would be more natural to include the formulas of the extended language in the replacement scheme. This is surely consistent with the intended meaning of the replacement principle, which only involves the 'size' of various collections, not the way that they are defined. The result seems to be the full impredicative second-order set theory,[33] as axiomatized by our $Z2$.

Notes

1. Quine reiterated this theme at a conference held in his honour at St Louis in April 1988.
2. Let R be a binary relation. The *ancestral* of R is a binary relation that holds of a pair x, y if there is a finite sequence $x_0, \ldots, x_n$, such that $x_0 = x$, $x_n = y$, and for each $i < n$, $Rx_i x_{i+1}$. In other words, y is an R-ancestor of x if y is in the minimal closure of $\{x\}$ under the relation R. The analogy, of course, is with the phrase 'ancestor of' in ordinary language, which represents the ancestral of the 'parent of' relation (if one takes individuals to be ancestors of themselves, and parents to be ancestors of their children). Frege (1884) introduced the ancestral with a second-order definition and brilliantly exploited it in his work in logic and foundations of arithmetic. For Frege, a 'natural number' is an extension that bears the ancestral of a certain successor relation to the empty extension. We return to the ancestral in Chapter 9 below.

   Here is an amusing exercise in applying the deductive system of second-order logic. Define a relation R to be *diamond-closed* if, for every x, y, z, if Rxy and Rxz then there is a w such that Ryw and Rzw. Then it can be stated in $L2$ and proved in $D2$ that for every relation R, if R is diamond-closed, then so is its ancestral.
3. This is one of a number of notions that have adequate accounts involving either natural numbers or variables ranging over sets (or properties). This suggests that the notion of set is intimately connected with that of number, or finitude. The connection is discussed in historical context in Chapter 7, and is pursued more directly in Chapter 9.
4. In constructive mathematics, inductive definitions are often taken to be primitive constructions, not characterized in terms of other things. This further underscores the importance of the minimal closure operation.
5. If, for example, the threefold application of p to the extension of Φ exhausts the minimal closure, then the latter would be characterized by $\exists y(\Phi(y)$ & $(x = y \vee x = py \vee x = ppy \vee x = pppy))$.

6. Let T be a set of formulas that do not contain a given non-logical item t (a constant, predicate letter, etc.). Let Γ be a set of formulas some of which do contain t. Then Γ is said to be *eliminable* if, for each formula Ψ, there is a formula Ψ' not containing t such that $T + \Gamma \vDash (\Psi \equiv \Psi')$, and Γ is said to be *non-creative* if, for every Ψ not containing t, if $T + \Gamma \vDash \Psi$ then $T \vDash \Psi$. Notice that both of these notions involve semantics, not deductive systems. It is widely held that implicit definitions of non-logical items ought to be eliminable and non-creative (see Mates 1972, Chapter 11). The result reported by Corcoran (1971) is that a given Γ is eliminable and non-creative if and only if every model of T can be extended to a model of $T + \Gamma$ in exactly one way.

7. The equivalence between infinite and Dedekind-infinite depends on a version of the axiom of choice. As noted above, a principle of choice is included in the metatheory, and there is an analogue of it in the deductive system $D2$ for second-order languages.

8. There is also a first-order formula that is satisfied by a given model if and only if Φ has *exactly n* elements in its extension.

9. This holds even if the underlying first-order language has enough set-theoretic terminology to express the common definitions of finitude. Such first-order theories have unintended models in which the extension of 'x is finite' contains 'sets' with infinitely many 'elements'. In short, the definition of finitude only 'works' in higher-order languages. This point is developed more fully in Chapter 9.

10. The $\leq$ in $|X| \leq |Y|$ and the $=$ in $|X| = |Y|$ are not relation symbols, and $|X|$ is not a term. These symbols are only part of the notation for the relations of 'smaller or equal cardinality' and 'equal cardinality' between sets (or properties).

11. It is sometimes said that R_x is the set 'projected by' R on x.

12. See Garland (1974) for extensions and refinements of results like these. A related theme is developed by Hodes (1988a, b).

13. Notice also that X has the cardinality of the continuum if there are two objects in X, and two binary functions and a linear order on X that make X a model of real analysis. A formula asserting this can be obtained from the second-order axiomatization of real analysis by the above (Ramsey) technique of replacing constants and function symbols with variables, and prefixing the result with existential quantifiers.

14. For the principle of real-determinacy, the 'games' are the same 'length' ω as those considered in the original principle, but the 'players' choose sets of natural numbers instead of natural numbers.

15. I am indebted to Matthew Foreman and Robert Solovay for pointing me to the relevant set theory. Incidentally, the foregoing discussion starts with a model m of real-determinacy and constructs a *Henkin model* out of it. An alternative would be to use the model m of real-determinacy as the universe of our semantics, and to work with standard models *within m*. That is, if m were the universe of our semantics, then the continuum would satisfy AC (and comprehension) but not WOP. Notice that AC is not a logical truth in this 'universe'. I have been informed that Günter Asser and Christine Gassner have established the independence of WOP from AC without the assumption of the consistency of real-determinacy. In Chapter 3, it was mentioned that Hilbert and Ackermann (1928) include a stronger version of the axiom of choice in their presentation of second-order logic. The scheme can now be put succinctly: $\forall x \exists X(\Phi(x, X)) \rightarrow \exists R \forall x(\Phi(x, R_x))$.

Asser and Gassner have established the independence of *WOP* from this as well. The independence would also follow from the existence of a model of determinacy in which the powerset of the continuum has continuum-choice. Models of determinacy in which every set has continuum-choice have in fact been studied (real-determinacy plus 'theta is regular') but they are rather strong (see Steele and van Wesep 1982).

16. See Büchi (1953) for a similar analysis comparing the axiom of choice with Zorn's lemma. Incidentally, the principle behind Zorn's lemma can also be stated in *L*2. It is implied by *AC*, but according to the aforementioned work by Asser and Gassner (note 15), it does not imply *AC*. As indicated above, in *D*2* global choice can be derived from *Z*2 and *AC*. There is also a converse. Working in *D*2*, take *Z*2 and global choice as premises, and assume $\forall x \exists y Rxy$. For each x, let $\alpha(x)$ be the smallest ordinal γ such that the rank V_γ contains at least one member of R_x. The requisite function is obtained by applying the global choice function to the members of the class of all $\{V_{\alpha(x)} \cap R_x \mid \alpha$ is an ordinal$\}$. Notice that this argument makes use of the axiom of foundation in that one extracts a sub*set* $V_{\alpha(x)} \cap R_x$ of each class R_x. Flannagan (1975) shows that this use of foundation is essential. Let Z_0 be the axioms of second-order set theory without the axiom of foundation. Then in *D*2*, Z_0 & *AC* implies global choice, but Z_0 and global choice does not entail *AC*. Similarly, Z_0 together with the existence of a well-ordering of the universe (our *WOP*) implies global choice, but again the converse fails. Flannagan shows that there are many versions of the axiom of choice that are equivalent in *Z*2 but not in Z_0. The next subsection deals with the central notion of well-foundedness.

17. A structure M satisfying the axioms of set theory is an *ω-model* if the extension of 'finite ordinal' in M is isomorphic to the natural numbers (of a standard model). I presume that Putnam would not put it this way. The notion of constructibility emerges in Gödel's proof of the consistency of the axiom of choice and the continuum hypothesis. See, for example, Jech (1971, 1973).

18. First-order real analysis is an interesting, but different, case to be considered shortly.

19. Consider the set *S*1 of formulas Φ of the language of first-order set theory such that $\vdash_{D2} Z2 \to \Phi$. Although *S*1 is recursively enumerable (and thus is recursively axiomatizable), I know of no natural elegant presentation of it that does not explicitly refer to the second-order axiomatization. The usual first-order extensions of first-order *ZFC* whose set of deductive consequences include *S*1 are much stronger (in terms of relative consistency) than *Z*2.

20. For example, let M be an uncountable model of the set *AR*-1 of first-order arithmetic truths. A compactness argument establishes that there are *countable* non-standard models. Consider the language of arithmetic augmented with one individual constant e, and let Γ be the set of formulas

$$AR\text{-}1 \cup \{e \neq 0, e \neq s0, e \neq ss0, e \neq sss0, \ldots\}.$$

Clearly, Γ is consistent. By compactness, Γ is satisfiable, and by the downward Löwenheim–Skolem theorem, there is a countable model that satisfies every member of Γ. Such a model must be non-standard, since the denotation of e cannot be in the minimal closure of the denotation of 0 under the denotation of the successor function.

21. Let $a \in m$. Then, since m is transitive, every member of a is a member of m. Thus $a \subseteq m$, and a is countable.

22. This follows from the comprehension scheme of second-order logic.

23. Other definitions can be introduced to arithmetic that do not result in conservative extensions. For example, one can introduce a truth predicate T with the axioms

$$T(t_n) \equiv \Phi$$

where t_n is a numeral for a number n and Φ is the sentence with Gödel number n. By Tarski's theorem, the extended theory is not a conservative extension of arithmetic, but it is *semantically* eliminable and non-creative (see Parsons 1983, Essay 3).

24. The theory $AR1_2$ can characterize the syntax and proof theory of formal languages. Thus, if semantics is excluded, $AR1_2$ is a reasonable metatheory.

25. Since $AR1_2$ is a conservative extension of $AR1_1$, the expanded theory is what Mates (1972) calls non-creative (see note 6). It follows that multiplication is not eliminable. For a similar result concerning addition, see McNaughton (1965).

26. In fact, logicians sometimes use the term 'analysis' to refer to second-order arithmetic. The insight behind this is that, with appropriate 'coding' techniques, a theory of natural numbers and sets of natural numbers is a much better representation of traditional analysis than the theory of real closed fields. The coding is rather awkward and does not reflect the natural progress from arithmetic to analysis through the theory of rational numbers.

27. We can also add a new predicate letter N to the language of real analysis to represent the natural numbers. The intended meaning of Nx would be 'x is a natural number'. The additional axioms would be straightforward variations of those of first-order arithmetic (including the induction scheme). If the completeness scheme is extended to include formulas of the expanded language, the resulting theory is a better formalization of classical analysis (but it still lacks the important minimal closure construction).

28. But this may very well be a straw man. Few theorists consider first-order arithmetic to be an adequate representation of even basic number theory.

29. A function f is provably recursive in a theory A if there is a number e such that (1) e is the Gödel number of a recursive derivation of f, and (2) it is provable in A that the function whose derivation is coded by e is a total function (see Rogers 1967, pp. 305–6).

30. See the last section of Chapter 1 for further discussion of sets and classes in the context of set theory.

31. The last section of Chapter 9 is devoted to first-order set theory as a foundation of mathematics.

32. Parsons goes on to show that there is an interesting analogy between the notion of class and that of truth (or satisfaction). The concept of class 'answers to a . . . need to generalize on predicate places in the language' and truth serves as a 'means for generalizing *sentence* places' (or formula places in the case of satisfaction). Parsons notes that these generalizations are readily made in ordinary non-mathematical contexts. The various antinomies indicate that some care is required in set theory.

33. Frankel *et al.* (1973, Chapter 2, Section 7) contains an extensive account of the role of classes in set theory, discussing the difference between predicative and impredicative versions of set/class theory. Bernays (1961) shows how simple

versions of rather strong set theories can be formulated with an axiom scheme of reflection involving the impredicative concept of classes. Both this section of Fraenkel *et al.* (1973) (which was written by Levy) and Bernays (1961) are reprinted in Müller (1976), where the latter is translated into English. The reader interested in set/class theory would do well to consult the papers in that volume.

6

Advanced metatheory

The purpose of this chapter is to report a potpourri of results about second-order logic, with standard semantics. Most of the questions have their roots in philosophy, but philosophical interest is sometimes (although not always) left behind. Recall that in standard semantics, a second-order language $L2K$ has the same class of models as its first-order counterpart $L1K=$. Most of the items presented here involve the ability to make distinctions within this common framework.

Up until now, the metatheory underlying the semantics for our languages has been left at an informal level, with only an occasional reference to the resources it requires. In parts of this chapter we must be more explicit, and so the opening section is a discussion of the set theory underlying the model-theoretic semantics. In Section 6.2, we turn to reductions. There is a sense in which nth-order logic, for $n \geq 3$, is reducible to second-order logic. Thus the present focus on second-order logic is not arbitrary. There is an important distinction between the expressive resources of first-order languages and second-order languages, but resources are not significantly increased at yet higher levels. Section 6.3 concerns the use of the set-theoretic hierarchy to provide the semantics of second-order languages. The plausibility of this depends on certain reflection principles, and we enter the realm of so-called 'small large cardinals'. In Section 6.4, analogues of the Löwenheim–Skolem theorems are presented, entering the domain of 'large large cardinals'. Section 6.5 concerns various properties of semantics that, in effect, characterize first-order logic. It is sometimes held that these are in fact desirable properties for logic, but this is questioned. Finally, Section 6.6 concerns definability, and a few diverse matters of interest.

Many proofs are omitted, but references are provided. In several places, a grasp of (first-order) set theory is assumed.

6.1 A word on semantic theory

The bulk of the present chapter can be regimented in second-order set theory, called $ZFC2$. Its axiom is the single sentence $Z2$ introduced in Chapter 4. For the most part, however, the full impredicative nature of theory is not needed. We occasionally refer to proper classes, and find it convenient to employ variables ranging over classes, but von Neumann–Gödel–Bernays (*NGB*) set theory, a conservative extension of first-order *ZFC*, will suffice for most purposes. Moreover, as noted in the last section of the previous chapter, one can paraphrase much of the talk of classes away. But there is no reason to bother doing so, and, as above, it is a distraction to check each class definition to see if it is predicative or first-order definable.

In places, we need a deductive system even stronger than *ZFC2*, one capable of formulating a notion of satisfaction over structures whose domains are proper classes. Some notation is needed for this. Assume a fixed arithmetization of the formulas of a second-order language *L2K*. For each natural number n, let Φ_n be the formula with Gödel number n.

Define a *first-order variable assignment* to be a function whose domain is the set of first-order variables.[1] If $\langle x \rangle_n$ is a sequence of first-order variables $x_1, \ldots, x_n$, and b is a first-order variable assignment, let $b\langle x \rangle_n$ be the corresponding sequence of sets $b(x_1), \ldots, b(x_n)$. Let $A1(p, q)$ be a (first-order) formula asserting that 'p is a first-order variable assignment whose range is contained in q'. In other words, $A1(p, q)$ holds if and only if p is a function that assigns a member of q to each first-order variable of *L2K*. We also need a formula asserting that p is a first-order variable assignment whose range is contained in the class Q. For convenience, call it $A1(p, Q)$.

A *second-order variable assignment* is a function from the set of relation variables to a collection of *classes* and a function from the set of function variables to a collection of functions. To avoid an ascent to a third-order language, each such assignment is to be coded as a single class. The idea is to replace a (small) collection of classes by a class of sets. In particular, a second-order variable assignment is a collection B of pairs, such that if $\langle p, q \rangle \in B$ then p is either a relation variable or a function variable. If p is an n-place relation variable then q is an n-tuple, and B assigns the relation $\{q \mid \langle p, q \rangle \in B\}$ to p. If p is an n-place function variable, then $\{q \mid \langle p, q \rangle \in B\}$ is the graph of a function, and B assigns that function to p. Notice that B may be a proper class. If $\langle X \rangle_n$ is a sequence $X_1, \ldots, X_n$ of relation variables, then let $B\langle X \rangle_n$ be the corresponding sequence of relations, as assigned by B, and if $\langle f \rangle_n$ is a sequence of function variables, then let $B\langle f \rangle_n$ be the corresponding sequence of functions. Let $A2(P, Q)$ be a formula asserting that Q is not empty and, for each n, P assigns an n-place relation on Q to every n-place relation variable and P assigns an n-place function on Q to every n-place function variable. That is, $A2(P, Q)$ asserts that P is a second-order variable assignment on the domain Q. Again, for convenience, $A2(P, q)$, $A2(p, Q)$, and $A2(p, q)$ are understood similarly, with terms denoting sets in place of terms denoting classes.

As is well known, the relation of 'satisfaction by structures whose domain is a set' is definable in first-order set theory. In particular, there is a formula

sats(p, q, r, s), with only the four free variables listed, which asserts that

$A1(q, p)$ & $A2(r, p)$ & 'p satisfies Φ_s under assignments q and r'.

Assume that the metalanguage contains the non-logical terminology in K, or analogues thereof (in addition to the terminology for sets and classes). Then the 'definability' of satisfaction can be expressed in it. Let Φ be a formula of $L2K$ and let t be a term for either a class or a set. That is, t is either a monadic predicate variable, a non-logical monadic predicate letter, or a first-order term denoting a set. In the first two cases, we sometimes write $x \in t$ for tx, so that membership and predication are expressed with the same terminology. If X^n is a relation variable, then let $X^n \subseteq t^n$ be an abbreviation of $\forall \langle x \rangle_n (X^n \langle x \rangle_n \rightarrow (x_1 \in t \, \& \dots \& \, x_n \in t))$, and if f^n is a function variable, then let $f^n \mid t$ be an abbreviation of the assertion that f is *closed on* t, $\forall \langle x \rangle_n ((x_1 \in t \, \& \dots \& \, x_n \in t) \rightarrow f^n \langle x \rangle_n \in t)$. Finally, we write Φ/t for the *relativization* of Φ to t:

if Φ is atomic, then Φ/t is Φ,

$(\Phi \rightarrow \Psi)/t$ is $\Phi/t \rightarrow \Psi/t$,

$(\neg \Phi)/t$ is $\neg(\Phi/t)$,

$(\forall x \Phi)/t$ is $\forall x (x \in t \rightarrow \Phi/t)$,

$(\forall X^n \Phi)/t$ is $\forall X^n (X^n \subseteq t^n \rightarrow \Phi/t)$, and

$(\forall f^n \Phi)/t$ is $\forall f^n (f^n \mid t \rightarrow \Phi/t)$.

In sum, Φ/t is a formula in the metatheory that asserts that Φ holds on the domain t. Let $\Phi_n(\langle X \rangle_s, \langle f \rangle_t, \langle x \rangle_u)$ have only the free variables indicated by the sequences $\langle X \rangle_s, \langle f \rangle_t, \langle x \rangle_u$. The *Tarski formula of set satisfaction* for Φ_n is

$$(A1(q, p) \, \& \, A2(r, p)) \rightarrow [\textbf{sats}(p, q, r, n) \equiv \Phi_n(r\langle X \rangle_s, r\langle f \rangle_t, q\langle x \rangle_u)/p].$$

These formulas are all provable in the metatheory.

The stage is now set to expand the metalanguage to include a predicate for class satisfaction. Add a (higher-order) relation constant $SATS(P, q, R, m)$ whose intended interpretation is 'class P satisfies Φ_m under the assignments q and R'. Among the new axioms are

$SATS(P, q, R, m) \rightarrow m \in \omega$, $SATS(P, q, R, m) \rightarrow (A1(q, P) \, \& \, A2(R, P))$,

and, for each formula Φ_n in both $L2K$ and the metalanguage, the *Tarski formula of class satisfaction*

$$(A1(q, P) \, \& \, A2(R, P)) \rightarrow [SATS(P, q, R, n) \equiv \Phi_n(R\langle X \rangle_s, R\langle f \rangle_t, q\langle x \rangle_u)/P].$$

The expanded metatheory is hereby dubbed $ZFC2+$. It is not finitely axiomatized. Notice that for each sentence Φ of second-order set theory, the *truth* of Φ amounts to the satisfaction of Φ by the entire universe. Thus, $ZFC2+$ can express the truth of sentences of $ZFC2$ and, hence $ZFC2+$ is a genuine extension of $ZFC2$ by Tarski's theorem on the undefinability of truth.

6.2 Reductions

In the proof of the completeness of second-order logic with first-order or Henkin semantics, the language $L2K$ is treated as a multi-sorted first-order language, and the 'predication' (or membership) relation between objects and relations is taken to be non-logical (see Chapter 4, Section 4.3). A similar technique works for higher-order languages in general (see Henkin 1950). Notice also that the set-theoretic membership relation can be successfully characterized in a *second-order* language. There is, for example, a second-order sentence whose models are all and, up to isomorphism, only ranks V_α, where α is an ordinal (see, for example, Montague 1965). It follows that the predication relation, as construed by standard semantics, can also be characterized in a second-order language. These observations can be combined to produce a reduction, of sorts, of higher-order logic with standard semantics to second-order logic (also with standard semantics). In effect, the higher-order predication relation is treated as non-logical, and is given a second-order axiomatization.

We now sketch the essentials of an nth-order language LnK and its semantics, for $n > 2$. Recall that the second-order language $L2K$ contains variables (and quantifiers) over relations and functions. For simplicity, only *monadic* predicate variables and quantifiers are included in LnK. There are, for example, variables ranging over predicates of predicates, but not variables ranging over m-place relations of predicates, for any $m > 1$, nor are there any variables ranging over functions.[2]

Begin with the first-order language $L1K=$, as above. For each natural number i, such that $2 \leq i \leq n$, we introduce a stock of ith-order variables and quantifiers. These variables are upper-case italic letters, and the 'order' of each variable is indicated with a subscript. Thus P_4 is a fourth-order variable and X_6 is a sixth-order variable. If the context makes it clear, the subscripts may be omitted. As above, first-order variables are lower-case italic letters. The following formation clauses are added.

If P is an mth-order variable and Q is an $(m+1)$th-order variable, then QP is a well-formed formula.

If Φ is a well-formed formula and X is an mth-order variable, then $\forall X \Phi$ is a well-formed formula.

Thus, for example, $X_6 Y_5$ is well-formed. It indicates that a sixth-order predicate X_6 applies to a fifth-order predicate Y_5. Similarly, $\forall X_6 \exists Y_5 (X_6 Y_5)$ is well-formed. It expresses the falsehood that for every sixth-order predicate X_6 there is some fifth-order predicate Y_5 such that X_6 applies to Y_5.

The semantics is extended in the straightforward way. If $M = \langle d, I \rangle$ is a model of LnK (i.e. a model of $L1K$), the second-order variables range over the powerset of d, the third-order variables range over the powerset of the powerset of d, etc.

We now begin the reduction. Let $T_1, T_2, \ldots$ be a stock of non-logical predicate letters, let PR be a non-logical binary relation letter, and assume that none of these occur in the given set K of non-logical terms. Let $K' = K \cup \{PR, T_1, T_2, \ldots\}$. The idea is that T_m is to represent the range of the mth-order variables, so that $T_m(x)$ asserts that x corresponds to an mth-order item. The formula $PR(t, u)$ asserts that t represents a property that is predicated of the item represented by u. We next construct several mappings of the formulas in LnK to those of the first-order $L1K' =$ and its second-order counterpart $L2K'$.

First, fix a one-to-one *rewording function* from the variables of LnK onto those of $L1K$. For each variable X (or x) of LnK, let X' (or x') be the corresponding variable of $L1K$. Keep in mind that both X' and x' are *first-order* variables. The correspondence of the rewording function can be extended to the terms of LnK in a straightforward way: if t is a constant, then t' is t, and if t is $ft_1 \ldots t_m$, then t' is $ft'_1 \ldots t'_m$. Now, for each formula Φ of LnK, assign a formula Φ' of $L1K' =$ as follows.

If R is an m-place non-logical relation letter, then $(Rt_1 \ldots t_m)'$ is $Rt'_1 \ldots t'_n$.

If T is an mth-order variable and Y is an $(m + 1)$th-order variable, then $(YT)'$ is $PR(Y', T')$. $(\neg \Phi)'$ is $\neg (\Phi')$ and $(\Phi \to \Psi)'$ is $(\Phi') \to (\Psi')$.

If X is an mth-order variable, then $(\forall X \Phi)'$ is $\forall X'(T_m(X') \to (\Phi'))$.

The task at hand is to express the relation of 'predication' (represented by PR) among the surrogate 'properties'. It is a matter of asserting the following: (i) for each $m < n$, the extension of T_{m+1} is isomorphic to the powerset of the extension of T_m (with PR interpreted as membership); (ii) T_1 is not empty; (iii) the various T_i together exhaust the domain. This can be accomplished for finite collections of non-logical terminology. If K^- is a finite subset of K, then let STAN(K^-, n) be the conjunction of the following sentences of $L2K'$:

(1a) $T_1(c)$, for each constant c in K^-;

(1b) $\forall x_1 \ldots \forall x_m((T_1(x_1) \& \ldots \& T_1(x_m)) \to T_1(fx_1 \ldots x_m))$ for each m-place function letter f in K^-;

(1c) $\forall x_1 \ldots \forall x_m(Rx_1 \ldots x_m \to (T_1(x_1) \& \ldots \& T_1(x_m)))$ for each m-place relation letter R in K^-;

(2) $\exists x T_1(x)$;

(3) $\forall x(T_1(x) \vee \ldots \vee T_n(x))$;

(4) $\forall x \forall y((PR(y, x) \,\&\, YT_{m+1}(y)) \rightarrow T_m(x))$ for each m, $1 \leq m < n$;

(5) $\forall y \forall z((\neg T_1(y) \,\&\, \neg T_1(z) \,\&\, \forall x(PR(y, x) \equiv PR(z, x))) \rightarrow y = z)$;

(6) $\forall X \exists y(T_{m+1}(y) \,\&\, \forall x(PR(y, x) \equiv (Xx \,\&\, T_m(x))))$ for each m, $1 \leq m < n$.

Item (1a) asserts that all constants (in K^-) are in T_1, the 'range' of the items associated with first-order variables of LnK, item (1b) asserts that the function symbols are closed over this extension, and item (1c) asserts that the relation symbols range over this domain. Item (2) states that the extension of T_1 is not empty.[3] Item (3) asserts that the extensions of the various T_i exhaust the domain, while (4) says that if y is 'predicated' of x, then the 'order' of x is one less than the 'order' of y. Item (5) asserts that the 'predication' relation is extensional. Notice that (1a)–(5) are all first-order sentences. The only second-order item is (6), which has a single second-order universal quantifier whose scope is the entire formula. It is a comprehension principle of sorts, stating that for each set X, there is an $(m + 1)$th-order item y such that y is 'predicated' of exactly those mth-order items x that are in X.

For each sentence Φ of LnK, let $\Phi+$ be $\text{STAN}(K^-, n) \rightarrow \Phi'$, where K^- consists of the items of K that occur in Φ. Notice that $\Phi+$ is a second-order sentence (of $L2K'$). This completes the reduction. Let us see how it works. Let $\mathcal{P}$ be the powerset operator, and for each m let $\mathcal{P}^m$ be the m-fold powerset That is, $\mathcal{P}^0(a)$ is a, and $\mathcal{P}^{m+1}(a)$ is $\mathcal{P}(\mathcal{P}^m(a))$.

LEMMA 6.1.   Let $M = \langle d, I \rangle$ be a model of the language LnK. Then there is a model $M+ = \langle d+, I+ \rangle$ of $L2K'$ such that $M+ \vDash \text{STAN}(K^-, n)$ for each finite $K^- \subseteq K$ and for every sentence Φ of LnK

$$M \vDash \Phi \quad \text{iff} \quad M+ \vDash \Phi' \quad \text{iff} \quad M+ \vDash \Phi+.$$

Proof.   Let the domain $d+$ be $d \cup \mathcal{P}(d) \cup \ldots \cup \mathcal{P}^{n-1}(d)$. In $M+$, the items in K receive the same interpretation that they have in M. That is, $I+(c) = I(c)$ for each constant c, $I+(R) = I(R)$ for each relation letter R, and $I+(f)$ agrees with $I(f)$ on d for each function letter f (and it is stipulated that $I+(f)(x) = x$ for any x that is not in d). As for the new terminology, $I+(T_m) = \mathcal{P}^{m-1}(d)$ for each m, $1 \leq m \leq n$, and $I+(PR)$ is the set

$$\{\langle y, x \rangle \mid \text{there is an } m \text{ such that } 1 < m < n, \, y \in \mathcal{P}^m(d), \text{ and } x \in y\}.$$

That is, PR is interpreted as the 'real' membership relation on $d+$. It is straightforward to verify that $M+ \vDash \text{STAN}(K^-, n)$ and that $M \vDash \Phi$ iff $M+ \vDash \Phi'$ iff $M+ \vDash \Phi+$.   □

Notice that if the domain d of M is infinite and has cardinality λ, then the domain $d+$ of $M+$ has cardinality $|\mathcal{P}^{n-1}(\lambda)|$, which is larger than λ. There is a converse, of sorts, to Lemma 6.1.

LEMMA 6.2.   Let $M = \langle d, I \rangle$ be a model of $L2K'$ such that $M \vDash \text{STAN}(K^-, n)$ for each finite $K^- \subseteq K$. Then there is a model $M' = \langle d', I' \rangle$ of LnK such that, for each sentence Φ of LnK, $M' \vDash \Phi$ iff $M \vDash \Phi'$ iff $M \vDash \Phi+$.

Proof.   Let d' be the extension of T_1 in M, i.e. $d' = I(T_1)$, and let I' be the restriction of I to d so that M' is a submodel of M. Once again, it is straightforward to verify that $M' \vDash \Phi$ iff $M \vDash \Phi'$ iff $M \vDash \Phi+$.   □

These two lemmas give the basis of a reduction of nth-order logic to second-order logic.

THEOREM 6.3.   For each nth-order sentence Φ there is a second-order sentence $\Phi+$ such that if Φ is satisfiable then so is $\Phi+$, and Φ is a logical truth of LnK if and only if $\Phi+$ is a logical truth of $L2K'$.

Similarly, for each nth-order sentence Φ, Φ is satisfiable in LnK if and only if $\text{STAN}(K^-, n)$ & Φ is satisfiable in $L2K$ where, as above, K^- contains the non-logical terminology in Φ.

In a sense, Frege mounted a 'reduction' like this. In the systems developed by Frege (1884, 1893), which are higher-order, he associated each concept with an object in the range of the first-order variable, its extension. The membership relation, among extensions, corresponds to the predication relation among concepts. And membership is given a *second-order* treatment. Of course, Frege's system is inconsistent. The difference between it and the above is that, for Frege, the 'reduced' and the 'reducing' languages are the same, so that the range of the first-order variables in the treatment of membership is the same as the range of the first-order variables in the language we start with. By contrast, in the present case the range of the variables in $M+$, which interprets $L2K'$, goes well beyond the range of the variables in M, which interprets LnK. In effect, the first-order variables of $\text{STAN}(K^-, n)$ range over the union of the ranges of the first-order, second-order, ..., and nth-order variables of LnK. Cantor's theorem entails that the models M, $M+$ cannot have the same domain (but Frege did not think in terms of domains of discourse).[4]

The non-logical terminology introduced to define $\Phi+$ can be eliminated by a technique introduced above. In $\Phi+$, replace each occurrence of T_i with a monadic predicate variable Y_i that does not occur in Φ', and replace PR with a binary relation variable P^2 that also does not occur in Φ'. Call the result $\Phi++$. It is a *formula* of $L2K$ with $Y_1, \ldots, Y_n$ and P^2 free. Then Φ is a logical truth of LnK if and only if $\forall P^2 \forall Y_1 \ldots \forall Y_n(\Phi++)$ is a logical truth of $L2K$. In a similar fashion, there is a sentence χ of $L2K$ such that Φ is satisfiable in LnK if and only if χ is satisfiable in $L2K$.

If the set K of non-logical terminology contains enough items to formulate a pairing function on the domain, then the binary relation variable P^2 can be replaced with a monadic variable. As above, a binary relation is equivalent to a (monadic) property of pairs. In general, however, binary relation variables cannot be eliminated (see Chapter 9, Section 9.1 and Gurevich (1985)). Montague (1965) reports a result, attributed to David Kaplan, that indicates that what may be called 'binary second-order logic' is all that one needs:[5]

THEOREM 6.4 (Kaplan).   For each sentence Φ in $L2K$, there is a sentence Ψ such that Ψ contains no m-place relation variables with $m > 2$, and Ψ contains no function variables, such that for each model M, $M \vDash \Psi$ if and only if the domain of M is infinite and $M \vDash \Phi$.

To sum up, there is a sense in which nth-order logic is reducible to second-order logic and that second-order logic is reducible to 'binary second-order logic'. A significant reduction indeed.

It must be reported, however, that the reductions developed here are not perfect. Define a cardinal λ to be *second-order describable* if there is a sentence Φ of $L2$ (with no non-logical terminology) such that $M \vDash \Phi$ iff the cardinality of M is λ. And, for $n \geq 3$, define λ to be nth-*order describable* if there is a sentence Φ of LnK, with no non-logical terminology, such that $M \vDash \Phi$ iff the cardinality of M is λ. In the light of the above reductions, one might think that the set of second-order describable cardinals is exactly the set of mth-order describable cardinals, for any $m > 1$. Alas, the following is stated, but not proved, by Montague (1965).

THEOREM 6.5.   Let $n \geq 3$ and let λ be the smallest cardinal that is not nth-order describable. Then λ is $(n + 1)$th-order describable.

See Hintikka (1955), Montague (1965), and van Benthem and Doets (1983) for extensions and refinements of these results.[6]

6.3   Reflection: small large cardinals

Kreisel (1967, pp. 152–7) presents and defends a provocative informal principle of logical theory. Let Φ be a formula and, for each $i \in \omega$, let Φ^i indicate that Φ is of at most order i. In present terms, Φ^1 indicates that Φ is in $L1K$ and Φ^2 indicates that Φ is in $L2K$, for some set K of non-logical terminology. Kreisel begins by introducing an *informal* predicate **Val**Φ to mean that Φ is 'intuitively valid' or that Φ is 'true in all structures'. This is contrasted with a more precise predicate **V**Φ asserting that Φ is 'valid in all set-theoretic structures' or that Φ is 'true in all structures of the cumulative hierarchy'. The property **V** is what we call 'logical truth' in standard semantics. An example is used to indicate that the models referred to in the definition of the informal **Val** include those whose domains are proper classes, while those of **V** are restricted to iterative sets.

Let *Kreisel's principle* be the thesis that the informal predicate **Val** and its precise counterpart **V** are coextensive:

$$\forall \Phi (\mathbf{Val}\Phi \equiv \mathbf{V}\Phi).$$

This principle is an insightful *presupposition* of the use of the set-theoretic hierarchy to provide the semantics of formal languages. It is a version of our thesis (1b2) of Chapter 2, Section 2.4, the 'sufficiency' of the semantics:

> There are 'enough' models in the set-theoretic universe to serve semantics. In particular, if Φ is satisfied by every set-theoretic model, then Φ is true under every interpretation of the language.

In practice, the adequacy of the set-theoretic semantics is rarely questioned. If, however, Kreisel's principle were false, then there would be a sentence Φ such that Φ is satisfied by all set-theoretic models, but Φ is false in some 'other' interpretation. In such a case, the formal semantics would entail that Φ is a logical truth, but that would be 'incorrect'. To put the matter differently, our use of the set-theoretic hierarchy as the essential ingredient in the semantics of formal languages presupposes that for any sort of interpretation at all, there is a set-theoretic model that is equivalent to it (in some appropriate sense of 'equivalent'). In short, nothing less than the plausibility of the prevailing model-theoretic semantics is at stake with Kreisel's principle.

Despite the inherent informality of the predicate **Val**, Kreisel points out that one can actually *prove* the *first-order* version of the principle:

$$\forall \Phi^1 (\mathbf{Val}\Phi \equiv \mathbf{V}\Phi).$$

Of course, the word 'proof' is not understood here as a sequence of formulas in a deductive system, but rather as a compelling argument, Kreisel's 'informal rigour'. The first premise is the 'obvious' $\forall i \forall \Phi^i (\mathbf{Val}\Phi \rightarrow \mathbf{V}\Phi)$, every set-theoretic model is a legitimate interpretation of the language. This is what we call the *conformity* of the model-theoretic semantics. Let $\mathbf{D}\Phi$ assert that Φ is a theorem of our first-order deductive system $D1$. The second premise is $\forall \Phi^1 (\mathbf{D}\Phi \rightarrow \mathbf{Val}\Phi)$. This is verified by a straightforward examination of the axioms and rules of $D1$; they are surely correct no matter what the range of the variables. The final premise is the Gödel completeness theorem:[7] $\forall \Phi^1 (\mathbf{V}\Phi \rightarrow \mathbf{D}\Phi)$.

This reasoning does not generalize since, as shown in Chapter 4, Theorem 4.14, there is no completeness theorem for higher-order logic. For the second-order case, Kreisel points out that 'we do not have a convincing proof of' $\forall \Phi^2 (\mathbf{Val}\Phi \equiv \mathbf{V}\Phi)$, but he adds that 'one would expect one'.

In this section, an articulation and an extension of the second-order Kreisel principle are formulated. Each of the principles we present is equivalent to a second-order version of a set-theoretic 'principle of reflection' (see Levy 1960) which, in turn, is equivalent to a 'strong axiom of infinity'. Thus the acceptance of Kreisel's principle has consequences concerning the 'size' of the set-theoretic hierarchy.[8]

The only sort of 'non-set-theoretic' structures considered here are those whose domains are proper classes. Thus we do not actually leave the province of set theory, but we do go beyond first-order set theory and the members of the iterative hierarchy. For the rest of this section, all formulas are assumed to be at most second-order. It is convenient to reformulate Kreisel's principle in terms of satisfaction rather than validity. So let **Sat**Φ assert that there is a structure whose domain is a class (i.e. a collection of members of the set-theoretic hierarchy) that satisfies Φ, and let **S**Φ assert that there is a set-theoretic structure, one whose domain is a set, that satisfies Φ. Since every set is a class, (**S**$\Phi \to$ **Sat**Φ) holds, and Kreisel's principle amounts to

$$\forall \Phi(\mathbf{Sat}\Phi \to \mathbf{S}\Phi).$$

Kreisel's principle states that if there is a class that satisfies Φ, then there is a set that satisfies Φ.

We can restrict attention here to the second-order language $L2$ which has no non-logical terminology. No generality is lost because the satisfiability of a formula Φ of any language $L2K$ is equivalent to the satisfiability of the result of replacing each non-logical term in Φ with a variable.

Notice that a model of $L2$ is simply a domain of discourse, a set or a proper class. There is nothing else to 'interpret'. Two models are isomorphic if they have the same cardinality.

Of course, each formula of $L2$ is also a formula of the metatheory $ZFC2$ (see Section 6.1). If Φ is a formula of $ZFC2$ and E is a binary relation variable that does not occur in Φ, then let $(\Phi[E])$ be the formula of $L2$ obtained from Φ by replacing each subformula of the form $t \in u$ by Etu. We call $(\Phi[E])$ a *logic translate* of Φ.

It is easily seen that Kreisel's principle implies the existence of inaccessible cardinals and thus it is independent of $ZFC2$ (if consistent with it). Consider, for example, the sentence

$$ZL: \exists E(Z2[E]),$$

the existential generalization of a logic translate of the axiom of $ZFC2$. Since ZL is satisfied by the entire set-theoretic hierarchy, **Sat**(ZL) holds. This, together with Kreisel's principle, entails **S**(ZL), which asserts that there is a *set* that satisfies ZL. In $ZFC2$ this is equivalent to the existence of an inaccessible cardinal.

Following Levy, for each ordinal α, let $P(\alpha)$ be the αth inaccessible cardinal, provided that there are that many. That is, $P(\alpha)$ is the smallest inaccessible cardinal greater than every member of $\{P(\beta) \mid \beta < \alpha\}$. Let $EP(\alpha)$ be a formula that asserts the existence of $P(\alpha)$.

As it stands, the above formulation of Kreisel's principle involves the notion of 'satisfaction by a class'. Thus, taken literally, it cannot be stated in the language of $ZFC2$, but requires the extended $ZFC2+$ introduced in Section 6.1. However, there is a scheme of $ZFC2$ that captures much of its content.

If Φ is a sentence of $L2$ and t is a term for a set or class, then, as indicated in Section 6.1, (Φ/t) amounts to 't satisfies Φ'. Thus, if the variables x and X do not occur in Φ, then 'Φ is satisfiable by a class' is rendered $\exists X(\Phi/X)$, and 'Φ is satisfiable by a set' is rendered $\exists x(\Phi/x)$. The first formulation of Kreisel's principle is the scheme

$$(KP1) \quad \exists X(\Phi/X) \rightarrow \exists x(\Phi/x)$$

for each sentence Φ of $L2$ containing neither x nor X. Let $ZFC2 + KP1$ be the theory obtained from $ZFC2$ by adding each instance[9] of $KP1$ as an axiom.

In $ZFC2$, $KP1$ is equivalent to a second-order version of Levy's (1960, p. 1) 'principle of sentential reflection' (see Shapiro 1987):

> [Let Ψ be] any sentence of set theory. If Ψ holds, then there exists a standard model of [set theory] in which Ψ holds also.

In the present context, the 'language of set theory' is that of $ZFC2$, and a 'standard model' is an inaccessible rank (i.e. a model that satisfies $Z2$). It follows that there is no single sentence Φ in the language of $ZFC2$ such that $Z2 \& \Phi$ is both consistent and deductively implies each instance of $KP1$. That is, $ZFC2 + KP1$ has no consistent finitely axiomatized extension in the same language.[10]

The results of Levy (1960) can be carried out in $ZFC2 + KP1$.

THEOREM 6.6. For each natural number n, one can deduce that there are at least n inaccessibles from $ZFC2 + KP1$. That is, for each n,

$$ZFC2 + KP1 \vdash EP(n).$$

In a sense, this is the strongest result of this kind. The quantifier 'for each natural number n' cannot be 'transposed' across the 'one can deduce ...' phrase.

THEOREM 6.7.

$$Z2 \vdash \forall n \in \omega EP(n) \rightarrow Con(ZFC2 + KP1),$$

where $Con(ZFC2 + KP1)$ is the statement that $ZFC2 + KP1$ is consistent. Thus, $\forall n \in \omega EP(n)$ cannot be deduced from $ZFC2 + KP1$ (if the latter is consistent). *A fortiori*, neither can $EP(\omega)$.

Proof sketch.   It can be shown that for each instance Ψ of $KP1$ there is a natural number n such that Ψ holds at the nth inaccessible rank $V_{P(n)}$ (see Levy 1960). Similarly, for any *finite* collection Γ of instances of $KP1$ there is a natural number m such that every member of Γ is satisfied by $V_{P(m)}$. So, if $\forall n \in \omega EP(n)$, then every finite collection of instances of $KP1$ is satisfiable. This establishes the *deductive* consistency of $ZFC2 + KP1$. It follows that if $\forall n \in \omega EP(n)$ could be deduced from $ZFC2 + KP1$, then so could the consistency of $ZFC2 + KP1$, contradicting Gödel's second incompleteness theorem.   □

This is one more instance of the ω-incompleteness of theories containing arithmetic.

There is more to be said, however. Since there is no completeness theorem for second-order logic, a given theory may have semantic consequences that are not deductive consequences. From Theorem 6.6, for each natural number n, $ZFC2 + KP1 \vdash EP(n)$ and so $ZFC2 + KP1 \models EP(n)$. In all models of $ZFC2$ (i.e. all inaccessible ranks), the 'set of finite ordinals' is isomorphic to ω. Thus, in contrast with Theorem 6.7,

$$ZFC2 + KP1 \models \forall n \in \omega EP(n).$$

In effect, the reasoning that $\forall n \in \omega EP(n)$ is a semantic consequence of $ZFC2 + KP1$ refers to infinitely many instances of $KP1$. Indeed, as just noted, this formula is not a consequence of any theory consisting of $ZFC2$ plus a finite number of instances of $KP1$. Once again, second-order logic is not compact.

Applying the principle of sentential reflection to $\forall n \in \omega EP(n)$, we obtain the existence of an inaccessible rank that satisfies $\forall n \in \omega EP(n)$. Such a rank must be at least $V_{P(\omega)}$. Thus

$$ZFC2 + KP1 \models EP(\omega).$$

Applying the principle of sentential reflection to $EP(\omega)$, we obtain the existence of an inaccessible rank satisfying $EP(\omega)$. This must be at least $V_{P(\omega+1)}$, and so $ZFC2 + KP1 \models EP(\omega + 1)$. Similarly, $ZFC2 + KP1 \models EP(\omega + 2)$ etc. Notice that if $V_{P(\alpha)}$ satisfies every instance of $KP1$, then $ZFC2 + KP1$ does not imply $EP(\alpha)$. So, to determine the semantic strength of $KP1$, we describe the smallest model of $ZFC2 + KP1$.

Let Φ be a sentence of $ZFC2$ and α an ordinal. Say that Φ *describes* α if V_α satisfies Φ and, for each $\beta < \alpha$, V_β does not satisfy Φ. That is, Φ describes α if V_α is the smallest rank that satisfies Φ. Define α to be Π_0^2 *indescribable without parameters* iff there is no sentence Φ of $ZFC2$ such that Φ describes α. Notice that there are only countably many ordinals that are not indescribable without parameters.[11] The following is almost immediate.

THEOREM 6.8. $V_\kappa \models ZFC2 + KP1$ if and only if κ is both inaccessible and Π_0^2 indescribable without parameters.

It follows that $ZFC2 + KP1$ is satisfied by all but countably many inaccessible ranks. Following a construction suggested by Drake (1974, p. 276), there is an ordinal γ such that, for each $\alpha > \gamma$, $V_{P(\alpha)} \vDash ZFC2 + KP1$. Roughly speaking, $KP1$ holds at all sufficiently large inaccessible ranks. Similar considerations show that, for any cardinal κ with uncountable cofinality, there is an ordinal $\gamma < \kappa$ such that for any α such that $\gamma < \alpha < \kappa$, $V_{P(\alpha)} \vDash ZFC2 + KP1$. Letting κ be ω_1, we see that there is a *countable* ordinal α such that $V_{P(\alpha)}$ is a model of $ZFC2 + KP1$. Consequently, $ZFC2 + KP1$ does not imply the existence of uncountably many inaccessble cardinals. Thus, for example, $EP(\omega_1)$ is not a semantic consequence of $ZFC2 + KP1$.

Our second version of Kreisel's principle concerns sets of formulas. On an informal level, here it is.

> Let Γ be a set of formulas. If there is a class and an assignment that satisfies every member of Γ, then there is a set and assignment that also satisfies every member of Γ.

Here we do invoke the expanded metalanguage $ZFC2+$, with its explicit reference to satisfaction by classes. Let $L(x)$ be a formula of $ZFC2$ asserting that x is the Gödel number of a formula of $L2$ (i.e. a formula with no non-logical terminology). Our second articulation of Kreisel's principle is a single sentence in the language of $ZFC2+$:

$$(KP2) \quad \forall x \subseteq \omega((\forall z \in x L(z) \ \& \ \exists Y \exists Z \exists w \forall m \in x \, \mathbf{SATS}(Y, w, Z, m))$$
$$\rightarrow \exists y \exists z \exists w \forall m \in x \, \mathbf{sats}(y, w, z, m)).$$

Let $ZFC2 + KP2$ be the theory obtained from $ZFC2+$ by adding $KP2$. Notice, first, that the Tarski formulas allow the deduction of each instance of $KP1$ from $ZFC2 + KP2$. To obtain the instance of $KP1$ involving a sentence Φ_n, apply $KP2$ to the set $x = \{n\}$.

The reflection principle equivalent to $KP2$ states that for every set Γ of formulas of the language of $ZFC2$, if there is an assignment to the free variables that makes every member of Γ true, then there is a standard model of $ZFC2$ and an assignment that also satisfies every member of Γ. Recall that the notion of set-theoretic truth is definable in terms of class satisfaction. In effect, 'truth' is 'satisfaction by the universe'.

It was mentioned in the previous chapter that it can be shown in $ZFC2$ that there is a (countable) set that is *first-order* equivalent to the universe. In $ZFC2 + KP2$, there is a second-order analogue. Let t be the set of Gödel numbers of the true sentences of $ZFC2$. Applying the reflection principle to t, we obtain an inaccessible cardinal κ such that V_κ satisfies the sentences coded in t. Thus we have the following theorem.

THEOREM 6.9.   In $ZFC2 + KP2$ one can deduce the existence of a rank that satisfies all the true (second-order) sentences of $ZFC2$.

We conclude this section with a brief account of the semantic strength of $ZFC2 + KP2$. Let $V_{P(\delta)}$ be the smallest (standard) model of $ZFC2 + KP2$, provided, of course, that there is one. If $\alpha < \delta$, then $ZFC2 + KP2 \vDash EP(\alpha)$, but $ZFC2 + KP2$ does not imply $EP(\delta)$. The interesting fact here is that the cardinality of δ and thus the number of inaccessibles whose existence is implied by $ZFC2 + KP2$ is *independent* of $ZFC2+$. It can be shown that, as an ordinal, $\delta > \omega_1$ and hence $|\delta| \geq \aleph_1$, and it can be shown that the cardinality of δ is at most that of the continuum. Thus, if the continuum hypothesis is true, then δ has the cardinality of the continuum. But there is no theorem of $ZFC2+$ that fixes the cardinality of δ, even relative to that of the continuum. In effect, within the aforementioned bounds almost anything is possible. Proofs of the following are sketched in Shapiro (1987), pursuing some suggestions of Andreas Blass.

THEOREM 6.10.   Under the assumption that there are 'enough' inaccessibles (e.g. that $\forall \beta \in \omega_2 EP(\beta)$), the following are jointly consistent: (a) the continuum is large (e.g. greater than $\aleph_2$) and (b) there is a (standard) model of $ZFC2 + KP2$ which contains fewer than $\aleph_2$ inaccessibles. That is, there is an ordinal $\alpha < \omega_2$ such that $V_{P(\alpha)} \vDash ZFC2 + KP2$.

COROLLARY 6.11.   Under the assumptions of the previous theorem, it is consistent with $ZFC2+$ that $\forall \beta \in \omega_2 EP(\beta)$ is not a semantic consequence of $ZFC2 + KP2$.

THEOREM 6.12.   Assume $EP(\alpha)$ for each ordinal α whose cardinality is that of the continuum. Then the following are jointly consistent: (a) $ZFC2 + KP2$ is satisfiable; (b) the continuum is large, as large as it can be consistent with $ZFC2$; (c) there are no models of $ZFC2 + KP2$ containing fewer than 'continuum many' inaccessibles.

COROLLARY 6.13.   It is consistent with the satisfiability of $ZFC2 + KP2$ that $ZFC2 + KP2 \vDash EP(\omega_2)$.

In short, second-order set theory does not decide these statements of second-order consequence.

6.4 Löwenheim–Skolem analogues: large large cardinals

We have seen that the Löwenheim–Skolem theorems do not hold in the standard semantics of second-order languages (Chapter 4, Section 4.2). However, there are analogues of these results. Let K be a set of non-logical terminology and let LK be a language that contains $L1K=$ and has a semantics with the same class of models as that of $L1K=$. Consider the following definitions.[12]

> *Löwenheim number* for LK: the smallest cardinal κ such that for every formula Φ of LK, if Φ is satisfiable at all, then Φ has a model whose domain has cardinality at most κ.

Set-Löwenheim number for LK: the smallest cardinal κ such that for every set Γ of formulas of LK, if there is a model (and assignment) that satisfies every member of Γ, then there is a model (and assignment) whose domain has cardinality at most κ that satisfies every member of Γ.

Hanf number for LK: the smallest cardinal κ such that for every formula Φ of LK, if Φ has a model whose domain has cardinality at least κ, then there is no upper bound on the size of the models of κ, i.e. if Φ has a model of cardinality κ or greater, then for each cardinal δ, Φ has a model whose domain has cardinality at least δ.

Set-Hanf number for LK: the smallest cardinal κ such that for every set Γ of formulas of LK, if there is a model (and assignment) whose domain has cardinality at least κ that satisfies every member of Γ, then for every cardinal δ, there is a model (and assignment) whose domain has cardinality at least δ that satisfies every member of Γ.

The Hanf number, the set-Hanf number, and the Löwenheim number of the first-order $L1K=$ (and $L1K$) are all $\aleph_0$, of course, and the set-Löwenheim number of $L1K=$ is the maximum of $\aleph_0$ and the cardinality of K. This is a summary of the Löwenheim–Skolem theorems. As we have seen, things are not this simple in the case of $L2K$, or higher-order languages in general.[13] Here, we again enter the realm of large cardinals, but this time we require so-called 'large large cardinals' (in contrast with the results of the previous section and Shapiro (1987), which only involve 'small large cardinals').

THEOREM 6.14.   If the collection of formulas of LK is a set (i.e. not a proper class), then LK has a Löwenheim number, a set-Löwenheim number, a Hanf number, and a set-Hanf number.

Proof.   For each formula Φ of LK, let $L(\Phi)$ be the cardinality of the smallest model of Φ, provided that Φ is satisfiable, and let $L(\Phi)$ be the empty set otherwise. Let $H(\Phi)$ be the least upper bound of the cardinalities of the models of Φ, provided that there is such a bound, and let $H(\Phi)$ be the empty set otherwise.[14] Similarly, for each set Γ of formulas of LK, let $L(\Gamma)$ be the cardinality of the smallest model of Γ, provided that Γ is satisfiable, and let $H(\Gamma)$ be the least upper bound of the cardinalities of the models of Γ, provided that there is such a bound. Then the Löwenheim number of LK is the least upper bound of $\{L(\Phi) \mid \Phi$ is a formula of $LK\}$, the set-Löwenheim number is the least upper bound of $\{L(\Gamma) \mid \Gamma$ is a set of formulas of $LK\}$, the Hanf number of LK is the least cardinal strictly larger than every member of $\{H(\Phi) \mid \Phi$ is a formula of $LK\}$, and the set-Hanf number of LK is the least cardinal strictly larger than every member of $\{H(\Gamma) \mid \Gamma$ is a set of formulas of LK $\}$.   □

Notice that this proof is extremely abstract. Although it is rather simple, the argument uses a substantial amount of set theory, involving impredicative use of the axiom of replacement. We have no idea, so far, how large these numbers are, even for a language like $L2$, pure second-order logic.

Barwise (1972) shows that in the case of the Hanf number of second-order logic, this impredicative proof is the best we can do. Consider the language of first-order set theory augmented with a function symbol $\mathscr{P}$ for the powerset operation. Let Z be the first-order axioms of *Zermelo set theory* formulated for this language. It is like ZFC except that, instead of replacement, it contains a separation scheme

$$\forall x \exists y \forall z (z \in y \equiv (z \in x \ \& \ \Phi(z)))$$

for each formula Φ of the language not containing y free.[15] There is also an axiom for the symbol $\mathscr{P}$:

$$\forall x \forall y (y \in \mathscr{P}(x) \equiv \forall z (z \in y \rightarrow z \in x)).$$

Call the opening quantifier in a formula of the form $\forall x (x \in t \rightarrow \Phi)$ a *bounded quantifier*. A formula in the present language is called $\Sigma_1(\mathscr{P})$ if it is in the form $\exists x \Psi$, where all the quantifiers in Ψ are bounded. Let $ZFC-$ be the (first-order) theory whose axioms are those of Z together with all instances of the replacement scheme

$$\forall x \forall y \forall z (\Phi(x, y) \ \& \ \Phi(x, z) \rightarrow y = z) \rightarrow$$

$$\forall x \exists y \forall z (z \in y \equiv \exists w (w \in x \ \& \ \Phi(w, z)))$$

in which the formula Φ is $\Sigma_1(\mathscr{P})$ (and does not contain y free).

Barwise suggests that even though $ZFC-$ falls short of first order ZFC, it is a rather strong theory: '[It] seems safe to claim that $[ZFC-]$ is strong enough to prove any theorem of classical mathematics provable in [first-order ZFC]'.[16] But $ZFC-$ is not strong enough to deduce the existence of the Hanf number of second-order logic—not by a long shot.

THEOREM 6.15 (Barwise 1972).   It can be deduced from $ZFC-$ that if κ is the Hanf number of $L2$, pure second-order logic, then its rank V_κ is a model of $ZFC-$. Moreover, there are κ-many cardinals δ such that $\delta < \kappa$ and V_δ is a model of $ZFC-$.

The fact that the existence of the Hanf number of $L2$ cannot be proved in $ZFC-$ is a corollary of this theorem and Gödel's second incompleteness theorem.

Here is another 'application' reported by Barwise (1972). Let F be a function on the class of cardinal numbers. Define F to be a *Löwenheim function* for a logic LK if for each sentence Φ of LK and each cardinal λ, if Φ has a model whose domain has cardinality at least λ, then Φ has a model whose domain has cardinality at least λ and at most $F(\lambda)$. The function that assigns $\lambda + \aleph_0$ to λ is a Löwenheim function for the first-order $L1K =$. Considerations like the proof of Theorem 6.14 indicate that there is such a function for $L2$, but it seems that there is no reasonable definition of one. Define G to be $\Sigma_1(\mathscr{P})$-*definable* if there is a $\Sigma_1(\mathscr{P})$ formula $\Phi(x, y)$ such that, for each cardinal λ, $G(\lambda)$ is the unique cardinal μ such that $\Phi(\lambda, \mu)$. Barwise (1972) shows that there is no $\Sigma_1(\mathscr{P})$-definable Löwenheim function for $L2$.

THEOREM 6.16. Let G be a $\Sigma_1(\mathscr{P})$-definable function on cardinals such that, for each λ, $G(\lambda) \geq \lambda$. Then there is a sentence Φ of $L2$ such that, for each cardinal κ, there is a cardinal $\lambda > \kappa$ such that Φ has a model whose domain has cardinality at least λ, but none whose domain has cardinality between λ and $G(\lambda)$.

Recall from Section 6.1 that if Φ is a formula of set theory and t a term for a set or class, then Φ/t is the result of restricting the bound variables of Φ to t. For convenience, we repeat the definition in the context of second-order languages. Let Φ be a formula of $L2K$ and T a predicate term (variable or constant). Then let Φ/T be the *relativization of Φ to T*:

if Φ is atomic, then Φ/T is Φ,
$(\Phi \to \Psi)/T$ is $\Phi/T \to \Psi/T$,
$(\neg \Phi)/T$ is $\neg(\Phi/T)$,
$(\forall x\Phi)/T$ is $\forall x(Tx \to \Phi/T)$,
$(\forall X^n\Phi)/T$ is $\forall X^n(\forall x_1 \ldots \forall x_n(X^n x_1 \ldots x_n$
$$\to (Tx_1 \& \ldots \& Tx_n)) \to \Phi/T), \text{ and}$$
$(\forall f^n\Phi)/T$ is $\forall f^n[\forall x_1 \ldots \forall x_n((Tx_1 \& \ldots \& Tx_n) \to Tfx_1 \ldots x_n) \to \Phi/T]$.

In short, Φ/T means that Φ holds when the extension of T is taken as the domain of discourse.

We now take up the *cofinality* of the various numbers for second-order languages with standard semantics. It happens that these are rather small. It is noted above (in several places) that the satisfaction of a formula of $L2K$ is equivalent to that of the sentence of $L2$ (pure second-order logic) obtained by replacing each non-logical term with an appropriate variable, and binding the result with existential quantifiers (Ramsey). Thus, for single formulas, we can focus on sentences of $L2$ without loss of generality.

THEOREM 6.17. The Löwenheim number and the Hanf number of $L2$ each have cofinality ω.

Proof.
1. The proof of Theorem 6.14 shows that the Löwenheim number of $L2$ is the least upper bound of a countable set $\{L(\Phi) \mid \Phi$ is a sentence of $L2\}$ of cardinals. We only need to establish that this set has no maximum. Suppose that Φ is a satisfiable sentence of $L2$ and that $L(\Phi) = \lambda$, so that

the smallest model of Φ has cardinality λ. Let X be a predicate variable that does not occur in Φ and consider the sentence

$$\Phi': \exists X[\exists x Xx \ \& \ \exists Z(|X| \leq |Z| \ \& \ \neg|X| = |Z| \ \& \ \Phi/X)].$$

This sentence asserts that there is a non-empty class X such that Φ holds relative to X, and X is smaller than the domain. Clearly, Φ' has a model of cardinality λ^+ and this is its smallest model. So $L(\Phi') > \lambda$.

2. It was also shown in the proof of Theorem 6.14 that the Hanf number of $L2$ is the least cardinal larger than every element of the countable set $\{H(\Phi) \mid \Phi$ is a sentence of $L2\}$. Again, it suffices to establish that this set has no maximum. So suppose that Φ is a sentence such that $H(\Phi) = \lambda$ and λ is not empty. The first step is to find a sentence Φ_1 such that $H(\Phi_1) = \lambda$ and Φ_1 has a model of cardinality λ (so that λ is the cardinality of the *largest* model of Φ_1). If Φ itself has a model of cardinality λ, then we let Φ_1 be Φ. Otherwise, λ is the union of the cardinalities of the models of Φ. In Chapter 5, Section 5.1.3, we define a formula $WO(R, X)$ of $L2$ that asserts that R is a well-order of X. Let $WO(R)$ be $\forall X(\forall x Xx \rightarrow WO(R, X))$, which asserts that R is a well-order of the whole domain. Let Φ_1 be the following sentence:

$$\exists R[WO(R) \ \& \ \forall x \exists y(Rxy \ \& \ \forall Z(\forall z(Zz \equiv Rzy) \rightarrow \Phi/Z))].$$

In words, Φ_1 asserts that there is a well-order R on the domain such that for every x there is a y such that Rxy (i.e. x is less than y in the well-order), and Φ holds relative to $\{z \mid Rzy\}$. Since λ is the limit of the cardinalities of models of Φ, there is a model of Φ_1 of cardinality λ, and there can be no larger model. Thus $H(\Phi_1) = \lambda$. Now consider the sentence

$$\Phi': \exists X\{\exists x Xx \ \& \ \forall Z[\forall z Zz \rightarrow (\neg|X| = |Z| \ \& \ \forall Y(|X| \leq |Y|$$
$$\rightarrow (|X| = |Y| \vee |Y| = |Z|)))] \ \& \ \Phi_1/X\}.$$

The sentence Φ' asserts that there is a set X such that Φ_1 holds relative to X, that X is smaller than the domain, and that there are no cardinalities between that of X and that of the domain. Clearly, Φ' has a model of cardinality λ^+, and has no larger model. Thus $H(\Phi') > \lambda$. □

We now turn to the set-Löwenheim number and the set-Hanf number of $L2K$. If the set K of non-logical terms is either finite or denumerably infinite, then no generality is lost in assuming that K is empty, since each non-logical item can be replaced with an appropriate variable.

THEOREM 6.18. The cofinalities of the set-Löwenheim number and the set-Hanf number of $L2$ are *at most* the cardinality of the continuum.

Proof.
1. The case of the set-Löwenheim number is similar to that of the Löwenheim number. The proof of Theorem 6.14 shows the set-Löwenheim number

to be the least upper bound of a set $S = \{L(\Gamma) \mid \Gamma$ is a set of formulas of $L2\}$ whose cardinality is that of the continuum. We only need to establish that this set has no maximum. Let Γ be a satisfiable set of formulas and let $L(\Gamma) = \lambda$, so that λ is the cardinality of the smallest model of Γ. If necessary, uniformly reletter the formulas in Γ so that the predicate variable X does not occur. Consider the set

$$\Gamma': \{\exists Z(|X| \leq |Z| \& \neg |X| = |Z|)\} \cup \{\Phi/X \mid \Phi \in \Gamma\}.$$

The *formulas* in Γ' together assert that every formula in Γ holds relative to X and that there is a set larger than X. Thus the smallest model of Γ' has cardinality λ^+, so $L(\Gamma') > \lambda$.

2. Again, the proof of Theorem 6.14 shows that the set-Hanf number of $L2$ is the smallest cardinal strictly greater than every member of a set $\{H(\Gamma) \mid \Gamma$ a set of formulas of $L2\}$ whose cardinality is that of the continuum. And again, we need to show that this set has no maximum. So let Γ be a set of formulas and let $H(\Gamma) = \lambda$. Assume that λ is not empty. We first find a set Γ_1 such that $H(\Gamma_1) = \lambda$ and Γ_1 has a model of cardinality λ, so that λ is the cardinality of the *largest* model of Γ_1. If Γ already has a model of cardinality λ, then we set $\Gamma_1 = \Gamma$. If not, uniformly reletter the formulas in Γ so that neither the binary relation variable R nor the predicate variable I occurs. Define $R'xy$ to be the formula

$$Rxy \& \neg Iy \& \forall z[(Rxz \& Rzy) \rightarrow \neg Iz].$$

If R is thought of as an ordering, then $R'xy$ asserts that y is greater than x in this ordering and nothing in the extension of I lies between x and y. For each x, let R'_x be $\{y \mid R'xy\}$, the set of elements between x and the 'next' element of I. Finally, let Γ_1 be the set of formulas consisting of the following: (i) the statement $WO(R)$ that R is a well-ordering of the whole domain; (ii) the statement that I holds of the 'first' element of R, $\forall x(\forall y(y \neq x \rightarrow Rxy) \rightarrow Ix)$; (iii) the statement that I is not 'bounded' in R, $\forall x \exists y(Rxy \& Iy)$; (iv) a formula asserting that for each x and y, if Rxy and Ix and Iy, then the cardinality of R'_x is smaller than that of R'_y; (v) for each $\Phi \in \Gamma$, a formula asserting that, for each x, if Ix then Φ is satisfied in R'_x. In other words, the formulas in Γ_1 together entail that R is a well-ordering and, in this order, I divides the domain into pieces, each of which is a model of Γ, and any two distinct pieces have different cardinalities. Thus, models of Γ_1 are obtained by 'piecing together' models of Γ with different cardinalities. Since $H(\Gamma) = \lambda$, there is a model of Γ_1 of cardinality λ, and there is no larger model. To complete the proof, reletter the formulas in Γ_1 so that the predicate variable W does not occur, and let Γ' be the set

$$\{\forall Z(\forall x Zx \rightarrow (\neg |W| = |Z| \rightarrow \forall Y((\neg |Y| = |Z|)$$
$$\rightarrow |Y| \leq |W|)))\} \cup \{\Phi/W \mid \Phi \in \Gamma_1\}.$$

Again these formulas entail that W is smaller than the domain, there is no set whose cardinality lies between that of W and that of the domain, and every member of Γ_1 holds relative to W. The largest model of Γ' has cardinality λ^+, so $H(\Gamma') > \lambda$.   ☐

THEOREM 6.19.   The cofinalities of the set-Löwenheim number and the set-Hanf number[17] of $L2$ are *at least* $\aleph_1$.

Proof.

1. Let $\Gamma_0, \Gamma_1, \ldots$ be a denumerably infinite sequence of (satisfiable) sets of formulas of $L2$. For each i, let $L(\Gamma_i) = \lambda_i$. In the light of the proof of the previous theorem, it suffices to establish the existence of a set Γ of formulas of $L2$ such that $L(\Gamma) \geq \lambda_i$ for each i. If necessary, uniformly reletter the formulas in $\Gamma_0, \Gamma_1, \ldots$ so that the binary relation variable R and the individual variables $m_0, m_1, \ldots$ do not occur. Let Γ be the set of formulas consisting of the following: (i) the statement $WO(R)$ that R is a well-ordering of the whole domain; (ii) for each i, the formula $Rm_i m_{i+1}$; (iii) for each i, the set of formulas asserting that each member of Γ_i is satisfiable in the domain $\{x \mid x = m_i \vee (Rm_i x \ \& \ Rxm_{i+1})\}$ (i.e. the set of elements of the domain between m_i and m_{i+1}). Again, models of Γ are obtained by 'piecing together' models of each Γ_i. Moreover, any model of Γ contains a model of each Γ_i. So $L(\Gamma) \geq \lambda_i$.

2. Let $\Gamma_0, \Gamma_1, \ldots$ be a denumerably infinite sequence of sets of formulas of $L2$. For each i, let $H(\Gamma_i) = \lambda_i$ and assume that λ_i is not empty. Again, in the light of the previous theorem, it suffices to find a set Γ' of formulas of $L2$ such that $H(\Gamma') \geq \lambda_i$, for each i. By a construction in the proof of the previous theorem, we can assume that each Γ_i has a model of cardinality λ_i. If necessary, uniformly reletter the formulas in $\Gamma_0, \Gamma_1, \ldots$ so that the binary relation variables R, S, the predicate variable I, and the individual variables $m_0, m_1, \ldots$ do not occur. Let Γ be the set of formulas obtained by the construction of part 1. For present purposes, we need to supplement this set with formulas indicating that m_0 is the 'first' element in the relation R and that the collection $\{m_0, m_1, \ldots\}$ is unbounded in R. This is readily accomplished. Let Γ' be the set obtained from Γ by adding (i) the formula $\forall x(x \neq m_0 \to Rm_0 x)$; (ii) the statements that S is one-to-one, I is the minimal closure of m_0 under S, and the extension of I is unbounded in R; (iii) for each i, the formulas Im_i and $Sm_i m_{i+1}$. The domain of any model of Γ' is precisely the union of sets $\{x \mid x = m_i \vee (Rm_i x \ \& \ Rxm_{i+1})\}$, each of which is a model of the respective Γ_i. Thus, a maximal model of Γ' is obtained by piecing together maximal models of each Γ_i for each i.   ☐

Theorem 6.15 indicates that the Hanf number of $L2$ is rather large. As will be seen, the other numbers are large as well. Yet the last three theorems indicate that their cofinalities are relatively small. In a sense, the size of these numbers is independent of ZFC (provided only that the existence of an inaccessible cardinal is consistent with it). Notice, first, that if there is a sentence Φ that is a categorical characterization of a model of cardinality λ, then all four numbers are larger than λ. As above, let $Z2$ be the conjunction of the axioms of second-order ZFC, and let NI be a sentence asserting that there are no inaccessible cardinals. Then $Z2$ & NI is a categorical characterization of the first inaccessible rank. Once again, there is a similar sentence in the language $L2$ (with no non-logical terminology). Thus, if there is an inaccessible cardinal, all four numbers are greater than the first one. If there are no inaccessible cardinals, then all four numbers are 'accessible'. Similarly, if there are at least twelve inaccessibles, then the four numbers are all larger than the twelfth, since the conjunction of $Z2$ with the statement that there are exactly eleven inaccessibles is a categorical characterization of the twelfth inaccessible rank. Again, if there is a Mahlo cardinal, then all four numbers are larger than the first, and if there is a fixed point in the hierarchy of Mahlo cardinals, then the numbers are larger than the first one. As promised, we enter the realm of 'large large' cardinals. Let κ be the first measurable cardinal, if there is one. There is a second-order categorical characterization[18] of $V_{\kappa + 2}$. Thus, if there is a measurable cardinal, then all four numbers are greater than the first one. Similarly, if there are nine measurable cardinals, then the numbers are above the ninth, and if there is a fixed point in the hierarchy of measurable cardinals, then the numbers are above the first one.

This feature of the Löwenheim and Hanf numbers is a direct result of the expressive power of second-order languages. See Hasenjaeger (1967) for an insightful discussion of the Löwenheim number (and set-Löwenheim number) of second-order logic (not by those names) and the role of metatheory in these considerations.

If the set-theoretic universe is large enough (so to speak), upper bounds for these numbers can be given. I am indebted to Robert Solovay and Matthew Foreman for their insight on these matters.

A property $P(x)$ of sets is said to be *local* if there is a formula $\Psi(x)$ of first-order set theory such that for each x, $P(x)$ holds if and only if $\exists\delta(V_\delta \vDash \Psi(x))$. The idea is that local properties are those with a characterization that only refers to the sets below a fixed rank. One does not need to refer to 'arbitrarily large' sets in order to state that a given set has the property. Local properties of cardinals include inaccessible, Mahlo, hyper-Mahlo, and measurable. As in the proof of Theorem 6.14, if Φ is a satisfiable formula of a second-order language, let $L(\Phi)$ be the cardinality of the smallest model of Φ, so that the Löwenheim number of this language is the least upper bound of $\{L(\Phi) \mid \Phi$ is a formula$\}$.

LEMMA 6.20. Let $P(x)$ be a local property of cardinals and let κ be the smallest cardinal that has this property. Then there is a sentence Φ of second-order set theory such that $\kappa \leq L(\Phi)$.

Proof. Suppose that P is characterized by $\exists\delta(V_\delta \vDash \Psi(x))$. By hypothesis, there is an ordinal δ such that $V_\delta \vDash \Psi(\kappa)$. Let α be the smallest ordinal β such that there is a cardinal $\lambda < \beta$ where $V_\beta \vDash \Psi(\lambda)$. Evidently, for any such λ, $P(\lambda)$ and so $\kappa \leq \lambda$. Thus $\kappa \leq \alpha$. Let R be a sentence of second-order set theory whose models are all and, up to isomorphism, only the ranks V_γ, where γ is an ordinal (such a sentence is given by Montague (1965)). Consider the sentence

$$\Phi: \quad R \ \& \ \exists x \Psi(x).$$

By hypothesis, α is the smallest ordinal β such that V_β satisfies Φ. Therefore $L(\Phi) = |V_\alpha|$, the cardinality of V_α. And $\kappa \leq \alpha \leq |V_\alpha| = L(\Phi)$. $\qquad\square$

There is also a converse.

LEMMA 6.21. Suppose that Φ is a satisfiable sentence of $L2$. Then there is a local property of cardinals P such that $\exists\delta P(\delta)$ and, for every cardinal λ, if $P(\lambda)$ then $L(\Phi) \leq \lambda$.

Proof. Let t be a term of set theory that does not occur in Φ. By techniques introduced above, it is straightforward to construct a formula, which we again call Φ/t, of first-order set theory that amounts to 'Φ is satisfied by the domain t'. Suppose that the variables x, δ, and κ do not occur in Φ. Consider the property $P(\kappa)$ characterized by a formula asserting that there is an ordinal δ such that κ is a cardinal, $\kappa \in \delta$, and there is an $x \in V_\kappa$ such that $V_\delta \vDash (\Phi/x)$. Clearly, P is local. If m is the domain of a model of Φ, then Φ/m will hold in any rank V_δ where δ is a limit ordinal greater than any cardinal κ such that m is in V_κ. Thus, for any such κ, $P(\kappa)$. Moreover, for any cardinal λ, if $P(\lambda)$, then V_λ contains a model of Φ and thus $\lambda \geq L(\Phi)$. $\qquad\square$

Define a cardinal λ to be *minimal-local* if there is a local property P of cardinals such that λ is the smallest cardinal that has the property P. For example, the first inaccessible cardinal, the first Mahlo cardinal, the first measurable cardinal, and the first fixed point in the list of measurable cardinals are all minimal-local (provided, of course, that such cardinals exist). The last two lemmas yield the following theorem.

THEOREM 6.22. The Löwenheim number of $L2$ is the least upper bound of the set of all minimal-local cardinals.

The notion of a *supercompact* cardinal is not locally defined. Solovay *et al.* (1978, p. 86) point out that if κ is supercompact and P is a local property of cardinals, then if any cardinal has P, there is a cardinal $\lambda < \kappa$ such that λ has P. It follows (from Lemma 6.21) that the first supercompact cardinal, if there is one, is (much) greater than the Löwenheim number of $L2$. In fact, Magidor (1971) established that the first supercompact cardinal has a certain downward Löwenheim–Skolem property for higher-order logic.[19]

THEOREM 6.23 (Magidor 1971, p. 151). Let κ be supercompact and let $M = \langle d, I \rangle$ be a model of an nth-order language (for some finite n). If Φ is a sentence of this language such that $M \vDash \Phi$, then there is a subset $d' \subseteq d$ such that the cardinality of d' is less than κ and the corresponding substructure $M' = \langle d', I' \rangle$ also satisfies Φ. Moreover, the first supercompact cardinal is the smallest cardinal that has this property.

Solovay has indicated that if the set K of non-logical terminology is countable and if there is a supercompact cardinal, then the set-Löwenheim number of $L2K$ is smaller than the first supercompact cardinal. In general, if λ is the cardinality of K, then the set-Löwenheim number of $L2K$ is smaller than the least supercompact cardinal greater than λ (provided, of course, that there is one).

An upper bound for the Hanf number and the set-Hanf number of second-order languages is a consequence of another result of Magidor (1971). He shows that a certain analogue of compactness applies to *extendible* cardinals.

If λ is a cardinal, then define a logic L to be λ-*compact* if for every set Γ of formulas of L, if every subset of Γ whose cardinality is smaller than λ is satisfiable, then Γ itself is satisfiable. Thus, for example, Gödel's completeness theorem entails that first-order logic is $\aleph_0$-compact (which, of course, is usually called 'compact'), and this justifies the upward Löwenheim–Skolem theorem (see Chapter 4, Section 4.1).

THEOREM 6.24 (Magidor 1971, p. 155). If κ is an extendible cardinal, then for any natural number n, nth-order logic is κ-compact.[20] Moreover, κ is the first extendible if and only if κ is the smallest cardinal λ such that any second-order language ($L2K$) is λ-compact.

COROLLARY 6.25. If there is an extendible cardinal, then the Hanf number and the set-Hanf number for any $L2K$ are at most the first extendible cardinal.

Proof. This is a compactness argument. Let κ be the first extendible cardinal and suppose that a set Γ of formulas of $L2K$ has a model M whose cardinality is at least κ. We need to show that if λ is any cardinal, then Γ has a model whose cardinality is at least λ. Add λ-many new constants $\{a_\alpha \mid \alpha < \lambda\}$ to the set K of non-logical terminology and consider the set of formulas

$$\Gamma' = \Gamma \cup \{a_\alpha \neq a_\beta \mid \alpha < \beta < \lambda\}$$

of the extended language. Let A be any subset of Γ' such that $|A| < \kappa$. Then, since the domain of the model M (of Γ) has cardinality at least κ, M can be extended to a model of A. Thus A is satisfiable. By Theorem 6.24, Γ' has a model. But any model of Γ' is a model of Γ whose domain has cardinality at least λ.   □

Of course, since the Hanf number of $L2$ has cofinality ω (Theorem 6.17), it must be less than the first extendible. Similarly, if the cardinality of K is finite, but less than the first extendible, then, since the cofinality of the set-Hanf number of $L2K$ has cofinality at most $2^{|K|}$ (a straightforward extension of Theorem 6.18), it must also be less than the first extendible. Notice, however, that Theorem 6.24 does not depend on the size of the language. The first extendible cardinal is a bound on the set-Hanf number of any second-order (or nth-order) language, no matter how large it is.

Solovay has indicated (in correspondence) that this upper bound is probably the best we can expect. Considerations like those mentioned above entail that if there are at least, say, 106 supercompact cardinals, then the Hanf number of $L2$ must be greater than the 106th supercompact cardinal. Moreover, the Hanf number must also be greater than the first of a large variety of supercompact cardinals (all of which exist if there is an extendible and, under that assumption, are less than the first extendible). He also indicated that the first extendible (if there is one) is *exactly* the set-Hanf number of what may be called 'full second-order logic', the logic of a second-order language with no restrictions on the non-logical terminlogy. It is equivalent to $L2K$ in which K is a proper class.

The interested reader may consult Garland (1974), Baldwin (1985), Barwise (1985), and Ebbinghaus (1985) in addition to the works already cited (Hasenjaeger 1967, Magidor 1971, Barwise 1972, Drake 1974, Solovay *et al.* 1978) for refinements and extensions of the concepts and results reported here.

6.5   Characterizations of first-order logic

As usual, let K be a set of non-logical terminology. It is convenient to assume that K contains infinitely many constants and relation symbols of each degree. Let LK be a language that contains $L1K=$, and assume that if Φ and Ψ are formulas in LK, then so are $\neg\Phi$, $\Phi \rightarrow \Psi$, and $\exists x\Phi$ for each first-order variable x. Assume that LK has a semantics with the same class of models as that of $L1K=$, and assume that the aforementioned connectives and quantifiers have the same role in the satisfaction of formulas as they have in $L1K=$. Thus, in particular, the semantics of LK agrees with that of $L1K=$ on the satisfaction of first-order formulas. We also assume that if $M1$ and $M2$ are isomorphic models and Φ is any formula of LK, then $M1 \vDash \Phi$ if and only if $M2 \vDash \Phi$. Of course, $L1K=$ and $L2K$ fit this mould.

We say that LK is *first-order equivalent* if for each sentence Φ of LK, there is a sentence Φ' of $L1K=$ such that $\Phi \equiv \Phi'$ is a logical truth or, in other words, Φ and Φ' are satisfied by the same models. Thus, if LK is first-order equivalent, then it is not capable of making any distinctions among models that cannot be made by the first-order $L1K=$. Clearly, the second-order $L2K$ (with standard semantics) is not first-order equivalent. Any categorical sentence with an infinite model is not equivalent to any first-order sentence. Of course, the burden of this book is to argue that the distinctions made by first-order languages are not sufficient. There are a number of results that characterize logics that are first-order equivalent, several of which are reported here. First, a few definitions are needed.

The logic LK has the *relativization property* if for each formula Φ in LK and each $\Psi(x)$ with x free, there is a formula $\Phi/\{x \mid \Psi(x)\}$ asserting that Φ holds when the domain is $\{x \mid \Psi(x)\}$. This is a theme we have encountered several times already. LK has the *substitution property* if, for each formula Φ containing an n-place relation constant R and each formula $\Psi(x_1, \ldots, x_n)$ (containing no free variables that occur in Φ, except possibly $x_1, \ldots, x_n$), there is a formula $\Phi(R \mid \Psi)$ that is equivalent to the result of substituting[21] $\Psi(t_1, \ldots, t_n)$ for $Rt_1 \ldots t_n$ in Φ. The logic LK is *effectively regular* if the collection of formulas of LK is a recursive set of strings, and if the aforementioned relativization and substitution functions are recursive. Finally, LK has the *finite occurrence property* if, for each formula Φ of LK, there is a finite subset K' of K such that Φ is in LK'. The idea is that if LK has the finite occurrence property, then each formula of LK involves only finitely many non-logical items. Both $L1K=$ and $L2K$ have the relativization property, the substitution property, and the finite occurrence property. If K is recursive, then they are both effectively regular.

Many common semantical notions can be formulated in this general setting. For example, LK is *compact* if for every set Γ of formulas of LK, if each finite subset of Γ is satisfiable, then Γ itself is satisfiable, and LK is *countably compact* if for every countable set Γ of formulas of LK, if each finite subset of Γ is satisfiable, then Γ itself is satisfiable.[22] The logic LK is *semantically effective* if the collection of logically true sentences of LK is a recursively enumerable set of strings, LK has the *downward Löwenheim–Skolem* property if each satisfiable countable set of sentences has a model whose domain is at most countable, and LK has the *upward Löwenheim–Skolem* property if, for each set Γ of sentences, if Γ has a model whose domain is infinite, then for each infinite cardinal κ, Γ has a model whose domain has cardinality at least κ. All these properties are possessed by $L1K=$ (provided that K is recursive), but decidedly not by $L2K$.

The most well-known characterizations of first-order equivalence are due to Lindström.

THEOREM 6.26 (Lindström 1969). If LK has the finite occurrence property, is countably compact, and has the downward Löwenheim–Skolem property, then LK is first-order equivalent.

THEOREM 6.27 (Lindström 1969).   Let LK be an effectively regular logic. Then if LK has the downward Löwenheim–Skolem property and the upward Löwenheim–Skolem property, then LK is first-order equivalent.

THEOREM 6.28 (Lindström 1969).   Let LK be an effectively regular logic. If LK has the downward Löwenheim–Skolem property and is semantically effective, then LK is first-order equivalent, and moreover there is a recursive function f such that for every sentence Φ of LK, $f(\Phi)$ is a sentence of $L1K =$ that has exactly the same models as Φ.

See Flum (1985, Section 1) for proofs of these theorems, and further refinements of them. It is shown that if LK has the finite occurrence property and the downward Löwenheim–Skolem property, and yet LK is not first-order equivalent, then it is possible to characterize the notion of *finitude* in LK. In particular, under these circumstances, there is a set Γ of formulas of LK containing a monadic predicate letter U such that (1) in every model of Γ the extension of U is finite and (2) for each natural number $n \geq 1$ there is a model of Γ in which the extension of U has cardinality n. As noted in Chapter 5, Section 5.1, there can be no such set Γ in any compact extension of a first-order language.

Tharp (1975) suggested that compactness, semantic effectiveness, and the Löwenheim–Skolem properties are consequences of features one would *want* a logic to have. If so, the Lindström results establish that first-order logic is all we want or need. But one person's proof is another's *reductio ad absurdum*. A major theme of this book is that, as far as expressive resources are concerned, the indicated properties establish that first-order languages are too weak. Wang (1974, p. 154) agrees:

> When we are interested in set theory or classical analysis, the Löwenheim–Skolem theorem is usually taken as a sort of defect (often thought to be inevitable) of the first-order logic. Therefore, what is established (by Lindström's theorems) is not that first-order logic is the only possible logic but rather that it is the only possible logic when we in a sense deny reality to the concept of uncountable . . .

Let $M^1 = \langle d_1, I_1 \rangle$ and $M2 = \langle d_2, I_2 \rangle$ be two models of LK (and of $L1K =$). A *partial isomorphism* between $M1$ and $M2$ is defined to be a one-to-one function f from a subset of d_1 onto a subset of d_2 that preserves the relevant structure. Thus, for example, if c is a constant and $I_1(c)$ is in the domain of f, then $f(I_1(c)) = I_2(c)$, and if R is a binary relation letter and a_1, a_2 are both in the domain of f, then $\langle a_1, a_2 \rangle$ is in $I_1(R)$ if and only if $\langle f(a_1), f(a_2) \rangle$ is in $I_2(R)$. We say that $M1$ and $M2$ are *partially isomorphic* if there is a set P of partial isomorphisms between $M1$ and $M2$ with the *back-and-forth property*: for each $f \in P$ and each $a \in d_1$ there is an $f_1 \in P$ such that $f \subseteq f_1$

and a is in the domain of f_1, and for each $f \in P$ and each $b \in d_2$ there is a $f_2 \in P$ such that $f \subseteq f_2$ and b is in the range of f_2.

A well-known technique due to Cantor establishes that if the domains d_1 and d_2 are both countable and $M1$ and $M2$ are partially isomorphic, then $M1$ and $M2$ are isomorphic. It is sometimes called the 'zig-zag' method. This does not hold for domains with higher cardinalities, since, for example, any two dense linear orderings with neither a first nor a last element are partially isomorphic. For example, the real numbers under the 'less than' relation are partially isomorphic to the rational numbers under the same relation.

A logic LK is said to have the Karp property if partially isomorphic structures are equivalent. That is, LK has the Karp property iff for any models $M1$ and $M2$, and any sentence Φ of LK, if $M1$ and $M2$ are partially isomorphic, then $M1 \vDash \Phi$ iff $M2 \vDash \Phi$. It is not difficult to establish that first-order logic has this property. It is part of another characterization of first-order logic.

THEOREM 6.29. Let LK be a logic with the relativization, substitution, and finite occurrence properties. If LK has the Karp property and is countably compact, then LK is first-order equivalent.

This is proved in Flum (1985, Section 2). In fact, it is shown that if a logic LK (with the relativization, substitution, and finite occurrence properties) has the Karp property and is not first-order equivalent, then the natural numbers under the 'less than' relation can be characterized up to isomorphism in LK.

There is an interesting relationship between partial isomorphism and first-order quantifiers. Suppose, for simplicity, that the non-logical terminology consists of a single binary relation. Say that the two models $M1 = \langle d_1, I_1 \rangle$ and $M2 = \langle d_2, I_2 \rangle$ are *n-partially isomorphic* if there is a sequence $P_0 \subseteq P_1 \subseteq \ldots \subseteq P_n$ of sets of partial isomorphisms such that for each $i < n$, each $f \in P_i$, and each $a \in d_1$ there is an $f_1 \in P_{i+1}$ such that $f \subseteq f_1$ and a is in the domain of f_1, and for each $i < n$, each $f \in P_i$, and each $b \in d_2$, there is an $f \in P_{i+1}$ such that $f \subseteq f_2$ and b is in the range of f_2.

Next, define the *quantifier depth* of a first-order formula to be a measure of how 'deep' quantifiers are 'nested' in it. The quantifier depth of an atomic formula is 0, the quantifier depth of $\neg \Phi$ is that of Φ, the quantifier depth $\Phi \to \Psi$ is the maximum of the quantifier depths of Φ and Ψ, and the quantifier depth of $\forall x \Phi$ is one greater than the quantifier depth of Φ. Van Benthem and Doets (1983) report the following result (attributed to R. Fraïssé): if $M1$ and $M2$ are n-partially isomorphic and Φ is a first-order sentence whose quantifier depth is at most n, then $M1 \vDash \Phi$ iff $M2 \vDash \Phi$.

Let $P(M)$ be a property of models (such as 'M has an infinite domain' or 'M has an uncountable domain'). Say that P is *first-order definable* if there is a formula Φ of $L1K=$ such that $P(M)$ if and only if $M \vDash \Phi$. It follows from the result just mentioned that a property P is first-order definable if and only if there is a natural number n such that P is preserved under n-partial isomorphism. That is, if $P(M1)$ and $M2$ is n-partially isomorphic to $M1$, then $P(M2)$.

One more example. The use of ultraproducts is an extremely fruitful technique in the model theory of first-order logic. In effect, this gives another characterization of first-order equivalence (for the relevant definitions, see Bell and Slomson (1971) or Chang and Keisler (1973)). If $\{M_i \mid i \in A\}$ is a family of models of $L1K=$ and U is an ultrafilter on A, then let $\Pi_U\{M_i\}$ be the resulting ultraproduct. Say that a logic LK preserves ultraproducts if for each sentence Φ of LK and each ultraproduct $\Pi_U\{M_i\}$, if $M_i \vDash \Phi$ for each $i \in A$, then $\Pi_U\{M_i\} \vDash \Phi$.

THEOREM 6.30 (Keisler, in Chang and Keisler 1973, Chapter 6). *LK* is first-order equivalent if and only if *LK* preserves ultraproducts.

The 'only if' part of this equivalence underwrites the ultraproduct construction in first-order logic; the 'if' part indicates that only first-order logic can be illuminated in this way.

It is surely significant that such a wide variety of properties all converge on first-order semantics. From such evidence, one might call first-order logic a 'natural kind'. But we should not forget the expressive poverty of first-order languages. First-order logic is important, but it does not have a monopoly on the attention of mathematical and philosophical logicians.

6.6 Definability and other odds and ends

6.6.1 Complexity

Let K be a recursive set of non-logical terminology and fix an effective arithmetization of the formulas of both $L2K$ and second-order arithmetic. If Φ is a formula, let $[\Phi]$ be its Gödel number.

It is a consequence of Gödel's completeness theorem that the set of (codes of) first-order logical truths is recursively enumerable. *A fortiori*, this set is definable in first-order arithmetic. In particular, there is a (first-order) formula $LT(x)$ of arithmetic such that for each formula Φ of $L1K=$, Φ is a logical truth iff $LT([\Phi])$ holds. Even more, Φ is a logical truth iff $LT([\Phi])$ is *deducible* in first-order Peano arithmetic. The same applies to the second-order $L2K$ with Henkin or first-order semantics, and to the *free-variable* second-order languages $L2K-$ with standard semantics (see Chapters 3 and 4). It follows from Tarski's theorem on the undefinablity of truth that the converses fail. There is, for example, no arithmetically definable function F such that, for each formula Ψ of first-order arithmetic, Ψ is true iff $F([\Psi])$

is (the Gödel's number of) a logical truth of $L1K$ (or even $L2K-$). If there were such a function F, then the formula $LT(F(x))$ would be an arithmetic definition of arithmetic truth. We would have $LT(F([\Phi])) \equiv \Phi$ for each sentence Φ of first-order arithmetic. This contradicts Tarski's theorem.

By contrast, the opposite of this applies to second-order logic. The notion of standard 'second-order logical truth' is not second-order arithmetically definable. Indeed, recall that there is a second-order sentence AR that is a categorical characterization of the natural numbers. It follows that for every sentence Φ of second-order arithmetic, Φ is true iff $(AR \to \Phi)$ is a logical truth (see Chapter 4, Theorem 4.8 and Corollary 4.9). So, if second-order logical truth were definable in second-order arithmetic, then second-order arithmetic truth would be definable in second-order arithmetic, contradicting Tarski's theorem. Moreover, it follows from the reductions of Section 6.2 that second-order logical truth is not definable in nth-order arithmetic,[23] for any natural number n.

Van Benthem and Doets (1983) report an amusing variation on this theme. Let K contain the terminology of arithmetic and let Φ be a formula of our free-variable second-order language $L2K-$ that has no free first-order variables. Define Φ to be *first-order equivalent* if there is a sentence Ψ of $L1K=$ such that $\Phi \vDash \Psi$ and $\Psi \vDash \Phi$.

THEOREM 6.31.   The set of first-order equivalent formulas of $L2K-$ is not arithmetic.

Proof.   Let χ be a sentence of first-order arithmetic and, as above, let AR be a categorical characterization of the natural numbers.

LEMMA. $AR \vDash \chi$ iff the disjunction $(AR \lor \chi)$ is first-order equivalent.

Proof.   If $AR \vDash \chi$ then $(AR \lor \chi) \vDash \chi$ and $\chi \vDash (AR \lor \chi)$. Conversely, suppose that Ψ is a formula of $L1K=$ such that $\Psi \vDash (AR \lor \chi)$ and $(AR \lor \chi) \vDash \Psi$. Let N be the standard model of arithmetic. Clearly, $N \vDash AR$, so $N \vDash (AR \lor \chi)$, so $N \vDash \Psi$. Now, applying the upward Löwenheim–Skolem theorem, let M be any structure that is not isomorphic to N, such that for any first-order sentence Φ of arithmetic, $M \vDash \Phi$ iff $N \vDash \Phi$. Since Ψ is first-order, $M \vDash \Psi$, so $M \vDash (AR \lor \chi)$. But, since M is non-standard, M does not satisfy AR, so $M \vDash \chi$. Finally, since χ is first-order and M and N are first-order equivalent, $N \vDash \chi$, so χ is true and $AR \vDash \chi$.

So, with this lemma, χ is true iff $AR \vDash \chi$ iff $(AR \lor \chi)$ is first-order equivalent. So if the notion of first-order equivalence were arithmetic, then so would the notion of arithmetic truth, contradicting Tarski's theorem.   □

On the other side of this coin, it is straightforward to see that the standard definition of satisfaction for $L2K$, a relation between sets, assignments, and (codes of) formulas, can be formulated in the language of (first-order) set theory. It follows that the notion of 'second-order logical truth' is set-theoretically definable. That is, there is a formula of $LT2(x)$ of first-order ZFC such that for each formula Φ of $L2K$, Φ is a logical truth iff $LT2([\Phi])$ holds. In fact, $LT2$ has the form $\forall x \Psi$ in which every quantifier in Ψ is bounded. Thus, by Tarski's theorem, there is no set-theoretically definable function G such that for each sentence Ψ of first-order set theory, Ψ is true iff $G([\Psi])$ is the Gödel number of a logical truth of $L2K$ (see also Boolos 1975).

The results reported here indicate that the semantic notions of second-order logic are quite rich and complex, but they are not quite as rich and complex as the notion of (first-order) set-theoretic truth. We return to the contrast between second-order logic and set theory in the concluding chapter.

6.6.2 Craig interpolation

As above, let LK be a logic based on the non-logical terms in K, and let $K = K_1 \cap K_2$. Then the logic is said to have the *Craig-interpolation property* if, for each pair of sentences Φ_1 in LK_1 and Φ_2 in LK_2, if $\Phi_1 \vDash \Phi_2$, there is a sentence Ψ in LK such that $\Phi_1 \vDash \Psi$ and $\Psi \vDash \Phi_2$. The sentence Ψ is called the *interpolant* of Φ_1 and Φ_2. It contains only the non-logical terms that occur in both Φ_1 and Φ_2.

The proof that first-order logic with identity $L1K=$ has the Craig-interpolation property is rather subtle and complex (see Boolos and Jeffrey 1989, Chapter 23). One special case, however, is almost immediate. Suppose that Φ_1 and Φ_2 have the same relation and function symbols, so that they only differ in their individual constants. Let $c_1, \ldots, c_n$ be the constants in Φ_1 that do not occur in Φ_2, and write Φ_1 as $\Phi_1(c_1, \ldots, c_n)$. Assuming that the variables $x_1, \ldots, x_n$ do not occur in Φ_1 or Φ_2, let Ψ be $\exists x_1 \ldots \exists x_n \Phi_1(x_1, \ldots, x_n)$. It is a straightforward exercise in first-order logic to verify that if $\Phi_1 \vDash \Phi_2$, then Ψ is an interpolant.

Second-order logic $L2K$ also has the Craig-interpolation property, but its proof is a simple extension of the first-order case involving constants alone. Let Φ_1 be a sentence of $L2K_1$, let Φ_2 be a sentence of $L2K_2$, and assume that $\Phi_1 \vDash \Phi_2$. Let Ψ be the result of replacing each non-logical item of Φ_1 with an appropriate variable, and let Ψ' be the result of prefixing Ψ with an existential quantifier over every free variable that occurs in it. Then, as above, it is a sraightforward exercise to show that Ψ' is an interpolant.

Ebbinghaus (1985) remarks that properties like Craig-interpolation 'indicate some sort of balance between syntax and semantics'. Here, the 'syntax' of a logic seems to be its deductive system. Ebbinghaus supports this claim with connections between interpolation and a few other properties, together with examples of logics for which interpolation fails. It should be noted, however, that $L2K$ has the Craig-interpolation property, but in no sense are its 'syntax' and semantics 'in balance'. A more accurate statement is that interpolation, *together with compactness*, indicates a 'balance' between 'syntax' and semantics. And, as expected, the results that Ebbinghaus cites all rely on compactness. I shall not comment further here on the extent to which it is desirable to have the 'syntax' of a logic in balance with its semantics.

6.6.3 Beth-definability

Once again, let LK be a logic based on the non-logical terminology in K. Let Γ be a set of sentences of LK, and let t be an element of K (i.e. a constant, relation letter, or function letter). We say that Γ is an *implicit definition* of t if, for any models $M1 = \langle d_1, I_1 \rangle$ and $M2 = \langle d_2, I_2 \rangle$ of Γ, if $d_1 = d_2$ and $I_1(p) = I_2(p)$ for each item p in $K - \{t\}$, then $I_1(t) = I_2(t)$ as well. In other words, if $M1$ and $M2$ have the same domain and give the same interpretation to everything but t, then $M1$ and $M2$ give the same interpretation to t (and thus $M1 = M2$). An individual constant c is *explicitly definable* from Γ if there is a formula $\Phi(x)$ of LK which has only x free and does not contain c, such that $\Gamma \vDash \forall x(\Phi(x) \equiv x = c)$; an n-place relation letter R is *explicitly definable* from Γ if there is a formula $\Psi(x_1, \ldots, x_n)$ which has only $x_1, \ldots, x_n$ free and does not contain R, such that $\Gamma \vDash \forall x_1 \ldots \forall x_n(Rx_1 \ldots x_n \equiv \Psi(x_1, \ldots, x_n))$; an n-place function letter f is *explicitly definable*[24] from Γ if there is a formula $\chi(x_0, \ldots, x_n)$ which has only $x_0, \ldots, x_n$ free and does not contain f, such that $\Gamma \vDash \forall x_1 \ldots \forall x_n(fx_1 \ldots x_n = x_0 \equiv \chi(x_0, \ldots, x_n))$.

It is immediate that if an item t is explicitly definable from Γ, then Γ is an implicit definition of t. Here, we are interested in the converse. A language/semantics LK is said to have the *Beth-definability* property if for every set Γ of sentences of LK and every non-logical term t, if Γ is an implicit definition of t, then t is explicitly definable from Γ.

It is well known that first-order logic $L1K=$ has the Beth-definability property. Boolos and Jeffrey (1989, Chapter 24) show this to be a consequence of the compactness of $L1K=$ and the fact that $L1K=$ has the Craig-interpolation property.

Second-order logic $L2K$, of course, is not compact, and in fact it does not enjoy the Beth-definability property. Let A be the non-logical terminology of arithmetic $\{0, s, +, \cdot\}$ and, for each natural number n, let t_n be an abbreviation for the corresponding numeral (i.e. a 0 preceeded by n occurrences of the successor symbol). Define a set S of natural numbers to be *second-order definable* (sometimes called Π_0^2) If there is a formula $\Phi(x)$ of $L2A$ with only x free, such that for each n, $n \in S$ iff $\Phi(t_n)$ is satisfied by the natural numbers. Clearly, there are only countably many second-order definable sets of natural numbers, so let G be any non-second-order definable set. For example, by Tarski's theorem, we can let G be the set of the Gödel numbers of all the true sentences of arithmetic. Let A' be the set A augmented with one monadic predicate letter P, and let Γ be the set of sentences consisting of AR (the single sentence that is a categorical characterization of the natural numbers) together with $\{Pt_n \mid n \in G\} \cup \{\neg Pt_m \mid m \notin G\}$. Since every model of Γ is isomorphic to the natural numbers, Γ is an implicit definition of P. But since G is not second-order definable, P is not explicitly definable from Γ.

On the other hand, it is virtually immediate that if Γ is a *finite set* of sentences of $L2K$, and Γ implicitly defines t, then t is explicitly definable from Γ. Suppose, for example, that t is a binary relation symbol R. Let Φ be the conjunction of the sentences in Γ and let Φ' be the result of replacing each occurrence of R in Φ with a binary relation variable X^2 (that does not already occur in Φ). Then

$$\Gamma \vDash \forall x \forall y [Rxy \equiv \exists X^2(\Phi' \ \& \ X^2xy)]$$

follows from the fact that R is implicitly defined by Γ.

Thus, like Craig-interpolation, it is easy to establish that this weak version of Beth-definability applies to the second-order $L2K$, even though the corresponding result for first-order logic is a deep and non-trivial theorem.

On yet another hand, both Craig interpolation and the weak Beth-definability feature depend on the fact that $L2K$ contains variables of the same type and degree as its non-logical terminology. The technique would fail if K contained so-called higher-order terminology, such as relations of properties. And, indeed the Beth-definability property does fail in such cases. Craig (1965) established that under very general conditions, a notion of satisfaction is implicitly definable in nth-order languages (see also Väänänen 1985). In a second-order language of arithmetic, for example, add a relation letter $S(X, x, y)$ for 'class X is the code of a sequence of classes and x is the code of a sequence of objects that satisfies the formula coded by y'. The recursive definition of S can then be formulated in a (more or less) straightforward manner. The result is a finite set of sentences that is an implicit definition of S. But Tarski's theorem on the undefinability of truth entails that S is not explicitly definable, thus refuting the Beth-definability property.

It follows that Craig interpolation also fails in such cases. The argument in Boolos and Jeffrey (1989, Chapter 24) that the Beth-definability property follows from the interpolation property can be executed here, and we take the contrapositive.[25]

6.6.4   A final curiosity

I close this part of the narrative with an independence result, due to Ajtai (1979) and M. Magidor. For virtually any reasonable language and logic LK, isomorphic models are equivalent. That is, if $M1$ and $M2$ are models and Φ is a sentence of LK, then $M1 \vDash \Phi$ iff $M2 \vDash \Phi$. If the collection of sentences of LK is a set, then a simple cardinality argument establishes that the converse of this fails: there are non-isomorphic models that are equivalent in LK.

It is easy to see that if the domains of $M1$ and $M2$ are both *finite* and if, for every sentence Φ of the first-order $L1K=$, $M1 \vDash \Phi$ iff $M2 \vDash \Phi$, then $M1$ and $M2$ are isomorphic. In short, any two finite first-order equivalent models are isomorphic. The compactness and Löwenheim–Skolem theorems entail that this cannot be extended to models whose domains are *countable*. There are non-isomorphic countable models that are first-order equivalent. For example, there are countable non-standard models of the collection of first-order arithmetic truths.

Is there a similar result for our second-order $L2K$? It turns out that the answer is independent of Zermelo–Fraenkel set theory. Ajtai (1979) first points out that if Gödel's axiom of constructibility ($V = L$) holds, then for any countable models $M1$, $M2$, if $M1$ is second-order equivalent to $M2$, then $M1$ is isomorphic to $M2$. On the other hand, within some models of set theory, obtained by straightforward forcing techniques, there are two countable well-orderings that are second-order equivalent but not isomorphic.

Notes

1. To take $ZFC2$ itself as a metatheory, one must think of the language under study and its ingredients (variables, connectives, etc.) as part of the iterative hierarchy. One may, for example, identify each syntactic item with an iterative set, its Gödel code.

2. The introduction of higher-order relation and function variables to this framework is conceptually straightforward, but it is a notational nightmare, and the added obscurity does not produce new insights. If n is large enough, no generality is lost by the restriction to monadic variables since the set-theoretic construction of ordered pairs can be simulated in nth-order languages. For example, let a and b be first-order terms. Then let S_a be the property that applies to a alone (i.e. $\forall x(S_a(x) \equiv a = x)$) and let D_{ab} be the property that applies to a and b, and to nothing else. The comprehension scheme entails the existence of these properties. Now let OP_{ab} be the property of properties that applies to S_a and D_{ab}, and to nothing else. The binary relation R (among indviduals) corresponds to a property of properties of properties P_R as follows: $P_R(X)$ iff there is a pair a, b such that R holds of a, b and X is OP_{ab}. Therefore a second-order binary relation variable corresponds to a fourth-order predicate variable. Similarly, a fifth-order binary relation between (monadic) predicates corresponds to a seventh-order predicate. Functions and, in general, m-place relations can also be accommodated. An inelegant feature of the restriction to monadic variables is that the present languages LnK are not extensions of the previous second-order $L2K$, since the latter has variables ranging over relations and functions. Since the reduction is (ultimately) to a second-order language, there would be little loss in allowing second-order relation and function variables in LnK, and simply not 'reducing' them.

3. This clause is not necessary if there are any individual constants in K^- (in the light of (1a)).

4. I am indebted to Nino Cocchiarella for pointing out the connection with Frege (see Cocchiarella 1987, Chapter 4).

5. The proof of this theorem proceeds by 'simulating' an unpairing function with two binary relation variables: R_1xy if y is the first element of the pair coded by x, and R_2xy if y is the second element of the pair coded by x. Then n-place relations and functions can be 'reduced' to monadic properties by continued pairing.

6. Montague (1965) also shows how one can extend the hierarchy of logics into the transfinite, and obtains many interesting reducibility results for what may be called αth-order logic, for transfinite ordinals α.

7. Virtually the same reasoning shows that for first-order languages, the informal notion **Val** is equivalent to one obtained on a semantics whose models all have countable domains. For example, one may restrict attention to models that are hereditarily countable, with no loss of generality concerning the notions of validity, satisfaction, and logical consequence. This is related to the expressive poverty of first-order languages—they cannot 'distinguish' between countable and uncountable models.

8. See Shapiro (1987) for more details. Kreisel (1965, Note 12) also suggests that a reflection principle is needed if the set-theoretic hierarchy is to serve as the semantics of formal languages.

9. It might be noted that $KP1$ entails that the standard notion of second-order logical truth is equivalent to what Boolos (1985a) calls 'supervalidity'. Conversely, the equivalence between these notions of validity entails $KP1$. See Chapter 9, Section 9.1.1, for more on Boolos (1985a).

10. Suppose that there were such a sentence Φ. Then, by an instance of the principle of sentential reflection, $Z2 \& \Phi$ would entail that there is a *set* that is a model of $Z2 \& \Phi$. So $Z2 \& \Phi$ would imply the consistency of $Z2 \& \Phi$, contradicting Gödel's second incompleteness theorem.

11. It follows that 'indescribability without parameters' is a much weaker notion than the more standard 'indescribability'. Every indescribable cardinal is inaccessible. See Drake (1974, p. 276).

12. A note on sentences and formulas. As above, in nth-order systems, the satisfiability of a single formula Φ is equivalent to that of the sentence obtained by prefixing Φ with existential quantifiers over its free variables. Thus the Löwenheim number and Hanf number could have been defined in terms of sentences. We could do the same for sets of formulas if the set K of non-logical terminology contains infinitely many constants and relation symbols of each type and degree (or, more precisely, if the set of constants and relation symbols of each type and degree is at least as large as the corresponding set of variables). Here, however, we work with formulas, preferably those with no non-logical terminology.

13. It follows from the reductions of Section 6.2 that the Löwenheim number and the Hanf number of second-order languages are the same as the respective numbers for higher-order languages in general. The combined Löwenheim–Skolem theorems entail that if a first-order sentence Φ has an infinite model, then for every infinite cardinal κ, Φ has a model whose domain has cardinality *exactly* κ. There is nothing analogous to this for second-order logic. As we have seen (Chapter 5, Section 5.1.2), there is a sentence COF-OMEGA which is satisfied by a model M if and only if the cofinality of the cardinality of the domain of M is ω. Thus, for every cardinal κ, there is a cardinal $\kappa_1 > \kappa$ such that *every* model whose domain has cardinality κ_1 satisfies COF-OMEGA, and there is a cardinal $\kappa_2 > \kappa$ such that *no* model whose domain has cardinality κ_2 satisfies COF-OMEGA.

14. That is, $H(\Phi)$ is empty if either Φ is not satisfiable at all or, for each cardinal κ, Φ has a model whose cardinality is at least κ.

15. The other axioms of Z are choice, extensionality, foundation, pairs, unions, powerset, and infinity (see Chapter 5, Section 5.2). Arithmetic, analysis, functional analysis, etc. can all be embedded in Z, but one cannot derive the existence of, say, $\aleph_\omega$ nor of the rank $V_{2\omega}$ from Z.

16. Along these lines, Mac Lane (1986) raises doubts about standard ZFC, suggesting that it might be 'too strong'. The present $ZFC-$ seems close to the set theory he does propose as a foundation of mathematics.

17. This theorem and the last entail that if the continuum hypothesis holds, then the set-Löwenheim number and the set-Hanf number of $L2$ both have cofinality $\aleph_1$. In general, the cofinality of these numbers is independent of set theory. That is, there are models of ZFC in which the continuum has cardinality greater than $\aleph_1$, but the cofinality of the set-Hanf number of $L2$ is still $\aleph_1$, and there are models of ZFC in which the cofinality of this set-Hanf number is itself greater than $\aleph_1$. I am indebted to Robert Solovay for pointing this out. Theorem 6.18 readily generalizes to cases in which the set K of non-logical terms is uncountable. Let λ be the cardinality of K. Then the set-Löwenheim number and the set-Hanf number of $L2K$ each have cofinality at most 2^λ. The first part of Theorem 6.19 also generalizes: the set-Löwenheim number has cofinality at least λ^+. The second part of Theorem 6.19 however, is not completely general. A painfully tedious argument establishes that if the language contains at least $\aleph_1$ individual variables or constants, then its set-Hanf number has cofinality at least $\aleph_2$. A similar statement holds for $\aleph_2$, $\aleph_3$, $\aleph_\omega$, and some other cardinalities. But there is a limit to this. It will be shown below that if the set-theoretic universe is large enough, then there is an absolute upper bound on the size of the set-Hanf number of second-order languages (independent of the size of K).

18. The indicated sentence is the conjunction of the assertions that the domain is a rank, that there is a measurable cardinal, that this cardinal has a powerset, and that this powerset has no powerset. Drake (1974) provides a good background in set theory, oriented towards large cardinals. Solovay *et al.* (1978) give a more advanced treatment of 'large large cardinals'.

19. Actually, if κ is supercompact and P is a local property of cardinals such that $\exists \delta P(\delta)$, then the cardinality of the set $\{\lambda \mid P(\lambda) \ \& \ \lambda < \kappa\}$ is κ. That is, κ is a fixed point in the hierarchy of cardinals that have P. Matthew Foreman has pointed out (in conversation) that if there is a supercompact cardinal, then a smaller upper bound for the Löwenheim number of $L2$ can be given. Define a cardinal κ to be *δ-strongly one extendible* if for every $\mu < \delta$ there is a $\lambda \geq \kappa$ and an elementary embedding $j: V_{\kappa+1} \to V_{\lambda+1}$ whose critical point is κ. One can show that if δ is supercompact, then there is a cardinal κ which is δ-strongly one extendible, such that κ is (much) less than δ and the Löwenheim number of $L2$ is less than κ.

20. Actually, Magidor (1971) shows that if κ is extendible, then the infinitary language obtained from an nth-order language by allowing conjunctions and disjunctions whose length is less than κ (i.e. $L_{\omega\kappa}$) is κ-compact. See Chapter 9, Section 9.1, for a rudimentary treatment of infinitary languages.

21. See Ebbinghaus (1985, Section 1.2) for more precise definitions of relativization and substitution.

22. Notice that the property 'countably compact' is not the same as '$\aleph_0$-compact' introduced in the previous section.

23. This indicates that the collection of (codes of) second-order logical truths does not occur in the Kleene analytic hierarchy. Montague (1965) extends this result to the transfinite: second-order logical truth is not definable in any transfinite extension of higher-order arithmetic in which the types of the variables are ordinals definable in some nth-order logic. Thus the collection of second-order logical truths does not occur in any natural extension of the Kleene hierarchy. But, for what it is worth, Montague reports that if λ is the Löwenheim number of $L2$, then second-order logical truth is definable in what may be called $(\lambda + 1)$th-order arithmetic.

24. Note the similarity between these notions of implicit and explicit definition and the criteria of 'unique extendibility' introduced above. See Chapter 5, note 6, and Corcoran (1971).

25. Actually, Boolos and Jeffrey's argument invokes the compactness theorem, but that is not necessary here since the aforementioned implicit definition of S is already a finite set of sentences.

Part III

HISTORY and PHILOSOPHY

The historical 'triumph' of first-order languages

If 'all' and 'there exists' are applied to variable propositional functions, the question arises: what is the totality of all propositional functions?
                                                    Skolem (1928)

It is true that the ... notion of consequence ... presupposes a certain absolute notion of ALL propositional functions ... But this is presupposed also in classical mathematics, especially classical analysis.
                                                    Church (1956, p. 326n)

7.1 Introduction

As we have seen, many philosophers hold, and some argue, that classical first-order languages, with their matching deductive sysems and model-theoretic semantics, are the strongest systems entitled to be called 'logic'. First-order logic also receives the great bulk (but not all) of the attention of contemporary mathematical logicians. But it has not always been this way. Almost all the systems developed in the first part of this century are higher-order; first-order logic was an afterthought. The purpose of this chapter is to trace the historical emergence of first-order languages as the *de facto* standard in logic. As will be seen, many of the contemporary debates surrounding higher-order logic have their roots in the historical development.

To reiterate a theme from previous chapters, the difference between first-order and standard higher-order logic lies in the *range* of the predicate and relation variables. In standard models, the predicate variables, for example, range over *every* subset, or every property of whatever is in the range of the first-order variables.[1] We have seen that it is also possible to interpret a formal language with relation or function variables as a many-sorted first-order language, as it is in Henkin or first-order semantics (see Chapters 3 and 4). In these non-standard semantics, the range of the predicate variables varies from model to model, even if the range of the first-order variables is held fixed. In effect, predication or membership is non-logical in Henkin and first-order semantics for higher-order languages.

On the view defended here, the border between logical and non-logical terminology cannot be 'read off' a natural or formal language, or even a language equipped with a deductive system (see Chapters 1 and 2). The soundness of higher-order deductive systems for faithful Henkin models indicates that, in a sense, a non-standard semantics is available for virtually any of the formal languages and deductive systems considered here, even those that contain variables that seem to range over relations or functions. In short, languages and deductive systems, by themselves, are neither first-order nor higher-order.

This observation leads to a difficulty in interpreting the work of either contemporary or historical authors who develop languages with relation or function variables. We must figure out what the variables are intended to range over.

To follow a theme introduced in Chapter 1, Section 1.2, consider, first, cases in which the range of the predicate variables, say, is somehow explicitly articulated. One possibility is that the language is presented with a model-theoretic semantics, but of course this is not the only way. The author may simply discuss the intended range of the predicate variables directly. In such cases, the situation may be straightforward. We only need to see if the *stated* range of the predicate variables is the entire powerset of the domain, or includes *all* its properties. If so, the logic is higher-order and standard semantics is an appropriate model of its logical relations.[2] Of course, one can still wonder whether the use of the word 'all' in the author's language really means '*all*', but this is perverse. More substantially, one can wonder whether the author has the same notion of 'property' that we do. The crucial question is whether or not every subclass (in the present sense) of the range of the first-order variables is the extension of a 'property'. Some authors (Poincaré and Russell, for example) are disposed to reject properties that are not definable, or are definable only impredicatively. The resulting languages are higher-order, but they differ from those presented here (see the brief introduction to ramified type theory in Chapter 3).

Things may not even be this clear if no model-theoretic semantics is articulated, or if the range of the predicate variables is not discussed. In historical studies, we are often left without an articulated semantics from the very beginning. In such cases, one possibility is that the predicate (or relation, or function) variables are not to range over anything. The author might be developing a 'meaningless' formal language, perhaps with a deductive system. Then, as noted, the logic is neither first-order nor higher-order. Another possibility is that the way parts of the language are to be understood is left informal or intuitive. Then it is a matter of exegesis. Some authors clearly intend their predicate variables to range over 'all' properties (of a given type), but, again, they may not mean by 'property' what we mean by 'property'. In most of the cases under study here before, say, 1930, even if a standard higher-order semantics distorts the author's intentions, Henkin semantics is a much greater distortion. In effect, standard semantics is usually the better model of the author's intentions.

Before the historical roots can be traced, we make a number of distinctions which concern the development of logic since the latter half of the last century. We attend to differing views on the scope of logic, and various conceptions of class, variable, and quantifier.

Three traditions can be distinguished in the history of modern logic (provided one does not insist on sharp boundaries). One of them originates with Boole and includes, among others, Peirce and Schröder. This *algebraic school* focused on the relationships, or analogies, between algebraic operations, like addition and multiplication, and canons of inference. A primary aim was to develop *calculi* common to the reasoning in different areas of mathematics. Boole's seminal work (Boole 1847, 1854), for example, was a formal calculus which could be interpreted among propositions, classes, and probabilities. The orientation is that of abstract algebra, along the same lines as group theory or field theory. One begins with some system of related operations and articulates a common *abstract* structure.[3] The result is a set of axioms which is satisfied by each of the systems and which illuminates all of them. In some of the cases at hand, the axioms are dubbed 'laws of thought'.

Our second tradition dates back at least to Euclid, and for the present purposes includes Dedekind, Peano, Hilbert, and the postulate theorists like Veblen and Huntington. The aim of this *mathematical school* is the axiomatization of particular branches of mathematics. Euclid, Hilbert (1899), and Veblen (1904) developed geometry, Dedekind (1888) and Peano (1889) developed arithmetic, and Hilbert (1900b) and Huntington (1902, 1905) developed analysis. As noted, an axiomatization produced by the algebraic school is intended to apply to several systems at once. In contrast, each axiomatization of the mathematical school is primarily intended to apply to a single system. It should be noted that this is a difference of emphasis rather than a difference of principle, in that mathematicians occasionally considered alternative interpretations of their axiom systems. Geometers, for example, took it to be important that the axiom of parallels is independent of the other axioms because the latter have a model in which the former is false. Some members of the mathematical school did not indicate interest in the study of logic *per se*. They are included here because of their role in the history of logic.

The third tradition, called the *logicist school*, includes Frege, Russell, and perhaps the early Wittgenstein. Their aim was to codify the underlying logic of *all* rational scientific discourse. For them, logic is *not* the result of abstractions from the reasoning in various disciplines, or in various systems. Logic concerns the most general features of actual (precise) discourse. The aim is a single universal language, applicable in all contexts without further interpretation. Frege's writings contain numerous comparisons between his work and that of the algebraists. For example, in 1883 he wrote:

> I did not wish to represent an abstract logic by formulas, but to express a content
> ... in more exact and clear fashion ... (Frege 1883)

The difference seems to be that the algebraists were concerned with certain structures, or algebras, and with features common to reasoning in these contexts, while the logicists were attempting to codify *unrelativized* reasoning, reasoning that is applicable in every context because of its generality.[4]

Goldfarb (1979) and van Heijenoort (1967b) argue that the aim of developing a universal language applicable in all contexts and the thesis that logic does not involve (a process of) abstraction separates the logicists not only from the algebraists (and the mathematicians), but also from contemporary model theory. Today, schematic letters are used for non-logical terminology, such as predicates, relations, and individual constants. These letters are given interpretations over different domains in the model-theoretic semantics. In this respect, the orientation is much like that of the algebraists. There also the languages are interpreted over several domains at once. On the other hand, instead of schematic letters, logicist languages have variables, with associated quantifiers, and the individual variables range over *all objects*, not over the objects of this or that model. Predicate variables thus range over all properties, and relation variables range over all relations. Since they did not think in terms of different 'interpretations', or different models of their languages, it is fair to state that logicist languages have no non-logical terminology. Moreover, the items in the languages they construct (variables, connectives, quantifiers, etc.) are regarded as logical terminology today. The only possible exception to this is the terminology for the predication relation. In standard semantics, that is also logical.

In summary, the algebraic school of logicians took variables to range over an unspecified but *fixed* domain. As in abstract algebra, this domain is an abstraction from more specific contexts. For the mathematical school, the variables of each language are intended to range over a fixed *and specified* domain, such as the natural numbers or Euclidean space. The logicists Frege, Russell, and the early Wittgenstein took their languages to represent the underlying logic of all rational discourse. For them variables range over *all objects whatsoever*.[5]

All the schools developed quantifiers, but they were understood differently. Frege and Peano, for example, took free variables and quantifiers in the contemporary sense except, perhaps, that they allowed (at least) second-order terminology. The algebraic school, on the other hand, took quantified propositions as extended conjunctions and disjunctions. For example, a statement in the form $\forall x \Phi(x)$ is understood as a conjunction of statements in the form $\Phi(a)$. This led to the consideration of infinitely long expressions, discussion of 'convergence', etc. Notice that a *domain* is needed to expand quantifiers into conjunctions and disjunctions, in that the variables are replaced by names of the objects being discussed. Thus, once again the algebraic school was relying on a fixed domain (see Leblanc 1976).

Finally, let us briefly review the discussion (from Chapter 1, Section 1.3) of the role of classes in logic. There is a tradition dating at least from Boole that takes classes (or intensional counterparts like properties or propositional functions) to be under the purview of logic. The algebraic school took subsets of a fixed domain to be under study by logic—this was one of the stated interpretations of their systems. Frege also took the study of concepts and their extensions to be within logic (see, for example, Frege 1893), as did Russell before his no-class period, and even afterwards variables ranging over attributes were part of his formal languages. What is crucial here is that the algebraic and logicist focus is on the subsets of a *fixed* universe or domain. That is, the context of the theory determines, or presupposes, a universe of discourse, a range of the (first-order) variables. A set is a subdomain of this universe. This is the *logical sense* of 'set'. Each logical set divides the domain into two parts: the elements that are in the set, and those that are not in it. Logical sets have a Boolean structure in that, for example, the complement of a logical set is itself a logical set. At least for the algebraists, 'logical set' is similar to an indexical expression in ordinary language because its extension depends on the context of its use. Thus, in arithmetic a logical set is a collection of natural numbers, in geometry a logical set is a collection of points, etc. To reiterate, there are no logical sets *simpliciter*, only logical sets within a given theory, although, of course, the context can be left unspecified.

On the other hand, current axiomatic set theory, as it developed from the work of Cantor, Zermelo, Skolem, Fraenkel, etc., fits the mould of the mathematical school. The axiomatization refers to a binary membership relation on a domain consisting of a (possibly empty) collection of urelements, sets of those, sets of sets of those, etc., with the 'set of' relation iterated into the transfinite. This is the *iterative sense* of 'set'. Iterative sets do not exhibit a Boolean structure, because the complement of an iterative set is not itself an iterative set.

In short, then, an iterative set is a member of the set-theoretic hierarchy— the domain of a single theory, axiomatic set theory. The symbol for the corresponding membership relation is a *non-logical* expression. The logical notion of set, on the other hand, always involves a domain fixed by context. A logical set is a subclass of the universe of discourse. Its membership relation is a part of the logical systems of the algebraic and logicist schools.[6]

7.2 Narrative

In the more direct sketches of the relevant histories, there are three major items, two of which overlap considerably. The first is the emergence of first-order *languages* (and semantics) as the major focus of mathematical and philosophical logic. The second is the development of *set theory* and the emergence of first-order *ZFC*. The third is the contemporary controversy over the status of second-order logic. The first two are presented in this section; the third is deferred to the next. Much of the historical material is based on the work of Moore (1980, 1988), and on several suggestions he made. Of course, I am responsible for any errors.

Once disagreements over these issues began in earnest, Skolem and Gödel were the main proponents of first-order languages. Each held that only axiomatizations in first-order formal languages are legitimate.[7] The higher-order language 'opposition' was championed by Zermelo, Hilbert, and Bernays. There is an interesting absence of correlation between the line-up across this battle line and that over more traditional philosophical matters. Gödel and Bernays were platonists (each in his own way), whereas Skolem and Hilbert embraced various versions of relativism, formalism, and finitism.

7.2.1 The development of first-order logic

Prior to Löwenheim's (1915) theorem, no one had discussed first-order logic as even a distinguished *part* of logic. Authors from all schools introduced variables ranging over both objects and properties (or propositional functions, or classes). As noted, one stated interpretation of the systems of Peirce and Schröder was the subclasses of a fixed domain. Each proposition (with a free variable) determines a class. This is in line with the comprehension scheme $\exists X \forall x (Xx \equiv \Phi(x))$ in our deductive system $D2$ (of Chapter 3). The algebraists also introduced second-order variables ranging over proposition-subclasses, but they did not carry this very far. By contrast, Frege (1879, 1884) introduced and brilliantly exploited second-order variables ranging over concepts. The notions of identity, equipollence, and the ancestral were all defined with second-order formulas, the latter playing a central role in the formulation of the natural numbers. Much of the present treatment is modelled after Frege's work. He did not separate the first-order part of the language, and in a sense he could not, since the language contains no predicate and relation symbols other than higher-order variables. A variation on this theme is Russell, who went on to develop ramified type theory, with different variable sorts for individuals, propositional functions, propositional functions of propositional functions, etc.

There are, to be sure, differences between these logicist systems and those of current higher-order logic. For one thing, the properties or propositional functions of the logicists may be intensional. Not much turns on this, however, since a precise notion of 'identity between properties' was not formulated. In Frege's case, the identity relation only applies to objects, the items in the range of the first-order variables. The closest thing to 'identity' that Frege applies to concepts is coextensiveness.[8] More important, perhaps, is the fact that metatheory and model-theoretic semantics are foreign to logicism. Indeed, the consequence relation was not articulated at all (see van Heijenoort 1967b, Goldfarb 1979).

Nevertheless, it does not take a major exegetical study to show that standard higher-order logic is a good model of the logicist systems, and it would be a major distortion to think of them as if they were first-order (for example, to impose a non-standard semantics). First, as noted above, the languages were not intended to be uninterpreted calculi. Second, and more important, in contemporary terms the languages do not have a non-logical terminology, much less a non-logical predication relation. Every item has a fixed meaning, and every variable a fixed range. It is true that Russell (at least) may not have envisaged the range of property variables in contemporary higher-order logics because he rejected impredicative definitions of propositional functions, but even this difference is not all that clear in the light of the axiom of reducibility. In contrast with non-standard semantics, Russell did not regard the range of higher-order variables as indeterminate—a given higher-order variable ranges over *all* propositional functions of appropriate type and level.

Peano also introduced variables ranging over 'classes' of natural numbers, and similar practices were adopted by other members of the mathematical school. The axiomatizations of geometry by Hilbert (1902) and Veblen (1904), and the axiomatizations of analysis by Huntington (1902, 1905), all contain essential reference to classes. Hilbert introduced an 'extremal' axiom asserting that the models of the other axioms are to have no proper extensions.[9] Veblen and Huntington employed the more usual second-order axioms of continuity, essentially due to Dedekind. To be sure, the consequence relation was not discussed, and in fact some of these authors had very little to say about logic at all. But the second-order variables were clearly intended to range over all classes or properties of the relevant domain. If, through an act of hindsight, one restricts these systems to first-order languages, Hilbert's extremal axiom is not satisfiable and the categoricity theorems proved by Veblen and Huntington are false.[10]

Our attempt to characterize the emergence of first-order languages and logic is complicated somewhat by the use or discussion of infinitary formulas. This dates back (at least) to the interpretaton of the quantifiers in the algebraic school, and continued through the period under study here. For example, Hilbert (1905) adopted such an interpretation (but later came to reject infinitary languages), and in the discussion surrounding *Principia mathematica* Lewis (1918) and Ramsey (1925) both introduced infinitary formulas. With hindsight, such systems provide a hierarchy of logics (see Chapter 9, Section 9.1.3).

The separation of first-order systems, or *sub*systems, is due to Löwenheim and Hilbert. I shall begin with the latter.

In a series of lectures in 1917, Hilbert applied the axiomatic method to geometry *and logic* (see Moore 1988). This is easily recognized as an extension of the methodology of the mathematical school. He explicitly developed primitive symbols and axioms for first-order logic, which he named 'the functional calculus'. Hilbert noted that this system is sufficient to model deductions *within* various branches of mathematics, but he added that it is not adequate when the 'foundations of mathematical theories themselves [become] an object of investigation'. An 'extended calculus', containing variables ranging over properties, was developed for 'foundational study'. This extended calculus is, in effect, a version of ramified type theory (with the axiom of reducibility). Hilbert's logical systems did not appear in print, however, until *Principles of mathematical logic*, by Hilbert and Ackermann, was published in 1928. Eventually, Hilbert came to accept the simple theory of types, an ω-order logic. The important point is that in both places Hilbert regarded first-order logic as a *distinct subsystem* of all logic. It was dubbed the '*restricted* functional calculus'. He indicated that set theory and arithmetic are incapable of an adequate treatment in the restricted system. Hilbert's point seems to be that the first-order systems cannot adequately formulate many of the propositions and concepts necessary for metamathematical study of various theories. Examples include the principle of induction for formulas, the membership relation, number, and cardinality. He showed how all these notions have straightforward formulations in the full higher-order system (see Chapters 4–6).

Hilbert's co-workers, such as Bernays (1918, 1928), Schönfinkel (1924) (and Bernays and Schönfinkel 1928), Ackermann (1924), and von Neumann (1927), all used essentially the same systems. Bernays (1918) formulated and proved the completeness of propositional logic. Within the Hilbert programme, this result was the first precise solution to a completeness problem for a *proper part* of logic. Similar problems for other subsystems of logic became crucial components of the programme, and represented stages towards what would ultimately be a consistency proof for all mathematics. In this spirit, the problem concerning the completeness of first-order logic was proposed by Hilbert (1929) (and Hilbert and Ackermann 1928). This, of course, was solved by Gödel (1930) (who also used the locution 'restricted functional calculus' to denote first-order logic.

In contrast with Hilbert, Löwenheim was firmly placed in the algebraic school. He names Schröder as the source of his interest in logic, and all Löwenheim's work concerns variants of Schröder's systems (see Thiel 1977, p. 237, Moore 1988). The landmark theorem, appearing in Löwenheim (1915), was no exception. Löwenheim first made a distinction between a 'relational expression' and an 'individual expression'. The latter has to be of finite length and can only contain variables over individuals. This is close to Hilbert's distinction between first-order and higher-order formulas, but in keeping with the algebraic school, Löwenheim thought of formulas with bound variables as expandable into infinitely long formulas. On this matter, however, the crucial difference between Löwenheim and his predecessors is that the only infinitary formulas envisaged were those that are equivalent (in the system) to finitary formulas. This variation on the algebraic theme permitted Löwenheim to distinguish carefully the first-order part of his system. His version of the Löwenheim–Skolem theorem concerned that part, but his *proof* relied heavily on the full system. That is, the proof involved both higher-order and infinitary formulas (in the metalanguage). Löwenheim also showed that the result does not hold for the full (higher-order) system.

It was Skolem who showed that Löwenheim's theorem could be proved *in* a first-order metalanguage (by using Skolem functions). He extended the theorem somewhat, applying it to countably infinite sets of formulas and to some infinitary languages (Skolem 1920). By 1922, however, he stopped mentioning the extensions of the theorem to infinitary languages and began to urge that first-order logic is the proper basis for set theory and, indeed, for all of mathematics (Skolem 1922). I say 'urge' here, not 'argue'. As far as I can determine, neither Skolem nor Gödel gave detailed *reasons* for their insistence on first-order logic. In both cases, the assertions were not merely directives that first-order logic is the most interesting or fruitful area for research; they were claims that higher-order variables do not belong in logic.

It was at this time that Skolem began discussing the 'Skolem paradox', which concerns the interpretation of axiomatic systems, notably set theory. It is to the axiomatization of set theory that we now turn.

7.2.2 Axiomatization of set theory

In this part of our story, the crucial item is the axiom of separation:

$$\forall x \exists y \forall z (z \in y \equiv z \in x \ \& \ Pz).$$

The issue concerns the status of the symbol P. In first-order Zermelo set theory, the axiom is a scheme, each instance of which is obtained by replacing the letter P with a first-order formula (not containing y free). In second-order treatments, the letter P is a predicate variable, regarded either as free or as bound by an initial universal quantifier.[11]

Here, we begin with Zermelo. Earlier set theorists, like Cantor, were not particularly concerned with axiomatization and logic. Late in 1904, Zermelo proved the well-ordering theorem (Zermelo 1904) and, almost immediately, the proof attracted intense resistance.[12] Virtually every aspect of Zermelo's treatment was attacked. During 1907, in a response to his critics, Zermelo composed his first axiomatization of set theory (Zermelo 1908a, b). Within the tradition of Hilbert's methods, and what we have called the 'mathematical school', the goal was to elucidate (and defend) the assumptions behind the proof of the well-ordering theorem.

The version of the axiom of separation that appeared in Zermelo's first formulation asserted that for every propositional function $P(z)$, if $P(z)$ is *definit* for a set S, then there exists a set containing exactly those elements of S for which $P(z)$ is true. Present concern, of course, is with the opening universal quantifier ranging over propositional functions, and with the word '*definit*'. At the time, Zermelo only noted that a given $P(z)$ is *definit* for S if the membership relation on the domain and the 'universally valid laws of logic' determine whether P holds for each element of S. The only 'laws of logic' that are even hinted at here are the principles of bivalence and excluded middle. Perhaps there is little point in speculating on this, but as Moore (1980, p. 109) notes, it is reasonably clear that Zermelo did not intend a restriction to anything like those properties definable in a given first-order language. First, the axiomatization occurred almost a decade before Löwen-heim and Hilbert separated first-order logic as a subsystem of logic; second, the axiom of separation was presented as a single sentence with a variable ranging over propositional functions; third, Zermelo later attacked Skolem's proposal to limit set theory to a first-order language.

Like the previous proof of the well-ordering theorem, this axiomatization attracted criticism, but now the critics had something more tangible to attack. The bulk of the criticism was directed at the axiom of choice, but separation was not ignored. For example, Russell, writing to Jourdain in 1908, called the principle of separation 'so vague as to be useless' (see Grattan-Guinness 1977, p. 109), and Poincaré (1909) objected that a property that is *definit* might not be well-defined.[13]

In attempting to improve the axiom of separation, Weyl (1910) proposed that a property is *definit* iff it can be characterized by a formula obtained from forms $x \in y$ and $x = y$ by finitely many uses of negation, conjunction, disjunction, existential quantification, and substitution of a constant for a variable. He did not indicate what sorts of existential quantification are permitted here. Again, recall that first-order languages had yet to be published as separate systems. Weyl (1917) contains a similar proposal, but there he explicitly stated that variables ranging over properties are not countenanced. He went on to assert that higher-order variables are unsuitable for logic, probably the first person to do so in print. However, one should not infer that Weyl (1917) *accepted* classical first-order logic, or that he had something like current first-order set theory in mind. Some time after this, Weyl adopted the intuitionist perspective in mathematics (see Moore 1988).

Weyl (1910) noted that his formulation of *definit* seems to presuppose the notion of *natural number*, as evidenced by the phrase 'finitely many uses of'. This raises a foundational issue concerning whether sets or numbers are more fundamental, the question being which of these are to be defined in terms of the other. If set theory is to serve as a foundation for all mathematics, which includes arithmetic, one ought to be able to develop set theory independently of arithmetic and *then* formulate the natural numbers with set theory (e.g. Dedekind 1888).[14] After several attempts to explicate *definit* without using the notion of number, Weyl came to reject Zermelo's (and

Dedekind's (1988) set-theoretic formulation of the natural numbers. Apparently, Weyl regarded numbers as more fundamental than sets.

The two critics who enjoyed the most influence on the development of set theory were, of course, Fraenkel and Skolem, both of whom began writing on the subject in the early 1920s. Although the systems they developed were remarkably similar, their attitudes towards logic, set theory, and foundations of mathematics were different.

Fraenkel (1922a,b, 1925) was rather sceptical of the whole enterprise of mathematical logic. He attacked Zermelo's notion of *definit* just because it relied on the imprecise basis of 'general logic'. Presumably, this is a reference to Zermelo's invoking the 'universally valid laws of logic' in the formulation of *definit* property. Fraenkel thus seemed to suggest that a sufficiently precise notion was not characterized. To improve it, he introduced an alternate: $f(x)$ is *definitorisch* if it can be obtained by the finite iteration of the operation of powerset, union, and unordered pair. Notice that, like Weyl's version, this formulation contains a reference to 'finitely many iterations'. With hindsight, it seems that Fraenkel also took the theory of natural numbers to be more basic than set theory.

Skolem (1922) formulated a revision of *definit* property similar to (but independently of) that given by Weyl. Like Weyl's later work (Weyl 1917), Skolem explicitly restricted the existential quantification to first-order variables, and he was the first to formulate separation as an axiom *scheme*, one instance for each *definit* property *definable in the first-order language*.[15] Skolem's proposal was, in effect, to treat the membership relation as non-logical, and, more radically, to formulate set theory in a first-order language. That is, Skolem was moving away from the algebraic and logicist view of class theory as part of logic.

In the same paper, Skolem began the attack on the absoluteness of set-theoretic notions, arguing that there is no single intended interpretation of set-theoretic concepts. The Löwenheim–Skolem theorem indicates that, like any first-order axiomatization, set theory has a countable model—a model within the natural numbers. This is despite the fact that, within set theory, one can prove that, say, the real numbers are uncountable. He concluded from this, the so-called 'Skolem paradox', that set-theoretic notations are 'unavoidably relative' (see Chapter 5, Section 5.2). For example, one cannot claim that a given domain D is uncountable *simpliciter*, but only uncountable relative to a given model (containing D) of set theory. For any such D, one cannot rule out the possibility that D may be countable relative to a richer model, one that contains a function from the natural numbers onto D. Skolem held that this relativity also applies to the Dedekind notions of 'finite' and 'simply infinite system'.[16] Given the modern trend of regarding virtually all mathematical notions as set-theoretic, Skolem's conclusions would entail the relativity of just about everything. Skolem eventually held such a view, but at the time he seemed content to reject the foundation of mathematics in axiomatic set theory (see Benacerraf 1985). Skolem (1922) seemed to accept Weyl's conclusion, and Fraenkel's apparent presupposition, that there is no gain in formulating intuitive mathematical notions, like that of natural number, in set-theoretic terms. Zermelo did not agree.

Questions concerning categoricity were often raised in this context. From contemporary perspectives, the discussion can be read as if it were full of confusion over the distinction between the semantics of first-order languages and the semantics of higher-order languages, confusion over the range of logic and the range of categoricity, and confusion over the applicability of the Löwenheim–Skolem theorems. Those whose minds concerning these matters are settled might understand it that way. The historical assertions that conform to one's views are to be praised as clear while those that are incompatible are dubbed 'confused'. On the other hand, most of the remarks by the historical figures have counterparts in the current debate over second-order logic.[17] Once presuppositions are noted, some of the pronouncements are at least relatively clear, and in some cases remarkably clear, even by modern lights.

With hindsight, there are several sources of fundamental disagreement. One concerns the distinction between syntax and semantics and, in particular, the distinction between deductive consequence and semantic consequence. A closely related matter concerns the status of the second-order variables, involving what I call above the 'logical notion of set'. On one level, the question of whether this notion is a legitimate part of logic is a matter of deciding where to draw a border. Is the (logical) notion of set in the jurisdiction of logic, or does it belong to mathematics proper? The deeper issue concerns the extent of our 'intuitive' understanding of the second-order variables and the extent to which they can be *used* in formulating the syntax and semantics of formal languages. Advocates of higher-order logic seem to hold that the terminology in question is serviceably clear, and does not need a further 'foundation'. Indeed, the claim is that this very terminology is at the heart of the foundational enterprise. Any successful attempt at formulating second-order logic would itself have terminology involving the logical notion of set (perhaps in presenting the semantics) and would thus beg the central question.[18] The first-order advocates, on the other hand, hold that (what I call) the 'logical notion of set' is not clear enough for use in foundational systems, at least not as it stands. To be used at all, the relevant notions must first be formulated as part of an axiomatic theory. In short, the notion of set must be regarded as non-logical. And any assertions about sets must follow from the axioms in first-order logic. With hindsight, the best candidate for such an axiomatic formulation is a theory of the iterative hierarchy. Thus the first-order camp rejects the distinction between the iterative notion and the logical notion of set. There are only iterative sets, and the terminology is non-logical.

Skolem (1922) launched, in effect, a twofold attack against the categoricity of set theory. One aspect was the general relativistic thesis that *no* theory with an infinite model can be categorical, and thus no unique candidate can be singled out by the axioms of set theory. This, of course, *follows* from the Löwenheim-Skolem theorems and presupposes that all theories are first order.[19] Skolem embraced this presupposition. The other critique was specific to set theory (and would apply to the second-order versions of it). Skolem pointed out that even when the axiom of replacement is added, Zermelo's system is consistent with the existence of various collections of non-well-founded sets and various collections of urelements.

The latter aspect of Skolem's critique seems to call for new axioms, some of which were suggested by Skolem itself. The way to attack the more general relativistic thesis would be to reject the presupposition that all languages are first-order. Both approaches were forthcoming, some in response to Skolem and others independently.

Fraenkel (1921) attempted to formulate a categorical version of set theory with an 'axiom of restriction' which was similar to Hilbert's axioms of completeness in geometry. Fraenkel's axiom asserted that the only sets to be considered are those whose existence follows from the other axioms. In short, no model of the theory is to have a proper substructure that is itself a model of the other axioms.[20] This seems to rule out models with non-well-founded sets and models with urelements (as well as models with inaccessible cardinals). Fraenkel seemed to believe that the intersection of all domains satisfying the rest of the axioms would be a model of the axiom of restriction.

By standards of modern logic, statements like the axiom of restriction and Hilbert's axiom of completeness conflate formal languages with their model-theoretic semantics. The axioms of a theory are to refer to the relevant subject matter, sets in this case. It is only in the metalanguage that one can refer to what follows from the axioms, or to its models. But perhaps it is not proper to impose such standards on historical figures.[21] A deeper problem with Fraenkel's axiom is similar to one of the 'problems' with second-order languages. It *presupposes* familiarity with sets or, as von Neumann (1925) put it, the axiom of restriction relies on 'naive' set theory. If the purpose of the axiomatization is to *clarify* the notion of set, and to do so while avoiding 'naive' set theory (and the antinomies), then the axiom of restriction is circular. It might be noted, however, that those who hold that the concept of set is sufficiently clear—and does not stand in (further) need of 'foundation'— could argue that the circularity is not vicious, no more so than the *use* of connectives and quantifiers in a metalanguage to explicate the corresponding items in the formal language. On such a view, the purpose of axiomatization is not to provide the security of a foundation, but to codify the reasoning in a theory, to characterize its models, and/or to forge connections with other fields. To echo a theme of this book, it is foundations with foundationalism.

Since the intended subject matter of the formal languages in question is sets, model-theoretic semantics can be developed within it. This is the insight behind the use of set theory as the background of model theory (see Chapter 6, Sections 6.1 and 6.3). One can thus formulate a statement in *the formal language* that there are no models of the other axioms, and then add such a statement to the axioms of set theory. Any model of *this* theory would satisfy a version of Fraenkel's axiom of restriction. Indeed, the resulting *second-order* theory *is* categorical—all its models are isomorphic to the first inaccessible rank. The resulting first-order theory, of course, is not categorical (if it is consistent) because no first-order theory with an infinite model is categorical.

Von Neumann (1925) puts the situation with first-order languages well. He suggested that at least some of the problems with the axiom of restriction can be overcome by precisely formulating the relevant (semantical) notions. His own axiomatization of set theory, which includes separate variables for sets and classes, is suited for this, but the language must be augmented. A 'model' of von Neumann set theory would be a collection of sets, i.e. a class, together with the collection of its subclasses. But in the original theory, proper classes are not to be elements of either sets or classes. Thus, as it stands, von Neumann set theory cannot be used to discuss its own (class) models. We require a more encompassing theory, one with the sets *and proper classes* of the original theory as *elements*, i.e. as sets. Of course, the higher theory would have its own (super)classes. Working in a model of such a theory, one can use the relations of subset and subclass (in the higher theory) to formulate the notion of a class satisfying various statements, and thus the notion of a class being a *model* of ordinary set theory. The axiom of restriction then has a precise meaning—one can state in the higher theory that a given class has no proper subclasses that are models of ordinary set theory. Von Neumann observed that the intersection (in the purported model of the higher theory) of all models of ordinary set theory might turn out to be itself a model of set theory. If so, then it also satsfies the axiom of restriction, and no other model does. He then argued, however, that even if this process succeeds in fixing a model of the axiom of restriction, the resulting theory—ordinary set theory together with the axiom of restriction—may still not be categorical. In some cases, perhaps, a single model has been characterized, but only *relative to* the choice of the higher set theory and the model satisfying it. If one had begun the construction with an even larger model of the higher set theory, there may be a different collection of models of ordinary set theory and thus a different intersection.

The last section of von Neumann (1925) is a general discussion of categoricity. He noticed, first, that it is easy to *prove* the categoricity of theories like Euclidean geometry, but he added, parenthetically, that to accept the arguments, one must 'disregard the fact that the axioms of geometry ... depend on those of set theory'. After all, the second-order axiom of continuity refers to the *subsets* of the plane, and Hilbert's axiom of completeness refers to models of the axioms. The point seems to be that the categoricity proofs are based on higher-order, or set-theoretic, premises and thus they are *relative* to a particular interpretation of set theory. Von Neumann then reiterated the aforementioned conclusion that set theory, as then formulated, is *not* categorical, and he argued that considerations like the Löwenheim–Skolem theorems indicate that

> no categorical axiomatization of set theory seems to exist at all; for probably no axiomatization will be able to avoid the difficulties connected with the axiom of restriction and the 'higher systems'. And since there is no system for mathematics, geometry, and so forth, that does not presuppose set theory, there probably cannot be any categorically axiomatized infinite system at all.

Von Neumann went on to suggest that the same conclusion seems to apply to the axiomatic treatment of basic notions of cardinality, since even these are formulated with variables which occur 'with reference to the entire [set-theoretic] system'. Like Skolem (1922), the Dedekind notion of finitude is given as an example (see note 14). Von Neumann concludes that if this relativity is sustained, then, of the notion of finitude,

> nothing but the shell of its formal characterization would ... remain ... It is difficult to say whether this would militate more strongly ... against its intuitive character, ... or its formulation as given by set theory.

We have seen this dilemma before, in the guise of whether sets or numbers are more fundamental. Von Neumann is ambivalent as to whether, say, finitude needs a higher-order or set-theoretic foundation. If it does, he sees no way to regard the notion as unequivocal.

It might be noted in passing that, by this time, Hilbert had repudiated the algebraic school's understanding of quantified formulas as infinitary. He also came to accept in part the intuitionistic—and Skolemite—claim that infinite sets cannot be treated uncritically like finite ones (see, for example, Hilbert 1923).[22] Nevertheless, he continued to hold that the *use* of class terminology is essential to the foundational enterprise (i.e. to the Hilbert programme). One cannot characterize the interrelations between theories without it. The proposed solution to this dilemma was finitary proof theory, in which the logic, the set theory, and the mathematics are to be developed simultaneously.

Zermelo was beginning to move in the opposite direction. In a lecture in 1929, he accepted a version of what he called the 'logicist' thesis that mathematics is 'a systematization of the provable and, as such, an applied logic', but he came to reject the view that proofs must be of finite length. Mathematics was dubbed 'the logic of the infinite'.[23]

The same year, Zermelo returned to his axiomatization of set theory (Zermelo 1929). In discussing his earlier work, and its critics, he indicated that the explication of the crucial notion of *definit* depended on the logical resources available:

> At the time there did not exist a generally recognized 'mathematical logic' to which I could appeal, any more than it does today, where every ... researcher has his own system. (Zermelo 1929, p. 340)

The irony in this remark is that today there is a (more or less) generally accepted mathematical logic, classical first-order predicate calculus, but Zermelo would be reluctant to appeal to it because it is too weak. He explicitly rejected Fraenkel's proposal concerning the notion of *definit* since it relied on a *construction*. Such 'procedures' contradicted what he took to be the essence of the axiomatic method. Evidently, Zermelo took an axiomatization to be a *characterization* of its subject, not a construction of it. In this spirit, he proposed to axiomatize the notion of *definit* property. The result was an essentially *second-order* formulation. For present purposes, a crucial clause is that if $P(g)$ is *definit* for each propositional function g, then so are $\forall f P(f)$ and $\exists f P(f)$. He then noted that this characterization does *not* rely on the notion of natural number. This remark seems to be aimed at Skolem and, perhaps, Weyl, and also at the foundational ambivalence between sets and numbers. For Zermelo, set theory is sufficient by itself to serve as foundation—as a theory in which to (re)formulate other mathematical theories, including arithmetic.

Skolem (1930) was quick to respond in print, pointing out that his own characterization of *definit* (Skolem 1922) is quite similar to Zermelo's 'new' one. The difference, of course, is that Skolem did not allow the clause concerning variables ranging over propositional functions. He believed this to be obscure and, possibly, contradictory. He asked whether Zermelo intended to characterize 'propositional functions' by composing even more axioms. Of course, if Zermelo did this,[24] and the axioms were first order, the Löwenheim–Skolem theorem would apply. Skolem then repeated his thesis of set-theoretic relativity. In this context, the claim is that an unequivocal notion of *definit* property, as Zermelo surely intended it, *cannot* be characterized by axioms. Categoricity is out of the question. This, it seems, is the closest that Skolem came to arguing for his insistence on first-order languages. Perhaps the underlying thesis is that any notion that is not cast in a first-order language is too vague or obscure to be useful in foundational studies.

In his rejoinder, Zermelo (1930) held his ground. He formulated a second-order version of what is today called Zermelo–Fraenkel set theory (with urelements).[25] In describing the theory, Zermelo presented the iterative hierarchy in virtually its present form. He then proved that all models of his system are characterized up to isomorphism by one cardinal number and one ordinal number, chosen independently of each other. The former is the number of urelements and the latter is the structure of the inaccessible cardinals. This is correct for current second-order *ZFC*, but, of course, not for any first-order set theory.

The dialogue ended with this stand-off. In an expository paper during this period, Skolem (1928) made a few remarks on second-order logic. After developing a language with first-order variables and quantifiers, he showed how variables ranging over 'propositional functions' could be introduced, and he raised the possibility of quantifiers over these second-order variables. I repeat the passage at the beginning of this chapter.

> If 'all' and 'there exists' are applied to variable propositional functions, the question arises: what is the totality of all propositional functions?

The latter question, of course, is the sort of thing that Zermelo did not think had to be raised. Once a domain is fixed, the range of the locution 'all subsets', or 'all propositional functions' is determined. After all, similar questions are not raised about the first-order variables and the other logical terminology. Moreover, from this perspective, the only way to answer such questions is to *use* the corresponding terminology in the metalanguage.

But for Skolem the question is legitimate and pressing. He asserted that only two conceptions for the range of the higher-order variables are 'scientifically tenable'. The first is, in effect, ramified type theory (see Chapter 3). The second is to introduce the notion of propositional function axiomatically.

> The axioms will then become first-order propositions, since the . . . 'propositional functions' . . . will assume the role of individuals. The relation between arguments and functions will then appear . . . as primitive.

This is a foreshadowing of non-standard semantics. Of course, these 'first-order propositions' would be subject to the Löwenheim–Skolem theorems and would thus have a variety of 'interpretations' or models. Second-order logic would itself suffer from the 'relativity' of set-theoretic notions.

In sum, the clash between Zermelo and Skolem was rather fundamental. Skolem took the second-order terminology to be obscure and in need of further axiomatization, which, of course, would have to be first-order. That would allow various 'interpretations' of the terminology—with the result being a confirmation of relativism. Zermelo took the higher-order terminology to be sufficiently clear and not to require a further 'foundation'. Such terminology is an essential part of the very framework for doing foundations, at least foundations without foundationalism.

Of course, neither propositional functions nor sets are the first controversial entities to be studied by mathematicians. Negative, irrational, and complex numbers readily come to mind (see Nagel 1979). In such cases, there are, to speak (very) roughly, three different stances that have been taken by proponents. Here, however, there are troubling circularities at every turn. The first stance is simply to *postulate* the existence of the entities. If any axioms are given, they are taken to *describe* the postulated entities. From this perspective, alternative interpretations of the axioms are regarded as irrelevant. It need hardly be mentioned that postulation, by itself, is not going to convince the wary. It begs the question, if anything does. Often, postulation is accompanied by arguments concerning the usefulness of the entities, or the fruitfulness of the resulting theory. Much of Zermelo's and Cantor's writings fit this mould. However, the fruitfulness would be exhibited by *any* structure that satisfies the axioms. Thus the second possibility is *implicit definition*. One first gives axioms and then holds that the defined entities 'are' or 'can be' anything that satisfies them. As noted above, for example, Dedekind (1888) *defined* a 'simply infinite system' to be any collection of objects that has an operation with certain properties. He then gave a categoricity proof and defined 'the natural numbers' to be one such system (see Kitcher 1986). Skolem's second 'scientifically tenable' presentation of propositional functions, the axiomatic treatment, seems to be an implicit definition. The problem here is that the very issue at hand concerns just which structures satisfy which axioms. Sets, properties, propositional functions, or the like are central items in that very enterprise, the enterprise of model theory. If the *axioms* used in the definitions are taken to be first-order, as Skolem explicitly intended, then many (non-isomorphic) systems are so defined, and there is no way to distinguish a preferred interpretation. This is relativism, and its confirmation. That is, relativism is the result of taking the axiomatizations of, say, arithmetic or set theory to be implicit definitions *and* insisting that axiomatizations must be first-order. If the axioms are (standard) second-order, as Zermelo intended, there is no relativism, but the implicit definitions are circular. One 'defines' the entities in question, sets, by using variables ranging over those same entities, or very similar ones. The third outlook towards problematic entities is *construction*. One shows how the objects in question can be taken as combinations of less problematic entities. Examples include the Dedekind construction of real numbers as sets of rationals, and the definition of complex numbers as pairs of reals. Skolem's conception of propositional functions along the lines of ramified type theory is of this form. Propositional functions are associated with formulas of a series of languages. From the perspective of the advocates of higher-order logic, this construction is inadequate. Only countably many propositional functions are constructed in this way. More importantly, virtually every construction appeals to the intuitive notion of set and, as Skolem acknowledged, natural number. Again, these are the 'problematic' entities under study.[26] As we have seen, Zermelo explicitly rejected 'construction' as incompatible with axiomatic method.

7.2.3 Gödel

The next items are certainly among the most important in the history of logic—Gödel's theorems. Influenced by the methodology of the Hilbert school, but himself no finitist, Gödel established the completeness of first-order logic in his 1929 Ph.D. Dissertation (see Gödel 1930) and he established the incompleteness of arithmetic a year later (Gödel 1931). The former only applies to the logic of first-order languages, while the latter concerns every recursive axiomatization of arithmetic and it implies the incompleteness of second-order logic (see Chapter 4, Section 4.1).

In a lecture in 1931—after he became aware of the incompleteness theorem—Zermelo developed a radically new perspective on the relationship between mathematics and logic (Zermelo 1931, see Moore 1980). He deplored what he called 'Skolemism, the doctrine that *every* mathematical theory . . . is satisfiable in a countable model'. This is certainly not a case of a stubborn refusal to accept the Löwenheim–Skolem theorems. Zermelo rejected the relativism of set theory, and he rejected the thesis that all mathematical theories should be formulated in first-order languages. He derided the view as the 'finitistic prejudice':

> . . . the true subject matter of mathematics is *not*, as many would have it, 'combinations of signs', but *conceptually-ideal* relations between elements of a conceptually determined *infinite manifold*. Thus our system of signs is always an *incomplete* device . . .

Zermelo went on to propose a massive infinitary logic. In accordance with the algebraic school, quantified formulas were to be replaced by infinite conjunctions and disjunctions, but he went on to allow for each ordinal α, formulas of length α. In this context, Zermelo defined 'proof' in terms of logical consequence. He took it as crucial that every true sentence be 'provable' and even suggested that Gödel's incompleteness theorem relied on an overly restrictive conception of quantification and proof. In fact, Zermelo argued that Gödel's reasoning shows that any finitary notion of 'proof' is inadequate. In short, compactness is an unacceptable property of logic.

Over a period of six weeks, Zermelo and Gödel carried on a spirited correspondence. Zermelo wrote to Gödel, Gödel responded, and Zermelo wrote once more.[27] After an initial confusion on Zermelo's part was cleared up, Gödel insisted on a finitary and first-order metalanguage, from which the essential incompletability of arithmetic could be established. Zermelo suggested 'new methods of proof', along the lines of his infinitary system. He was clear on the source of the problem:

> . . . a 'finitistically restricted' proof-scheme does not suffice to 'decide' the propositions of an uncountable mathematical system . . . For what 'proof' is

cannot be 'proved', but must be *presupposed* or *assumed* in some form ... What does one understand by a 'proof'? In complete generality one understands thereby *a system of propositions such that from the assumption of the premises the validity of the conclusion can reasonably be asserted.* And still the question remains, what is 'reasonable'? In any case, *not merely* (and this you [Gödel] have shown) the propositions of a finististic scheme ... from the beginning, I have been working on the basis of a *more general* scheme, .. (Translated in Moore 1980, p. 128)

Gödel's proof is Zermelo's *reductio ad absurdum* against first-order finitary languages. Zermelo and Gödel were at cross purposes here. Gödel held that logic, or at least this part of logic, should focus on the *formal*. I presume that he had something like proof theory in mind. As discussed above, derivations within deductive systems should be mechanically checkable. But the collection of second-order logical truths is not recursively enumerable (see Chapter 6, Section 6.6), and the consequence relation enumerated by Zermelo is even more complex than that of higher-order logic. On the other hand, according to Wang (1987), Gödel accepted many of Zermelo's conclusions, or at least something close to them (see also Gödel's correspondence reported by Wang (1974)). In particular, Gödel held that the human ability to understand and work with mathematical concepts goes beyond the mechanical, or the 'formal'. As far as I know, Gödel never objected to Euclidean geometry, or even set theory formulated with reference to proper classes, taken as face value. Far from it. Recall, for example, that Gödel had a role in the development of set-class theory, often called von Neumann–Gödel–Bernays set theory. We use such theories, we work in them, and we understand what we do. It is only that they are not 'formal', in that they have a non-effective consequence relation. As discussed in Chapters 1 and 2, however, there is more to logic than proof theory.

Zermelo published a few articles developing his infinitary logic, but did not carry it very far. In 1935 he was dismissed for failing to salute Hitler and his proposal was not pursued by anyone else until, perhaps, the revival of infinitary languages in the 1950s.[28]

In a conference in 1938, Skolem returned to his discussion of the Löwenheim–Skolem theorems and extended his relativism to mathematics as a whole (Skolem 1941). At the same conference, Bernays still resisted both the relativism and the restriction to first-order languages. He suggested that the limitations of the Löwenheim–Skolem theorems are due to the 'restrictiveness' of the formalism and proposed this this reveals 'a certain inadequacy of the method under discussion ... for making axiomatizations precise' (Gonseth 1941).

Gödel, of course, did not accept the relativism, but he did insist on first-order languages. This combination prevailed. From this point, the explicit controversy over higher-order languages subsided, and most logicians began to accept the Skolem–Gödel proposal that only first-order languages are appropriate for their work. For example, the vast majority of textbooks in logic written after 1940 hardly mention higher-order terminology.[29]

It seems that this general consensus was not based on a philosophy of foundational studies. It was more of a research programme, suggesting that first-order model theory is the best place to focus intellectual attention. In short, first-order logic became a Kuhnian paradigm (see Kuhn 1970). Given the apparent lack of explicit arguments from the major figures in the first-order camp, one can only speculate on the reasons. Surely, Gödel's completeness theorem makes first-order logics attractive for many purposes. The theorem shows, in effect, that the proof theory and the model-theoretic semantics of first-order logic are a perfect match. This entails that there is but one consequence relation, one sort of 'independence' statement, etc., and it allows one (automatically) to transfer results about the semantics of a system to its proof theory and vice versa. Thus, one can reliably study semantics in order to shed light on deducibility. First-order model theory is still the most powerful tool we have for studying *deductive* relations between various statements and various theories. Even in this book, Henkin models have been employed to shed light on (second-order) deducibility relations. So it may be that first-order languages were adopted in part because the resulting proof theory is more fruitful, more conceptually clear, and more elegant.

In any case, the range of the locution 'all subclasses' was (and is) widely regarded as sufficiently problematic to suggest that the corresponding terminology be non-logical. This amounts to an insistence that only the resources of first-order languages and semantics can serve logic. I do not know the extent to which this ambivalence towards class terminology is the cause or the effect of the 'triumph' of first-order languages.

To close this section, it is to be noted that higher-order logic never quite died out. For example, interest in type theory remained (and remains) alive, perhaps prompting Skolem (1961) to reiterate his support for its interpretation in many-sorted first-order languages (referring to Gilmore (1957)). Church (1951) is a rather straightforward higher-order system, and, by way of transition to the next section, Church (1956) contains a technical and philosophical discussion of second-order logic.

7.3 To the present

I conclude this chapter with a few remarks on the contemporary controversy concerning second-order languages. From one perspective, the discussion continues the border dispute as to whether any notion of 'set' belongs to logic. In those terms, however, the question does not seem to amount to much. The best resolution, perhaps, is simply to hold that there is no sharp border between logic and mathematics. The analogy, of course, is with political boundaries, but unlike those, our lines can be drawn and moved at will, unless emotions of sovereignty run high. As in the previous section, the deeper issues concern the epistemic and semantic status of the high-order terminology, especially the ranges of the variables. Once again, advocates of first-order logic hold that second-order terminology is not sufficiently clear, or is otherwise inappropriate to play a role in logic. In some cases, the underlying thesis seems to be that notions used in logic should not have any possible obscurity or avoidable uncertainty. The set-theoretic antinomies are still used to defend this claim.

As noted in several places already, the central advocate of first-order languages is W. V. O. Quine, but not on foundationalist grounds. His critique of higher-order logics dates back (at least) to Quine (1941). The bulk of those remarks, however, were directed at the *intensional* character of the 'attributes' of Russell and Whitehead's *Principia mathematica*. Quine proposed that the higher-order terminology be supplanted with a primitive membership relation among sets. Other higher-order logics, however, such as those presented in this book, take 'properties' or 'classes' to be extensional (see Chapter 1, Section 1.3; on Frege and extensionality, see note 8 to this chapter). Quine (1970) contains a full elaboration of his attack on contemporary second-order logic (see also Quine 1969, Part 3). The thesis is that so-called 'second-order logic' is not part of logic, but rather is 'set theory in disguise'. He points out that some rather substantial set-theoretic theses can be formulated in second-order logic. This much is sustained in Chapter 5. It is a consequence of the expressive power of second-order languages.

It should be noted that Quine is not a critic of set theory (unlike, say, Skolem (1922)). He was (and remains) an advocate of the theory, and has contributed to its development. Quine's claim is that set terminology does not belong to *logic*. In speaking of classes, we cross the border to mathematics. To state the obvious, Quine (1941, 1970) follows Skolem's later work in taking membership to be non-logical. The thesis seems to be that logic, properly so-called, should be topic neutral and should not presuppose anything about any subject matter. There are no 'logical objects' or, in other words, logic should not have an ontology:[30]

> Set theory's staggering existential assumptions are ... hidden ... in the tacit shift from schematic predicate letter to quantifiable set variable. (Quine 1970, p. 68)

Notice the divergence between this view of logic and that held by both the algebraic school and the logicists, all of whom took classes or properties to be under the purview of logic. As we have seen, historically the 'shift' was in the direction opposite to that suggested by Quine. It went from the quantifiable variables of higher-order languages to the non-logical schematic predicate letters of first-order formal languages.

Tharp (1975) joined the border dispute. He (and others) bolstered the preference for first-order logic by quoting the theorems of Lindström (1969), which show that, in some sense, first-order logic is the only logic that is compact and has Löwenheim–Skolem properties. Presumably, the latter are regarded as 'desirable', or, at any rate, the convergence of those properties on a single consequence relation indicates that the first-order logic is natural. Lindström's theorems are presented and discussed in Chapter 6, Section 6.5.

Meanwhile, a few voices were raised in the tradition of Hilbert, Zermelo, and Bernays, arguing that first-order languages do not capture important aspects of pre-formal mathematical practice. An interesting example is the last chapter of Church (1956), which is devoted to second-order logic. Either explicitly or through exercises, it is shown how many mathematical theories have natural and straightforward formulations in higher-order languages, and that first-order counterparts are awkward and inadequate. In short, first-order languages are inadequate to the task of *describing* the intended interpretations of various theories. Church points out that second-order semantic notions (e.g. consequence, satisfaction, and logical truth) must be distinguished from their proof-theoretic counterparts (deductive consequence, consistency, and theoremhood). The important semantic notions are not recursively axiomatizable. He concedes in a footnote (Church 1956, p. 326n) that this raises doubts in some minds.[31] Part of the response is quoted at the top of this chapter. Here is a wider context:

> Objections may indeed be made to this new point of view, on the basis of the sort of *absolutism* it presupposes . . . But it should be pointed out that this . . . is already inherent in classical mathematics generally, and it is not made more acute or more doubtful, but only more conspicuous, by its application to theoretical syntax [i.e. logic]. For our definition of the consequences of a system of postulates . . . can be seen to be not essentially different from [those] required for the . . . treatment of classical mathematics . . . It is true that the non-effective notion of consequence, as we have introduced it . . . presupposes a certain absolute notion of ALL propositional functions of individuals. But this is presupposed also in classical mathematics, especially classical analysis, and objections against it lead to such modifications . . . as intuitionism . . .

With the exception of Weyl, none of the aforementioned critics of higher-order logic favour intuitionism. All accept classical mathematics as it stands.

To echo Church's point, Montague (1965) proposed that the informal, but much used, notion of the 'standard model' of arithmetic, analysis, and even set theory is explicated by the notion of the 'model of the respective second-order theory'. Another influential item was Kreisel's (1967) 'Informal rigour and completeness proofs', which is discussed in Chapter 5, Section 5.3. The attack is directed at first-order versions of theories, like arithmetic and analysis (and set theory), that have schemes with infinitely many instances in place of second-order axioms. It is argued that such theories allow only unnatural epistemologies and are not true to the informal meaning, the 'informal rigour', of actual mathematical practice. Corcoran (1973, 1980), Boolos (1975), and Shapiro (1985a) are studies of aspects of mathematical practice that resist first-order treatments. Corcoran focuses on the historical importance of categoricity which, of course, cannot be attained in a first-order language.[32]

I concede that many of the arguments in favour of higher-order logic, including my own, are not successful against a thorough relativism like that of Skolem (and perhaps von Neumann). Such views, in effect, deny outright that these structures and concepts are unequivocal. They claim that most mathematical theories *do not have* unique 'standard interpretations', even up to isomorphism. Thus the failure of the categoricity of first-order theories accurately reflects the semantic and ontological situation. But, in large part, this view is a straw man, at least today.[33] Many contemporary advocates of first-order languages seem to reject Skolemite relativism and thus presumably agree that we do succeed in the description (up to isomorphism) and communication of at least some infinite structures. The prevailing attitude seems to be that *informal* mathematics is somehow sufficient to describe and communicate the structures and concepts in question, but that model-theoretic semantics must fail where informal practice succeeds. Such a view is explicitly articulated by Myhill (1951).

The latter combination, first-order logic without relativism, is the target of this book. With Church (1956), the proposal is that the consequence relation of higher-order logic, or something equivalent, is a good model of classical mathematical practice or, better, that higher-order logic provides the best explication of classical mathematics.

This is *not* to say that the consequence relation of second-order logic is completely understood, nor is it as well-understood as first-order logic. But we do have a serviceable grasp of second-order logic. There are, to be sure, deep philosophical and mathematical problems associated with it. For example, there are problems concerning reference and problems concerning how the language can be learned. But these are present in classical mathematics as well, and, as noted, proponents of first-order logic are not willing to give that up, or even to modify it or take it at other than face value. To follow Church, the problems are more perspicuous in the case of higher-order logic, but they are not more troublesome.[34] The thesis is that the language *and semantics* used to model various mathematical theories should be in line with the (presumed) descriptive and communicative power of the language of mathematics.

A common response from the first-order camp is that the (semantic) 'benefits' of second-order languages are the results of the (naive) set theory hidden in the metalanguage. This is an elaboration of von Neumann's (1925) remark that the categoricity of, say, Euclidean geometry is won by temporarily ignoring problems with the underlying set theory. This is correct, but it tells against classical mathematics as much as it does against second-order logic.

Another suggestion is that it would be more natural, and more revealing, to formulate various mathematical theories within (first-order) set theory. This raises again the issue concerning the border between mathematics and its logic (see Chapter 9, Section 9.3). No doubt, the consequence relation of second-order logic, as articulated here, is not a suitable ingredient in the early foundationalist programmes, logicism and the Hilbert programme, at least for the epistemic agenda. One who takes logic to be the last outpost of foundationalism might be inclined toward first-order logic. However, Quine and his followers are thoroughly anti-foundationalist, even concerning logic (see, for example, Quine 1960). Quine also holds that there is no sharp border between logic/mathematics and natural science. In many places, he has shown how mathematical concepts, involving a 'commitment' to its ontology, are essential in virtually all sciences. This is his anti-nominalism. But he also seems to believe that logic—indeed, the logic of mathematics—is different.

To sum up, the period between the 1930s and the present has produced a detailed elaboration of the various positions and, consequently, not as much discussion is obviously at cross purposes. Nevertheless, the present stand-offs are not all that different from their historical counterparts. The higher-order advocates claim that what we call the 'logical notion of set'—variables ranging over the subclasses of a fixed domain—is sufficiently clear for use in logic and, moreover, the use of such terminology is essential to at least part of the foundational enterprise, if not the foundational*ist* enterprise. The first-order advocates reject the use of set terminology, regarding it as problematic or as not sufficiently topic neutral to serve logic. The alternative, once again, is that membership be treated as non-logical. The task of characterizing structures and the 'higher-order' concepts (like finitude and well-foundedness) is passed to *first-order* set theory (pretty much as Skolem formulated it). The latter, of course, has a rather steep ontology (as conceived informally), but it is associated with the mathematical theory of sets, not with logic. Of course, first-order set theory is itself subject to the Löwenheim–Skolem theorems and thus has a wealth of non-standard models. The 'first-order' options are either to embrace relativism and deny that there is a single range to the locution of 'all subclasses' (even after a domain is fixed) or to insist that model-theoretic semantics must ignore the inherent success of mathematical understanding, practice, and communication. In short, the foundational 'goals' for which higher-order terminology is invoked are regarded as unattainable in semanics, either because they cannot be attained at all—there is nothing unequivocal to describe—or because communication is attained only 'informally'.

The stand-off is particularly frustrating because there is no apparent common standpoint from which to evaluate and adjudicate the matter. What one side regards as an integral part of the whole foundational enterprise— including the enterprise of 'logic choice'—the other side rejects as obscure or problematic.

Notes

1. As understood here, every collection of objects is the extension of a property. See Chapter 1, Section 1.3.
2. Standard higher-order and first-order (or Henkin) interpretations do not exhaust the possibilities. If, for example, the range of the predicate variables is the collection of all *finite* subsets of the domain, then the logic is, in a sense, intermediate between first-order and second-order. This is called 'weak second-order logic' (see Chapter 9, Section 9.1, and Barwise and Feferman (1985)).
3. In the axioms for group theory, for example, the variables range over a fixed, but unspecified, group. The purpose is to make statements applicable to all groups. Today, the term 'abstract' has taken on a different meaning in discussions of ontology. It is a synonym for 'immaterial'. Here, however, the term refers to the result of a process of abstraction, the determination of structures common to different systems of objects. For the present, questions concerning the ontological status of the results of abstraction are not considered (see Shapiro 1989b).
4. It is not claimed that this taxonomy of logicians is exclusive or comprehensive. In fact, members of the different schools drew from each other. Moreover, the division is limited to the period under study here. Contemporary logic has elements of all three, and there is no need to force earlier logicians, such as Aristotle, the Stoics, and the Scholastics, into this classification.
5. With techniques of contemporary logic, this difference can be overcome, at least in part. The logicist can restrict the quantifiers in formulas to particular structures. When an algebraist, or a mathematician, says 'for all x, . .' in reference to a domain d, a logicist could write 'for all x, if x is in d, then. . .'. On the other hand, the notion of unrelativized reasoning was foreign to the algebraic approach. As noted in Chapter 1 above, Schröder (1890, p. 245) remarked that one cannot, without contradiction, let the fixed domain consist of all objects (although his reasons for this were rather obscure). Something similar to unrelativized reasoning might be obtained if, conceivably, one could invoke a notion of 'all structures whatsoever' and abstract 'laws of thought' from it. Similarly, a mathematician cannot literally capture what the logicists intend, unless the entire universe can somehow be regarded as a single system and given an axiomatic treatment. However, once set theory, and the general notion of model, have themselves been developed axiomatically, at least some of the logicists' universality can be expressed. A statement about 'all properties', for example, might correspond to a statement, within set theory, about all sets.
6. As noted in Chapter 1, confusion between these two notions of set should arise only in set theory, since in that case the 'fixed domain' (for the logical notion) is itself the set-theoretic hierarchy. An iterative set is a member of that hierarchy and, in this context, a logical set is a *collection* of iterative sets—what is called a 'class'. The argument yielding Russell's paradox shows that in set theory, there are logical sets (classes) that are not iterative sets or, in other words, there are collections of iterative sets that are not members of the set-theoretic hierarchy. Following common terminology, a *proper class* is a collection of iterative sets that is not itself a member of the set-theoretic hierarchy. The entire hierarchy, for example, is a proper class. The effect of Russell's paradox on various historical figures is briefly treated in Chapter 1. For the most part, only the logicists were

affected, since they envisaged a universal domain which at least prima facie includes all sets, or the extensions of all properties.

7. John Corcoran has informed me that Tarski eventually favoured first-order logic, even though much of his work in the 1930s concerns higher-order languages.

8. Coextensiveness, of course, is the criterion of identity among extensional items. It is consistent with Frege's view that coextensiveness is a *congruence* relation among concepts. That is, if $\forall x(Xx \equiv Yx)$ and $\Phi(X)$ then $\Phi(Y)$ (provided that Y is free for X in $\Phi(X)$). I am grateful to Harold Hodes for pointing this out.

9. As Moore (1988) notes, this 'completeness axiom' did not appear in the original German edition (Hilbert 1899), but was added in the French (Hilbert 1902) and English translations.

10. Again, no first-order theory with an infinite model is categorical. Thus, if the categoricity statements proved by Veblen and Huntington are applied to first-order theories, they are false. As noted, Hilbert's extremal axiom states that the intended models are 'maximal'—there are to be no proper extensions of the models. But if the theory without the extremal axiom is first-order then, since it has an infinite model, the theory has no maximal model. Every model is contained in a larger one. To put this historical point in Quinean terms, suppose that we were engaged in 'translating' the languages of these authors into current mathematical dialect. If it is insisted that the 'output' of the translation be rendered in the corresponding first-order languages, then we must attribute some rather elementary mistakes to the authors.

11. The same goes for the stronger axiom of replacement, to be discussed presently. See Chapter 6, Section 6.4 for a brief discussion of Zermelo set theory.

12. The well-ordering theorem states that for every set x, there is a well-ordering on x (see Chapter 5, Section 5.1). In current Zermelo–Fraenkel set theory, it is equivalent to the axiom of choice. See Moore (1982) for an extended discussion of Zermelo's work on set theory, and its subsequent influence on mathematics.

13. See also Schoenflies (1911). Poincaré's attack was based in part on his rejection of the actual infinite and of impredicative definition (see Goldfarb 1988). These are two of many issues related to the proper treatment of infinite collections. The resolutions led to what is today called 'classical mathematics', including the use of classical logic, impredicative definition, and set theory. For an illuminating presentation of the 'transition', see Stein (1988).

14. Dedekind defined a set S to be *finite* if there is no one-to-one correspondence between S and a proper subset of S. This is at least prima facie higher-order, since it uses what I call the 'logical notion of set'. Harold Hodes suggested (in correspondence) that, conceivably, one could attempt a bootstrap construction. First formulate a rudimentary set theory without separation and define 'the natural numbers' to be say, the finite von Neumann ordinals. Then, with this as metatheory, one might employ the newly defined notion of natural numbers to formulate a set theory containing a principle of separation, perhaps along the lines of Weyl (1910). However, it is not clear that the arithmetic formulated in the rudimentary set theory is sufficient, since the usual way to derive a general induction scheme within set theory uses separation. Moreover, the elementary set theory does not appear to be capable of coding some collections necessary to do metatheory (e.g. the collection of well-formed formulas). If an induction principle were explicitly stated and added as an axiom scheme, it would seem

that one is taking the natural numbers as fundamental after all. In any case, this sort of thing was not attempted by anyone during the period under study here. The relationship between the notion of set and that of number is developed in Chapter 9, Section 9.1.

15. Skolem and Fraenkel (independently) also realized the need for an axiom of replacement. Skolem's version was an axiom scheme formulated in terms of his (first-order) notion of *definit* property, much like contemporary first-order *ZFC*. Fraenkel first gave a rather imprecise account:

> If *M* is a set, and *M'* is obtained by replacing each member of *M* with some object, then *M'* is a set.

Thus the name 'replacement'. The principle was soon recast in terms of Fraenkel's notion of the *definitorisch* function, but then it was too weak to serve its purpose. Von Neumann (1928) demonstrated that this version of the axiom of replacement could be proved in Zermelo's original system.

16. For Dedekind, a *simply infinite system* is, in effect, a countable set and a successor operation. At least conceptually, the Dedekind notion of finitude (see note 14) differs from the usual one, which refers to or presupposes the natural numbers. A set *S* is *Cantor finite* if there is a natural number *n* such that *S* has exactly *n* elements. Thus we have a choice between a set-theoretic and a number-theoretic foundation for the notion of finitude.

17. This is elaborated in the next section and the next chapter.

18. As shown in Chapter 5, Section 5.4 (see also Chapter 9, Section 9.3), one can give a set-theoretic definition of second-order logical consequence in contemporary set theory, even first-order set theory. But this pushes the question back one level, to the issue of whether first-order set theory is adequate.

19. As far as I can determine, the first explicit observation that first-order theories of arithmetic are not categorical did not occur until Skolem (1933, 1934), but it follows from the incompleteness of arithmetic and the completeness of first-order logic.

20. Fraenkel's axiom of restriction might be called a 'minimal principle' since it attempts to rule out the existence of proper substructures that are models of the other axioms. In contrast, Hilbert's axiom of completeness is 'maximal' in that it attempts to rule out proper superstructures that are models of the other axioms. For an extensive treatment of such 'extremal axioms', see Carnap and Bachmann (1936). On the axiom of restriction, see Fraenkel *et al.* (1973, pp. 113–19).

21. If one allows the metatheoretic principle of restriction to count as an axiom of set theory, then in a sense it does provide a categorical characterization, whether or not the other axioms are first-order. It can be shown that the only models of first-order *ZFC* that have no proper submodels are those isomorphic to the minimal constructible model—a countable set. The only standard models of second-order *ZFC*, our sentence *Z*2, that have no proper submodels are those that are isomorphic to the first inaccessible rank.

22. Of course, the claim that infinite collections are problematic did not originate with Skolem or the intuitionists.

23. Zermelo's lecture is published in Moore (1980, Section 10.2).

24. In fact, around this time, Hilbert and Ackermann (1928) did provide an axiomatic treatment of propositional functions. As noted in the previous subsection, they characterized ω-order logic.

25. This version of the theory contains the axiom of replacement and the axiom of foundation. The axiom of choice was not included, however, but it seems to have been assumed as a general logical principle. As noted in Chapters 4 and 5, a (global) principle of choice can be proved in second-order Zermelo–Fraenkel set theory (our axiom $Z2$) from the axiom of choice $\forall R(\forall x \exists y Rxy \rightarrow \exists f \forall x Rxfx)$ in the deductive system $D2$ of second-order logic.

26. Skolem (1928) also states that both of his 'scientifically tenable' characterizations (of propositional functions) make essential use of the notion of natural number. He then concedes that we cannot characterize *this* notion without using propositional functions (in the induction axiom). He concludes:

    The attempt to base the notions of logic upon those of arithmetic, or vice versa, seems to me to be mistaken. The foundations of both must be laid simultaneously and in an interrelated way.

27. The first of these letters is reprinted (in Zermelo's hand) and translated in Dawson (1985a). The other two letters are published in Grattan-Guinness (1979).

28. See Chapter 9, Section 9.1.3, for a brief summary of infinitary languages.

29. Some (very) notable exceptions will be discussed presently. The debate over *relativism* continued throughout Skolem's career. See, for example, the exchange between Tarski and Skolem in Skolem (1958) (reprinted in part in Moore (1988)).

30. A similar assault on second-order logic was recently made by Field (1984), who suggested that logic should not have substantial existence theorems. Field embraces the Kantian thesis that there should be no a priori, or purely logical, arguments for the existence of anything (e.g. *Critique of pure reason*, B622–623, on 'ontological arguments').

31. Church states that there would be cogent objections to a logic whose very grammar is not effective, because there would then be no mechanical way to determine if a given string is a well-formed formula. But objections to a non-effective consequence relation are on a different level. In the note in question, Church uses the word 'platonism' to describe the attitude shared by the employment of the second-order consequence relation and the pursuit of classical mathematics generally (referring to Bernays (1935)). This can be misleading. The matters at hand are methodological, concerning things like non-effective relations, the law of excluded middle, and impredicative definition. The issues surrounding platonistic epistemology are not raised, nor, for that matter, are traditional matters of ontology. See Shapiro (1989a).

32. Boolos (1975) goes on to challenge Quine's claim that the ontological presuppositions of second-order logic are excessive. In two recent articles, Boolos (1984, 1985a) proposes that second-order quantifiers be regarded as 'plural quantifiers' are in ordinary language, and has developed a semantics along these lines. The claim is that, understood this way, second-order variables and quantifiers introduce *no* ontology beyond that of a corresponding first-order theory, but only new expressive resources for the same ontology. This is briefly presented in Chapter 9, Section 9.1.

33. On the other hand, the relativism of von Neumann and Skolem is not dead. Weston (1976) claims that the non-categoricity that pervades first-order systems reappears in the *set-theoretic semantics* of higher-order languages. The proposal is that the powerset operation is not unique in an absolute sense. If this is correct, then the very semantics for second-order languages is itself not unique. In fact,

there would be a wealth of such semantics—one for each 'powerset' operation. Quine, for his part, has articulated and defended a general relativism in ontology, but not on Skolemite grounds. He has often criticized the use of the Skolem paradox in ontology. An extended treatment of the connections between this and his views on first-order logic would go beyond the scope of this book.

34. Completeness is not a cure-all for the sorts of philosophical problems indicated here. First-order logic is not immune, nor is propositional logic. One group of issues concerns the extent to which explicit or implicit, formal or informal, rules for using a language determine what it 'means'. Carnap (1943) shows in great detail that even the eminently complete deductive system for *propositional* logic is consistent with different 'interpretations' of it.

Second-order logic and rule-following

Not empiricism and yet realism in philosophy, that is the hardest thing.

And the picture that might occur to someone here is that of a short bit of handrail, by means of which I am to let myself be guided further than the rail reaches. (But there *is* nothing there; but there isn't *nothing* there!)

The difficult thing here is not, to dig down to the ground; no, it is to recognize the ground that lies before us as the ground.

Wittgenstein (1978, pp. 325, 430, 333)

This penultimate chapter concludes the polemics of the book. Its purpose is to cast some of the issues surrounding higher-order logic in philosophical terms, relating them to current matters of general ontology, epistemology, and semantics. In the last section, the problem of higher-order logic is related to Wittgensteinian issues of rule-following.

In a recent conference proceedings, Corcoran (1987) defends second-order logic by arguing that discourse about properties and relations is a natural, and inevitable, extension of discourse about objects, as indicated by the presence of common nouns and straightforward grammatical constructions. In present terminology, the thesis is that languages with variables ranging over properties and relations are natural extensions of languages with variables ranging over objects.[1] In this book, I have argued at some length that this is especially so in the development of formal languages to model the underlying logic of mathematical discourse.

On the other hand, there is nothing to prevent a first-order language from being 'about' relations, functions, sets, or anything else for that matter, provided only that there are coherent statements about such items to model. As we have seen, this is not the same as a higher-order language with standard semantics. The issue lies in the extension, or range, of the variables in question.

There is a striking affinity between Corcoran's remarks and Quine's analysis of ontological commitment in language (see, for example, Quine 1960, Resnik 1982). Both focus on the development of linguistic techniques for acknowledging and referring to objects. Quine, of course, is a steadfast *opponent* of second-order logic *as logic*, but he is not an opponent of set theory as mathematics. This indicates that the analysis of language that shows that talk of sets is natural does not thereby determine the totality of the range of the relevant variables. In the present framework, the Quine–Corcoran analysis does not, by itself, decide among the different semantics for the extended languages. Many of Corcoran's arguments in favour of second-order *languages* equally support standard semantics and Henkin semantics.

To reiterate, the proponents of second-order logic *as logic* hold that second-order terminology with standard semantics is sufficiently clear, intuitive, or unproblematic to serve the underlying framework for axiomatization and foundations of mathematics. The claim is that once a domain (for the first-order variables) is fixed, there is a reasonably clear and unambiguous understanding of such locutions as 'all relations' or 'all subsets' thereof. We have a decent grasp on such locutions, and they play central roles in foundations of mathematics.

The first-order 'opposition', on the other hand, rejects this. Most do not claim that sets do not exist, nor that discourse about sets or properties is somehow illegitimate. Indeed, many of the major proponents of first-order logic, such as Skolem, Quine, and Gödel, have explicitly acknowledged set theory and contributed to its development. Moreover, Quine and Gödel adopted and defended attitudes of realism towards set theory (each in his own way). Their claim seems to be that variables ranging over all the properties of a fixed domain are not sufficiently clear to serve *foundational* studies, and that this terminology itself stands in need of further 'foundation'. That is, the relevant theory of sets ought to be formulated as an axiomatic theory in its own right, presumably a *first-order* theory. As we have seen, Quine (1970) calls second-order logic 'set theory in disguise'. The issue here is a difficult one and it seems impossible to avoid begging at least some of the questions.

8.1 The regress

Imagine a dialogue between an advocate of second-order logic, call him 'Second', and an advocate of first-order logic, call her 'First'. Second begins by developing a formal language with variables ranging over properties, and he explains, informally, the intuitive standard 'semantics', the idea that the property variables range over all properties, or all sets, of whatever is in the range of the first-order variables. He then proves that arithmetic and real analysis, as formulated in second-order languages, are categorical (along the lines of Chapter 4, Section 4.2), and he shows that the real numbers are not countable (Cantor's theorem). At this point, First raises a question concerning the range of the second-order variables. She asserts that the meaning of the second-order terminology is not very clear and she requests that it be developed more fully. Second could retort that First knows perfectly well what locutions like 'all subsets' mean, and he may accuse her of making trouble for the sake of making trouble. They would then be at a stand-off.

On the other hand, Second may regard the request for clarification as legitimate. One can, indeed, do rigorous model-theoretic semantics and, in effect, provide a foundation for the background metatheory. So Second proceeds to develop a version of axiomatic set theory sufficient to formulate the standard semantics of the second-order theories. Call the formal meta-theory *MT*. Second shows how the proofs of the categoricity and cardinality theorems can be rendered in *MT*.

At this point, things become interesting. First applauds the effort. She agrees that the development of *MT* is a significant event and clarifies things considerably. She even contributes to the development of *MT* by proving some theorems and suggesting new axioms. But she takes *MT* as a *first-order* theory. In particular, she claims that the semantical theory is itself subject to Löwenheim–Skolem theorems and the like. Thus *MT* has many models. First argues that the categoricity theorems only show that *within* each model of the semantics *MT*, all models of arithmetic are isomorphic and, similarly, within each interpretation of the semantics, all models of real analysis are isomorphic. Also, within each model of the semantics, the extension of 'the real numbers' is uncountable *in that model*. Such is relativism.

Second retorts that *MT* is not to be regarded as just another theory with various models of various cardinalities. And it is not an implicit definition of its subject matter. On the contrary, *MT* has an *intended interpretation*—the semantics of the original languages. Foundational studies are not done with uninterpreted theories. In short, the categoricity results should be taken at *face value*, referring to possible domains for the original languages, not to this or that model of the metatheory. The results are that arithmetic and real analysis are *really* categorical, not just categorical in each model of *MT*, and Second insists that the real numbers are really uncountable. Moreover, he points out that the argument that First makes crucially depends on the Löwenheim–Skolem theorems, which are *demonstrably false* for the second-order languages under study. Remember the categoricity theorems.

The reply at this point is predictable. First claims that the 'refutations' of the Löwenheim–Skolem theorems are themselves relative to a model. To repeat, they only show that *within* each model *M* of *MT* each model *m* of, say, real analysis, is uncountable in *M*. It does not rule out the possibility that this same model *m* is countable in some more encompassing model of *MT* (but of course *m* would not be a model of real analysis in the more encompassing structures). The theorems only show that the same structure cannot be both countable and a model of real analysis *from the same perspective*. As for the assertion that *MT* is 'already' interpreted, First requests clarification of this 'intended semantics for the original languages'. Second reminds First that he has already accomplished this. *MT* is the characterization, and First accepted it. But she seems to insist that *MT* must itself be interpreted. We seem to have reached another stand-off.

Upon further examination (since neither Second nor First are stubborn), it is seen that the dispute centres on the axiom of separation (in *MT*), which states that if x is a set and P a property that is well-defined on the members of x, then there is a subset y of x that contains all and only the members of x that have the property P. As above, its straightforward formulation is

$$\forall x \exists y \forall z[z \in y \equiv (z \in x \mathbin{\&} Pz)].$$

This, of course, is a second-order sentence. Second insists that it be given a *standard* reading, with the variable P ranging over all properties of the universe (i.e. all classes), while First insists on a first-order (or Henkin) interpretation. She claims that the locution 'all classes' is not unequivocal, and certainly is not part of the logic. At this point, Second can respond to the challenges by developing a semantics for *MT*, a metasemantics. Call it *MMT*. But then First would understand *MMT* as a first-order theory and Second would not. Our desire to avoid (or postpone) the stand-off between First and Second has led to a regress.

The scepticism, or relativism, that First advocates is not limited to second-order logic. It is linked to a remarkably similar regress or stand-off concerning the range of the *first-order* variables in rather basic theories. They can be regarded as subject to a wide variety of standard and non-standard modelling, or else one can insist that there is an unambiguous intuitive understanding of the range of the variables, unique up to isomorphism. Suppose, for example, that First asks what one means by 'the natural numbers', the intended domain of arithmetic. Second responds with an axiomatization of Peano arithmetic, the crucial item of which is the induction axiom

$$(P0 \mathbin{\&} \forall x(Px \rightarrow Psx)) \rightarrow \forall x Px.$$

First raises the (by now) usual question concerning the range of the property variable P. She takes induction to be a first-order *axiom scheme*, and points out that the theory, thus construed, has many models of various cardinalities. Of course, Second rejects this construal and replies that the understanding he has in mind—the intended model—is the 'smallest' of the models. It is the structure that is an initial segment of all of the first-order models. First asks for a characterization of 'smallest model' or 'initial segment of all models', claiming that the quantifiers in these locutions are too problematic to serve foundations without further ado. Perhaps in frustration, Second asserts that by 'natural number', he means 'member of the sequence 0, 1, 2, 3, 4, . . .'. First asks about the '. . .'.

In sum, our advocate of second-order logic holds that reference to, say, the natural numbers is clear and unambiguous, at least now. Any two mathematicians who discuss arithmetic are talking about the same (or isomorphic) structures. Suppose that First and Second agree, at least for the sake of argument, that formal arithmetic adequately models pre-theoretical discourse—as they agreed that MT models informal semantics. Second takes the categoricity results to *confirm* his prior belief that arithmetic is unambiguous. But these results involve locutions like 'all properties' or 'all subsets', and the 'confirmation' depends on those locutions themselves being unambiguous. First insists that there is no reason to believe this for the second-order variables and thus no reason to accept the confirmation of the original belief that arithmetic is unequivocal.

In sum, the scepticism or relativism concerning second-order languages applies (or not) just as well to mathematical theories whose intended domains are infinite. Relativism concerning second-order variables goes with what may be called 'object language relativism'. On the other hand, one who is willing to accept classical mathematics, more or less as it stands, should also accept second-order languages. As we have seen, Church (1956, p. 326n) makes a similar point. Let us repeat the passage:

> Objections may indeed be made to this new point of view, on the basis of the sort of *absolutism* it presupposes . . . But it should be pointed out that this . . . is already inherent in classical mathematics generally, and it is not made more acute or more doubtful, but only more conspicuous, by its application to [logic] . . . It is true that the non-effective notion of consequence, as we have introduced it . . . presupposes a certain absolute notion of ALL propositional functions of individuals. But this is presupposed also in classical mathematics, especially classical analysis, . . .

As shown in the previous chapter, parts of these dialogues can be found in exchanges between major figures earlier this century. Zermelo (1908a, b) who corresponds to Second, formulated axiomatic set theory. Skolem (1922) pointed out that the proposed axioms have many models, even countable ones. Like our character First, he formulated the central principle of separation as a scheme, one instance for each formula of the (first-order) language. This, of course, is in line with the set theories of today. When Zermelo (1929) returned to his axiomatization, he produced an explicit second-order characterization with variables ranging over propositional functions. In response, Skolem (1930) noted that this reformulation of set theory was similar to his own (Skolem 1922), the only difference being Zermelo's use of variables ranging over propositional functions. Skolem wondered whether Zermelo intended to provide still more axioms to characterize those. Presumably, Zermelo did not think that a further formulation was needed—this is the material of which foundations are made. Clearly, he could have provided axioms to characterize the propositional functions, or else he could refer to Hilbert and Ackermann's (1928) treatment of higher-order logic. But Skolem stands ready to interpret anything Zermelo might say as thoroughly first-order, and thus subject to reinterpretation via the Löwenheim–Skolem theorems.

8.2 Options

In philosophy, regresses like the ones encountered here are familiar. One cannot forever continue to define one's terms using other terms, one cannot forever continue to prove one's premises from still more premises, and in the cases at hand one cannot forever continue to model the meaning of one's discourse by providing more model-theoretic semantics. The hope of foundationalism was that such regresses would end at the bedrock of self-evidence, but this was not to be. In the present situation, it looks as if questions must be begged. The first-order camp rejects, or at any rate challenges, the very framework that the higher-order advocates use in explicating the meaning of informal mathematical discourse.

Several options are available at this point. One is to maintain that most of the discourse of informal mathematics can be taken at face value (i.e. not reinterpreted) and that it successfully refers to structures that are unique, up to isomorphism. Such structures include those of the natural numbers, the real and complex numbers, and perhaps the set-theoretic hierarchy. As in Chapter 5, this may be called 'working realism' because no position is taken (so far) concerning the metaphysical nature of the indicated structures.

The previous chapters of this book *assume* working realism and argue from that perspective that first-order languages are inadequate models of mathematical practice. In other words, it has been presupposed all along that there is something for the formal languages of foundational studies to describe. If the natural language of mathematics is cast in a first-order language, then one cannot account for the characterization and communication of the presumed structures. There is a clear sense in which the non-standard models do not capture what is intended. *One* 'solution', the one pursued here, is to maintain that the languages of informal discourse are well modelled by second-order languages with standard semantics. This is to assume or presuppose that the second-order terminology is itself understood unambiguously. With Church, this is no more problematic than working realism in informal mathematics. The presuppositions of second-order logic are those of classical mathematics, taken at face value.

Another option, still within the rubric of working realism, is to hold that mathematical structures are successfully characterized (up to isomorphism) and communicated, but to maintain that this occurs only intuitively, or only in *informal* practice. That is, the communication of mathematics is somehow inherently informal.[2] This view denies a significant role to *any* rigorous semantics in explicating mathematical description and communication. One may then hold that, to the limited extent that mathematics can be modelled, the logic to employ is first-order. Against Church, this combination rejects the connection between the presuppositions of classical mathematics, as practised, and second-order logic. The former is accepted; the latter is not.

A third option is to reject working realism and to embrace a version of Skolemite relativism. One maintains that mathematical theories do not have unequivocal interpretations—or even interpretations unique up to isomorphism. With a moderate amount of set theory, one can characterize models of various theories, and in some cases it is possible to use the resources of set theory to specify an 'intended' interpretation for a theory. For example, one shows that the standard model of arithmetic is isomorphic to the set of finite ordinals. But, and here is the rub, this view invariably insists that the mathematical theories *and metatheories* are implicit definitions, and their languages can only be modelled with first-order semantics. Thus any theory at any level, if satisfiable in an infinite domain, has models of every infinite cardinality, and ultimately there is no principled way to identify an intended one. In other words, the underlying model theory is yet another theory with many 'interpretations'. There is no unequivocal understanding of such terms as 'set', 'subset', or 'finite', and quantifiers like 'all models' or 'all propositional functions'.

Benacerraf (1985) shows that Skolem shifted from the 'mathematics is inherently informal' view, which he held in Skolem (1922), to such a relativism. We have seen that von Neumann (1925) registers ambivalence. After discussing Fraenkel's attempt to provide a categorical characterization of set theory with the axiom of restriction, von Neumann encountered the sort of regress, or relativism, presented above. He concluded that

> ... no categorical axiomatization of set theory seems to exist at all; for probably no axiomatization will be able to avoid the difficulties connected with the axiom of restriction ... And since there is no axiom system for mathematics, geometry, and so forth that does not presuppose set theory, there probably cannot be any categorically axiomatized infinite systems at all.

Von Neumann then noted that a similar relativism seems to apply to basic notions of cardinality, like finitude, since even these concepts are formulated with variables which occur 'with reference to the entire system'. This strikes close to home. If the relativity is sustained, then, of the notion of finitude,

> ... nothing but the shell of its formal characterization would ... remain ... It is difficult to say whether this would militate more strongly against its intuitive character ... or its foundation as given by set theory.

Von Neumann expresses two parts of the present tri-lemma.

1. One can reject the assertion that the fundamental notions of number, cardinality, subset, etc., as formulated in practice, are unequivocal. The best grasp we have of these concepts is that codified in axiomatic set theory, taken to be an implicit definition and first-order. This is relativism.

2. One can maintain that we have an intuitive unequivocal grasp of the notions and reject the adequacy of the axiomatic set-theoretic foundation.

We add another option.

3. One can maintain the intuitive character of the notion of subset and *use* this to provide second-order characterizations.

In the cases at hand, second-order implicit definitions succeed in characterizing their subjects up to isomorphism.

8.3   Rules and logic

In practice, of course, the present regresses do not go on very long. No one, for example, has bothered to formulate a meta-meta-metalanguage and then wonder how to understand or interpret it. The regresses end, on all accounts, in the discourse of informal mathematics. At this level, there is no further codification, perhaps because it is realized that this would only push the problems further back. It is not that we cannot precisely formulate the next metalanguage, but we see little point in doing so.

There is also almost universal agreement among present-day mathematicians concerning the practice of informal mathematics and the use of informal discourse. With the exception of traditional constructivists, there is no widespread and systematic disagreement over examples of correct *proof*, at least not now. There is at most an occasional skirmish. The more philosophical disputes noted here do not concern the correctness of informal mathematics, but rather things like how the discourse should be described, what it means, what it refers to, and what its non-logical terminology is. None of the real or fictional disputants of this chapter should be regarded as advocating the revision of current practice.[3]

This explains why the proof theories of the logics under examination here are remarkably similar, and underscores the foregoing thesis that the differences between first-order logic and higher-order logic lie primarily in the different views on the totality of the range of the extra variables—in the model theory. Indeed, one cannot deduce more *theorems* using a second-order language than one can with a multi-sorted first-order language with set variables. Both have admirably succeeded in 'saving appearances' concerning the correct use of informal discourse.[4]

Thus, to borrow a Quinean phrase, the regress ends in practice when we 'lapse into the mother tongue' of informal mathematical discourse, and there things proceed rather smoothly, at least for now. This observation is rather congenial with the view held by some philosophers that there is no more to understanding concepts than knowing how to use the relevant language. Variations on this theme have been championed by the later Wittgenstein (1958, 1978), Dummett (1973), and Putnam (1980). There is a much discussed remark of Wittgenstein's that seems to fit the situation well:

> It can be seen that there is a misunderstanding here from the mere fact that in the course of our argument we gave one interpretation after another, as if each

one contented us for at least a moment, until we thought of another standing behind it. What this shews is that there is a way of grasping a rule which is *not* an *interpretation*... (Wittgenstein 1959, Section 201)

A slogan often associated with such views is 'meaning is use', but I believe that this is misleading. For present purposes, it is a thesis about *understanding*, not a thesis about meaning or semantics, at least not directly. The claim is that understanding should not be ineffable. One understands the concepts embodied in a language to the extent that one knows how to use the language correctly. Call this the *Use Thesis*.

In the philosophy of language, the most straightforward opponents of the Use Thesis are those who tie understanding to a grasp of something that transcends use, or is conceptually independent of use. One example, perhaps, is Frege, who held that each meaningful expression of an interpreted language is associated with a timeless, eternal, objective, and mind-independent entity called its *sense*. On such views, presumably, the concepts associated with a part of language are understood only if the requisite senses are grasped. To be sure, a given person's ability to use a language, such as that of arithmetic, is *evidence* for his having grasped the senses, but use and understanding are two different things. Against such views, the Use Thesis is that the ability to use a language *constitutes* understanding and thus grasping the concepts.

As Dummett (1973) puts it:

> An individual cannot communicate what he cannot be observed to communicate: if an individual associated with a mathematical symbol or formula some mental content, where the association did not lie in the use he made of the symbol or formula, then he could not convey that content by means of the symbol or formula, for his audience would be unaware of the association and would have no means of becoming aware of it.

Moreover, in learning a language, such as that of arithmetic, one does not directly learn the sense of each expression, much less the denotation of each term. One learns, in effect, how to *use* each expression. This includes performing the computations that underlie simple equations, applying arithmetic to everyday problems, and, later, proving and refuting arithmetic statements and reasoning hypothetically in the language:

> These things are all that we learn when we are learning the meanings of the expressions of a language of the mathematical theory in question, because they are all that we can be shown.

Perhaps another way to characterize the present contrast is to note that, on Fregean views, it is possible, at least in principle, for someone (or some machine) to be able to use a language correctly and still not grasp the relevant concepts. One can fake it. Dummett writes:

To suppose that there is an ingredient of meaning which transcends the use that is made of that which carries the meaning is to suppose that someone might have learned all that is directly taught when the language of a mathematical theory is taught to him, and might then behave in every way like someone who understood the language, and yet not actually understand it, or understand it only incorrectly.

Conversely, on the views under attack, it seems to be possible to grasp concepts and yet not be able to *say* anything correct about them. Again, understanding is conceptually independent of use, even if the gap is usually not very large in practice. The Use Thesis rejects both of these possibilities out of hand.[5]

It is often thought that the Use Thesis stands opposed to realism, the view that the variables of the language range over a realm of objects that exist independent of the mathematician and her mental life. Indeed, the slogan 'meaning is use' is often taken as a hallmark of anti-realism. Dummett, for example, argues that the Use Thesis suggests, or even demands, that model-theoretic semantics, with domains of discourse, a satisfaction relation, and truth conditions, is inappropriate. He proposes that 'use' replace 'truth' or 'satisfaction' as the main *ingredient* of a compositional semantics. One provides 'proof conditions' instead of 'truth conditions' (and thus his defence of intuitionistic logic).

This broad conclusion is not warranted, and in fact I urge the opposite. The Use Thesis is quite plausible, and places sensible constraints on *any* theory of meaning. But, by itself, it does not demand an anti-realist ontology, nor a non-model-theoretic semantics. It does not follow from the Use Thesis that 'use' must be the central item in semantics. What does follow is that the ontology and truth conditions of semantics must be *compatible* with the learnability and understanding of a language through its use. Truth conditions should not be that far removed from the knowledge implicit in the correct use of a language, and from whatever it is that one learns when acquiring facility with a language. There should be a natural (if not inevitable) link between use and truth conditions. Ideally, it should be clear, or at least defensible, that a theory in a formal language, plus its semantics, is a further articulation of the natural language being modelled, not an abrupt shift away from it. To use a Wittgensteinian metaphor (out of place),[6] it should be plausible that in adding semantics to a theory, one has 'gone on as before'. Otherwise, Dummett is correct that meaning is ineffable, or at least the charge is left unrefuted.[7]

In a similar context, Putnam (1980, p. 479) notes that an advocate of the Use Thesis does not have to reject notions like model and reference. It is a question of understanding the roles that these play in philosophy of mathematics. The *grasp* of particular models cannot be the central criterion of understanding. The model theory is itself formulated (originally) in informal language, which is understood through *its* use. Once one

... has succeeded in understanding a rich enough language to serve as a meta-language for some theory *T*, he can define 'true in *T*' ... he can talk about 'models' for *T*, etc. He can even define 'reference' ... exactly as Tarski did.

The central observation is that semantics comes *after* the original natural language of mathematics is understood, and the original understanding does not consist of grasping a model, intended or otherwise. Understanding the language is knowing how to use it.

At the level of discourse in natural languages, prior to semantics, one can ask about the meanings and referents of certain words. Many of the answers turn out to be platitudes like '12 is a natural number' or '6 is the sixth natural number after zero'. Similarly, the informal metalanguage is capable of distinguishing standard from non-standard models (or semantics): 'Standard models of arithmetic are those that are isomorphic to the natural numbers. Non-standard models begin with a copy of the natural numbers, followed by other elements of the domain.' We do say things like this, and people understand it, or seem to. From the perspective of the regress above, of course, it begs the question. The 'problems' concerning meaning and reference apply to those very statements. We cannot rule out unintended interpretations of the metalanguage unless we can somehow fix its semantics, and we cannot do that without using more language, in which case we must worry about *its* interpretation. And on it goes. But the Use Thesis blocks this regress or, at any rate, decides to stop by refusing to carry it on. We use the languages without further interpretation, but to echo Wittgenstein (also out of place), it does not follow that we use them without right. The (informal) metalanguage and the original natural language are understood when we know how to use them. *We* make the statements, we understand them, and we mean what we say. It makes no sense to ask for the meaning and reference of the *entire* natural language and to expect the answers to be somehow independent of that language.

Recall that two of the options in the above tri-lemma accept working realism, the view that mathematical discourse is to be taken at face value. Arithmetic is about natural numbers, real analysis is about real numbers, set theory is about sets, etc. This much is compatible with the Use Thesis and, indeed, seems to *follow* from it. What else is the Use Theorist going to hold? To be explicit about it, the natural language of mathematics has a predicate N for 'is a natural number'. It is a basic item of the lexicon. The mathematician says that four is a natural number, $N4$. It follows, by existential generalization, that $\exists x N x$, numbers exist, and that is that. I propose that, on the Use Thesis, Skolemite relativism is to be rejected out of hand. The possibility of *re*interpretation of the formal language has nothing to do with original use and thus nothing to do with understanding. To paraphrase Wittgenstein, there is a way of understanding which is not an interpretation. The informal language, as it is used, is not equivocal.

At some point, it seems, we asked for a model-theoretic semantics to be used in accounting for how structures are apprehended, characterized, and communicated. As Putnam (1980) notes, this is a fatal step. It is not that the desire for a model theory is somehow illegitimate. Quite the contrary. The problem is with the idea that model-theoretic semantics is needed to give an account of what we grasp when we learn the meaning of a language:

> To adopt a theory of meaning according to which a language whose whole use is specified still lacks something—viz. its 'interpretation'—is to accept a problem which *can* only have crazy solutions. To speak as if *this* were my problem, 'I know how to use my language, but, now, how should I single out an interpretation?' is to speak nonsense. (Putnam 1980, pp. 481–2)

If this conception of understanding is to be sustained, there is an interesting problem analogous to that of reference and non-standard models. Use Theorists are often criticized for leaving the concept of 'use' vague. Surely an account is needed, even if problems of interpreting that account inevitably arise. As Wittgenstein (1978, pp. 366–7) puts it:

> It all depends [on] *what* settles the sense of a proposition ... The use of the signs must settle it; but what do we count as the use?

It might appear that the Use Thesis demands a shift of attention from model-theoretic semantics to deductive systems, but this is misleading. The problem is to account for how the understanding of a language of mathematics, through its use, constrains the *future* use of the language. How do we 'go on as before'? Specifically, what is the relationship between derivation in deduction systems and broad global 'use', as it figures in understanding?

There is an important aspect of mathematical practice—the *use* of mathematical discourse—that is not captured by first-order languages or by effective deductive systems, namely the sense in which the discourse outstrips, or even 'transcends', its previous manifestations. In fact, many of the considerations in favour of second-order languages can be straightforwardly understood in these terms. The arguments that certain concepts and theories resist first-order treatment amount to claims that first-order languages are not adequate to capture important aspects of the *use* of the relevant languages. We take up an example presently. To anticipate the conclusion, even if the Use Thesis dissolves the above regress of semantics, it does not dissolve the issue of second-order logic. The problem of interpreting the interpretations is replaced with the problem of rules for following rules.

There is an interesting affinity between the way that the problem of second-order languages is posed above and Wright's (1980, Chapter 2) discussion of rule-following.[8] In the above scenarios, the two characters Second and First seemed (at times) to be in agreement. They accepted the same verbal *description* of the interpretation of the language. But they later discovered that they were interpreting the description (of the interpretation) differently. Thus begins the regress. Wright presents a thought experiment involving two people who agree on a description of a rule, and yet go on to apply it differently. There is a hidden divergence on the interpretation of the description of the rule. Let us pursue the analogy.

Kripke (1982) formulates an interesting problem on Wittgenstein's behalf. Most of us were taught how to add in primary school, and we now employ the symbol $+$. The problem is to account for our meaning the addition function by $+$. The thesis at hand is that the meaning of the term is fixed by our use of it and other expressions. But 'what do we count as the use?' The addition function has infinitely many arguments and values. We have not 'used' all of them yet, nor will we ever. Let 'quus' denote a binary function that agrees with addition for all arguments less than some large number N, but differs thereafter. I suggest that the role of the quus function here is analogous to the role of non-standard models in the regress. Kripke's version of the problem is to show how we can refute a 'sceptic' who tries to claim (*ad hominem*) that, in the past, we really meant quus by $+$. The analogy is with a sceptic (i.e. First or Skolem) who tries to claim that our past use of mathematical discourse may have referred to a non-standard model.

If the value of N is large enough, both the plus function and the quus function are consistent with all our past activities—all the numbers that we have added (or quadded) so far. Both are also consistent with our *physical* dispositions to add (assuming that there is some limit to the size of numbers we are disposed to consider). Moreover, anything we have *said* about our practice, such as the recursive definition of $+$, is subject to alternate interpretations supporting either the 'plus' or the 'quus' reading.

Putting aside the exegetical and philosophical merits of Kripke's proposed (anti-realist) solution, the problem points to a difficulty for the Use Thesis or, at any rate, a *presupposition* behind the use of ordinary language. Virtually every (non-fictitious) person believes that we do mean plus, and not quus, by $+$. It follows that our ability to add, and our knowledge of arithmetic, somehow go beyond our previous performance, our dispositions to behave, etc., or at least we *assume* that they do. When we encounter new instances of addition and handle them correctly, we have 'gone on as before'. Wittgenstein's problem is to maintain the Use Thesis and yet have the pattern of 'use' of an expression at a given time go beyond its previous manifestations. We need a plausible account of what it is to 'go on as before'. This may be related to the first passage quoted at the beginning of this chapter. The problem is to maintain realism in the sense that we do mean something by our terms—Skolemite relativism is surely absurd—and yet not be limited by the 'observation' of our previous behaviour, not 'empiricism'.

The same sort of difficulty arises in the present situation, but now on a grand scale. Consider, for example, real analysis and, to make the analogy better, think of the completeness axiom as sanctioning a *rule*:

> When one learns that a set *S* of real numbers is bounded from above, one can infer that *S* has a least upper bound.

Suppose that some mathematician, or some community of mathematicians, formulates arithmetic and real analysis, learns the completeness rule, and uses it successfully for several decades. Call him (or them) 'Karl'. Suppose that during those decades, real analysis is the most powerful theory Karl has. In particular, suppose that Zermelo–Fraenkel set theory has not been developed.

Now, a first-order formulation of real analysis takes the completeness rule as a scheme, one instance for each open formula of *Karl's language*. Like Kripke's quus function, first-order analysis characterizes (1) Karl's past (correct) use of the completeness rule and (2) his physical dispositions to apply the rule (correctly). But it captures much more: (3) every use of the rule he *can* make given his expressive resources, and here the modal term 'can' is not limited to physical possibility—the first-order scheme includes every application of the rule in Karl's *present* language; (4) his ability to describe his possible uses; (5) our ability to describe his ability to apply the rule (correctly), etc.

It should come as no surprise, then, that from Karl's perspective, there is no significant difference between the class of theorems he can prove in first-order analysis and the class he can prove in second-order analysis. The first-order scheme has instances covering just about any use he can make given his (or their) resources,[9] i.e. any use he can make *at this stage* in his development. Yet, as with Kripke's quus function, this is not enough. The *problem* is to maintain the Use Thesis and yet hold that the 'use' of at least some expressions (like the completeness rule) goes *beyond*, say, (1)–(5) above.

Suppose that Karl now develops, or becomes aware of, new expressive resources. For example, he may formulate some set theory and model the real numbers therein. Suppose also that he uses his extended language to define sets of real numbers that he could not define prior to the new deveopments. He then applies the completeness rule to these sets and thereby learns more analysis—he learns more about the real numbers. It seems clear that he (or they) has 'gone on as before'. Karl's reaction to the newly defined sets of real numbers is exactly analogous to ours when we encounter a particular sum for the first time. We apply the same rule to a new case.

Along similar lines, Parsons (1990) describes a scenario in which two (communities of) mathematicians meet and learn each other's languages. Each *proves* that the other's natural and real numbers are isomorphic to his own (essentially by reproducing the categoricity proofs of Chapter 4). They conclude, correctly, that they have been speaking of the same things all along. This meeting of the minds, so to speak, is not accomplished by an esoteric appeal to intuition. Rather, each uses the resources of the *combined* languages to define sets of numbers, and then applies the relevant axiom (of induction or completeness) to these sets. Each mathematician applies the relevant 'rule' to cases he *could not formulate* before the meeting, before he learned the other's language. As with Karl and set theory, the combined language expands the resources and provides new cases to which the rule can be applied, but the rule itself is not changed.

Second-order real analysis captures this intuition of 'going on as before'. For Karl, the terminology of set theory is involved in extending the comprehension scheme (of second-order logic) which is used to describe and establish the existence of the 'new' sets of real numbers. Once this is accomplished, the completeness rule is applied to these sets—the same completeness rule that Karl used before. The rule itself is not extended and not reinterpreted.

With first-order real analysis, the situation is not as straightforward. To derive the new theorems, the set-theoretic terminology must be used to produce new instances of the completeness *scheme* itself. That is, Karl must produce new cases of the very *defining statements* of analysis. In effect, the new *language* entails that Karl is working in a new *theory* with a new set of rules. It is an extension of the old one, to be sure, but that theory has many extensions. What is lacking is a principled account of how the chosen new theory is the 'same'—how Karl went on as before.

In sum, the first-order view and the second-order view seem to diverge *in practice* when the expressive resources are expanded. As discussed in several places above, the first-order schemes are limited to the sets that are definable in the original first-order languages. The second-order account applies the same rule to the newly defined sets. Perhaps we did not note the potential divergence in the above scenarios because it was assumed that the total expressive resources are held constant throughout the regress, or maybe we silently allowed our advocate of first-order logic to reconstruct the basic theories at each level.[10]

I do not claim that adopting higher-order logic somehow *solves* the twin problems of rule-following and Skolemite relativism. If our character First were reintroduced at this point, she would argue that the second-order language creates a false *appearance* of 'going on as before'. With the adoption of the set theory, the completeness rule is the same, perhaps, but there are new instances of the comprehension scheme. She would thus claim that there is a shift in the range of the second-order variables. Recall that she denies that this range is fixed. It changes from one model of the *semantics* to another.[11]

The thesis here is that for better or worse (well, for better), the attitude underlying the practice of mathematics is that this sort of scepticism is false. We do go on as before, both in following rules and in extending our theories. At any rate, we talk and act that way, even if we cannot rule out the possibility that it may be an illusion. Second-order languages echo this *presupposition*. It is in line with Church's statement that the assumptions of second-order logic may be more conspicuous than those behind the practice of classical mathematics, but they are not more troublesome.

The same considerations rule out a 'formalistic' account of the 'use' of mathematical discourse. No single *explicitly formulated* algorithm, and thus no effective deductive system, can capture Karl's prior understanding and use of his language. No effective deductive system can account for Karl's 'going on as before' when his resources are expanded. At best, a deductive system can model Karl's theories in their present state of articulation—in their present languages.

Benacerraf (1985, pp. 110–11) puts the situation well:

> We *do* need a metaphysically and epistemologically satisfactory account of the way mathematical practice determines or embodies the meaning of mathematical language. (We could also use a satisfactory account for areas other than mathematics). We may even need to devise new concepts of meaning to forge such an account.
>
> ... mathematical practice reflects our intuitions and controls our use of mathematical language in ways in which we may not be aware at any given moment, but which transcend what we have explicitly set down in any given *account*—or may ever be able to set down.
>
> With Gödel, I incline toward this view. But I am sufficiently aware of its vagueness and inadequacy not to be tempted into thinking it constitutes a *view*. It is merely a direction.

I also incline to this 'view'. The argument over Gödelian platonism, and for that matter the argument over formalism, is the extent to which we are able to fix the use of our terms *completely*. What is needed is a synthesis between 'relativism', which holds that the constraints on the use of our language do not extend much beyond our present ability to describe and apply our rules, and traditional platonism, which holds that our minds can somehow directly grasp infinite structures and that the concepts are thereby fixed completely, once and for all. The question concerns the *extent* to which our present practice in, say, real analysis determines the future use of the terms or, to use another Wittgensteinian phrase, the extent to which meaning and use are and are not fixed 'throughout logical space'.

However this is resolved, I make the proposal that we can shed some light on the requisite concepts of meaning and reference, and the sense in which these can outstrip prior manifestations, by studying the use of the second-order concepts in mathematics.

Notes

1. As shown in the previous chapter, the presentation of second-order languages as *extensions* of first-order ones does not reflect the history of logic, nor was it intended to. First-order logic was first studied as a distinct *subsystem* of higher-order logic.
2. See Myhill (1951) for a lucid presentation of this option. Similar views have been suggested (in correspondence or conversation) by several prominent logicians.
3. Hermann Weyl, who played a significant role in the events described in the previous chapter, eventually adopted intuitionism.
4. See Chapters 4 and 5, and Chapter 9, Section 9.3, for a comparison of the deductive systems of common second-order theories with their first-order counterparts.
5. Admittedly, these possibilities in principle invoke a rather broad metaphysical modality. It is open to a Fregean to defend a thesis that a *complete* fake, or even a large fake, is impossible in some, perhaps epistemic, sense. Plato may have held such a view in that the Socratic method seems to presuppose that, if a person fails to grasp a concept, then there are situations in which he cannot give intelligent responses.
6. That later Wittgenstein seemed to be hostile to *all* foundational studies, whether first-order or otherwise. He held that mathematics, as practised, does not have a common core to characterize and study. It is a loose collection of techniques that have only a family resemblance to each other. In effect, Wittgenstein rejected the entire Fregean foundational programme, not just its conception of meaning. It is ironic, perhaps, that the present chapter invokes a broadly Wittgensteinian line of argument in favour of another aspect of the Fregean programme, higher-order logic. I am grateful to Mark Steiner for pointing this out.
7. Parsons (1983, Essay 3) gives an insightful discussion of the theory of arithmetic truth. The question is the extent to which the arithmetic within this theory is the same or different from arithmetic alone. In Shapiro (1989b). I argue that a structuralist philosophy of mathematics is congenial with both the Use Thesis and realism, even model-theoretic semantics.
8. I owe this observation to Barbara Scholz.
9. As indicated in Chapter 5, second-order analysis is deductively stronger than first-order analysis, but when the latter contains terminology for natural numbers and certain functions, the differences are minor.
10. There is an interesting analogy between these considerations and the major argument that Friedman (1983) brings for the reality of space–time. Friedman concedes that if we focus attention exclusively on the most powerful and complete physical theory we have, general relativity for example, the 'substantival' versions that refer to space–time are equivalent to the 'relationalist' versions that do not. But space–time is needed to see the smooth relationships between, say, gravitational theory alone and gravitational theory plus electrodynamics. The separate relationalist theories do not fit together that well. In short, the reality of space–time is confirmed in the *historical* advance from the weaker theory to its more comprehensive successor.
11. Weston (1976) contains a close approximation of this retort by First.

9

The competition

One of the main themes of this book is a thorough anti-foundationalism (see Chapter 2). The view under attack is the thesis that there is a unique best foundation of mathematics, and the concomitant view that there is a unique best logic—one size that fits all. We have gone to some lengths to identify inadequacies of first-order logic, and we have shown how second-order logic, with standard semantics, overcomes many of these shortcomings. But first-order logic and higher-order logic do not exhaust the possibilities that have been considered. The purpose of this concluding chapter is to explore some alternatives (without attempting to be exhaustive).

Section 9.1 concerns other logics, and in particular other model-theoretic semantics. Recall that the bulk of the inadequacies of first-order logic is a result of its compactness, which is a corollary of completeness, the existence of an effective complete deductive system. Most of the alternatives considered here are not compact and not complete. Each one is more expressive than first-order logic, but not quite as powerful as second-order logic, and the various model theories are, in a sense, more manageable than that of higher-order logic. Section 9.2 contrasts second-order languages with what I have above called free-variable second-order languages, languages with free, but not bound, relation and function variables. Section 9.3 concerns the use of first-order set theory as a foundation of mathematics. Parts of this chapter require a basic grasp of axiomatic set theory.

9.1 Other logics

The articles in Barwise and Feferman (1985) present a wealth of model theories. In the opening piece, Barwise endorses the present thesis that first-order logics are too impoverished to capture and study many serious 'mathematical concepts':

> As logicians, we do our subject a disservice by convincing others that logic is first-order and then convincing them that almost none of the concepts of modern mathematics can really be captured in first-order logic. (Barwise and Feferman 1985, p. 5)

He concludes, 'One thing is certain. There is no going back to the view that logic is first-order logic' (Barwise and Feferman 1985, p. 23). But this is not to accept second-order logic which, apparently, is thought to have an intractable model theory. As Cowles puts it:

> It is well-known that first-order logic has a limited ability to express many of the concepts studied by mathematicians ... However, first-order logic ... does have an extensively developed and well-understood model theory. On the other hand, full second-order logic has all the expressive power needed to do mathematics, but has an unworkable model theory. Indeed, the search for a logic with a semantics complex enough to say something, yet at the same time simple enough to say something *about*, accounts for the proliferation of logics ... (Cowles 1979, p. 129)

I leave it to the reader to judge how intractable second-order logic really is, and the extent to which that is a defect for various purposes. Most of the alternatives presented here are treated in Barwise and Feferman (1985), but some are not as prominent as others.

9.1.1   *Monadic second-order logic*

A first-order language $L1K$ is *monadic* if the set K of non-logical terminology does not contain any function symbols or any n-place relation symbols, for $n > 1$. It is well known that the set of logical truths of each such language is recursive (see, for example, Dreben and Goldfarb 1979, Section 8.3), but the languages are too weak to express substantial mathematics. The notion of function is central to modern mathematics; it is hard to do much without it.

Monadic second-order languages lie between first-order and second-order languages. No restrictions are placed on the non-logical terminology, but there are to be no *variables* ranging over functions or n-place relations, for any $n > 1$. That is, all second-order variables are monadic.[1] Gurevich (1985) gives an extensive treatment of such languages, arguing that they are 'a good source of theories that are both expressive and manageable'.

There is an important restriction on this statement. A *pair function* on a given domain d is a one-to-one function from $d \times d$ into d. A theory *admits pairing* if there is a formula $\Phi(x, y, z)$, with only the free variables shown, such that in every model M of the theory, there is a pair function f on the domain of M such that for every assignment s on M, $M, s \vDash \Phi(x, y, z)$ if and only if $f(s(x), s(y)) = s(z)$. In short, a theory admits pairing if there is a definable pair function in it. Following a theme introduced in several places above, if a theory cast in a monadic second-order language admits pairing, then it is equivalent to the same theory formulated in an unrestricted second-order language. There is no loss of expressive power and no gain in manageability.[2] The reason, of course, is that a relation can be thought of as a property of pairs. Let f be a pair function. Then a given binary relation R is equivalent to the property that holds of an element x iff there is a y and z such that $f(y, z) = x$ and R holds of y and z.

In arithmetic, the function $f(x, y) = 2^x 3^y$ is a pair function, and in set theory $g(x, y) = \{\{x\}, \{x, y\}\}$ is. For this reason, monadic second-order arithmetic and monadic second-order set theory are equivalent to their second-order versions. Shelah (1975) shows that first-order arithmetic can be reduced to the monadic second-order theory of the real numbers under the order relation. Thus the latter is a rich undecidable theory. More substantially, Gurevich and Shelah (1983) have established that second-order logic can be reduced to what is called the monadic second-order theory of order, cast in a language with a single non-logical relation symbol $<$. In particular, they show that there is a recursive function F such that, for each sentence Φ of the second-order language $L2$, $F(\Phi)$ is a sentence in the monadic second-order language of order, and Φ is a logical truth iff $F(\Phi)$ is satisfied by every linear order. Thus the monadic second-order theory of order is just as rich (and unmanageable) as second-order logic.

On the positive side, Gurevich (1985) points out that there are theories that do not admit pairing whose monadic second-order theories are interesting. One is arithmetic formulated with the successor function alone. Although the monadic second-order theory is categorical and the natural order can easily be defined in it, the theory is decidable. A second example, also decidable, is the monadic theory of the binary tree.[3] Another is the monadic second-order theory of countable ordinals.

Boolos (1984, 1985a; see also 1985b) has proposed an alternative way of understanding monadic second-order languages (with or without pairing). It promises to overcome at least some of the philosophical objections to second-order logic. According to standard semantics, as developed in Chapter 3, a monadic second-order existential quantifier can be read 'there is a class' or 'there is a property', in which case, of course, the locution invokes classes or properties. Against this, Boolos suggests that the quantifier be considered a counterpart of a *plural* quantifier, 'there are (objects)' in natural language. The following illustration is called the Geach–Kaplan sentence:

Some critics admire only one another.

It has a (more or less) straightforward second-order rendering, taking the class of critics to be the domain of discourse:

$$\exists X(\exists x Xx \ \& \ \forall x \forall y((Xx \ \& \ Axy) \rightarrow (x \neq y \ \& \ Xy))).$$

Kaplan has observed that there is no first-order sentence that is equivalent to this.[4] According to standard semantics, the formula would correspond to 'there is a non-empty *class* X of critics such that for any x in X and any y, if x admires y, then $x \neq y$ and y is in X'. But this implies the existence of a class, while the original 'some critics admire only one another' does not, at least prima facie.

Natural languages, like English, allow the plural construction and, in particular, English contains the plural quantifier 'there are objects'. Boolos argues that the informal metalanguage, the one we use in developing formal semantics, also contains this construction, and it can be employed to interpret second-order monadic existential quantifiers. The relevant locution is 'there are objects X, such that . . .'. As in the first-order case, the variable serves as a place-holder for purposes of cross reference. It is similar to a pronoun in ordinary language. Construed this way, a monadic second-order language has *no* ontology beyond that of its first-order counterpart. In set theory, for example, the 'Russell sentence' $\exists X \forall x (Xx \equiv x \notin x)$ is a consequence of the comprehension scheme. According to standard semantics, it corresponds to a statement that there is a *class* that is not coextensive with any *set*. Admittedly, this takes some getting used to. On Boolos' interpretation, however, the Russell sentence reads, 'there are some sets such that any set is one of them just in case it is not a member of itself'. In set theory, this is no more than a truism. Similarly, the second-order principle of foundation $\forall X (\exists x Xx \rightarrow \exists x (Xx \ \& \ \forall y (y \in x \rightarrow \neg Xy)))$ comes to 'it is not the case that there are some sets such that every one of them has a member that is also one of them'. Again, proper classes are not invoked.

There is a complication here which is due to the fact that a sentence in the form 'there are some objects with a certain property' implies that there is at least one object with this property, while a sentence that begins with a standard second-order existential quantifier does not have a similar implication. In particular, in standard semantics, a sentence in the form $\exists X \Phi(X)$ is satisfied by a model even if Φ holds only of the empty class in that model.[5] To accommodate this, Boolos takes the comprehension scheme $\exists X \forall x (Xx \equiv \Phi(x))$, for example, to correspond to 'either $\neg \exists x \Phi(x)$ or else there are some objects such that any object is one of them just in case Φ holds of it'. Again, the latter seems to be a correct statement, provided only that Φ is meaningful (and does not contain the variable X free). It does not invoke classes unless, of course, Φ itself does.

Boolos (1985a) shows how a rigorous model-theoretic semantics for monadic second-order languages can be developed along these lines. The plural quantifier is used in the metalanguage. Recall that in standard semantics, the central relation is *satisfaction* $M, s \vDash \Phi$, in which Φ is a formula, $M = \langle d, I \rangle$ is a model, and s is an assignment of an element of d to each first-order variable *and* an n-place relation (or function) on d to each n-place relation (or function) variable. But this invokes relations and functions. Assume that the formal language under consideration is monadic second-order. Let p be a fixed pair function in the metalanguage. Its domain includes both the objects in the domains of the various models and the syntactic items of the formal language, the predicate variables in particular. Boolos shows how a single predicate R (in the metalanguage) can code an assignment of 'values' to the second-order variables of the formal language. To use the terminology of classes, the item $p(U, u)$ is in R iff U is a second-order variable and u is in the class[6] to be assigned to U. But this is heuristic, for those of us who need to be weaned from class terminology in the metalanguage. The ladder is to be kicked away, since the monadic second-order terminology is ultimately to be understood in terms of plurals. Boolos defines a relation $M, s, R \vDash \Phi$, in which Φ is a formula of the formal language, M is a model, s is an assignment to the first-order variables (only), and R is a second-order predicate in the metalanguage. The major new clauses of the semantics are as follows.

$M, s, R \vDash Uu$ iff $Rp(U, u)$.

$M, s, R \vDash \exists V \Phi$ iff $\exists X \exists T (\forall x (Xx \equiv Tp(V, x))$ & $\forall u((u$ is a second-order
variable other than $V) \rightarrow \forall x (Tp(u, x) \equiv Rp(u, x)))$
& $M, s, T \vDash \Phi)$.

The initial second-order quantifiers in the last formula are to be understood as plural quantifiers, but we shall not venture a translation into less formal English.

The main advantage of this semantics is that if it can be sustained, then one can accept monadic second-order languages without thereby being committed to the existence of proper classes. Indeed, plural quantifiers do not involve any ontology other than the range of the first-order variables.

In Chapter 1, Section 1.3, we made a distinction between logical sets and iterative sets. The locution 'logical set' is similar to an indexical expression in that it is relative to a fixed context, a domain of discourse. In arithmetic a logical set is a collection of natural numbers, in geometry a logical set is a collection of points (or a collection of regions), etc. An iterative set, on the other hand, is a member of the set-theoretic hierarchy, the intended interpretation of axiomatic set theory. In the context of set theory, then, a logical set is a collection of iterative sets, what is called a 'class'. Russell's paradox shows that in set theory there are logical sets that are not coextensive with any iterative set. The collection of all iterative sets, for example, is a logical set (and it has a name V), but there is no iterative set that contains every iterative set.

In the present study, monadic second-order variables are understood to range over logical sets—the subdomains of the domain of discourse. On the Boolos interpretation, this understanding is not necessary. One is free to accept second-order logic and still reject logical sets. The only collections that Boolos countenances are iterative sets, members of the set-theoretic hierarchy.

In most fields, this difference does not amount to much. According to the Boolos proposal, second-order arithmetic (or analysis) presupposes numbers, but not sets of numbers, and second-order geometry presupposes points, but not sets of points (or regions but not sets of regions). This may be an important distinction for tracking the separate presuppositions of different fields, but ultimately it is not crucial, at least not here. Boolos, being a major advocate of the ontological presuppositions of set theory (see, for example, Boolos 1971), is certainly not out to reject sets altogether. Moreover, if certain reflection principles hold (along the lines of Chapter 6, Section 6.3), the second-order consequence relation is the same on both standard semantics and his interpretation.[7]

The difference between the interpretations comes to the fore in set theory itself. Boolos does not accept the existence of proper classes (and thus does not regard V as a proper noun).[8]

> ... we [do not] want to take the second-order variables as ranging over some set-like objects, sometimes called 'classes', which have members, but are not themselves members of other sets, supposedly because they are 'too big' to be sets. Set theory is supposed to be a theory about *all* set-like objects. (Boolos 1984, p. 442)

The Boolos programme, then, accomplishes a reduction of ontology by employing plural quantifiers which are found in ordinary language. It is thus a trade-off between ontology and ideology, and, as such, it is not clear how the case is to be adjudicated. The prevailing criterion for assessment of ontology is the Quinean assertion that the ontology of a theory is the range of its bound variables. Quine insists that the theory in question first be regimented in a *first-order* language, but the criterion is readily extended to *standard* higher-order languages since, in such systems, higher-order variables have (more or less) straightforward ranges, namely classes, relations, or functions. In this respect, second-order variables are on a par with first-order variables. Boolos, however, proposes a certain asymmetry between first-order and monadic second-order variables. The latter do not have 'ranges' in the same sense that the former do.

Resnik (1988) argues against the Boolos programme, suggesting that the plural quantifiers of natural language be understood (after all) in terms of classes. Both Resnik (1988) and Boolos (1985a) acknowledge that this sort of dispute leads to a stand-off, or a regress. It is similar to the stand-off or regress between advocates of second-order logic and advocates of first-order logic noted in Chapters 7 and 8 above. Indeed, it may be the same. Anything that either side says can be *re*interpreted by the other. In the first-order/second-order case, the issue turns on whether we have a serviceable grasp of second-order variables and quantifiers, taken at face value, sufficient for use in foundational studies. Here, the issue concerns whether we have a serviceable grasp of plural quantifiers, sufficient for use in the metalanguages of model-theoretic semantics. Resnik seems to claim that we do not. What

understanding we do have of plural quantifiers is mediated by our understanding of sets. Boolos claims that we do have a reasonable grasp on plural
quantifiers, citing the prevalence of plurals in ordinary language. It might
be noted, however, that plurals *in general* seem to be rather complex, and
there is no consensus among linguists concerning how they are to be
understood (see, for example, Landman 1989). But Boolos does not invoke
the full range of plural nouns, only plural *quantifiers*. It must be admitted
that these seem to be understood reasonably well, about as well as (monadic)
second-order quantifiers. Resnik might retort that even this is mediated by
set theory, *first-order* set theory, in which case we have indeed entered the
regress and stand-off of Chapters 7 and 8.

9.1.2 *Finitude*

The next four logics each presuppose the notion of finitude, or something
very similar. After characterizing each of them, we show how there is a sense
in which they are equivalent to each other. Then their expressive resources
are assessed, and they are compared with second-order logic.

   Weak second-order logic employs the same languages as second-order
logic, namely $L2K$, except that there are no function variables. The semantics
is different. Let $M = \langle d, I \rangle$ be a model. Define s to be a *finite assignment*
on M if s assigns a member of d to each first-order variable and a *finite*
n-place relation on d to each n-place relation variable. That is, for each X^n,
$s(X^n)$ is a finite subset of d^n. The semantics of weak second-order logic is
restricted to finite assignments. In particular, if s is a finite assignment on
M, then $M, s \vDash \forall X \Phi$ iff $M, s' \vDash \Phi$ for every finite assignment s' that agrees
with s except possibly at X. The result is that the relation variables of weak
second-order logic range over the *finite* relations on the domain. If the
context does not make it clear which logic is under discussion, we employ
the symbol $\vDash_w$ for the satisfaction and consequence relation of weak
second-order logic.

   Some instances of the comprehension scheme

$$\exists X^n \forall \langle x_i \rangle [X^n \langle x_i \rangle \equiv \Phi(\langle x_i \rangle)]$$

are not logical truths of weak second-order logic. In fact, a sentence in the
form $\exists X \forall x (Xx \equiv \Phi(x))$ is satisfied by a structure M if and only if the
extension of Φ in M is finite. It follows that weak second-order logic is more
expressive than first-order logic, since the latter cannot express finitude (see
Chapter 5, Section 5.1). The definition of identity, $t = u$ as $\forall X (Xt \equiv Xu)$,
can be maintained in weak second-order logic, but it is convenient here to
include identity as a (logical) primitive.

   The next logic $L(Q_0)$ employs the language of first-order logic with identity
($L1K=$), augmented with another quantifier Q called a *cardinality quantifier*.
Let M be a model of $L1K=$ and s an assignment. The new clause in the

semantics is

$M, s \vDash Qx\Phi$ iff there are infinitely many distinct assignments s' such that
$\quad\quad$ s agrees with s' on every variable except possibly x,
$\quad\quad$ and $M, s' \vDash \Phi$.

The formula $Qx\Phi$ may be read 'for infinitely many x, Φ' or 'Φ holds of infinitely many x'. The sentence $Qx(x = x)$ asserts that the domain is infinite, $Qx\Phi$ asserts that the extension of Φ is infinite, and $\neg Qx\Phi$ asserts that the extension of Φ is finite. As above, it follows that $L(Q_0)$ is more expressive than first-order logic.[9]

Assume, for the moment, that the set K of non-logical terms contains a binary relation symbol $<$. Let M be a model of the language $L1K=$. Define M to be an ω-*model* if the field of $<$ in M (i.e. the set $\{s(x) \mid M, s \vDash \exists y(x < y \lor y < x)\}$) is isomorphic to the natural numbers under the usual less-than relation. We say that a set Γ of formulas of $L1K=$ is ω-*satisfiable* if there is an ω-model M and an assignment s on M such that $M, s \vDash \Phi$, for every Φ in Γ. A single formula Φ is ω-*satisfiable* if the singleton $\{\Phi\}$ is ω-satisfiable. And if $\langle \Gamma, \Phi \rangle$ is an argument, we say that Γ ω-*implies* Φ, or $\langle \Gamma, \Phi \rangle$ is ω-*valid*, written $\Gamma \vDash_\omega \Phi$, if for every ω-model M and assignment s, if M, s satisfies every member of Γ, then M, s satisfies Φ. A formula Φ is an ω-*logical truth* if the empty set ω-implies Φ. The resulting system is called ω-*logic* (see Ebbinghaus 1985).

Let Sxy be an abbreviation of

$$x < y \mathbin{\&} \neg\exists z(x < z \mathbin{\&} z < y).$$

That is, Sxy asserts that y is the successor of x in the relation $<$. In an ω-model, the statement 'x is in the field of $<$' is equivalent to $\exists y(x < y)$. Notice that $\forall x(\exists y(x < y) \rightarrow \exists! y Sxy)$ is an ω-logical truth.

In Chapter 5, the *ancestral* R^* of a relation R was defined. To reiterate, R^*xy holds if there is a finite sequence $a_0 \ldots a_n$ such that $a_0 = x$, $a_n = y$, and, for each i, $0 \le i < n$, $Ra_i a_{i+1}$ holds. Equivalently, R^*xy if y is in the minimal closure of $\{x\}$ under R. Consider the first-order language $L1K=$, augmented with an *ancestral operator* A. If Φ is a formula in which x and y occur free, and if t_1, t_2 are terms, then $Axy(\Phi)t_1 t_2$ is a well-formed formula in which the variables x, y are bound. If M is a model and s an assignment, then $M, s \vDash Axy(\Phi)t_1 t_2$ if the denotation of t_2 is an ancestor of the denotation of t_1 under the relation (in M) expressed by $\Phi(x, y)$. Call the resulting system *ancestral logic*.[10]

This completes the list of logics for this subsection. They are weak second-order logic, $L(Q_0)$, ω-logic, and ancestral logic. The next item on the agenda is to compare their expressive power.

The four systems are all extensions of the first-order $L1K=$. Each can characterize the natural numbers, up to isomorphism, with a single sentence.

THEOREM 9.1.   Let A' be $\{0, s, +, \cdot, <\}$, the non-logical terminology of arithmetic, plus the $<$ symbol. Each of the languages described in this subsection contains a sentence Φ such that, for each model M of $L1A'$, $M \models \Phi$ iff M is isomorphic to the natural numbers (with the usual operations and relations). In the terminology of Barwise and Feferman (1985), the collection of structures isomorphic to the natural numbers is an *elementary class* (*EC*) of weak second-order logic, $L(Q_0)$, ω-logic, and ancestral logic.

Proof.   Let Ψ be the conjunction of the following (first-order) sentences (see Chapter 4, Section 4.2):

$$\forall x(sx \neq 0) \ \& \ \forall x \forall y(sx = sy \rightarrow x = y)$$
$$\& \ \forall x(x \neq 0 \rightarrow \exists y(sy = x)) \qquad \text{(successor axiom)}$$
$$\forall x(x + 0 = x) \ \& \ \forall x \forall y(x + sy = s(x + y)) \quad \text{(addition axiom)}$$
$$\forall x(x \cdot 0 = 0) \ \& \ \forall x \forall y(x \cdot sy = x \cdot y + x) \quad \text{(multiplication axiom)}$$
$$\forall x \forall y(x < y \equiv \exists z(x + sz = y)) \qquad \text{(order axiom)}$$

The order, successor, and addition axioms entail that in any model of Ψ, the field of $<$ is the entire domain. Notice that, if M is an ω-model, then M is isomorphic to the natural numbers. Thus, Ψ itself characterizes the natural numbers, up to isomorphism, in ω-logic. In the other cases, Ψ must be augmented with a statement that entails that $0, s0, ss0, \ldots$ (i.e. the minimal closure of 0 under s) is the whole domain. In ancestral logic, there is a formula that says this. Let Φ_A be the following ancestral sentence:

$$\forall z(Axy(Sxy)0z)$$

where Sxy is the successor relation of $<$, defined above. In effect, Φ_A asserts that everything is a successor-ancestor of 0. So, $\Psi \ \& \ \Phi_A$ characterizes the natural numbers up to isomorphism. Notice that it would also suffice to conjoin Ψ with an assertion that for every object x there are only finitely many elements smaller than x. Let Φ_Q be the following sentence of $L(Q_0)$:

$$\forall y \neg Qx(x < y).$$

Then $\Psi \ \& \ \Phi_Q$ is a categorical characterization of the natural numbers. Finally, for weak second-order logic, we add a statement asserting that for each x there is a *finite* set X that contains all the elements smaller than x. Let Φ_w be

$$\forall x \exists X \forall y(y < x \rightarrow Xy).$$

Once again, $\Psi \ \& \ \Phi_w$ is a categorical characterization of the natural numbers. $\qquad\square$

It follows that each of these characterizing sentences has a countable model, and no uncountable model. Recall that the refutations of compactness and completeness for second-order logic (in Chapter 4, Section 4.2) only depend on the existence of a categorical characterization of the natural numbers.

COROLLARY 9.2.   Let L be weak second-order logic, $L(Q_0)$, ω-logic, or ancestral logic. Then the *upward* Löwenheim–Skolem theorem fails for L, and L is not compact. Moreover, let D be any effective deductive system that is sound for L. Then D is not (weakly) complete: there is a logical truth of L that is not a theorem of D. In short, L is *inherently incomplete*.

Let LK and $L'K$ be languages based on the set K of non-logical terminology, and let each be equipped with a model-theoretic semantics involving the same class of models as the first-order $L1K$. Then $L'K$ is said to *include* LK, written $LK \leq L'K$, if for each sentence Φ of LK there is a sentence Φ' of $L'K$ such that for every model M, $M \vDash \Phi$ in LK iff $M \vDash \Phi'$ in $L'K$. The idea is that $L'K$ is capable of expressing any distinctions among models that is expressible in LK. In the terminology of Barwise and Feferman (1985), $L'K$ includes LK if every elementary class of LK is an elementary class of $L'K$, in which case they say that $L'K$ is 'as strong as' LK, and Cowles (1979) says that $L'K$ is an 'extension' of LK. The languages are said to be *equivalent*[11] if both $LK \leq L'K$ and $L'K \leq LK$.

We must extend this notion a bit to accommodate ω-logic, since it does not have the same class of models as the first-order $L1K$. Assume that the set K contains the binary relation symbol $<$. Then we say that $L'K$ *includes* ω-*logic* if, for each sentence Φ of the first-order $L1K=$, there is a sentence Φ' of $L'K$ such that for each model M, $M \vDash \Phi'$ in $L'K$ if and only if M is an ω-model and $M \vDash \Phi$.

LEMMA 9.3.   Suppose that $L'K$ contains the connectives and quantifiers of the first-order $L1K=$. Then $L'K$ includes ω-logic if and only if there is a sentence Ψ of $L'K$ whose only non-logical term is $<$, such that for each model M, $M \vDash \Psi$ in $L'K$ if and only if the field of $<$ in M is isomorphic to the natural numbers (i.e. M is an ω-model).

Proof.   If Φ is a sentence of $L1K=$, then the relevant sentence of $L'K$ is $\Phi \& \Psi$. The converse is immediate.   □

THEOREM 9.4.   Weak second-order logic, $L(Q_0)$, and ancestral logic all include ω-logic.

Proof.   According to Lemma 9.3, for each case, we need a sentence Ψ whose only non-logical term is $<$, and which is satisfied by all and only ω-models. Let Ψ' be a (first-order) sentence asserting that the field of $<$ is a non-reflexive linear order of its field, and that every element in the field of $<$ has a unique successor. For ancestral logic, we conjoin Ψ' with an assertion that there is an element x such that every element in the field of $<$ is an ancestor of x under the successor relation:

$$\exists x \forall y (\exists z (y < z \lor z < y) \rightarrow (Apq(Spq)xy)).$$

For $L(Q_0)$, we conjoin Ψ' with an assertion that for each y there are only finitely many x such that $x < y$:

$$\forall y \neg Qx(x < y).$$

And for weak second-order logic, we conjoin Ψ' with an assertion that for each y, there is a finite set X containing every element that 'precedes' y under $<$:

$$\forall y \exists X \forall x(x < y \rightarrow Xx). \qquad \square$$

THEOREM 9.5. Weak second-order logic includes $L(Q_0)$.

Proof. For each formula Φ of $L(Q_0)$, we define a formula Φ' of weak second-order logic by induction on the complexity of Φ.

> If Φ is atomic, then Φ' is Φ.
> $(\Phi \rightarrow \Psi)'$ is $\Phi' \rightarrow \Psi''$.
> $(\neg \Phi)'$ is $\neg \Phi'$.
> $(\forall x \Phi)'$ is $\forall x \Phi'$.
> $(Qx\Phi)'$ is $\neg \exists X(\forall x(Xx \equiv \Phi'))$, where X is the alphabetically first
>   monadic predicate variable that does not occur in Φ'.

A straightforward induction shows that for any sentence Φ of ancestral logic, if M is any model, s is any M-assignment to the first-order variables, and s' any M-assignment in weak second-order logic that agrees with s on the first-order variables, then $M, s \vDash \Phi$ iff $M, s' \vDash \Phi'$. $\qquad \square$

THEOREM 9.6. Weak second-order logic includes ancestral logic.

Proof. A similar proof suffices here. We need a correlate of each formula of the form $Axy(\Phi)t_1 t_2$ in weak second-order logic. It is somewhat tedious, and we shall not write it out fully. Suppose, first, that f is a *function* on a subset of the domain. Then 't_2 is an ancestor of t_1 under f' can be expressed in weak second-order logic as follows: (1) there is a finite set X such that Xt_1, and if Xx and $x \neq t_2$, then Xfx, and (2) t_2 is in every finite set Z such that Zt_1 and for every x, if Zx and $x \neq t_2$, then Zfx. In general, let Φ' be the correlate in weak second-order logic of a formula Φ. Then the correlate of $Axy(\Phi)t_1 t_2$ can be expressed as follows: there is a finite binary relation Y^2 such that (1) for every x, y, if $Y^2 xy$ then $\Phi'(x, y)$, (2) the extension of Y^2 is the graph of a function f on a subset of the domain (i.e. $\forall x \forall y \forall z((Y^2 xy \ \& \ Y^2 xz) \rightarrow y = z)$), and (3) t_2 is an ancestor of t_1 under f. $\qquad \square$

This completes the list of inclusion relations among the logics of this subsection. The other possibilities fail.

THEOREM 9.7 (Cowles 1979). $L(Q_0)$ does *not* include weak second-order logic.

Proof.   Let B be the terminology of real analysis $\{0, 1, +, \cdot, <\}$, and let Φ be the conjunction of the (first-order) axioms for an ordered field (see Chapter 4, Section 4.2). Let Φ_w be

$$\forall x \exists X (X1 \ \& \ \forall y((y < x \ \& \ Xy) \rightarrow X(y+1))).$$

In weak second-order logic, this sentence asserts that for each x there is a finite set that contains all the positive integers less than x plus one more. In effect, Φ_w entails that the structure is *Archimedean*. Thus $M \vDash \Phi \ \& \ \Phi_w$ iff M is an Archimedean field. On the other hand, Cowles (1979) shows that Tarski's theorem concerning the completeness of first-order analysis can be extended to $L(Q_0)$ (see Tarski (1948, 1967); see also Chapter 5, Section 5.3). In particular, for each formula χ of $L(Q_0)$ whose non-logical terminology is in B, there is a formula χ', with the same free variables as χ, such that χ' has no quantifiers and $\chi \equiv \chi'$ holds in all models of the theory of real closed fields—first-order analysis. Now, if $L(Q_0)$ included weak second-order logic, it would contain a sentence Φ' that is a correlate of $\Phi \ \& \ \Phi_w$ above. That is, Φ' would be satisfied by all and only Archimedean fields. Let Φ'' be its quantifier-free equivalent. But as shown in Chapter 5, a compactness argument establishes that there is no first-order sentence that is satisfied by all and only Archimedean fields, which is a contradiction.   □

THEOREM 9.8. $L(Q_0)$ does not include ancestral logic.

Proof.   As above, let Φ be the conjunction of the (first-order) axioms for an ordered field, and let Φ_A be

$$\forall x(1 < x \rightarrow \exists y[Apq(q = p + 1)1y \ \& \ x < y]).$$

The sentence Φ_A asserts that, for every x, there is a 'natural number' y that is larger than x. Thus $M \vDash \Phi \ \& \ \Phi_A$ iff M is an Archimedean field. The rest of the proof is the same as that of the previous theorem.   □

THEOREM 9.9.   Ancestral logic does not include $L(Q_0)$ or weak second-order logic.

Proof.   Let the set K contain only monadic predicate letters, and let Φ be a formula of the first-order $L1K=$. Then it can be shown that there is a natural number n such that, for any model M and assignment s on M,

$$\begin{aligned}
M, s \vDash Axy(\Phi)pq \ \text{iff} \ M, s \vDash \ &\exists x_1 \ldots \exists x_n (x_1 = p \ \& \ x_n = q \\
&\& \ (\Phi(x_1, x_2) \lor x_1 = x_2) \ \& \ (\Phi(x_2, x_3) \lor x_2 = x_3) \\
&\& \ldots \& \ (\Phi(x_{n-1}, x_n) \lor x_{n-1} = x_n))
\end{aligned}$$

(where $x_1 \ldots x_n$ do not occur in $Axy(\Phi)pq$, relettering if necessary). The implication from right to left is immediate. The converse is a consequence of the proof of the decidability of the monadic predicate calculus (see Dreben and Goldfarb 1979, Section 8.3). Thus, for this set K of non-logical terminology, ancestral logic is equivalent to the first-order $L1K=$. Let D be a monadic predicate letter in K. It follows from this, and another result reported by Dreben and Goldfarb, that there is no sentence of ancestral logic equivalent to either the sentence $QxDx$ of $L(Q_0)$ or the sentence $\neg \exists X \forall x(Xx \equiv Dx)$ of weak second-order logic.   □

The following diagram summarizes the results so far. Each logic includes those below it, and no logic includes any of those at the same or a higher level.

weak second-order logic

$L(Q_0)$ ancestral logic

ω-logic

I would suggest that the 'non-inclusions' here are artefacts of an unnatural restriction on the non-logical terminology. To illustrate this, we show that $L(Q_0)$ can express the notion of an Archimedean field if the non-logical terminology is slightly expanded. Let B' be $\{0, 1, +, \cdot, <, N\}$, the terminology of ordered fields plus a monadic predicate letter N. As above, let Φ be the conjunction of the (first-order) axioms for an ordered field, and let Φ_1 be $[N0 \;\&\; \forall x(Nx \rightarrow N(x + 1))]$. Let Φ_2 be $\forall x \neg Qy(Ny \;\&\; y < x)$. It is straightforward to verify that every model of $\Phi \;\&\; \Phi_1 \;\&\; \Phi_2$ is an Archimedean field. Conversely, in every Archimedean field F, there is a set P (namely, the 'natural numbers' of F) such that if P is made the extension of N, then F satisfies $\Phi \;\&\; \Phi_1 \;\&\; \Phi_2$. In the terminology of Barwise and Feferman (1985), this shows that the class of Archimedean fields is a *projective class* (*PC*) of $L(Q_0)$.

It might be added that in a context as rich as set theory, there are essentially no differences between the logics of this subsection. As above, let *ZFC* be *first-order* Zermelo–Fraenkel set theory.[12] To formulate useful versions of set theory in the languages of this subsection, we must add principles that relate the new terminology (i.e. A, Q, $<$, and the higher-order variables) to the membership relation. For weak second-order logic, $L(Q_0)$, and ancestral logic this is accomplished by expanding the replacement scheme of *ZFC* to include every instance in the respective expanded language. Let *Z2w*, *ZQ*, and *ZA* be the resulting theories in weak second-order logic, $L(Q_0)$, and ancestral logic respectively. For ω-logic, things are almost this simple. The binary relation letter $<$ is added to the language, together with an assertion that the empty set is the initial element of $<$, and for each x in the field of $<$, the 'ordinal successor' of x, $x \cup \{x\}$, is the successor of x in $<$:

$$\forall x [\exists y (x < y \vee y < x) \to \exists z (\neg \exists w (w \in z) \& (z = x \vee z < x))]$$
$$\& \; \forall x \forall y [Sxy \to \forall z (z \in y \equiv (z \in x \vee z = x))].$$

Let $Z\omega$ be the result of adding this sentence to ZFC and including every instance of the replacement scheme in the expanded language.

Let omega(x) be a formula of ZFC asserting that x is a subset of every set that contains the empty set and is closed under the ordinal successor relation. In effect, omega(x) asserts that x is the set of finite ordinals. It can be seen that $\exists ! x (\text{omega}(x))$ follows from the axioms of ZFC. Let $M = \langle d, I \rangle$ be a model of ZFC. Define M-*omega* to be the unique member p of d such that $M, s \models \text{omega}(x)$ iff $s(x) = p$. In effect, M-omega is the element that plays the role of ω in M. However, there are models M such that M-omega is not isomorphic to the natural numbers. Indeed, there are models M in which M-omega has uncountably many 'elements'. A model M of set theory is sometimes said to be an 'ω-model' if M-omega is in fact isomorphic to the natural numbers. We have used this term before, of course, in connection with ω-logic.[13] It is straightforward to see that there is no conflict.

THEOREM 9.10.   Let $M = \langle d, I \rangle$ be a model of ZFC. Then M-omega is isomorphic to the natural numbers if and only if there is a way to interpret $<$ in d such that the result is a model of $Z\omega$ in ω-logic.

Proof. Suppose that $M = \langle d, I \rangle$ is any model of set theory. Let p be M-omega and assume that p is isomorphic to the natural numbers. Let the field of $<$ be the members of d that are 'elements' of p in M. Let $x < y$ be $x \in y$, restricted to this field. All told, then, $u < v$ is defined as

$$\exists x (\text{omega}(x) \& v \in x \& u \in v).$$

It is straightforward to verify that the resulting structure satisfies the new axiom of $Z\omega$, and since $<$ is definable in terms of membership, the new instances of the replacement scheme hold as well. By hypothesis, the field of $<$ is isomorphic to the natural numbers. Thus the structure is a model of $Z\omega$ in ω-logic. Conversely, suppose that $M' = \langle d', I' \rangle$ is a model of $Z\omega$ in ω-logic. Let p' be M'-omega. It follows from (the new instances of) the replacement scheme that there is an element q' of d' whose 'members' in M' are all and only the 'members' of p' that are in the field of $<$. It is easy to verify that the 'empty set' of M' is a 'member' of q', and that q' is closed under the ordinal successor relation in M'. Thus p' is a subset of q', and so $p' = q'$. So p' is isomorphic to the natural numbers. $\square$

We are now in position to characterize the other theories.

THEOREM 9.11.   A structure M is a model of $Z2w$ iff M is a model of ZQ iff M is a model of ZA iff M is an ω-model of ZFC.

Proof.   Suppose that M_1 is a model of $Z2w$ or ZQ, and let p_1 be M_1-omega. An instance of the replacement scheme (in the extended language) entails that there is a q_1 in the domain of M_1 whose 'members' in M_1 are all and only the 'members' of p_1 that have finitely many 'elements'. As above, it is easy to see that $p_1 = q_1$, and so q_1 is isomorphic to ω. Now let M_2 be a model of ZA and let p_2 be M_2-omega. Again, it follows from an instance of the replacement scheme that there is a q_2 in the domain of M_2 whose 'members' in M_2 are the 'members' of p_2 that are ancestors of the empty set under the ordinal successor relation. And again, $p_2 = q_2$ and q_2 is isomorphic to ω. Let us turn to the converses. There are straightforward definitions of finitude in the languages of ZFC. For example, let FIN(w) be a formula asserting that there is an x and y such that omega(x) and $y \in x$ and there is a one-to-one function from w to y. As noted in Chapter 5, the problem is that in general this definition does not 'work'. A compactness argument establishes that there are models of ZFC containing items w such that FIN(w), but w has infinitely many 'elements' in the model. Notice, however, that in any model M, the extension of FIN(w) depends only on the sets that are 'members' of M-omega. It follows that the definition of finitude does 'work' in ω-models. That is, if $M = \langle d, I \rangle$ is an ω-model of ZFC and $p \in d$, then FIN(p) iff p has finitely many 'elements' in M. Next, notice that if X is any finite n-place relation on d, then there is an element p_X of d whose 'members' in M are the ordered n-tuples of the items in X. In other words, for every finite relation, there is a set that corresponds to it. Although we shall not provide the tedious details, it follows that for each formula Φ in the language of weak second-order set theory, there is a formula Φ' of first-order ZFC such that Φ and Φ' are equivalent in all ω-models. Thus, if M is an ω-model of ZFC, then M satisfies the instances of the replacement scheme in $Z2w$. The same holds for ZQ and ZA since weak second-order logic includes $L(Q_0)$ and ancestral logic (Theorems 9.5 and 9.6).   □

The moral of all this, I believe, is that the four logics under study are equivalent in contexts in which there are enough resources to express the notion of 'finite set', or something equivalent to this. This observation can be made precise.

Let K and K' be sets of non-logical terminology such that $K \subseteq K'$. Let $M = \langle d, I \rangle$ be a model of the language $L1K$, and let $M' = \langle d', I' \rangle$ be a model of $L1K'$. We say that M' is an *expansion* of M if $d = d'$, and for each item k in K, $I(k) = I'(k)$. That is, M' is an expansion of M if M and M' have the same domain and agree on the interpretation of the items in K. In the above example, K is the set of non-logical items of real analysis $\{0, 1, +, \cdot, <\}$ and K' is the same set augmented with a predicate letter N, and we presented expansions of some of the models of $L1K$ in $L1K'$.

Let LK and $L'K$ be languages built on a set K of non-logical terminology, and assume that each is equipped with a semantics involving the usual class of models. We say that $L'K$ *quasi-projects* LK if for each sentence Φ of LK, if Φ has only infinite models, then there is a set $K' \supseteq K$ and a sentence Φ' of $L'K'$ such that, for each model M, $M \vDash \Phi$ in LK iff there is an expansion M' of M such that $M' \vDash \Phi'$ in $L'K'$. In the terminology of Barwise and Feferman (1985), $L'K$ quasi-projects LK iff every elementary class of LK that contains only infinite sets is a projective class of $L'K$. We say that LK and $L'K$ are *quasi-projectively-equivalent* if LK quasi-projects $L'K$ and $L'K$ quasi-projects LK.

Once again, we must modify this notion to accommodate ω-logic, since it does not have the same class of models as the others. We say that $L'K$ *projects* ω-*logic* if, for each sentence Φ of the first-order $L1K=$, in which K includes the symbol $<$, there is a set $K' \supseteq K$ and a sequence Φ' of $L'K'$, such that (1) for each model M' of $L1K=$, if $M' \vDash \Phi'$ in $L'K'$ then M' is an ω-model and $M' \vDash \Phi$, and (2) for each ω-model M of $L1K=$, if $M \vDash \Phi$ then there is an expansion M' of M such that $M' \vDash \Phi'$ in $L'K'$.

Conversely, we say that ω-*logic projects* LK if, for each sentence Φ of LK in which K does *not* include the symbol $<$, if Φ has only infinite models, then there is a set $K' \supseteq K$ such that the symbol $<$ is in K', and there is a sentence Φ' of the first-order $L1K'=$ such that, for each model M, $M \vDash \Phi$ in LK iff there is an ω-model M' that is an expansion of M and $M' \vDash \Phi'$. And we say that LK is *projectively equivalent* to ω-*logic* if ω-logic projects LK and LK projects ω-logic.

Finally, we come to the equivalence of the logics of this subsection.

THEOREM 9.12.   Weak second-order logic, $L(Q_0)$, and ancestral logic are quasi-projectively equivalent to each other, and all three are projectively equivalent to ω-logic.

Proof.   Notice, first, that if $L'K$ includes LK, then $L'K$ quasi-projects LK, and if $L'K$ includes ω-logic, then $L'K$ projects ω-logic. It follows from this, Theorems 9.4, 9.5, and 9.6, and the various definitions that it suffices to show that ω-logic projects weak second-order logic. This is accomplished by adding terminology for coding 'finite sets'. In Chapter 5, it was shown how a binary relation can be used to represent some subsets of a domain. To reiterate, let E be a binary relation, and define E_x to be the set $\{y \mid Exy\}$. We say that E_x is the set *coded by* x *in* E, and the relation E *represents* the collection of all the sets E_x, where x ranges over the domain of discourse. Of course, no relation can represent every subset of the domain (Cantor's theorem), but if a domain is infinite, then there is a relation that represents the collection of its *finite* subsets. The plan here is to show that such a relation can be characterized in ω-logic. Let E be a binary *non-logical* relation symbol and let $\Psi_1[E]$ be the following formula:

$$\exists x \forall y (\neg Exy) \ \& \ \forall x \forall y \exists z \forall w (Ezw \equiv (Exw \lor w = y)).$$

The first conjunct of Ψ_1 asserts that the empty set is coded by something in E, and the second conjunct asserts that if a set X is coded in E then, for any element y, $X \cup \{y\}$ is coded in E. Thus Ψ_1 entails that *every* finite subset of the domain is coded in E. It remains to assert that *only* finite sets are coded in E. For this, the resources of ω-logic are employed. We introduce a non-logical binary relation N such that Nxy entails that x is in the field of $<$, and the cardinality of E_y is the natural number corresponding to x. In particular, let $\Psi_2[E, N]$ be the conjunction of (1) the assertion that if x is the initial element of $<$, then Nxy holds iff $\forall z(\neg Eyz)$ (i.e. E_y is the empty set), and (2) if x' is the successor of x in $<$, then $Nx'y$ holds iff there is a w and a z such that Nxw, z is not in E_w, and E_y is $E_w \cup \{z\}$. Finally, let $\Psi_3[N]$ be $\forall y \exists x(\exists z(x < z) \,\&\, Nxy)$. That is, $\Psi_3[N]$ asserts that for every y there is an x in the field of $<$ that represents the cardinality of E_y. So let $\Psi[E, N]$ be $\Psi_1[E] \,\&\, \Psi_2[E, N] \,\&\, \Psi_3[N]$. In any ω-model of Ψ, E represents the set of all finite subsets of the domain. Let Φ be a sentence of weak second-order logic that has no finite models. Then terminology for a pairing function can be introduced, and there is a sentence Φ' containing only monadic second-order variables that has the same models as Φ. Assume that the relation letters $<, E, N$ do not occur in Φ' (relettering if necessary). To each second-order variable X that occurs in Φ', associate a unique first-order variable x_X that does not occur in Φ'. Let Φ'' be the result of replacing each subformula Xt of Φ' with $Ex_X t$ (i.e. the formula asserting that t is in the set represented by x_X in E) and replacing each quantifier $\forall X$ by $\forall x_X$. The result is a first-order sentence. Finally, let χ be $\Psi[E, N] \,\&\, \Phi''$. It is routine to establish that for each model M, $M \vDash \Phi$ iff there is an expansion of M that satisfies χ.   □

Before turning to an assessment of the logics, it must be noted that the restriction to sentences with no finite models is inelegant. The possibility of removing it is an interesting aside.

As above, let $L'K$ and LK be languages with model-theoretic semantics. We say that $L'K$ *projects* LK if, for each sentence Φ of LK, there is a set $K' \supseteq K$ and a sentence Φ' of $L'K'$ such that, for each model M, $M \vDash \Phi$ in LK iff there is an expansion M' of M such that $M' \vDash \Phi'$ in $L'K'$. In the terminology of Barwise and Feferman (1985), $L'K$ projects LK if and only if every elementary class of LK is a projective class of $L'K$. It is written $LK \leq_{PC} L'K$. The logics LK and $L'K$ are *PC-equivalent* if $LK \leq_{PC} L'K$ and $L'K \leq_{PC} LK$. The counterpart of this for ω-logic has already been defined.

First, we show that ancestral logic projects $L(Q_0)$. Let s be a unary function letter, and let INF be the (first-order) assertion that s is one-to-one and that there is an element that is not in the range of s. If s is not in K, then for any model M of $L1K =$ the domain of M is infinite if and only if there is an expansion of M that satisfies INF. Let FIN_A be a sentence asserting that there is an x such that everything (including x) is an ancestor of sx under s. If s is not in K, then for every model M of $L1K=$, the domain of M is finite if and only if there is an expansion of M that satisfies FIN_A. Now let Φ be a sentence of $L(Q_0)$ and assume that s does not occur in Φ (relettering if necessary). Since ancestral logic quasi-projects $L(Q_0)$ (Theorem 9.12), let Φ' be a sentence of ancestral logic corresponding to $\Phi \& Qx(x = x)$. So if M is infinite, then M satisfies Φ iff there is an expansion of M that satisfies Φ'. Now let Φ^* be a (first-order) sentence obtained by systematically replacing each subformula of Φ in the form $Qx\Psi$ with a logical contradiction. If M is finite, then $M \vDash \Phi$ iff $M \vDash \Phi^*$. Combined, for any model M (of any cardinality), $M \vDash \Phi$ iff there is an expansion of M that satisfies

$$(\text{INF} \& \Phi') \lor (\text{FIN}_A \& \Phi^*).$$

A similar argument establishes the converse, that $L(Q_0)$ projects ancestral logic.[14] So $L(Q_0)$ and ancestral logic are PC-equivalent.

The question of whether $L(Q_0)$ and ancestral logic project weak second-order logic, and thus whether all three are PC-equivalent, is equivalent to a long-standing open problem in complexity theory. As above, the crucial proposition is this:

> For every sentence Φ of weak second-order logic, there is a sentence Φ^* of $L(Q_0)$ such that, for each *finite* M, $M \vDash \Phi$ iff there is an expansion M' of M such that $M' \vDash \Phi^*$.

When attention is restricted to finite models, then weak second-order logic is the same as second-order logic[15] and, as above, each sentence of $L(Q_0)$ is equivalent to a first-order sentence. Thus our proposition becomes:

> For every sentence Φ of the second-order $L2K$, there is a sentence Φ^* of the first-order $L1K'=$ such that for each finite M, $M \vDash \Phi$ iff there is an expansion M' of M such that $M' \vDash \Phi^*$.

A second-order sentence Ψ is said to be *existential* if it has the form $\exists X_1 \ldots \exists X_n \chi$, where χ has no bound higher-order variables. If some of the non-logical items in a first-order sentence are systematically replaced with (new) variables of appropriate type and then bound by an initial existential quantifier, the result is an existential second-order sentence. This (Ramsey) technique has been used several times already. It follows that the foregoing proposition is equivalent to:

> For every sentence Φ of the second-order $L2K$, there is an existential second-order sentence Φ^* (also of $L2K$) such that, for each finite M, $M \vDash \Phi$ iff $M \vDash \Phi^*$.

For any higher-order sentence Ψ, there is an algorithm that decides, of any finite model M, whether $M \vDash \Psi$. Leivant has indicated that the foregoing proposition, and thus the question of whether $L(Q_0)$ projects weak second-order logic, depends on the complexity of these algorithms. Existential second-order formulas coincide with properties of finite structures recognized by so-called NP algorithms (and vice versa), while second-order formulas in general coincide with properties recognized by another class of algorithms, the full polynomial–time hierarchy. It is not known whether the latter is coextensive with the former. For this, and similar results, see Fagin (1974), Immerman (1983), Gurevich (1988), and Leivant (1989), as well as the wealth of papers cited therein.

Enough comparison.[16] It should be clear that the languages in this subsection do not have all the shortcomings of first-order languages. Finitude can be characterized in them, but if anything has the advantages of theft over toil, this does. The notion of finitude is explicitly 'built in' to the systems in one way or another. Similarly, the natural numbers can be characterized up to isomorphism, and minimal closures of definable sets and relations can be characterized (e.g. in terms of the ancestral). Slightly less trivially, the rational numbers can be characterized up to isomorphism as an infinite field whose domain is the minimal closure of $\{1\}$ under the field operations and their inverses. As noted above, the logics are not compact and the upward Löwenheim–Skolem theorem fails.

There are, however, limitations to the expressive power of these languages. They fall well short of second-order languages. First, the *downward* Löwenheim–Skolem theorem holds for ω-logic: for any ω-model M there is a countable substructure M' that is also an ω-model and is equivalent to M. It follows from the proofs of the above comparison results that a similar theorem holds for weak second-order logic, ancestral logic, and $L(Q_0)$. Thus the Löwenheim number (see Chapter 6, Section 6.4) of each logic is $\aleph_0$.

Thus the real numbers cannot be characterized up to isomorphism in these languages. Nevertheless, the versions of real analysis in these languages are improvements over the first-order variety. As above, one can guarantee that every model is Archimedean (employing extra terminology if needed), and so every model is isomorphic to a *subset* of the real numbers. To speak loosely, with the present languages we cannot establish the existence of every real number, but at least extraneous 'numbers', infinitesimals for example, can be excluded. Moreover, the 'natural numbers' and the 'rational numbers' of each model can be characterized.

As we have seen, the class of models of set theory as formulated in the present languages is the class of ω-models and this is an improvement over first-order ZFC. There are, however, countable models of the set theories formulated in the present languages and, moreover, there are models in which the membership relation is not well-founded. Similarly, the general notion of well-ordering cannot be characterized. In particular, let δ be the least upper bound of all ordinals α such that there is a recursive well-ordering of the natural numbers whose order type is α. If Φ is a sentence of one of our languages, all of whose models are well-orderings, then there is no model of Φ whose order type is δ or any ordinal greater than δ. In the terminology of Barwise and Feferman (1985), δ is not 'pinned down' by weak second-order logic, ancestral logic, ω-logic, or $L(Q_0)$, and in fact δ is the 'bound' of these languages.

As indicated in Chapter 7, in the history of foundational research there was some controversy, or uncertainty, as to whether the notion of natural number (or an equivalent, like finitude) is more fundamental than the membership relation of set theory or the predication relation of higher-order logic. Recall, for example, that Skolem (1928) suggested that the foundations of both must be laid out simultaneously in an interrelated manner. The present languages take the notion of natural number, or finitude, as 'primitive'. The structures and notions that can be captured in these languages are precisely those that can be characterized *in terms of* natural numbers. We saw, for example, that a membership relation on *finite* sets can be simulated (if the domain is infinite and certain non-logical terms are added). But the logics are weaker than second-order logic.

The comparison results above entail that the present languages all have the same Hanf number (see Chapter 6, Section 6.4). Let $B(0) = \aleph_0$, $B(\alpha + 1) = 2^{B(\alpha)}$, and, if λ is a limit ordinal, $B(\lambda) = \bigcup \{B(\alpha) \mid \alpha < \lambda\}$. Then the Hanf number of the present languages is $B(\delta)$, with δ as just above. Barwise (1985) indicates that the Beth definability property (see Chapter 6, Section 6.6) fails for the logics of this subsection, for much the same reason that the general property fails for second-order logic. The interpolation property also fails.

Details of the results reported here, and a host of other information about weak second-order logic, ω-logic, and $L(Q_0)$ can be found in the papers published in Barwise and Feferman (1985), especially Barwise (1985), Ebbinghaus (1985), and Väänänen (1985).

Before moving on, let us briefly consider one extension of the present logics. Define *quasi-weak second-order logic*, abbreviated $L2q$, to be like weak second-order logic, but with variables ranging over *countable* relations. Thus $L2q$ has the same formulas as weak second-order languages, but in the semantics each variable assignment consists of a function from the first-order variables to the domain, as usual, and a function from the relation variables to countable relations. So $\forall X \Phi$ can be read 'for all countable X, Φ'. It is equivalent to augmenting ω-logic with a sort of variable representing functions whose domain is the field of $<$ (i.e. the collection of 'natural numbers').

Let $\text{FIN}(X)$ be a formula asserting that there is no (countable) function whose domain is X and whose range is a proper subset of X. Clearly, $\text{FIN}(X)$ is satisfied by a model and assignment if and only if the set assigned to X is finite. It follows that $L2q$ includes weak second-order logic.[17] The converse fails, however. For example, in the $L2q$ version of analysis, one can state that every bounded countable set has a least upper bound. This, with the other axioms, is sufficient to establish the categoricity of the theory—all its models are isomorphic to the real numbers. Let $Z2q$ be the axioms of ZFC formulated in the present language (so that appropriate formulas in $L2q$ occur in the replacement scheme). If $M = \langle d, I \rangle$ is a model of $Z2q$ and c is a countable subset of d, then there is a member of d whose 'elements' in M are the members of c. In other words, every countable *class* is a *set*. It follows from this and the axiom of foundation (and choice) that the membership relation of M is well-founded. Thus, M is isomorphic to a transitive set m, and m contains all its countable subsets.

In general, the notion of well-foundedness can be formulated in $L2q$. Let $WO(R)$ be the assertion of $L2q$ that R is a linear order and that every countable set has a 'least element' under R. Then, assuming the axiom of choice in the metatheory, $WO(R)$ is satisfied by a structure if and only if R is a well-ordering of the domain. In short, $L2q$ is a significant improvement. There is, however, a downward Löwenheim–Skolem theorem of sorts. A construction similar to the proof of the first-order case establishes that for every structure $M = \langle d, I \rangle$ there is a substructure $M' = \langle d', I' \rangle$ such that the cardinality of d' is at most that of the continuum, and for every formula Φ of $L2q$ and assignment s on M', $M, s \vDash \Phi$ iff $M', s \vDash \Phi$.

9.1.3 *Infinitary languages*

We next consider languages that have formulas of infinite length. There is some justification for rejecting these out of hand as serious candidates for foundational research. If nothing else, language is an instrument for communication, and one cannot do much communicating if it takes an infinite amount of time and space to write or speak or comprehend a single sentence. On a related matter, Hilbert (1925) wrote:

> ... the literature of mathematics is glutted with ... absurdities which have had their source in the infinite. For example, we find writers insisting, as though it were a restrictive condition, that in rigorous mathematics only a finite number of deductions are admissible in a proof—as if someone had succeeded in making an infinite number of them.

This is beyond dispute, but it is not inconceivable that mathematicians are able to *refer* to infinite sentences (and deductions), themselves construed as abstract objects. Communication is accomplished in natural languages, and we are dealing here with formal languages and model-theoretic semantics. In general, there is always a gap between formal languages and the natural languages they model. One suggestion is to regard the natural language of mathematics as an informal metalanguage for an infinitary language whose models are the various structures under study. It may not be too much of a distortion to view the proposal in Zermelo (1931) that way. Less exotically, one might suggest that infinitary languages capture important relations and features underlying mathematics as practised.

In any case, infinitary logic has received some attention from mathematical logicians in recent decades. One reason is that such systems seem to do well in the aforementioned trade-off between expressive ability and tractable model theory. We take a passing glance at infinitary languages here.

If K is a set of non-logical terminology and $\kappa \geq \lambda$ are two cardinal numbers, then $L\kappa\lambda K$ is an infinitary language based on K. For convenience, we shall omit the K in most contexts. The formation rules of $L\kappa\lambda$ are those of the first-order $L1K=$, augmented with the following clauses.

If Γ is a set of well-formed formulas whose cardinality is less than κ, then $\bigwedge \Gamma$, the conjunction of the formulas in Γ, is a well-formed formula.

If A is a set of variables whose cardinality is less than λ, and Φ is a well-formed formula, then $\forall A\Phi$ is a well-formed formula. In $\forall A\Phi$, every variable in A is bound.[18]

For convenience, it is stipulated that the formulas in the set Γ of the first clause contain fewer than λ free variables total. This allows one to bind the variables of any formula with initial quantifiers. If Γ is a set of formulas, let $\neg\Gamma$ be $\{\neg\Phi \mid \Phi \in \Gamma\}$. Then define $\bigvee \Gamma$, the infinitary disjunction of Γ, to be $\neg\bigwedge \neg\Gamma$. If A is a set of variables, then define $\exists A\Phi$ to be $\neg\forall A\neg\Phi$. If the restriction on the size of the set Γ in the above clauses is dropped, the language is called $L\infty\lambda$, and if the restriction on the cardinality of the set A of variables is also dropped, the language is called $L\infty\infty$. In $L\kappa\lambda$, the collection of well-formed formulas is a set, while $L\infty\lambda$ and $L\infty\infty$ each have a proper class of formulas. The latter has a proper class of variables.[19] Notice that $L\omega\omega K$ is just the first-order $L1K=$. The 'smallest' infinitary language is $L\omega_1\omega$, which allows countable conjunctions and only finitary quantifiers. The semantics for infinitary languages is a straightforward extension of the semantics of first-order languages. The new clauses are as follows.

$M, s \vDash \bigwedge \Gamma$ if $M, s \vDash \Phi$ for every $\Phi \in \Gamma$.

$M, s \vDash \forall A\Phi$ if $M, s' \vDash \Phi$ for every assignment s' that agrees with s
on the variables not in A.

The expressive power of infinitary languages is often a matter of 'brute force'. One simply 'says' what is required. For example, let $\Phi_1(x)$ be the infinitary disjunction of $x = 0, x = s0, x = ss0, \ldots$ (in $L\omega_1\omega$). Any model of the axiom for the successor function and $\forall x\Phi_1(x)$ is isomorphic to the natural numbers. Similarly, let $\Phi_2(x)$ be the disjunction of $x < 1, x < 1 + 1, \ldots$. Then $\forall x\Phi(x)$ is satisfied by an ordered field F if and only if F is Archimedean. The real numbers can be characterized up to isomorphism in $L\omega_1\omega_1$ (but not in $L\omega_1\omega$).

Let $\Phi(x, y)$ be any formula with x and y free. Then 'w is an ancestor of x under Φ' is characterized as the disjunction of $w = x$, $\Phi(z, w)$, $\exists x(\Phi(z, x)$ & $\Phi(x, w))$, $\exists x_1 \exists x_2(\Phi(z, x_1)$ & $\Phi(x_1, x_2)$ & $(x_2, w))$, etc. This, and similar reasoning, shows that the smallest infinitary language $L\omega_1\omega$ includes all the logics of the last subsection. That is, if Φ is any sentence of weak second-order logic, $L(Q_0)$, or ancestral logic, then there is a sentence Φ' of $L\omega_1\omega$ such that, for any model M, $M \vDash \Phi$ iff $M \vDash \Phi'$ (and similarly for ω-logic; see Cowles (1979) and Barwise (1979) for more details on these results). Also, $L\omega_2\omega_1$ includes the system called quasi-weak second-order logic $L2q$ (see Section 9.1.2).

Cardinality considerations show that none of the finitary languages developed here includes any infinitary language. For example, if the set K consists of the single binary relation letter, a straightforward transfinite induction establishes that if α is any ordinal whose cardinality is less than κ, then there is a sentence Φ_α of $L\kappa\omega K$ such that any model M satisfies Φ_α iff M is isomorphic to α (under the membership relation). Thus there are uncountably many different structures that can be characterized up to isomorphism in $L\omega_1\omega$. On the other hand, if K is countable, then the second-order $L2K$ has only countably many sentences, and so only countably many structures can be characterized up to isomorphism. Thus second-order logic does not include $L\omega_1\omega$ and, *a fortiori*, neither does weak second-order logic, $L2q$, $L(Q_0)$, ancestral logic, or ω-logic. It might be added that no infinitary language $L\kappa\lambda$ includes second-order logic. For example, the notions of compact space and complete linear order can be characterized in a second-order language, but not in any $L\kappa\lambda$ (see Dickmann 1985, p. 323). The reason is that there is no bound on the cardinality of the relations in the range of second-order variables.

If the deductive system $D1$ for $L1K=$ is augmented with plausible infinitary rules of inference, then the smallest infinitary logic $L\omega_1\omega$ enjoys a certain completeness property. In particular, if Γ is a *countable* set of formulas and Φ is a single formula, then $\Gamma \vDash \Phi$ in $L\omega_1\omega$ iff Φ can be 'deduced' from Γ in the expanded deductive system.[20] There is also an analogue of the downward Löwenheim–Skolem theorem. If κ is uncountable and Φ is any sentence of $L\kappa\omega$, then if Φ has a model at all, it has a model whose cardinality is less than κ. It follows that the Löwenheim number of $L\kappa\omega$ is at most κ. The Löwenheim number of $L\omega_1\omega$ is $\aleph_0$. As in the previous subsection, let $B(0) = \aleph_0$, $B(\alpha + 1) = 2^{B(\alpha)}$, and, if λ is a limit ordinal, $B(\lambda) = \bigcup \{B(\alpha) \mid \alpha < \lambda\}$. Then the Hanf number of $L\omega_1\omega$ is $B(\omega_1)$. In general, the Hanf number of $L\kappa^+\omega$ is at least $B(\kappa^+)$ and is less than $B((\kappa^+)^+)$.

Even though, as noted above, any ordinal $\alpha < \kappa$ can be characterized up to isomorphism in $L\kappa\omega$, there is no sentence of $L\infty\omega$ whose models are all and only well-ordered structures, nor is there any sentence of $L\infty\omega$ whose models are all and only well-founded structures. On the other hand, the notion of well-foundedness can be characterized in $L\omega_1\omega_1$. Let $A = \{x_0, x_1, \ldots\}$ be a denumerably infinite set of variables and let Γ be $\{Rx_1x_0, Rx_2x_1, \ldots\}$. Then the relation R is well-founded iff $\forall A \neg(\bigwedge \Gamma)$. The latter directly 'says' that there is no infinite descending R-chain. The conjunction of this with the (first-order) axioms of a linear order constitutes a characterization of well-ordering (assuming the axiom of choice in the metalanguage) in $L\omega_1\omega_1$.

The interested reader is referred to the essays in Barwise and Feferman (1985), especially Dickmann (1985), Kolaitis (1985), and Nadel (1985), and to the wealth of references provided there.

9.1.4   *Substitutional quantifiers*

A number of philosophers have developed an alternative to model-theoretic semantics for formal languages. The idea is to replace the 'satisfaction' of formulas with the 'truth' of sentences. For present purposes, the truth of atomic sentences under an 'interpretation' is regarded as primitive; it is not defined in terms of other things. The crucial clause in the definition is as follows:

Let $\Phi(x)$ be a formula whose only free variable is x. Then $\forall x \Phi(x)$ is *true substitutionally in interpretation I* if for every term t of the language, $\Phi(t)$ is true substitutionally in I.

The main role of this *substitutional semantics* is to reduce ontology. If the programme were successful, one could have variables and quantifiers in an interpreted formal language without thereby taking on 'ontological commitment'. Presumably, variables and quantifiers, as understood substitutionally, do not have 'ranges' (see, for example, Leblanc 1976, Gottlieb 1980). Our purposes here are different. In this section, we are examining languages and semantics capable of expressing substantial mathematical concepts and describing mathematical structures, like the natural and real numbers. Since this presupposes that there is something to describe, we are not out to reduce 'ontological commitment', at least not in this way. When adapted to present purposes, however, substitutional semantics has some interesting advantages. It happens that the semantics is not compact, and no effective deductive system is both sound and complete for it.

The idea of model theory, as such, is foreign to substitutional semantics, but an accommodation can be made. Let $M = \langle d, I \rangle$ be a model of a first-order language $L1K=$. Define M to be a *substitution model* if for every $b \in d$, there is a term t of $L1K=$ such that t denotes b in M. In other words, M is a substitution model if every element of its domain is denoted by a term of the language. Substitution models are good candidates for what may be called 'substitutional interpretations' of a formal language like $L1K=$.

Define a set Γ of sentences to be *substitutionally satisfiable in $L1K=$* if there is a substitution model M such that, for every $\Phi \in \Gamma$, $M \models \Phi$, and define a single sentence Φ to be *substitutionally satisfiable in* $L1K=$ if the singleton $\{\Phi\}$ is substitutionally satisfiable in $L1K=$. An argument $\langle \Gamma, \Phi \rangle$ is *substitutionally valid in* $L1K=$, or Φ is a *substitutional consequence of* Γ in $L1K=$, if for every substitution model M, if $M \vDash \Psi$ for every $\Psi \in \Gamma$, then $M \vDash \Phi$. And a sentence Φ is a *substitutional logical truth in* $L1K=$, if Φ is a substitutional consequence of the empty set.

In the usual semantics for first-order languages, the properties of a formula, a set of formulas, or an argument depend only on the non-logical items it contains. For example, if a formula Φ is in both $L1K=$ and $L1K'=$, then Φ is a logical truth in $L1K=$ iff Φ is a logical truth in $L1K'=$. The same goes for higher-order languages, and the other logics developed in this section. This is not the case for substitutional semantics, since the extension of 'substitutional model' depends on the terminology of the language. For example, if K consists only of the individual constants p and q, then $\forall x(x = p \lor x = q)$ is a substitutional logical truth, as is $\exists y \exists z \forall x(x = y \lor x = z)$. Neither of these sentences is a substitutional logical truth if there is a third constant, or a function letter, in K.

Unless noted otherwise, it is stipulated that the set K of non-logical terminology contains infinitely many individual constants. This attenuates the impact of the close tie between the non-logical terms and the semantic properties, but as will be seen, it does not eliminate it.

THEOREM 9.13. A sentence Φ of $L1K=$ is substitutionally satisfiable if and only if Φ is satisfiable. *A fortiori*, Φ is a substitutional logical truth if and only if Φ is a logical truth.

Proof. Clearly, if Φ is substitutionally satisfiable, then Φ is satisfiable, since every substitution model is a model. For the converse, let $M = \langle d, I \rangle$ be a model such that $M \vDash \Phi$. Applying the downward Löwenheim–Skolem theorem, let $M_1 = \langle d_1, I_1 \rangle$ be a model such that d_1 is countable and $M_1 \vDash \Phi$. Then let $M_2 = \langle d_2, I_2 \rangle$ be a substitution model such that $d_1 = d_2$ and I_1 agrees with I_2 on every non-logical item that occurs in Φ. The model M_2 is obtained by reassigning the non-logical individual constants that do not occur in Φ, so that every element of d_2 is assigned to at least one constant. It is straightforward to verify that $M_2 \vDash \Phi$. □

COROLLARY 9.14. Substitutional semantics is *weakly complete* for the deductive system $D1$ for $L1K=$. That is, Φ is a substitutional logical truth if and only if $\vdash_{D1} \Phi$.

On the other hand, substitutional semantics is not strongly complete for any effective deductive system. Let A_1 be the union of the terminology of arithmetic $\{0, s, +, \cdot\}$ and the infinite list of individual constants $\{p_0, p_1, \ldots\}$. Let Γ consist of the successor, addition, and multiplication axioms (see Section 9.2), together with the sentences $p_0 = 0, p_1 = s0, p_2 = ss0, \ldots$. Then a substituion model M satisfies every member of Γ if and only if M is isomorphic to the natural numbers, with $p_0, p_1, \ldots$ as the numerals. In other words, in substitutional semantics Γ is a categorical characterization of the natural numbers. It follows that for every sentence Φ, Φ is a substitutional consequence of Γ if and only if Φ is true of the natural numbers. As above, it is a corollary of the incompleteness of arithmetic that substitutional semantics is inherently incomplete.[21]

The upward Löwenheim–Skolem theorem fails, trivially. If there are only countably many terms of the language, then there are no uncountable substitution models.[22] There is a more substantial result.

THEOREM 9.15. There is a set Γ of sentences such that for every $n > 0$, Γ has a substitution model whose domain has cardinality n, but Γ has no substitution model whose domain is infinite.

Proof. Let K consist of the unary function letter f and the individual constants $t_0, t_1, \ldots$. Let Γ consist of the sentences $f(t_0) = t_1$, $f(t_1) = t_2$, $f(t_2) = t_3, \ldots$, and $\exists x (f(x) = t_0)$. For each $n > 0$, let d_n consist of the natural numbers $\{0, 1, \ldots, n - 1\}$. For each i, let $I_n(t_i)$ be the remainder when i is divided by n, and let $I_n(f)$ be the function whose value at j is the remainder when $j + 1$ is divided by n. Then $M_n = \langle d_n, I_n \rangle$ is a substitution model that satisfies every member of Γ. Now, let $M = \langle d, I \rangle$ be any substitution model of this language that satisfies every member of Γ. If d is infinite, then the denotations in M of the terms $t_0, f(t_0), f(f(t_0)), \ldots$ must all be distinct and must exhaust the domain. Thus $M \vDash \neg \exists x (f(x) = t_0)$, which is a contradiction.[23]
□

THEOREM 9.16. Substitutional semantics is not compact.

Proof. This is a corollary of the above theorem, but there is a direct way to establish it. Let the non-logical terms consist of the constants $t_0, t_1, \ldots$, and the monadic predicate letter D, and let Γ consist of $Dt_0, Dt_1, \ldots$, together with $\exists x \neg Dx$. Then every *proper* subset of Γ is substitutionally satisfiable and so every finite subset is satisfiable. But Γ itself is not.
□

No structure whose domain is uncountable can be characterized in substitutional semantics, unless uncountably many non-logical terms can be used. On the other hand, every structure whose domain is countable can be characterized up to isomorphism. In general, any structure can be characterized in a language that has as many individual constants as the domain has members. Indeed, let $M = \langle d, I \rangle$ be any model at all. Assume that no element of d is a non-logical term of the associated language (relettering if necessary). Now expand the language so that every element of d is a non-logical constant, and expand I so that if $b \in d$ then $I(b) = b$ (so that b denotes itself). Call the result M'. Clearly, M' is a substitution model for the expanded language.

Let Γ be the set of sentences Φ such that $M' \vDash \Phi$. Clearly, any substitution model in the expanded language is isomorphic to M' iff it satisfies every member of Γ.

Recall that the main problem of characterizing the natural numbers is to state, somehow, that $0, 1, 2, \ldots$ are all the numbers that there are. We have seen how to accomplish this with a higher-order language and with the other languages developed in this section, and we have seen that in a first-order language it cannot be done. If a first-order theory of arithmetic has an infinite model at all, then it has models that contain elements different from all of $0, 1, 2, \ldots$. With substitutional semantics, categoricity is achieved by simply excluding those non-standard models from the semantics by fiat. Every element of every model must be denoted by something. If a set Γ has a substitution model at all, then one can construct such a model from equivalence classes of the terms of the language. Thus a theory that is substitutionally satisfiable carries a model in its syntax.

9.2   Free relation variables

The language, semantics, and deductive system for free-variable second-order languages $L2K-$ are presented in Chapters 3 and 4, alongside those of second-order languages $L2K$. The logics share the same class of models, and the variables are treated in the same way. The difference is that $L2K-$ does not contain *bound* relation or function variables. The effect is the same as allowing only initial universal quantifiers over second-order variables. See Corcoran (1980) for an extensive discussion of similar languages.

Notice that even though there is a negation sign in the language, $L2K-$ is not closed under what may be called 'contradictory opposition'. If Φ is a formula with a free relation variable, then there may be no formula of $L2K-$ that is the contradictory opposite of Φ. Indeed, $\Phi(X)$ is equivalent to $\forall X \Phi(X)$, while $\neg \Phi(X)$ is equivalent to $\forall X \neg \Phi(X)$. Along similar lines, there is, in general, no formula equivalent to $\exists X \Phi(X)$. It follows that the Boolos interpretation (which formulates monadic existential second-order quantifiers in terms of plural quantifiers) of Section 9.1 is not available for $L2K-$.

As we have seen, many thinkers, notably Quine, balk at the automatic assumption of the existence of relations and functions, no matter how these are construed. As noted in several places above, there is a tradition, also due to Quine, that regards the ontology of a theory to consist precisely of the range of its *bound* variables. The point is a simple one. The existential quantifier is a gloss on the ordinary word for existence; it is how existence is expressed in formal languages. Thus an interpreted theory in a formal language entails the existence of whatever falls under the range of an existential quantifier, and this is the range of the bound variables. In free-variable second-order languages, one cannot say that relations and functions *exist*, since relation and function variables are not bound by quantifiers.

In another context, Hilbert (e.g. 1925) made a similar distinction. A formula with a free variable expresses a certain generality in that such a formula can be used to assert *each* of its instances. This is not the same as formulas with bound variables (called 'apparent variables'). Those represent genuine claims of existence. Hilbert wished to develop theories that avoid reference to completed infinite sets, and in doing so he banned bound (i.e. 'apparent') variables but not free variables. Skolem (1923) expressed a similar idea:

> [Arithmetic] can be founded in a rigorous way without the use of Russell and Whitehead's notions 'always' and 'sometimes'. This can also be expressed as follows: A logical foundation can be provided for arithmetic without the use of apparent logical variables.

Free-variable second-order languages exploit this distinction in the context of sets, relations, and functions, the items of second-order logic.

A number of logicians have expressed (in correspondence) the belief that for a given infinite domain d, there is no clear understanding of the totality of the subsets of d (i.e. the powerset of d). The independence results in set theory suggest this. The powerful axioms of ZFC do not suffice to fix the powerset of the set of natural numbers, the simplest infinite powerset. But this is part of the range of the higher-order variables in arithmetic, the logical notion of set. The argument (sometimes) continues that the purported range may not even be unambiguous, but even if it is, the range is too problematic to serve foundational research. We do not have even a serviceable grap of the phrase 'all subsets of natural numbers'. Can one claim to have an intuitive grasp of statements in the form $\forall X \exists Y \forall Z \Phi$, even in a simple context like arithmetic?

We have seen arguments like this before (Chapters 2, 7, and 8) and dealt with them. I maintain that we have a reasonable grasp of such locutions, but not one that is incorrigible or self-evident. It can be added that virtually all the force of these objections to higher-order logic is deflected from free-variable second-order logic. Such systems do not presuppose a far-reaching grasp of the range of the second-order variables. In fact, one need not even presuppose that there is a fixed extension of the predicate (and relation) variables. It is often enough to recognize *unproblematic* definitions of subsets of the domain, as they arise. In effect, the only higher-order rule of inference allowed in $L2K-$ is universal instantiation: from $\Phi(X)$, infer $\Phi(S)$, where S is any set.[24] If, in a given case, there is no unclarity about the set S, then there is no unclarity about the inference. In short, $\Phi(X)$ can be interpreted as 'Φ holds of any *given* set X', or 'once a set S is determined, Φ holds of it'.

Consider the axiom of induction in arithmetic, as formulated in a free-variable second-order language,

$$(X0 \ \& \ \forall x(Xx \rightarrow Xsx)) \rightarrow \forall x Xx$$

and consider the corresponding axiom of completeness in analysis

$$\exists y \forall x(Xx \rightarrow x \leq y) \rightarrow \exists y \forall z(\forall x(Xx \rightarrow x \leq z) \rightarrow y \leq z).$$

As interpreted here, the former asserts that any *given* set of natural numbers that contains 0 and is closed under the successor function contains all the natural numbers. The second asserts that any given bounded set of real numbers has a least upper bound. These axioms, so construed, are enough to establish the categoricity of the respective theories. Recall the proof of the categoricity of analysis (Chapter 4, Section 4.2). We consider two models $M = \langle d, I \rangle$ and $M' = \langle d', I' \rangle$ of the theory. Using only weak and uncontroversial principles of set theory, we define certain subsets of d *in terms of* M' and certain subsets of d' in terms of M. Then these sets are taken as instances of the completeness axiom. In each case, we have an application of universal instantiation. Consider the step that occurred after it was shown that the 'rationals' of M are in one-to-one correspondence with the 'rationals' of M'. Let c be an arbitrary element of d and let C be the collection of rationals in M that are less than c. Then we let C' be the set of rationals in M' that correspond to the members of C. To apply the completeness axiom to C', we need only recognize that C' is a (bounded) subset of d'. This, I suggest, is patently obvious (even though C' may not be definable in M' alone). I conclude that one can work with theories formulated in free-variable second-order languages, and one can coherently maintain the categoricity of arithmetic and analysis, without claiming some sort of absolute grasp on the range of the relation and function variables—or even claiming that there is a fixed range. One only needs the ability to recognize subsets as they are defined, and in the context of the interpreted formal languages in question this is not problematic. This is a rather weak hold on the range of the second-order variables. Similar remarks apply to set theory, as formulated in a free-variable second-order language.

Notice that, in effect, *first-order* consequence, logical truth, etc. are often defined in terms of free-variable second-order logic. We may read, for example, that a sentence Φ is a logical truth if Φ is satisfied by every model *under every interpretation* of its non-logical terminology. This is the same as treating the non-logical terminology as free variables. Tarski (1935) exploits this in his celebrated treatment of logical consequence.

Along similar lines, notice also that a single formula of $L2K-$ is a logical truth if and only if the result of uniformly replacing each relation variable with a different non-logical term (of appropriate degree) is a logical truth. But the latter is first-order. Thus, as noted in Chapter 4, the set of logical truths of $L2K-$ is recursively enumerable (if K is), and $L2K-$ is weakly complete (even without the substitution rule). In the light of the categoricity results, however, $L2K-$ is not strongly complete. Indeed, the set of 'quasi-consequences' of the single formula that characterizes the natural numbers (with addition and multiplication) is not recursively enumerable—it is not even arithmetic.

Let A be a monadic predicate letter and R a binary relation (both non-logical). Then, as in Chapter 5, there is a formula of $L2K-$ equivalent to 'x is in the minimal closure of A under R':

$$MC(x): [\forall y(Ay \rightarrow Xy) \,\&\, \forall y \forall z((Xy \,\&\, Ryz) \rightarrow Xz)] \rightarrow Xx.$$

But one cannot state in $L2K-$ that *there is* a minimal closure of A under R (which, in the second-order $L2K$, is an instance of the comprehension scheme). Also, one cannot directly state in $L2K-$ a conditional whose antecedent is 'x is in the minimal closure of A under R'. Indeed, in such a conditional, the variable X would be implicitly bound by a universal quantifier whose scope is the *entire formula*. In general, $\forall X(MC(x)) \rightarrow \Phi$ is not equivalent to $\forall X(MC(x) \rightarrow \Phi)$. In some cases, however, this problem can be circumvented. Introduce a new non-logical predicate letter B, with the axiom

$$\forall y(Ay \rightarrow By) \,\&\, \forall y \forall z((By \,\&\, Ryz) \rightarrow Bz) \,\&\, \forall x(Bx \rightarrow MC(x)).$$

This entails that the extension of B is coextensive with the indicated minimal closure. To model the assertion that 'if x is a minimal closure of a under R, then Φ' one would write $\forall x(Bx \rightarrow \Phi)$.

Many of the second-order characterizations presented in Chapter 5 (and elsewhere) do not have straightforward equivalents in $L2K-$. The formula expressing infinitude, for example, has an *existential* quantifier ranging over functions:

$$\text{INF}(X): \exists f [\forall x \forall y(fx = fy \rightarrow x = y) \,\&\, \forall x(Xx \rightarrow Xfx)$$
$$\&\, \exists y(Xy \,\&\, \forall x(Xx \rightarrow fx \neq y))].$$

The opposite, finitude, can be expressed[25] if attention is fixed on a single predicate A:

$$\text{FIN}(A): \neg(\forall x \forall y(fx = fy \rightarrow x = y) \,\&\, \forall x(Ax \rightarrow Afx)$$
$$\&\, \exists y(Ay \,\&\, \forall x(Ax \rightarrow fx \neq y))).$$

Similarly, one can assert in $L2K-$ that a given relation is well-founded, or is a well-ordering of its field, but the well-ordering *principle* that every set has a well-ordering cannot be stated. The latter requires an existential quantifier ranging over relations.

Many of these features are a consequence of the fact that $L2K-$ is not closed under contradictory opposition. It is clearly inconvenient to be unable to express the complements of otherwise definable properties and relations, and to be unable to use definable notions in the antecedents of conditionals. In a sense, the second-order $L2K$ is the result of 'closing' $L2K-$ under contradictory opposition. But then, it seems, we do have 'apparent variables' over sets of relations and, presumably, the 'troubling matters of ontology'. This is another trade-off.

9.3   First-order set theory

This concluding section is devoted to what is probably the most common foundation of mathematics, first-order set theory. Let T be a theory formulated in a higher-order language. If the set of axioms of T is definable in set theory, then it is straightforward to construct a formula $T(x)$ of first-order set theory that asserts 'x is a model of T'. If Φ is a sentence of the language of T that does not contain occurrences of x, then Φ can be 'translated' into a sentence $\Phi' = \forall x(T(x) \rightarrow \Phi/x)$ in the language of set theory, where Φ/x is obtained from Φ by uniformly replacing the non-logical terminology with appropriate set-theoretic items referring to constructions from x (predicates with sets, n-place relations with sets of n-tuples, etc.), and then replacing all bound first-order variables with set variables ranging over (i.e. relativized to) the 'domain' of x, and replacing all bound relation and function variables with variables ranging over appropriate relations and functions on x. It can be tedious, but the replacements are straightforward. We have encountered similar constructions several times already. In sum, the sentence Φ' amounts to 'Φ holds in all (set-theoretic) models of T'. If T is categorical, or at least semantically complete,[26] then Φ' amounts to 'Φ is true in T'. Also, given the usual way that theories are formulated, a proof of Φ in T can be 'translated' into a proof of Φ' in set theory. That is, concerning deductions, set theory can do anything that a higher-order theory can do and usually more (for example, the consistency of T may be deducible in set theory).

It was noted above (in several places) that the set-theoretic hierarchy provides the model-theoretic semantics of formal languages. From that perspective, the sentence Φ' corresponds to 'Φ is a semantic consequence of T'. In effect, the set-theoretic formulation makes explicit the model-theoretic semantics of each theory. Moreover, virtually any of the common semantical statements about T can be cast in these terms. For example, the sentence $\exists x T(x)$ asserts that T is satisfiable, and the categoricity of T is equivalent to a set-theoretic statement of the form

$$C(T): \forall x \forall y((T(x) \ \& \ T(y)) \rightarrow (x \text{ and } y \text{ are isomorphic})).$$

If T has been proved categorical then, given the relative strength of set theory over the metatheory of T, $C(T)$ is a theorem of set theory.

It should be pointed out that, for theories like arithmetic and analysis whose intended models are all isomorphic, these 'semantic' interpretations are not the usual set-theoretic formulations of them. It is more common to stipulate a *particular set* to be the domain of the theory. For example, by convention, the natural numbers *are* the finite ordinals, the integers *are* certain equivalence classes of pairs of finite ordinals, etc. If the original higher-order theory is satisfiable and categorical (or semantically complete) and if the stipulated set is a model of that theory, then the approaches are the same. A sentence Φ of arithmetic is satisfied by the structure of the finite ordinals if and only if Φ holds in all models of second-order arithmetic. Not so for first-order arithmetic. Here we have one more instance of the usefulness of categoricity (see Chapter 5, Section 5.3, and Corcoran (1980)).

Notice also that the other concepts and properties discussed in Chapter 5 have straightforward characterizations in first-order set theory. For example, if b is a set and c is a set of binary relations, then 'x is in the minimal closure of b under the members of c' is characterized by the following formula, a mechanical transformation of the second-order formulation:

$$MC(b, c, x): \forall y([b \subseteq y \ \& \ \forall z \forall s \forall w((z \in y \ \& \ s \in c \ \& \ \langle z, w \rangle \in s) \rightarrow w \in y)]$$
$$\rightarrow x \in y).$$

And $\forall b \forall c \exists! y \forall x (x \in y \equiv MC(b, c, x))$ is a theorem of first-order ZFC. That is, it is provable that, for every b and c, there is a unique closure of b under the members of c. Similarly, the notion of well-foundedness can be formulated in set theory, and it can be shown that the membership relation is well-founded. And the various cardinality notions, and comparisons, can be cast in set-theoretic terms.

The set-theoretic foundation of mathematics is quite natural and fruitful. It provides a uniform semantics for all (or almost all) formal languages, and thus it establishes a smooth link between theories in formal languages and their model-theoretic semantics. In short, the set-theoretic hierarchy is a uniform foundation for all mathematics (or, perhaps, all mathematics short of set theory itself and maybe category theory).

The above set-theoretic formulations are all first-order, in that none of them have variables ranging over proper classes. Thus it might seem that first-order logic has been revived. But this depends on whether the background set theory is itself a first-order theory; or, to avoid the rhetoric of foundationalism, it depends on whether it is feasible or insightful or fruitful to model the entire background set theory in a first-order language.

There are a number of ways to understand or regiment or model the background metatheory. One of them is to take it to be *second-order ZFC*, as developed in Chapter 6, Section 6.1. To state the obvious, in this case first-order logic has not been revived. The above formulas are all first-order, but they are regarded as part of a higher-order background theory.

A second possibility is to take the background set theory to be a first-order theory, regarded as an implicit definition of its terminology. In particular, the background theory is itself cast in a first-order language, which is to be understood in terms of *its* models. In Chapter 5, a number of inadequacies of first-order set theory were pointed out. Foremost among them is the fact that first-order *ZFC* does not fix the subject matter of the theory, its 'standard models'. In the present programme, the model theory of first-order *ZFC* does not sufficiently fix the underlying model-theoretic semantics of the other mathematical theories.

Let us be a bit more precise. Since, in this option, the background theory is first-order, it has a wealth of models, some of which are clearly non-standard. There are models, for example, in which the membership relation is not well-founded, and, by hypothesis, we have no principled way to 'rule out' the unintended ones. This observation undermines the 'advantages' of the present set-theoretic programme. To focus on an example, consider the formula $N(x)$ of set theory that asserts that 'x is a model of second-order arithmetic'. The fact that second-order arithmetic is categorical corresponds to a set-theoretic *theorem* of the form

$$\forall x \forall y((N(x) \,\&\, N(y)) \rightarrow (x \text{ and } y \text{ are isomorphic})).$$

As von Neumann (1925) pointed out in a similar context, it follows from this that, for each model M of the background set theory, if a and b are in the domain of M, and $M \vDash N(a)$ and $M \vDash N(b)$, then M satisfies the statement that a and b are isomorphic. In other words, the categoricity theorem entails that *within the same model* M of set theory, any two sets satisfying $N(x)$ are isomorphic *in the model* M. This is not enough. The natural understanding of the categoricity result is that *any* two models of arithmetic are isomorphic, not just any two within the same model of set theory. A compactness argument, similar to the ones presented above, establishes that if the set theory is consistent, then it has a model M' with an element b (of the domain thereof) such that $M' \vDash N(b)$, but the collection of M' 'elements' of b is not isomorphic to the natural numbers. Indeed, there are models in which the set in question has uncountably many 'elements'.

Similar considerations apply to the set-theoretic versions of various mathematical notions. Consider, for example, the formula $MC(b, c, x)$ corresponding to 'x is in the minimal closure of b under the members of c'. The aforementioned model M' of set theory contains elements p, q, r such that $M' \vDash \forall x(x \in p \equiv MC(q, r, x))$, but the collection of M' 'elements' of p is not the indicated minimal closure.

We have before us another variant of the Skolem paradox, now applied to the background set theory. As we have seen, Skolem's conclusions cannot be resisted if the background theory is regarded as a first-order implicit definition, to be understood in terms of its models. This orientation does not

preclude non-standard or unintended interpretations of the various theories
and concepts. These occur in non-standard models of the background set
theory. Here, if nowhere else, the result is an unavoidable relativity of
virtually all mathematical notions. Once more, I submit that mathematical
practice does not reflect this. In fact, the option under consideration may be
something of a straw man.

A third possibility is to regard the background set theory to have an
intended interpretation. Just as the natural number structure is the intended
interpretation of arithmetic and the real number structure is the intended
interpretation of analysis, there is a structure, call it M, that is *the*
intended interpretation of our background first-order set theory. As above,
the background theory need not be ZFC. For many cases, a weaker variation
will do. Let us stipulate, for simplicity, that M contains no urelements.
Presumably, M is to be a *standard* model of set theory, in that it is well-
founded and extensional. It follows that M is isomorphic to a transitive set
(or class) m under membership. We also assume that m is closed under the
subsets of its elements (i.e. if $b \in m$ and $a \subseteq b$, then $a \in m$). This is also part
of what it is to be a standard model (see Chapter 5, Section 5.2). It follows
that m is a limit rank V_λ or else m is V itself. If m is to be adequate for
arithmetic, geometry, analysis, functional analysis, etc., then the ordinal λ
must be at least 2ω (in which case, m is a model of Zermelo set theory). If
the structure is to accommodate second-order set theory (and perhaps
category theory), then λ must be larger than an inaccessible cardinal.
It follows from the considerations in Chapter 6, Section 6.3, that if m is to
represent the semantics of second-order theories adequately, then it must
satisfy certain reflection principles and so must be larger than some (small)
large cardinals.

Notice that this option avoids the considerations against first-order set
theory as an implicit definition. The fact that the background theory has
unintended models is irrelevant. The theory is regarded as fully interpreted;
it is about M or m. The only relevant feature is that the theory be true of
m. It does not have to characterize m uniquely (or up to isomorphism). For
example, the formula $N(x)$ is now interpreted as 'x is a set *in m* that is a
model of the natural numbers'. Since m is standard, if $c \in m$ and M satisfies
$N(c)$, then c is in fact isomorphic to the natural number structure.

It was pointed out in Section 9.1.2 that weak second-order logic, $L(Q_0)$,
ancestral logic, and ω-logic all presuppose the natural numbers, or something
similar. Thus it is not more than a truism that the natural number structure
can be characterized up to isomorphism in such systems. It is analogous to
the observation that each axiom of a deductive system is deducible in it. One
might say that structures that are characterized in, say, ω-logic are characterized 'up to the natural numbers'. A similar, but more far-reaching, consideration can be directed at the present use of interpreted set theory. To say that

a structure *P* is characterized up to isomorphism by the language of set theory as interpreted is only to say that *P* is characterized in terms of *m*, or 'up to *m*'. Surely, this is no major insight, at least not now. Virtually every (other) structure studied in mathematics can be characterized in the set-theoretic hierarchy. The problem as to how *m* is itself grasped, understood, or communicated is left mysterious, and it is all the more perplexing since *m* is so complex. Without an independent characterization of *m*, it is not clear how the language of set theory overcomes the problems with characterizing structures in first-order languages.

At this point, perhaps, it might be suggested that one need not actually *characterize* the structure *M*. It is sufficient to let *M* be *any fixed* model of the background set theory. However, not just any model will do, if the problems with using first-order set theory as an implicit definition are not to be reintroduced. To characterize the requisite structures and concepts correctly, *M* must be a *standard* model of set theory. At the very least, it must be well-founded and closed under the subsets of its elements. As above, these concepts are not first-order definable.

Our final option is a variant on the Wittgensteinian theme that there is a way to understand a rule which is *not an interpretation*. The background set theory is taken literally, at face value, and it is used without benefit of a meta-metatheory that characterizes its intended model or models. In Quinean terms, the present proposal is that set theory is a regimented version of the natural language of mathematics normally used as metalanguage, the 'mother tongue' of logical theory. The regimented version has explicit syntax and a uniform ontology.

The outlook towards this final language is the 'working realism' described in the last section of Chapter 8. The language of set theory is employed, without apology, and no anti-realist interpretation or reduction its envisaged. Indeed, no explicit interpretation is envisaged at all. There is no perspective outside this language from which to discuss its interpretations, or its models, or at least none is contemplated. The set-theoretic universal quantifier reads 'for all sets' and the existential quantifier reads 'there is a set'. Thus sets are in the ontology of the background theory. If asked 'which sets?' or 'how many?', there is only one answer: 'all of them'. This is what it is to take the language literally. Notice that if there are no variables ranging over proper classes, then it follows *in* the background theory that there is no collection of all sets: $\neg \exists x \forall y (y \in x)$ is a theorem. Thus, from this perspective, any talk of an 'intended interpretation' of the background set theory is ill founded. There is none.

The set-theoretic programme, taken from this perspective, is unobjectionable. Set theory *is* a natural stopping place in the regress of metalanguages. We have assumed something like this all along, as witnessed by the continued use of set theory in stating and proving metatheoretic results. But, given the overriding anti-foundationalism, it does not follow that second-order logic is undermined. In the absence of model-theoretic semantics for the background theory, it is not significant that the theory is cast in a first-order language. If anything, second-order logic is confirmed.

Let me elaborate. From the perspective of second-order logic, it is assumed that if one countenances a domain d, one also countenances each subset of d, and each relation and function on d. That is what the second-order quantifiers, taken literally, range over. But this also holds for the set-theoretic programme, as presently construed. The powerset axiom states that, for each set x, there is a set consisting of all the subsets of x. One can also show that for each set x and each natural number n, there is a set consisting of the n-place relations and n-place functions on x. So both set theory, as presently construed, and second-order logic presuppose that, for any domain d, one can speak coherently of 'all subsets' of d and 'all relations' on d. This, I believe, is the crucial feature of both programmes. To put it baldly, the perspective of second-order logic assumes that reference to subsets, or relations, or something structurally similar to them, is helpful in accounting for, or modelling, mathematical practice. The set-theoretic programme, as presently construed, does just that. It does not matter whether one employs sets, or properties, or whatever.

One might retort that the background theory is still first-order. All *its* variables range over sets. No proper classes are countenanced. In almost all cases, however, this is not significant. Arithmetic, for example, only involves reference to natural numbers and sets of (and relations and functions on) natural numbers, and perhaps sets of sets of numbers, but not much more. For arithmetic, reference to the entire hierarchy is not necessary, let alone reference to proper classes.[27] The same goes for analysis, point-set topology, geometry, and just about any theory short of set theory itself (and perhaps category theory). As for set theory, the differences between the first-order and the second-order versions are discussed above, but even those differences can be attenuated if certain reflection principles are assumed (see Chapter 6, Section 6.3).

A consideration from the previous chapter is relevant here. The reason that there is not much difference between the first-order and the second-order versions of the background set theory, as presently construed, is that it is assumed that this theory is capable of modelling *all* the resources available in mathematics, and that these resources are held fixed. We have argued at length (e.g. Chapter 5) that it will not do to restrict the induction scheme to the language of arithmetic. The same goes for analysis, complex analysis, etc. We cannot restrict the crucial axiom to the languages of these theories. It will do, at least for the present, to 'restrict' the replacement scheme to the language of the background set theory, because this is the most general framework envisaged.

One major advantage of the set-theoretic programme is that it provides a single uniform foundation for all (or most) mathematics. To reiterate, it is common to take mathematical theories and structures to be interrelated, and this suggests the propriety of a common semantics with a single language. Set theory provides this. With this uniform foundation, however, comes a uniform group of presuppositions, the range of the variables of the background set theory. This, I suggest, is unnatural, at least for some purposes. Informally at least, the presuppositions of arithmetic are less than those of real analysis, and the presuppositions of analysis are less than those of set theory. Arithmetic has the relatively modest commitment to denumerably many natural numbers (plus the relations and functions thereof), while analysis is committed to the members of an uncountable continuum (plus *its* relations and functions). One who is doing arithmetic *alone* does not appear to be committed to, say, the existence of the powerset of the continuum, much less the set-theoretic hierarchy. From this perspective, a *decision* to use real analysis to study the natural numbers involves an expanded commitment. A desire to keep track of presuppositions provides a reason to keep the theories separate.

A related advantage of the set-theoretic programme is that it provides a clear and straightforward connection between a theory and its model-theoretic semantics—both are cast in set theory. However, it follows from Tarski's theorem on the undefinability of truth that, in some sense, the semantics of a branch of mathematics is stronger than (or otherwise different from) the original theory of that branch. Once again, for the purpose of tracking presuppositions, it is worthwhile keeping theory and metatheory separate.

To extend the point, let us briefly recapitulate the ontological presuppositions of a given theory as formulated in a second-order language, as opposed to those of the same theory as formulated in set theory (see Chapter 1, Section 1.3). Instrumentalism and formalism aside, it seems safe to say that a second-order theory presupposes at least one model, or at least the elements of a model.[28] As above, I follow the Quinean view that the ontology of a theory is the range of its bound variables. If second-order variables are on a par with first-order variables (putting aside the suggestion of Boolos discussed in Section 9.1), a second-order version of a theory T has presuppositions beyond those of its first-order counterpart. If M is an intended model of T, and d is the domain of M, then the first-order theory of T presupposes each element of d. The second-order version also presupposes each relation and function on d. Since this exhausts the variable ranges, it exhausts the ontological presuppositions of the second-order version of T.

The point here is that a second-order theory only presupposes the relations and functions on a domain whose elements are already presupposed.[29] The latter are the range of the first-order variables. One could, I suppose, formulate a (new) second-order theory whose first-order variables range over the subsets of (or relations and functions on) d, in which case sets of sets of d and the like would be in one's ontology (see Church 1976). But this move is not forced on a theorist who accepts a second-order formulation of d. One only develops theories as needed. In any case, a second-order version of a theory short of set theory does not presuppose any more than a small fragment of the set-theoretic hierarchy.

By contrast, the ontology of a theory as formulated in the set-theoretic programme is the ontology of the background set theory. Presumably, the latter contains an infinite set, say ω, and the theory has a powerset axiom. Recall that on the perspective under consideration, the background theory is taken literally at face value. Thus, its ontological presuppositions include at least the powerset of ω, the powerset of the powerset of ω, etc. If the replacement principle is also assumed, then this process can be carried into the transfinite. The ontology contains every element of an inaccessible rank. This is certainly more than one needs for arithmetic, analysis, or just about any theory short of set theory.

To reiterate a theme from Chapter 1, second-order logic does not have a 'staggering ontology', against Quine. The ontological presuppositions of a second-order theory are not much greater than those of its first-order counterpart (and if the aforementioned Boolos programme can be sustained, the presuppositions of some second-order theories are exactly those of their first-order counterparts). It is set theory that has a staggering ontology.

Although second-order logic does not, of itself, presuppose large domains, it does make it possible to presuppose large domains. Indeed, that is the main advantage of second-order languages. By way of analogy, recall that first-order logic does not, of itself, presuppose an infinite ontology. But there are first-order sentences that are satisfied only in infinite domains. By using a corresponding sentence in natural language, one accepts, or assumes, an infinite ontology. In short, first-order logic does not mandate an infinite domain, but it does provide the resources to presuppose the elements of one. With second-order logic, many more options are available. One can establish a commitment to the elements of a denumerably infinite domain, a domain whose cardinality is that of the continuum, a domain of inaccessible cardinality, Mahlo cardinality, etc. Moreover, up to isomorphism, one can *limit* ontology to any of these domains (with its subdomains, relations, and functions). But second-order logic does not mandate any of these options.

As emphasized in several places, the set-theoretic hierarchy provides a natural domain for the model-theoretic semantics of formal languages, be they first-order, higher-order, infinitary, etc. Notice also that the *sentences* of a language can themselves be construed as sets, as members of the set-theoretic hierarchy. Even basic syntax can be cast in set theory. If so, then the notion of *satisfaction*, $M \vDash \Phi$ can be defined in pure set-theoretic terms as a relation between *sets* Φ and M. In the case of first-order logic, the connection between the satisfaction relation and set theory is quite innocent. If Φ is first-order, then in the straightforward formulation of the relation $M \vDash \Phi$ every bound variable is restricted to the domain of M. In other words, for first-order sentences the relation $M \vDash \Phi$ depends only on matters 'internal' to M, namely its elements, the elements of its elements, etc. No sets whose rank is greater than that of M (and Φ) are involved. It follows that the satisfaction relation is *absolute* in transitive sets. To be precise, if t is any transitive set that contains both M and Φ, then we say that t *satisfies* $M \vDash \Phi$ if the formula defining $M \vDash \Phi$ holds when its variables are restricted to t. Informally, 't satisfies $M \vDash \Phi$' means that if t were the entire set-theoretic universe, then $M \vDash \Phi$ would hold. It follows from the above considerations that if Φ is first-order and t is any transitive set containing M and Φ, then $M \vDash \Phi$ if and only if t satisfies $M \vDash \Phi$. In short, the first-order satisfaction relation is the same in any transitive domain, and thus in virtually any reasonable 'universe' for the semantics. This indicates that few substantial set-theoretic presuppositions are involved in characterizing first-order satisfaction.

This property of first-order logic is admittedly desirable, and it must be reported that second-order logic does not enjoy it.[30] If Φ is second-order, then the relation $M \vDash \Phi$ depends not only on the elements of the domain of M, but also on the subsets, relations, and functions on this domain. Thus the relation may depend on sets whose rank is larger than that of M. Notice also that since the powerset relation is not absolute on transitive sets, there may be two transitive sets that both contain M and Φ, but do not contain the same subsets of the domain of M. And, in fact, the satisfaction relation of second-order logic is not 'absolute' in the above sense. It follows from several of the results reported in this book that there are models M and second-order sentences Φ such that the statement that $M \vDash \Phi$ is independent of set theory (for example, Φ may be a version of the continuum hypothesis). This entails that there are transitive sets t, u, such that t and u are both models of our first-order background set theory such that t satisfies $M \vDash \Phi$ but u satisfies $M \vDash \neg \Phi$.

Thus it seems that, for some purposes, it is not so easy to separate second-order logic and set theory, but, as argued above, there is no reason to. It turns out that the *absoluteness* of the satisfaction relation of first-order logic is linked to the expressive *poverty* of first-order languages. In fact, the absoluteness is connected to a version of the downward Löwenheim–Skolem theorem. Väänänen (1985, p. 611) reports a theorem that if the satisfaction relation for a language LK has a certain absoluteness property (or, alternatively, if the set of sentences of LK and the satisfaction relation are both Σ_1 in set theory) and if the sentences of L are hereditarily countable sets, then for every sentence Φ of L, if Φ is satisfiable, then Φ has a model whose domain is countable.

It might be pointed out that if M is a model, Φ is a *second-order* sentence, and t is a transitive set that is closed under subsets and contains M and Φ, then $M \vDash \Phi$ iff t satisfies $M \vDash \Phi$. That is, the second-order satisfaction relation is in fact absolute in transitive sets that are closed under subsets. In other words, if the powerset operator is 'standard' on a transitive set t, then the second-order satisfaction relation is in fact absolute in t. This should not be surprising in the light of the close link between second-order variables and the subset relation, involving what we call the 'logical notion of set'. Väänänen (1985, p. 616) reports that the second-order satisfaction relation is indeed absolute if the background set theory is augmented with a powerset operator.[31] This is a formal analogue of the foregoing theme that second-order languages presuppose that locutions like 'all subsets' or 'all relations' are unequivocal. Given the major thesis of this book, it further underscores the importance of the powerset operation in classical mathematics.

Notes

1. Löwenheim (1915) contains a decision procedure for monadic second-order languages in which the only non-logical relation letters are monadic. See Gandy (1988, p. 61).
2. In Chapter 6, Section 6.2, it is shown that there is a sense in which what may be called monadic nth order logic (for sufficiently large n) admits pairing. Thus the manageability of monadic second-order logic does not apply to monadic higher-order logic in general.
3. The binary tree is the structure of the set of all strings on a two-letter alphabet. Rabin (1969) showed how to interpret the theory of strings on a countable alphabet in the monadic second-order theory of the binary tree.
4. If Axy is interpreted as $x = 0 \lor x = y + 1$ in the language of arithmetic, then the Geach–Kaplan sentence is satisfied by all *non-standard* models of first-order arithmetic, but not by the natural number structure itself. But, as pointed out above, there is a non-standard model M such that for any sentence Φ of first-order arithmetic, $M \vDash \Phi$ if and only if Φ is satisfied by the natural numbers.
5. Actually, it seems to me that the locution 'there are objects with a certain property' implies that there are at least *two* objects with the property. However, this detail can be handled in a straightforward manner, if desired.
6. This is similar to the technique developed in Chapter 6, Section 6.1, to accommodate models whose domains are proper classes. In standard semantics, an assignment to the second-order variables is, in effect, a sequence of classes. This is coded by a class of pairs.
7. Boolos's notion of 'supervalidity' seems to be the 'informal validity' **Val** of Kreisel's principle discussed in Chapter 6, Section 6.3 (and in Shapiro 1987). To put it in terms of classes, a formula Φ is 'supervalid' if Φ holds in every model, whether the domain is a set or a class.
8. Boolos (1975) resists the idea of formulating set theory in a second-order language, for the lack of *sets* to serve as assignments of second-order variables. This is corrected in the work under discussion here (Boolos 1984, 1985a).

In Boolos (1985a), it is stated that 'the difficulty of interpreting second-order quantifiers is most acute when the underlying language is the language of set theory . . .'.

9. In general, for each ordinal α, there is a logic $L(Q_\alpha)$, with the same language as $L(Q_0)$. The semantics of $L(Q_\alpha)$ includes a clause like

$M, s \vDash Qx\Phi$ if there are at least $\aleph_\alpha$ distinct assignments s' such that s agrees with s' on every variable except possibly x, and $M, s' \vDash \Phi$.

In $L(Q_\alpha)$, $Qx\Phi$ amounts to 'there are $\aleph_\alpha$ many x such that Φ'. It turns out that there is a complete effective deductive system for $L(Q_1)$. See Ebbinghaus (1985) and, for a more extensive treatment of $L(Q_1)$, Kaufmann (1985).

10. According to the definition, R^*xx holds (vacuously), no matter what R is. If one wishes, this can be excluded, with minor adjustments to what follows. Immerman (1983) is an interesting treatment of (what amounts to) ancestral logic, restricted to finite models.

11. In these terms, the results reported in Chapter 6, Section 6.5, provide conditions under which a logic is equivalent to the first-order $L1K=$.

12. Actually, the results reported here can be established for weaker set theories, such as that of Zermelo (see Chapter 7).

13. See also the discussion of Putnam (1980) in Chapter 5.

14. The crucial step in the argument is the proposition that, for each ancestral sentence Φ, there is a first-order Φ^* such that, for each *finite* M, $M \vDash \Phi$ iff there is an expansion M' of M such that $M' \vDash \Phi^*$. This can be accomplished by introducing terminology for a linear order, which allows objects in the domain to play the role of (some) natural numbers. Then for any binary relation R, a relation $R'xyn$ for 'y is an ancestor of x by a chain whose length corresponds to n' can be formulated, and the ancestral of R can be defined from this.

15. Variables ranging over functions do not introduce any complexity into the treatment. As above, they can be eliminated in favour of variables ranging over relations.

16. One more. Let U be a monadic predicate, and assume that the set K does not contain U. A language $L'K$ *projects* LK *relativized* if, for each sentence Φ of LK, there is a set $K' \supseteq K$ and a sentence Φ' of $L'K'$ such that, for each M, $M \vDash \Phi$ in LK iff there is a model M' such that $M' \vDash \Phi'$ in $L'K'$ and the extension of U in M' is isomorphic to M. The idea here is that $L'K$ can make any distinctions among models that LK can make provided that more non-logical terminology *and more elements* can be invoked. An argument similar to that of the previous theorem establishes that the logics of this subsection all project each other relativized.

17. Recall that $L(Q_1)$ is the logic based on the same language as $L(Q_0)$, except that $Qx\Phi$ means 'for uncountably many x, Φ' (see note 9). It is easy to see that L2q includes $L(Q_1)$. The converse does not hold, however. As noted, the set of logical truths of $L(Q_1)$ is recursively enumerable. It follows that there is no $L(Q_1)$ sentence that characterizes the natural numbers up to isomorphism. On the other hand, L2q includes weak second-order logic and thus it does contain a characterization of the natural numbers.

18. If κ is not regular, then there are, in effect, conjunctions of size κ in $L\kappa\lambda$. And if λ is not regular, there are formulas with λ-many bound variables. For this reason, some authors require κ and λ to be regular cardinals.

19. More exotic languages have been studied. Some have infinite alternations of quantifiers, for example, $\forall x_1 \exists y_1 \forall x_2 \exists y_2 \ldots \Phi$. It is also possible to restrict the sets of formulas that can be combined into single formulas, for example, to recursive sets or definable sets.

20. The infinitary 'rules of inference' are that from an infinitary conjunction, one can infer any conjunct, and from $\Phi \to \Psi$, for all Ψ in Γ, one can infer $\Phi \to \bigwedge \Gamma$. The restriction to countable sets of premises is necessary. For each $\alpha < \omega_1$, let c_α be an individual constant, and let f be a unary function symbol. Let Γ be $\{c_\alpha \neq c_\beta \mid \alpha < \beta\}$ and let Φ be a statement that f is one-to-one and the range of f is $\{c_\alpha \mid \alpha < \omega\}$ (i.e. $\forall x(f(x) = c_0 \vee f(x) = c_1 \vee \cdots))$. Then Γ entails that the domain is uncountable while Φ entails that the domain is countable. Thus $\Gamma \cup \{\Phi\}$ has no models, and so $\Gamma \cup \{\Phi\} \vDash c_0 \neq c_0$. But a deduction from $\Gamma \cup \{\Phi\}$ can involve only countably many members of $\Gamma \cup \{\Phi\}$, and any such collection is satisfiable and thus consistent. So $c_0 \neq c_0$ cannot be deduced from $\Gamma \cup \{\Phi\}$.

21. Notice that each instance of the induction scheme is also a substitutional consequence of Γ. If the requirement that there be infinitely many individual constants is waived, then the characterization of the natural numbers can be accomplished by a single sentence. Let the set of non-logical terminology be $\{0, s, +, \cdot\}$ and let Φ be the conjunction of the successor, addition, and multiplication axioms. Then for every substitution model M, $M \vDash \Phi$ if and only if M is isomorphic to the natural numbers. It follows that if finite sets of non-logical terms are allowed, then substitutional semantics is not weakly complete.

22. Recall that the proof of the upward Löwenheim–Skolem theorem involves adding individual constants to the language. This is not allowed here, since the semantic properties are dependent on the non-logical terminology available. Adding new constants would change the extension of 'substitution model'.

23. Despite this result, there is no characterization of *finitude* in substitution semantics. In particular, for every set Γ of formulas, if every finite substitution model satisfies every member of Γ, then there is an infinite substitution model that also satisfies every member of Γ. On the other hand, if the requirement that there be infinitely many individual constants is waived, then the notion of finitude can be characterized with a single sentence. Let the non-logical terminology consist of only the individual constant 0 and the unary function letter f. Then, for any substitution model for this language, $M \vDash \exists x(f(x) = 0) \vee \exists x \exists y(x \neq y \; \& \; f(x) = f(y))$ if and only if the domain of M is finite.

24. In the deductive system $D2-$ for $L2K-$, the central item is the 'substitution rule' allowing one systematically to replace subformulas Xt in a formula Φ with $\Psi(t)$, where Ψ is another formula (avoiding a clash of variables, of course). Since Ψ determines a subclass $\{x \mid \Psi(x)\}$ of the domain, the substitution rule is a version of universal instantiation.

25. Another group of examples are the cardinality comparison relations. The formulation of 'the cardinality of A is less than the cardinality of B' involves an initial existential quantifier, and so cannot be characterized directly in $L2K-$. But its complement 'the cardinality of B is greater than or equal to the cardinality of A' can be. Again, the notion 'A and B have the same cardinality' cannot be directly characterized, but its complement 'A and B have different cardinality' can be.

26. A theory T is *semantically complete* if for any sentence Φ in the language of T, either $T \vDash \Phi$ or $T \vDash \neg \Phi$. Every categorical theory is semantically complete.

27. There are, however, arithmetic theorems of second-order ZFC that are not theorems of first-order ZFC. One is the consistency of first-order ZFC.

28. Here in the informal metalanguage, we speak of a model as an existing structure, but this model may not be in the ontology of the theory under consideration, or at least not in the range of its *first-order* variables. To reiterate, a metatheory can have ontological presuppositions beyond those of the theory it models. Notice also that the presuppositions of the elements of a model apply to a theory formulated in a first-order language, and in this case it could be added that a *standard* model is presupposed. Suppose that it should happen that a dramatic event causes the mathematical community to believe that, although first-order analysis is consistent, it does not have a standard model (for example, it may be that every model has an undefinable bounded subset that has no least upper bound). Of course, the consistency of the theory entails that it has a model—in fact the theory can be interpreted as a complex structure of natural numbers. But this fact would give little comfort to one who has devoted her life to studying a non-existent real number structure.

29. The principle of accepting collections (if not functions, relations, and sets of sets) of previously accepted entities is held by such nominalists as Goodman (1972) and Field (1980).

30. I am indebted to Matthew Foreman for pointing out the significance of this.

31. Väänänen (1985) contains many other interesting results relating various model-theoretic notions to set theory.

REFERENCES

Ackermann, W. (1924). Begründung des 'Tertium non datur' mittels der Hilbertschen Theorie der Widerspruchsfreiheit. *Mathematische Annalen*, **93**, 1–36.

Ajtai, M. (1979). Isomorphism and higher-order equivalence. *Annals of Mathematical Logic*, **16**, 181–203.

Baldwin, J. (1985). Definable second-order quantifiers. In J. Barwise and S. Feferman (1985) (q.v.), pp. 445–77.

Barwise, J. (1972). The Hanf number of second-order logic. *Journal of Symbolic Logic*, **37**, 588–94.

Barwise, J. (1985). Model-theoretic logics: Background and aims. In J. Barwise and S. Feferman (1985) (q.v.), pp. 3–23.

Barwise, J. and Feferman, S. (1985). *Model-theoretic logics*. Springer-Verlag, New York.

Bell, J. and Slomson, A. (1971). *Models and ultraproducts: An introduction*. North-Holland, Amsterdam.

Benacerraf, P. (1985). Skolem and the skeptic. *Proceedings of the Aristotelian Society, Supplementary Volume*, **59**, 85–115.

Bernays, P. (1918). *Beiträge zur axiomatischen Behandlung des Logik-Kalküls*. Habilitationsschrift, Göttingen.

Bernays, P. (1928). Die Philosophie der Mathematik und die Hilbertsche Beweis-theorie. *Blätter für Deutsche Philosophie*, **4**, 326–67.

Bernays, P. (1935). Platonism in mathematics. *Philosophy of mathematics*, 2nd edn. (ed. P. Benacerraf and H. Putnam) Cambridge University Press (1983) pp. 258–71.

Bernays, P. (1961). Zur Frage der Unendlichkeitsschemata in der axiomatischen Mengenlehre. *Essays on the foundation of mathematics* (ed. Y. Bar-Hillel *et al.*) pp. 3–49. Magnes Press, Jerusalem.

Bernays, P. and Schönfinkel, M. (1928). Zum Entscheidungsproblem der mathematischen Logic. *Mathematische Annalen*, **99**, 342–72.

Blackburn, S. (1984). *Spreading the word*, 2nd edn. Clarendon Press, Oxford.

Bolzano, B. (1817). *Rein analytischer Beweis des Lehrsatzes, dass zwischen je zwei Werthen, die ein entgegengesetztes Resultat gewaehren, wenigstens eine reelle Wurzel der Gleichung liege*. Gottlieb Hasse, Prague.

Boole, G. (1847). *The mathematical analysis of logic, being an essay toward a calculus of reasoning*. London.

Boole, G. (1854). *An investigation of the laws of thought on which are founded the mathematical theories of logic and probabilities*. London.

Boolos, G. (1971). The iterative concept of set. *Philosophy of mathematics*, 2nd edn. (ed. P. Benacerraf and H. Putnam), Cambridge University Press (1983), pp. 486–502.

Boolos, G. (1975). On second-order logic. *Journal of Philosophy*, **72**, 509–27.

Boolos, G. (1981). For every A there is a B. *Linguistic Inquiry*, **12**, 465–7.

Boolos, G. (1984). To be is to be a value of a variable (or to be some values of some variables). *Journal of Philosophy*, **81**, 430–49.

Boolos, G. (1985a). Nominalist platonism. *Philosophical Review*, **94**, 327–44.

Boolos, G. (1985b). Reading the *Begriffsschrift*. *Mind*, **94**, 331–44.

Boolos, G. (1987). A curious inference. *Journal of Philosophical Logic*, **16**, 1–12.

Boolos, G. and Jeffrey, R. (1989). *Computability and logic*, 3rd edn. Cambridge University Press.

Büchi, J. (1953). Investigation of the equivalence of the axiom of choice and Zorn's lemma from the viewpoint of the hierarchy of types. *Journal of Symbolic Logic*, **18**, 125–35.

Carnap, R. (1943). *Formalization of logic*. Havard University Press, Cambridge, MA.

Carnap, R. and Bachmann, F. (1963). Über Extremalaxiome. *Erkenntnis*, **6**, 166–88. (Translated by H. G. Bohnert, *History and Philosophy of Logic*, **2** (1981), 67–85).

Chang, C. and Keisler, H. J. (1973). *Model theory*. North-Holland, Amsterdam.

Chuaqui, R. (1972). Forcing for the impredicative theory of classes. *Journal of Symbolic Logic*, **37**, 1–18.

Church, A. (1951). A formulation of the logic of sense and denotation. In *Structure, method and meaning* (ed. P. Henle *et al.*) pp. 3–24. Liberal Arts Press, New York.

Church, A. (1956). *Introduction to mathematical logic*. Princeton University Press.

Church, A. (1976). Schröder's anticipation of the simple theory of types. *Erkenntnis*, **10**, 407–11.

Cocchiarella, N. (1986). Frege, Russell and logicism. In *Frege synthesized* (ed. L. Haaparanta and J. Hintikka). pp. 197–252. Reidel, Dordrecht.

Cocchiarella, N. (1987). *Logical studies in early analytic philosophy*. Ohio State University Press, Columbus, OH.

Cocchiarella, N. (1988). Predication versus membership in the distinction between logic as language and logic as calculus. *Synthese*, **77**, 37–72.

Cocchiarella, N. (1989). Review of *The philosophy of W. V. Quine*. *History and Philosophy of Logic*, **10**, 77–83.

Coffa, A. (1982). Kant, Bolzano, and the emergence of logicism. *Journal of Philosophy*, **79**, 679–89.

Corcoran, J. (1971). A semantic definition of definition. *Journal of Symbolic Logic*, **36**, 366–7.

Corcoran, J. (1972). Completeness of an ancient logic. *Journal of Symbolic Logic*, **37**, 696–702.

Corcoran, J. (1973). Gaps between logical theory and mathematical practice. In *The methodological unity of science* (ed. M. Bunge), pp. 23–50. Reidel, Dordrecht.

Corcoran, J. (1980). Categoricity. *History and Philosophy of Logic*, **1**, 187–207.

Corcoran, J. (1983). Editor's introduction to the revised edition. In A. Tarski, *Logic, semantics, metamathematics*, 2nd edn (ed. J. Corcoran), pp. xv–xxvii. Hackett, Indianpolis, IN.

Corcoran, J. (1987). Second-order logic. *Proceedings Inference OUIC 86* (eds D. Moates and R. Butrick), pp. 7–31. Ohio University Press, Athens, OH.

Corcoran, J., Frank, W., and Maloney, M. (1974). String theory. *Journal of Symbolic Logic*, **39**, 625–37.

Cowles, J. (1979). The relative expressive power of some logics extending first-order logic. *Journal of Symbolic Lobic*, **44**, 129–46.

Craig, W. (1965). Satisfaction for nth-order languages defined in nth-order languages. *Journal of Symbolic Logic*, **30**, 13–25.

Dawson, J. (1985). Completing the Gödel–Zermelo correspondence. *Historia Mathematica*, **12**, 66–70.

Dedekind, R. (1888). The nature and meaning of numbers. *Essays on the theory of numbers* (ed. W. W. Berman), Dover Press, New York, (1963), pp. 31–115.

Detlefsen, M. (1986). *Hilbert's program*. Reidel, Dordrecht.

Detlefsen, M. (1990). Brouwerian intuitionism. *Mind*, **99**, 501–34.

Dickmann, N. A. (1985). Larger infinitary languages. In J. Barwise and S. Feferman (1985) (q.v.), pp. 317–63.

Drake, F. (1974). *Set theory: an introduction to large cardinals*. North-Holland, Amsterdam.

Dreben, B. and Goldfarb, W. (1979). *The decision problem: solvable classes of quantificational formulas*. Addison-Wesley, London.

Dummett, M. (1973). The philosophical basis of intuitionistic logic. In *Truth and other enigmas* (M. Dummett), Harvard University Press, Cambridge, MA (1978), pp. 215–47.

Ebbinghaus, H. D. (1985). Extended logics: the general framework. In J. Barwise and S. Feferman (1985) (q.v.), pp. 25–76.

Etchemendy, J. (1988). Tarski on truth and logical consequence. *Journal of Symbolic Logic*, **53**, 51–79.

Fagin, R. (1974). Generalized first-order spectra and polynomial-time recognizable sets. *SIAM-AMS Proceedings*, **7**, 43–73.

Field, H. (1980). *Science without numbers*. Princeton University Press.

Field, H. (1984). Is mathematical knowledge just logical knowledge? *Philosophical Review*, **93**, 509–52.

Flannagan, T. B. (1975). Axioms of choice in Morse–Kelley class theory. *Lecture Notes in Mathematics*, Vol. 499, pp. 190–247. Springer-Verlag, Berlin.

Flum, J. (1985). Characterizing logics. In J. Barwise and S. Feferman (1985) (q.v.), pp. 77–120.

Fraenkel, A. (1921). Über die Zermelosche Begründung der Mengenlehre. *Jahresbericht der Deutschen Mathematiker-Vereinigung*, **30**, 97–8.

Fraenkel, A. (1922a). Zu den Grundlagen der Mengenlehre. *Jahresbericht der Deutschen Mathematiker-Vereinigung*, **31**, 101–2.

Fraenkel, A. (1922b). Der Begriff 'definit' und die 'Unabhängigkeit des Auswahl-axioms. *Sitzungsberichte der Preussichen Akademie der Wissenschaften, Physikalisch-mathematische Klasse*, 253–7. Translated as 'The notion 'definite' and the independence of the axiom of choice', in J. van Heijenoort (1967a) (q.v.), pp. 284–9.

Fraenkel, A. (1925). Untersuchungen über die Grundlagen der Mengenlehre. *Mathematische Zeitschrift*, **22**, 250–73.

Fraenkel, A., Bar-Hillel, Y., and Levy, A. (1973). *Foundations of set theory*, 2nd rev. edn. North-Holland, Amsterdam.

Frege, G. (1879). *Begriffsschrift, eine der arithmetischen nachbegildete Formelsprache des reinen Denkens*, Louis Nebert, Halle. Translated in J. van Heijenoort (1967a) (q.v.), pp. 1–82.

Frege, G. (1883). Über den Zweck der Begriffsschrift. *Sitzungsberichte der Jenaischen Gesellschaft für Medicin and Naturwissenschaft*, **16**, 1–10.

Frege, G. (1884). *Die Grundlagen der Arithmetik*, Koebner, Breslau. Translated by J. Austin as *The foundations of arithmetic*, 2nd edn, Harper, New York, (1960).

Frege, G. (1893). *Grundgesetze der Arithmetik 1*. Hildescheim, Olms.

Frege, G. (1895). Review of Schröder's 'Vorlesungen über die Algebra der Logik', *Archiv für systematische Philosophie*, **1**, 433–56. Translated in *Translations from the philosophical writings of Gottlob Frege* (ed. P. Geach and M. Black), Basil Blackwell, Oxford (1980), pp. 86–106.

Frege, G. (1903). *Grundgesetze der Arithmetik 2*. Hildescheim, Olms.

Frege, G. (1906). On Schoenflies *Die logischen Paradoxien der Mengenlehre* (tr.

P. Long and R. White). In G. Frege, *Posthumous writings* (eds H. Hermes, F. Kambartel, and G. Kaulbach), University of Chicago Press (1979), pp. 176–83.

Friedman, M. (1983). *Foundations of space–time theories: relativistic physics and philosophy of science*, Princeton University Press.

Gandy, R. (1988). The confluence of ideas in 1936. In *The universal Turing machine* (ed. R. Herken), pp. 55–111. Oxford University Press, New York.

Garland, S. (1974). Second-order cardinal characterizability. *Proceedings of Symposia in Pure Mathematics*, **13** (II), 127–46.

Gilmore, P. (1957). The monadic theory of types in the lower-predicate calculus. In *Summaries of talks presented at the Summer Institute of Sybolic Logic at Cornell*, pp. 309–12. Institute for Defense Analysis.

Gödel, K. (1930). Die Vollständigkeit der Axiome des logischen Funktionenkalkuls. *Monatshefte für Mathematik und Physik*, **37**, 349–60. Translated as 'The completeness of the axioms of the functional calculus of logic', in J. van Heijenoort (1967a) (q.v.), pp. 582–91.

Gödel, K. (1931). Über formal unentscheidbare Sätze der Principia Mathematica und verwandter Systeme I, *Monatshefte für Mathematik und Physic*, **38**, 173–98. Translated as 'On formally undecidable propositions of the *Principia Mathematica*', in J. van Heijenoort (1967a) (q.v.), pp. 596–616.

Gödel, K. (1934). On decidable propositions of formal mathematical systems. In *The undecidable* (ed. M. Davis), pp. 39–74. The Raven Press, New York.

Gödel, K. (1936). Über die Länge von Beweisen. *Ergebinsse eines mathematischen Kolloquiums*, **7**, 23–4.

Gödel, K. (1944). Russell's mathematical logic. In *Philosophy of Mathematics* (eds P. Benacerraf and H. Putnam), 2nd edn, Cambridge University Press (1983), pp. 447–69.

Gödel, K. (1964). What is Cantor's continuum problem? In *Philosophy of Mathematics* (eds P. Benacerraf and H. Putnam), 2nd edn, Cambridge University Press (1983), pp. 470–85.

Goldfarb, W. (1979). Logic in the twenties: the nature of the quantifier. *Journal of Symbolic Logic*, **44**, 351–68.

Goldfarb, W. (1988). Poincaré against the logicists. In *History and philosophy of modern mathematics* (eds W. Aspray and P. Kitcher). Minnesota studies in the philosophy of science, Vol. 11, 61–81, University of Minnesota Press.

Gonseth, F. (1941). *Les entretiens de Zurich, 6–9 décembre 1938*. Leeman, Zurich.

Goodman, N. (1962). *Problems and projects*. Bobbs-Merrill, Indianapolis, IN.

Gottlieb, D. (1980). *Ontological economy: substitutional quantification and mathematics*. Oxford University Press.

Grattan-Guinness, I. (1977). *Dear Russell—Dear Jourdain*. Columbia University Press, New York.

Grattan-Guiness, I. (1979). In memoriam Kurt Gödel: his 1931 correspondence with Zermelo on his incompletablity theorem. *Historia Mathematica*, **6**, 294–304.

Gurevich, Y. (1985). Monadic second-order theories. In J. Barwise and S. Feferman (1985) (q.v.), pp. 479–506.

Gurevich, Y. (1988). Logic and the challenge of computer science. *Trends in theoretical computer science* (ed. E. Börger), pp. 1–57. Computer Science Press, Rockville, MD.

Gurevich, Y. and Shelah, S. (1983). Interpretating second-order logic in the monadic theory of order. *Journal of Symbolic Logic*, **48**, 816–28.

Hasenjaeger, G. (1967). On Löwenheim–Skolem-type insufficiencies of second-order logic. *Sets, models and recursion theory* (ed J. Crossley), pp. 173–82. North-Holland, Amsterdam.

Hazen, A. (1983). Predicative logics. *Handbook of philosophical logic 1* (ed. D. Gabbay and F. Guenthner), pp. 331–407. Reidel, Dordrecht.

Henkin, L. (1950). Completeness in the theory of types. *Journal of Symbolic Logic*, **15**, 81–91.

Henkin, L. (1953). Banishing the rule of substitution for functional variables. *Journal of Symbolic Logic*, **18**, 201–8.

Hilbert, D. (1899). *Grundlagen der Geometrie*. Leipzig. Foundations of geometry (tr. E. Townsend), Open Court, La Salle, IL, 1959.

Hilbert, D. (1900a). Mathematische Probleme. *Bulletin of the American Mathematical Society*, **8** (1902), 437–79.

Hilbert, D. (1900b). Über den Zahlbegriff. *Jahresbericht der Deutschen Mathematiker-Vereinigung*, **8**, 180–94.

Hilbert, D. (1902). *Les principes fondamentaux de la géometrie*. Gauthier-Villars, Paris. (French translation of Hilbert (1899).)

Hilbert, D. (1905). Über die Grundlagen der Logik und der Arithmetik. *Verhandlungen des dritten internationalen Mathematiker-Kongresses in Heidelberg vom 8 bis 13 August 1904*, pp. 174–85. Teubner, Leipzig. Translated in J. van Heijenoort (1967a), (q.v.), pp. 129–38.

Hilbert, D. (1923). Die logischen Grundlagen der Mathematik. *Mathematische Annalen*, **88**, 151–65.

Hilbert, D. (1925). Über das Unendliche. *Mathematische Annalen*, **95**, 161–90. Translated as 'On the infinite' in J. van Heijenoort (1967a) (q.v.), pp. 369–92.

Hilbert, D. (1929). Probleme der Grundlegung der Mathematik. *Mathematische Annalen*, **102**, 1–9.

Hilbert, D. and Ackermann, W. (1928). *Grundzüge der theoritischen Logik*. Springer, Berlin.

Hilbert, D. and Bernays, P. (1934). *Grundlagen der Mathematik*. Springer, Berlin.

Hintikka, J. (1955). Reductions in the theory of types. *Acta Philosophica Fennica*, **8**, 61–115.

Hintikka, J. (1988). On the development of the model-theoretic viewpoint in logical theory. *Synthese*, **77**, 1–36.

Hodes, H. (1984). Logicism and the ontological commitments of arithmetic. *Journal of Philosophy*, **81**, 123–49.

Hodes, H. (1988a). Cardinality logics, Part I: Inclusions between languages based on 'exactly'. *Annals of Pure and Applied Logic*, **39**, 199–238.

Hodes, H. (1988b). Cardinality logics, Part II: Inclusions between languages based on 'exactly'. *Journal of Symbolic Logic*, **53**, 765–84.

Huntington, E. (1902). A complete set of postulates for the theory of absolute continuous magnitude. *Transactions of the American Mathematical Society*, **3**, 264–79.

Huntington, E. (1905). A complete set of postulates for ordinary complex algebra. *Transactions of the American Mathematical Society*, **6**, 209–29.

Immerman, N. (1987). Languages that capture complexity classes. *SIAM Journal of Computing*, **16**, 760–78.

Jech, T. (1971). *Lectures in set theory: With particular emphasis on the method of forcing, Lecture Notes in Mathematics*, Vol. 217. Springer-Verlag, Berlin.

Jech, T. (1973). *The axiom of choice*. North-Holland.

Kaufmann, M. (1985). The quantifier 'there exists uncountably many' and some of its relatives. In J. Barwise and S. Feferman (1985) (q.v.), pp. 123–76.

Kitcher, P. (1983). *The nature of mathematical knowledge*. Oxford University Press, New York.

Kitcher, P. (1986). Frege, Dedekind, and the philosophy of mathematics. In *Frege synthesized* (eds L. Haaparanta and J. Hintikka), pp. 299–343. Reidel, Dordrecht.

Kolaitis, P. (1985). Game quantification. In J. Barwise and S. Feferman (1985) (q.v.), pp. 365–421.

Kraut, R. (1980). Indiscernibility and ontology. *Synthese*, **44**, 113–35.

Kreisel, G. (1965) Mathematical logic. *Lectures on Modern Mathematics 3* (ed. T. L. Saaty), pp. 95–195. Wiley, New York.

Kreisel, G. (1967). Informal rigour and completeness proofs. *Problems in the philosophy of mathematics* (ed. I. Lakatos), pp. 138–86. North-Holland, Amsterdam.

Kripke, S. (1982). *Wittgenstein on rules and private language*. Harvard University Press, Cambridge, MA.

Kuhn, T. (1970). *The structure of scientific revolutions*, 2nd edn. University of Chicago Press.

Landman, F. (1989). Groups. *Linguistics and Philosophy*, **12**, 559–605, 723–744.

Leblanc, H. (1976). *Truth-value semantics*. North-Holland, Amsterdam.

Leibnitz, G. (1686). Universal science: Characteristic XIV, XV. In *Monadology and other philosophical essays* (tr. P. Schrecker) Bobbs-Merill, Indianapolis, IN (1965), pp. 11–21.

Leivant, D. (1989). Descriptive characterizations of computational complexity. *Journal of Computer and System Sciences*, **39**, 51–83.

Levy, A. (1960). Principles of reflection in axiomatic set theory. *Fundamenta Mathematicae*, **49**, 1–10.

Lewis, C. I. (1918). *A survey of symbolic logic*. University of California Press.

Lindström, P. (1969). On extensions of elementary logic. *Theoria*, **35**, 1–11.

Löwenheim, L. (1915). Über Möglichkeiten im Relativkalkül. *Mathematische Annalen*, **76**, 447–79. Translated in J. van Heijenoort (1967a) (q.v.), pp. 228–51.

Mac Lane, S. (1986). *Mathematics, form and function*. Springer-Verlag, New York.

Mac Lane, S. and Birkhoff, G. (1967). *Algebra*. MacMillan, New York.

Magidor, M. (1971). On the role of supercompact and extendible cardinals in logic. *Israel Journal of Mathematics*, **10**, 147–57.

Mates, B. (1972). *Elementary logic*, 2nd edn. Oxford University Press, New York.

McCarthy, T. (1981). The idea of a logical constant. *Journal of Philosophy*, **78**, 499–523.

McCarty, C. and Tennant, N. (1987). Skolem's paradox and constructivism. *Journal of Philosophical Logic*, **16**, 165–202.

McNaughton, R. (1965). Undefinablity of addition from one unary operator. *Transactions of the American Mathematical Society*, **117**, 329–37.

Mendelson, E. (1987). *Introduction to mathematical logic*, 3rd edn. Van Nostrand, Princeton, NJ.

Montague, R. (1965). Set theory and higher-order logic. *Formal systems and recursive functions* (eds J. Crossley and M. Dummett), pp. 131–48. North-Holland, Amsterdam.

Moore, G. (1978). The origins of Zermelo's axiomatization of set theory. *Journal of Philosophical Logic*, **7**, 307–29.

Moore, G. (1980). Beyond first-order logic, the historical interplay between logic and set theory. *History and Philosophy of Logic*, **1**, 95–137.

Moore, G. (1982). *Zermelo's axiom of choice: Its origins, development, and influence.* Springer-Verlag, New York.

Moore, G. (1988). The emergence of first-order logic. In *History and philosophy of modern mathematics,* (eds W. Aspray and P. Kitcher). Minnesota Studies in the Philosophy of Science, Vol. 11, pp. 95–135. University of Minnesota Press.

Mostowski, A. (1952). *Sentences undecidable in formalized arithmetic: an exposition of the theory of Kurt Gödel.* North-Holland, Amsterdam.

Müller, G. (1976). *Sets and classes: on the work by Paul Bernays.* North-Holland, Amsterdam.

Myhill, J. (1951). On the ontological sgnificance of the Löwenheim–Skolem theorem. In *Academic freedom, logic and religion* (ed. M. White), pp. 57–70. American Philosophical Society, Philadelphia, PA. Also in *Contemporary readings in logical theory* (eds I. Copi and J. Gould), MacMillan, New York (1967), pp. 40–54.

Nadel, M. (1985). $L\omega_1\omega$ and admissible fragments. In J. Barwise and S. Feferman (1985) (q.v.), pp. 271–316.

Nagel, E. (1979). Impossible numbers: a chapter in the history of modern logic. In *Teleology revisited and other essays in the philosophy and history of sciences,* pp. 166–94. Columbia University Press, New York.

Neurath, O. (1932). Protokollsätze. *Erkenntnis,* **3,** 204–14.

Parsons, C. (1977). What is the iterative conception of set? In *Logic, foundations of mathematics and computability theory* (eds R. Butts and J. Hintikka), pp. 335–67. Reidel, Dordrecht.

Parsons, C. (1983). *Mathematics in philosophy.* Cornell University Press, Ithaca.

Parsons, C. (1990). The uniqueness of the natural numbers. *Iyyun,* **39,** 13–44.

Peano, G. (1889). *Arithmetrices principia, nova methodo exposita.* Turin. Translated as 'The principles of arithmetic, presented by a new method', in J. van Heijenoort (1967a) (q.v.), pp. 85–97.

Poincaré, H. (1908). *Science and method, Foundation of Science* (tr. G. Halsted), Science Press, New York (1921), pp. 349–546.

Poincaré, H. (1909). La logique de l'infini. *Revue de métaphysique et morale,* **17,** 461–82.

Presburger, M. (1930). Über die Vollständigkeit eines gewissen Systems der Arithmetik ganzer Zahlen, in welchem die Addition als einzige Operation hervortritt. *Sprawozdanie z I Kongresu matematyków krajów slowianskich, Warszawa 1929,* pp. 92–101, 395.

Putnam, H. (1980). Models and reality. *Journal of Symbolic Logic,* **45,** 464–82.

Quine, W. V. O. (1941). Whitehead and the rise of modern logic. In P. A. Schilpp, *The philosophy of Alfred North Whitehead,* pp. 127–63. Tudor, New York.

Quine, W. V. O. (1960). *Word and object.* MIT Press, Cambridge, MA.

Quine, M. V. O. (1969). *Set theory and its logic.* rev. edn. Harvard University Press, Cambridge, MA.

Quine, W. V. O. (1970). *Philosophy of logic.* Prentice-Hall, Englewood Cliffs, NJ.

Rabin, M. (1969). Decidability of second-order theories and automata on infinite trees. *Transactions of the American Mathematical Society,* **141,** 1–35.

Ramsey, F. (1925). The foundations of mathematics. *Proceedings of the London Mathematical Society,* **25** (2), 338–84.

Rang, B. and Thomas, W. (1981). Zermelo's discovery of the 'Russell paradox', *Historia Mathematica,* **8,** 15–22.

Resnik, M. (1980). *Frege and the philosophy of mathematics.* Cornell University Press, Ithaca, NY.

Resnik, M. (1982). Mathematics as a science of patterns: epistemology. *Nous*, **16**, 95–105.

Resnik, M. (1985). Logic, normative or descriptive? The ethics of belief or a branch of psychology. *Philosophy of Science*, **52**, 221–38.

Resnik, M. (1988). Second-order logic still wild. *Journal of Philosophy*, **85**, 75–87.

Rogers, H. (1967). *Theory of recursive functions and effective computability.* McGraw-Hill, New York.

Rosser, B. (1936). Extensions of some theorems of Gödel and Church. *Journal of Symbolic Logic*, **1**, 87–91.

Russell, B. (1903). *The principles of mathematics.* Allen & Unwin, London.

Schoenflies, A. (1911). Über die Stellung der Definition in der Axiomatik. *Jahresbericht der Deutsche Mathematiker-Vereinigung*, **20**, 222–55.

Schönfinkel, M. (1924). Über die Bausteine der mathematischen Logik. *Mathematische Annalen*, **92**, 305–16. Translated in J. van Heijenoort (1967a) (q.v.), pp. 355–66.

Schröder, E. (1890). *Vorlesungen über die Algebra der Logik 1.* Teubner, Leipzig.

Shapiro, S. (1981). Understanding Church's thesis. *Journal of Philosophical Logic*, **10**, 353–65.

Shapiro, S. (1983). Remarks on the development of computability. *History and Philosophy of Logic*, **4**, 203–20.

Shapiro, S. (1985a). Second-order languages and mathematical practice. *Journal of Symbolic Logic*, **50**, 714–42.

Shapiro, S. (1985b). *Intensional mathematics.* North-Holland, Amsterdam.

Shapiro, S. (1987). Principles of reflection and second-order logic. *Journal of Philosophical Logic*, **16**, 309–33.

Shapiro, S. (1988). The Lindenbaum construction and decidability. *Notre Dame Journal of Formal Logic*, **29**, 208–13.

Shapiro, S. (1989a). Logic, ontology, mathematical practice. *Synthese*, **79**, 13–50.

Shapiro, S. (1989b). Structure and ontology. *Philosophical Topics*, **17**, 145–71.

Shelah, S. (1975). The monadic theory of order. *Annals of Mathematics*, **102**, 379–419.

Skolem, T. (1920). Logisch-kombinatorische Untersuchungen über die Erfüllbarkeit oder Beweisbarkeit mathematischer Sätze nebst einem Theoreme über dichte Mengen. *Videnskapsselskapets skrifter I. Matematisk-naturvidenskabelig klasse*, no. 4, 1–36. Section 1 translated in J. van Heijenoort (1967a) (q.v.), pp. 252–63.

Skolem, T. (1922). Einige Bemerkungen zur axiomatischen Begründung der Mengenlehre, *Matematikerkongressen i Helsingfors den 4–7 Juli 1922*, pp. 217–32. Akademiska Bokhandeln, Helsinki. Translated as 'Some remarks on axiomatized set theory', in J. van Heijenoort (1967a) (q.v.), pp. 291–301.

Skolem, T. (1923). Begründung der elementaren Arithmetik durch die rekurrierende Denkweise. *Videnskapsselskapents skrifter I. Matematisk:naturvidenskabelig klasse.* no. 6. Translated as 'The foundations of arithmetic established by the recursive mode of thought', in J. van Heijenoort (1967a) (q.v.), pp. 303–33.

Skolem, T. (1928). Über die mathematische Logik. *Norsk matematisk tidsskrift*, **10**, 125–42. Translated in J. van Heijenoort (1967a) (q.v.), pp. 508–24.

Skolem, T. (1930). Einige Bemerkungen zu der Abhandlung von E. Zermelo: 'Über die Definitheit in der Axiomatik'. *Fundamenta Mathematicae*, **15**, 337–41.

Skolem, T. (1933). Über die Unmöglichkeit einer vollständigen Charakterisierung der Zahlenreihe mittels eines endlichen Axiomsystems. *Norsk matematisk forenings skrifter*, Ser. 2, no. 10, 73–82.

Skolem, T. (1934). Über die Nicht-charakterisierbarkeit der Zahlenreihe mittels endlich oder abzählbar unendlich vieler Aussagen mit ausschliesslich Zahlenvariablen. *Fundamenta Mathematicae*, **23**, 150–61.

Skolem, T. (1941). Sur la portée du théoréme de Löwenheim–Skolem. In F. Gonseth (1941) (q.v.), pp. 25–52.

Skolem, T. (1950). Some remarks on the foundation of set theory. *Proceedings of the International Congress of Mathematicians, Cambridge, Massachusetts*, pp. 695–704. American Mathematical Society, Providence, RI (1952).

Skolem, T. (1958). Une relativisation des notions mathématiques fondamentales. *Colloques Internationaux du Centre National de la Recherche Scientifique*, pp. 13–18. Paris.

Skolem, T. (1961). Interpretation of mathematical theories in the first-order predicate calulus. In *Essays on the foundations of mathematics, Dedicated to A. A. Fraenkel* (eds Y. Bar-Hillel *et al.*), pp. 218–25. Magnes Press, Jerusalem.

Solovay, R., Reinhardt, N., and Kanamori, A. (1978). Strong axioms of infinity and elementary embeddings. *Annals of Mathematical Logic*, **13**, 73–116.

Statman, R. (1978). Bounds for proof-search and speed-up in the predicate calculus. *Annals of Mathematical Logic*, **15**, 225–87.

Steel, J. and van Wesep, R. (1982). Two consequences of determinacy consistent with choice. *Transactions of the American Mathematical Society*, **272**, 67–85.

Stein, H. (1988). *Logos*, logic, and *Logistiké*: Some philosophical remarks on the nineteenth century transformation of mathematics. In *History and philosophy of modern mathematics*, (eds W. Aspray and P. Kitcher). Minnesota Studies in the Philosophy of Science, 11, pp. 238–59. University of Minnesota Press.

Steiner, M. (1975). *Mathematical knowledge*. Cornell University Press, Ithaca, NY.

Tait, W. (1981). Finitism. *Journal of Philosophy*, **78**, 524–46.

Takeuti, G. and Zaring, W. (1971). *An introduction to axiomatic set theory*. Springer-Verlag, Berlin.

Tarski, A. (1935). On the concept of logical consequence. *Logic, semantics and metamathematics*, pp. 417–29. Clarendon Press, Oxford (1956).

Tarski, A. (1948). *A decision method for elementary algebra and geometry*. University of California Press (1951).

Tarski, A. (1967). *The completeness of elementary algebra and geometry*. Institut Blaise Pascal, Paris.

Tarski, A. (1986). What are logical notions? *History and Philosophy of Logic 7* (ed. J. Corcoran), pp. 143–54.

Tharp, L. (1975). Which logic is the right logic? *Synthese*, **31**, 1–31.

Thiel, C. (1977). Leopold Löwenheim: life, work, and early influence. In *Logic Colloquium 76* (eds R. Gandy and M. Hyland), pp. 235–52. North-Holland, Amsterdam.

Väänänen, J. (1985). Set-theoretic definability of logics. In J. Barwise and S. Feferman (1985) (q.v.), pp. 599–643.

Van Benthem, J. and Doets, K. (1983). Higher-order logic. *Handbook of philosophical logic 1* (eds D. Gabbay and F. Guenthner), pp. 275–329. Reidel, Dordrecht.

Van Heijenoort, J. (1967a). *From Frege to Gödel*. Harvard University Press, Cambridge.

Van Heijenoort, J. (1967b). Logic as calculus and logic as language. *Synthese*, **17**, 324–30.

Veblen, O. (1904). A system of axioms for geometry. *Transactions of the American Mathematical Society*, **5**, 343–84.

Von Neumann, J. (1925). Eine Axiomatisierung der Mengenlehre. *Journal für die reine und angewandte Mathematik*, **154**, 219–40. Translated in J. van Heijenhoort (1967a) (q.v.), pp. 393–413.

Von Neumann, J. (1927). Zur Hilbertschen Beweistheorie. *Mathematische Zeitschrift*, **26**, 1–46.

Von Neumann, J. (1928). Über die Definition durch transfinite Induktion und verwandte Fragen der allgemeinen Mengenlehre. *Mathematische Annalen*, **99**, 373–91.

Wagner, S. (1987). The rationalist conception of logic. *Notre Dame Journal of Formal Logic*, **28**, 3–35.

Wagner, S. (1991). Logicism. *On proof: philosophical investigations concerning the nature of mathematical reasoning*. Routledge, London.

Wang, H. (1974). *From mathematics to philosophy*. Routledge and Kegan Paul, London.

Wang, H. (1987). *Reflections on Kurt Gödel*. MIT Press, Cambridge, MA.

Weston, T. (1976). Kreisel, the continuum hypothesis and second-order set theory. *Journal of Philosophical Logic*, **5**, 281–98.

Weston, T. (1977). The continuum hypothesis is independent of second-order ZF. *Notre Dame Journal of Formal Logic*, **18**, 499–503.

Weyl, H. (1910). Über die Definitionen der mathematischen Grundbegriffe. *Mathematisch-naturwissenschaftliche Blätter*, **7**, 93–95, 109–13.

Weyl, H. (1917). *Das Kontinuum*. Veit, Leipzig.

Wittgenstein, L. (1958). *Philosophical investigations* (tr. G. E. M. Anscombe). Macmillan, New York.

Wittgenstein, L. (1978). *Remarks on the foundations of mathematics* (tr. G. E. M. Anscombe). MIT Press, Cambridge, MA.

Wright, C. (1980). *Wittgenstein on the foundations of mathematics*. Harvard University Press, Cambridge, MA.

Zermelo, E. (1904). Beweis, dass jede Menge wohlgeordnet werden kann. *Mathematischen Annalen*, **59**, 514–16. Translated in J. van Heijenoort (1967a) (q.v.), pp. 139–41.

Zermelo, E. (1908a). Neuer Beweis für die Möglichkeit einer Wohlordnung. *Mathematische Annalen*, **65**, 107–28. Translated in J. van Heijenoort (1967a) (q.v.), pp. 183–98.

Zermelo, E. (1908b). Untersuchungen über die Grundlagen der Mengenlehre. I. *Mathematische Annalen*, **65**, 261–81. Translated in J. van Heijenoort (1967a) (q.v.), pp. 199–215.

Zermelo, E. (1929). Über den Begriff der Definitheit in der Axiomatik. *Fundamenta Mathematicae*, **14**, 339–44.

Zermelo, E. (1930). Über Grenzzahlen und Mengenbereiche: Neue Untersuchungen über die Grundlagen der Mengenlehre. *Fundamenta Mathematicae*, **16**, 29–47.

Zermelo, E. (1931). Über Stufen der Quantifikation und die Logik des Unendlichen. *Jahresbericht der Deutschen Mathematiker-Vereinigung (Angelegenheiten)*, **31**, 85–8.

INDEX